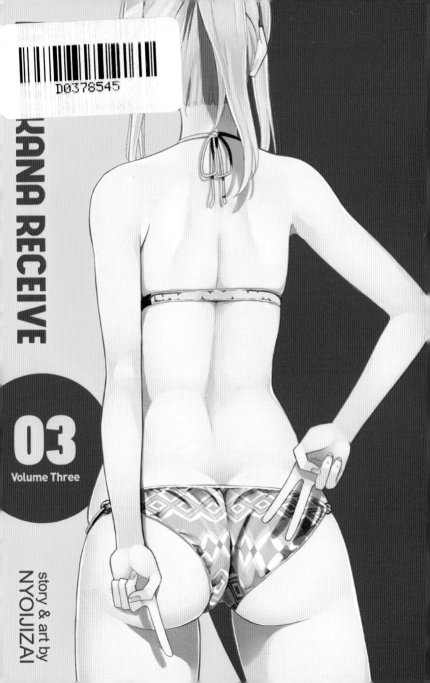

KANA RECEIVE

03

Volume Three

story & art by
NYOIJIZAI

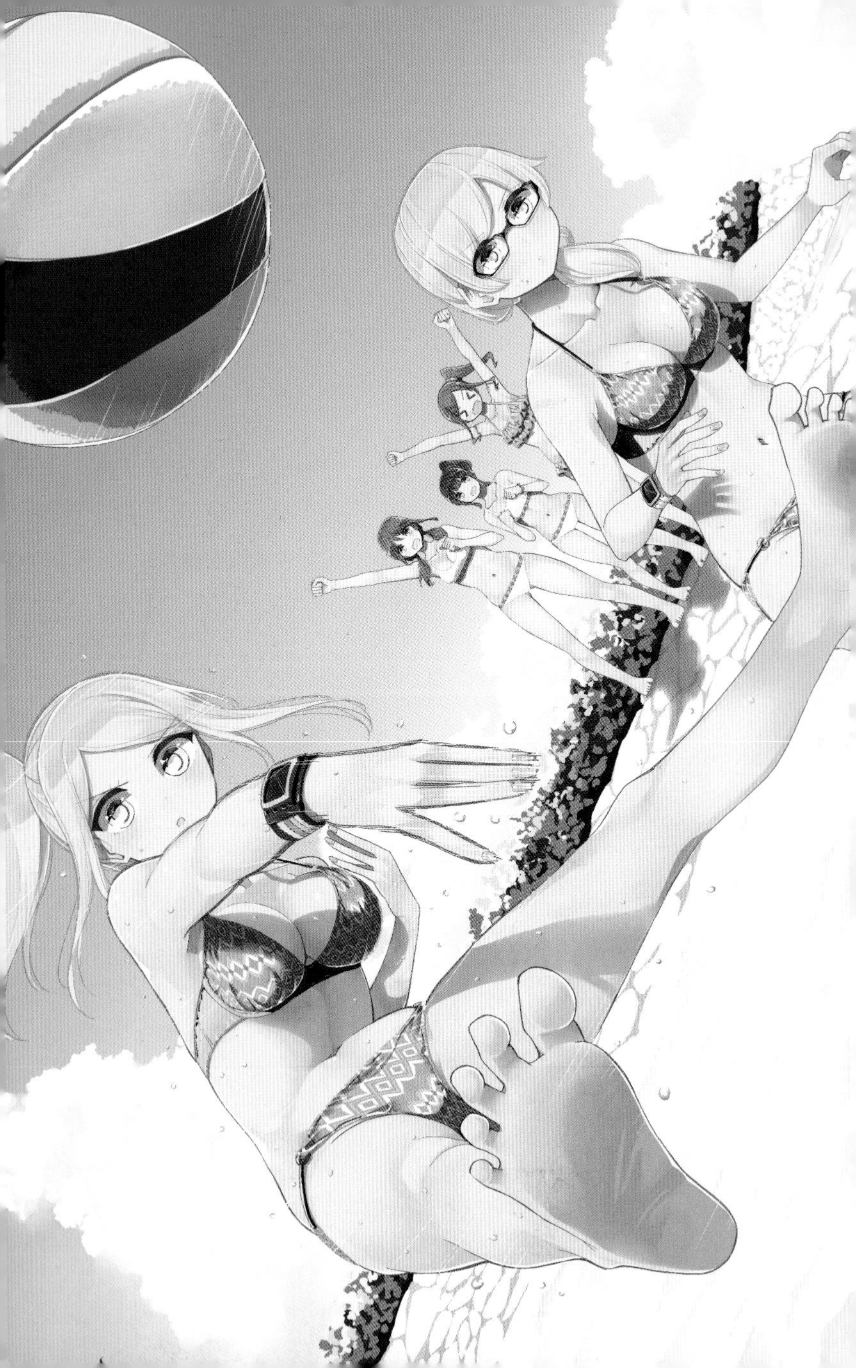

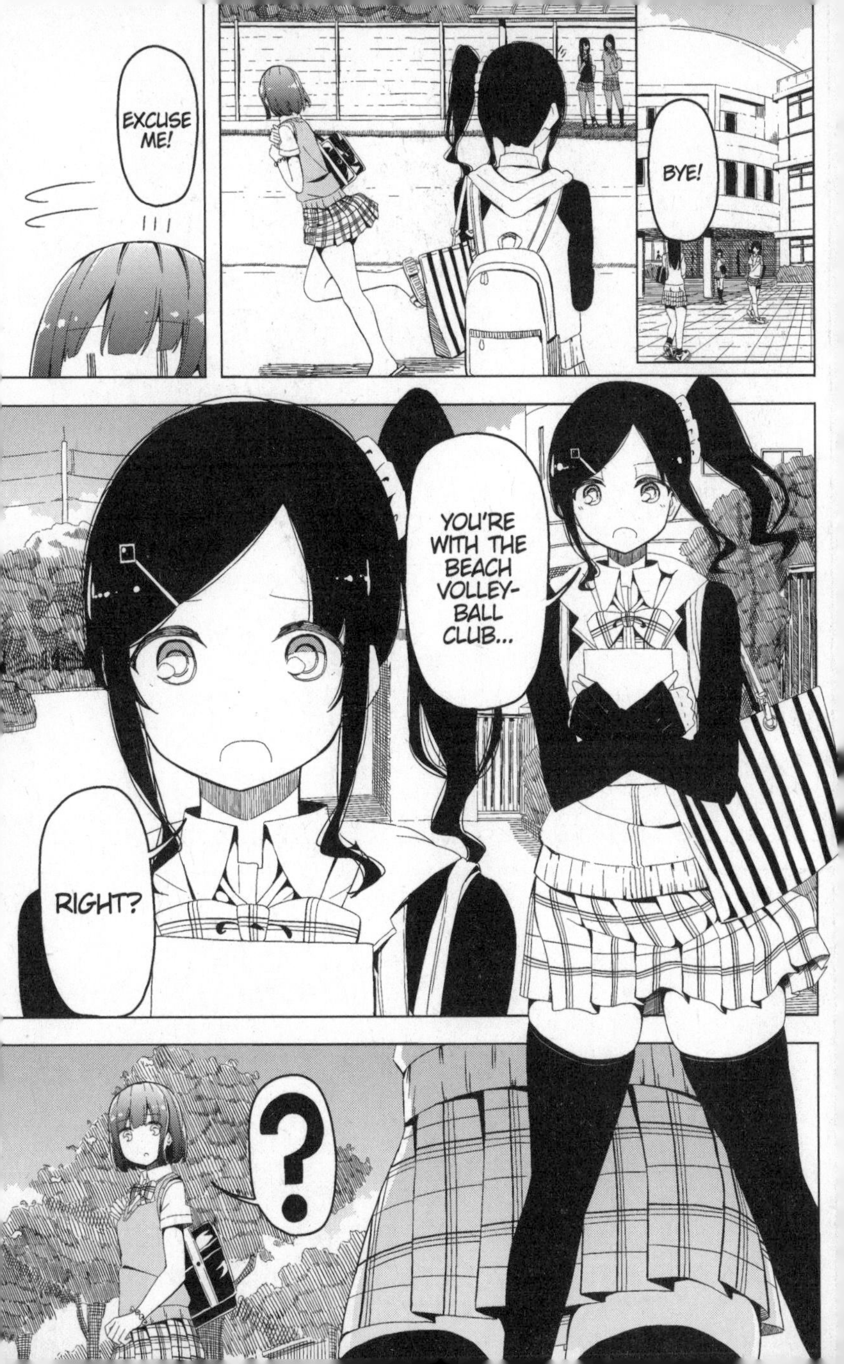
BYE!
EXCUSE ME!
YOU'RE WITH THE BEACH VOLLEY-BALL CLUB...
RIGHT?
?

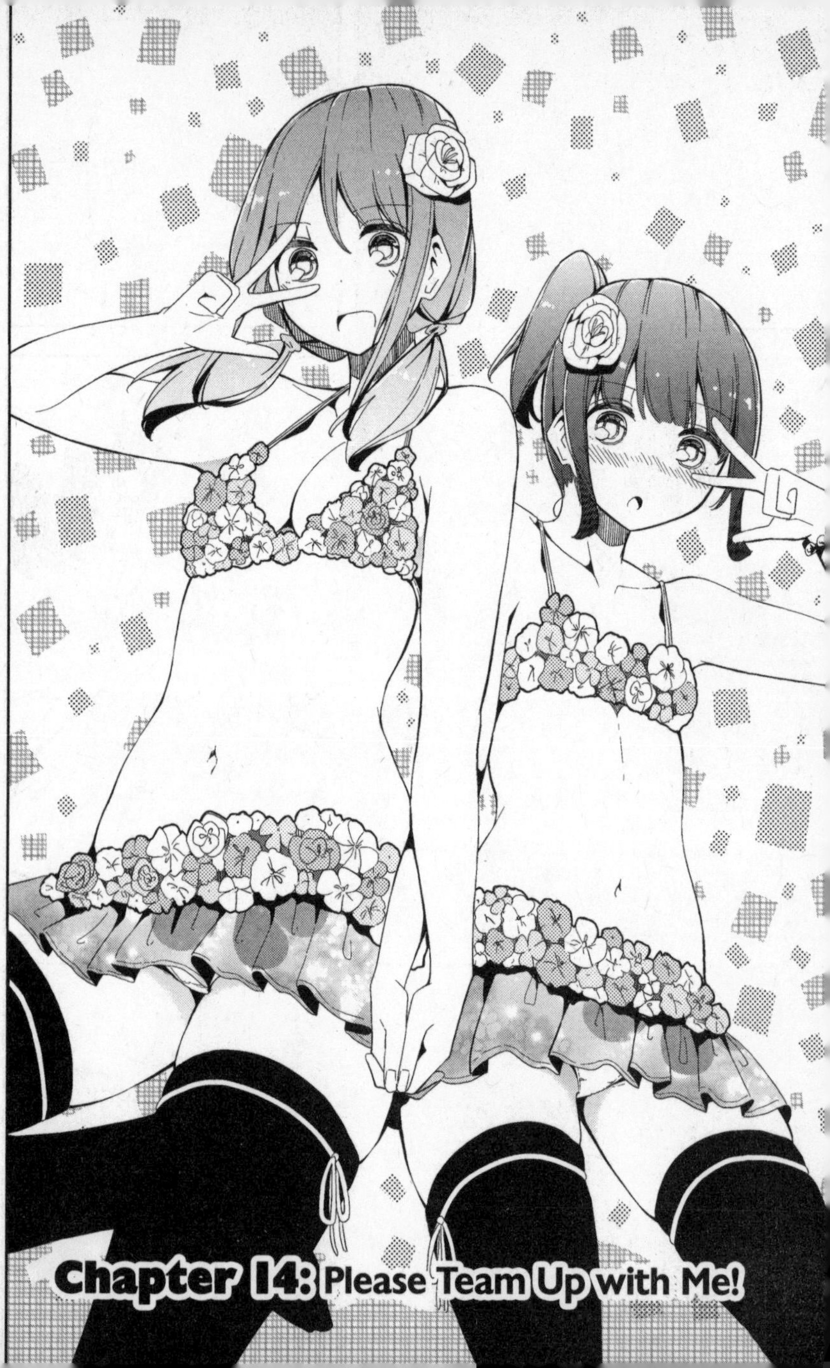

Chapter 14: Please Team Up with Me!

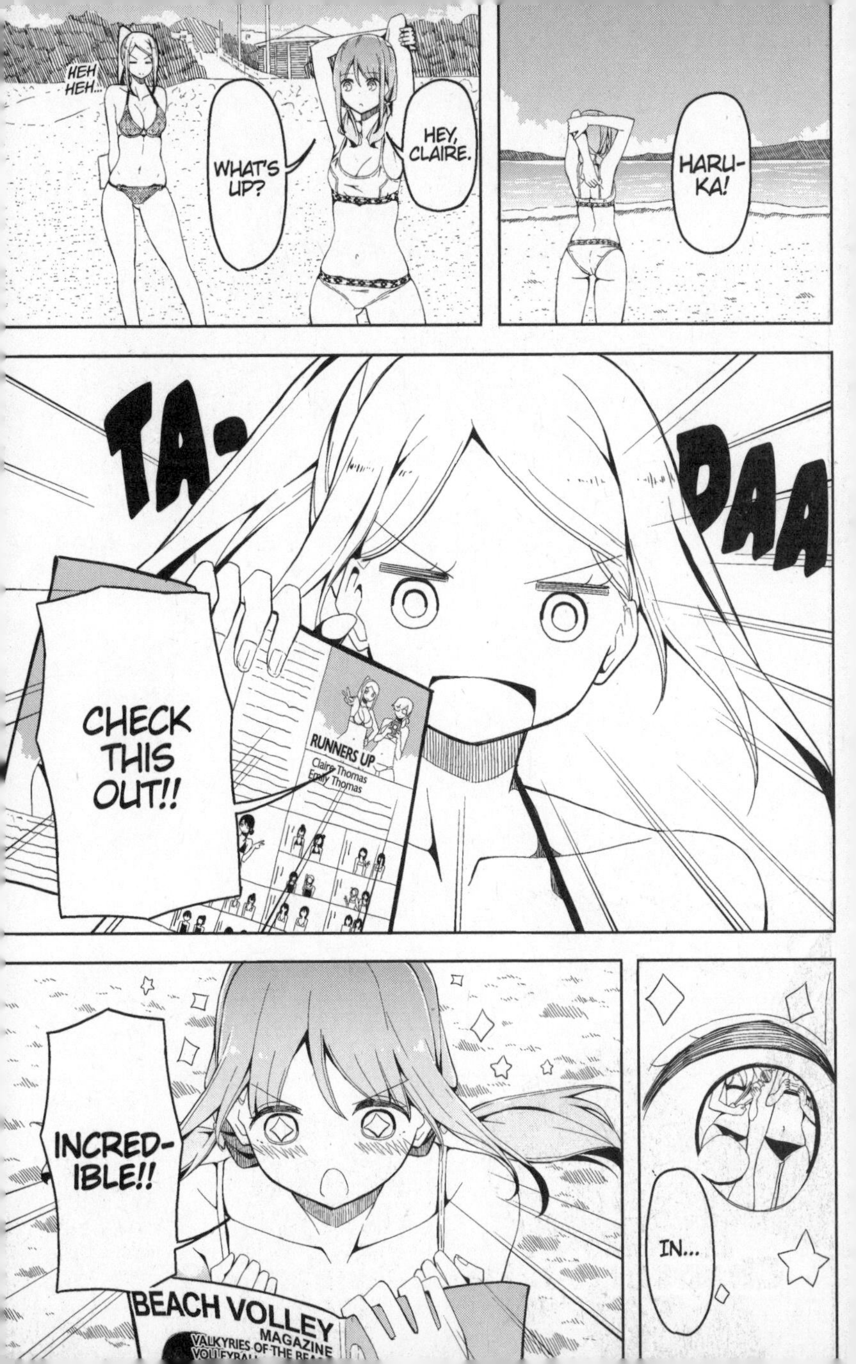
HARU-KA!
HEY, CLAIRE.
WHAT'S UP?
HEH HEH...
TA-DAA
CHECK THIS OUT!!
RUNNERS UP
Claire Thomas
Emily Thomas
IN...
INCRED-IBLE!!
BEACH VOLLEY
MAGAZINE

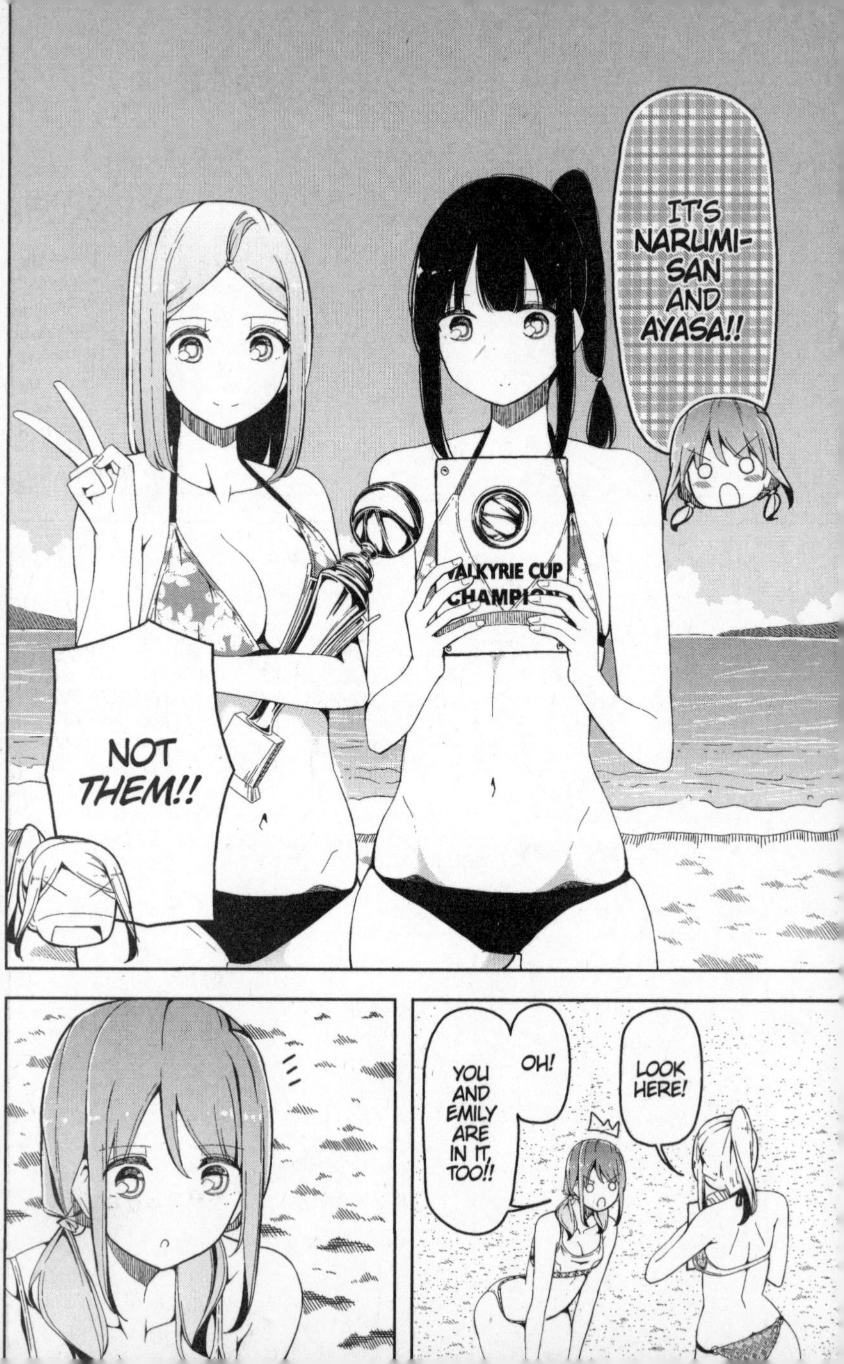
IT'S NARUMI-SAN AND AYASA!!
VALKYRIE CUP
NOT THEM!!
LOOK HERE!
OH!
YOU AND EMILY ARE IN IT, TOO!!

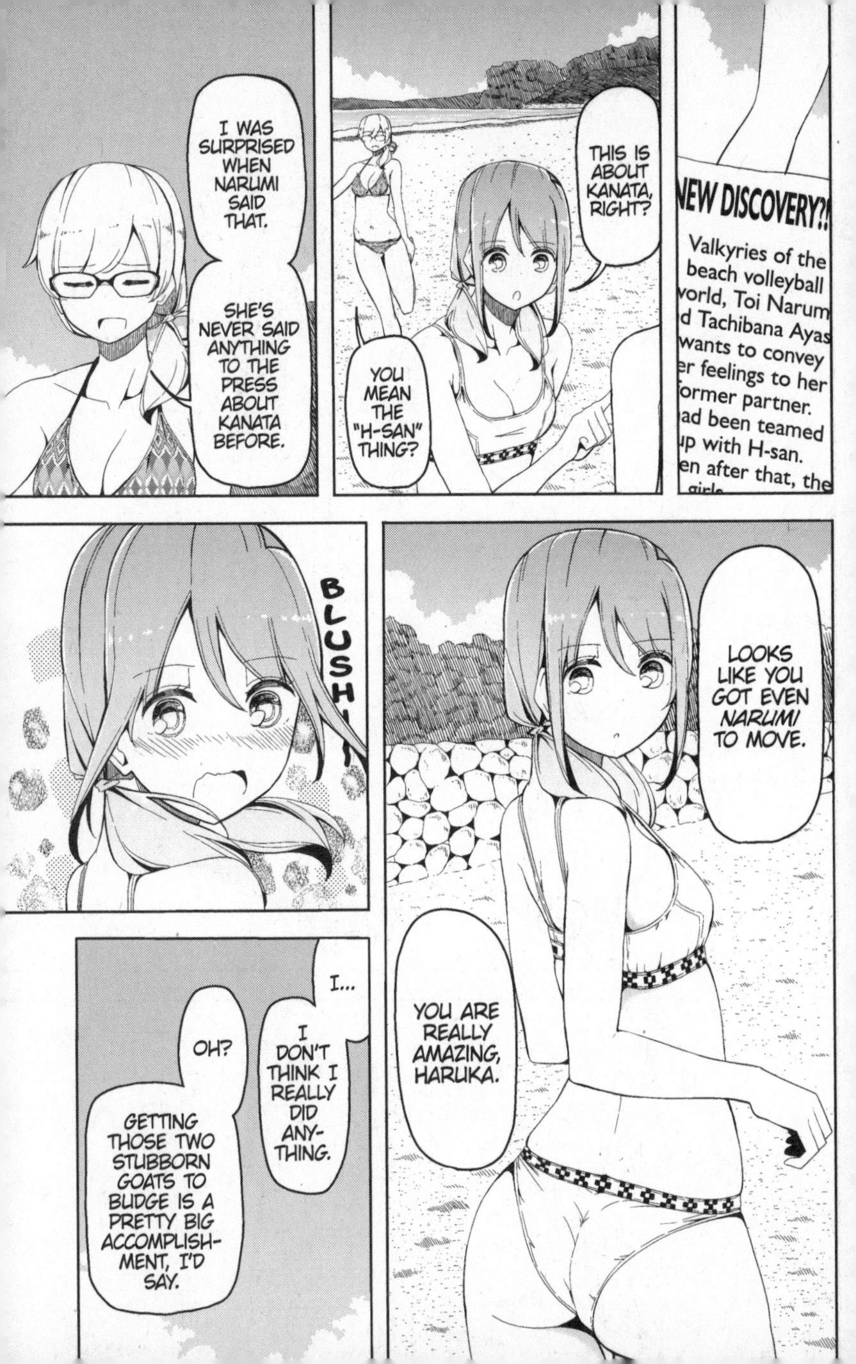
NEW DISCOVERY?!
Valkyries of the beach volleyball world, Toi Narum d Tachibana Ayas wants to convey er feelings to her former partner. ad been teamed up with H-san. en after that, the
THIS IS ABOUT KANATA, RIGHT?
YOU MEAN THE "H-SAN" THING?
I WAS SURPRISED WHEN NARUMI SAID THAT.
SHE'S NEVER SAID ANYTHING TO THE PRESS ABOUT KANATA BEFORE.
LOOKS LIKE YOU GOT EVEN *NARUMI* TO MOVE.
YOU ARE REALLY AMAZING, HARUKA.
BLUSH!!
I...
I DON'T THINK I REALLY DID ANY-THING.
OH?
GETTING THOSE TWO STUBBORN GOATS TO BUDGE IS A PRETTY BIG ACCOMPLISH-MENT, I'D SAY.

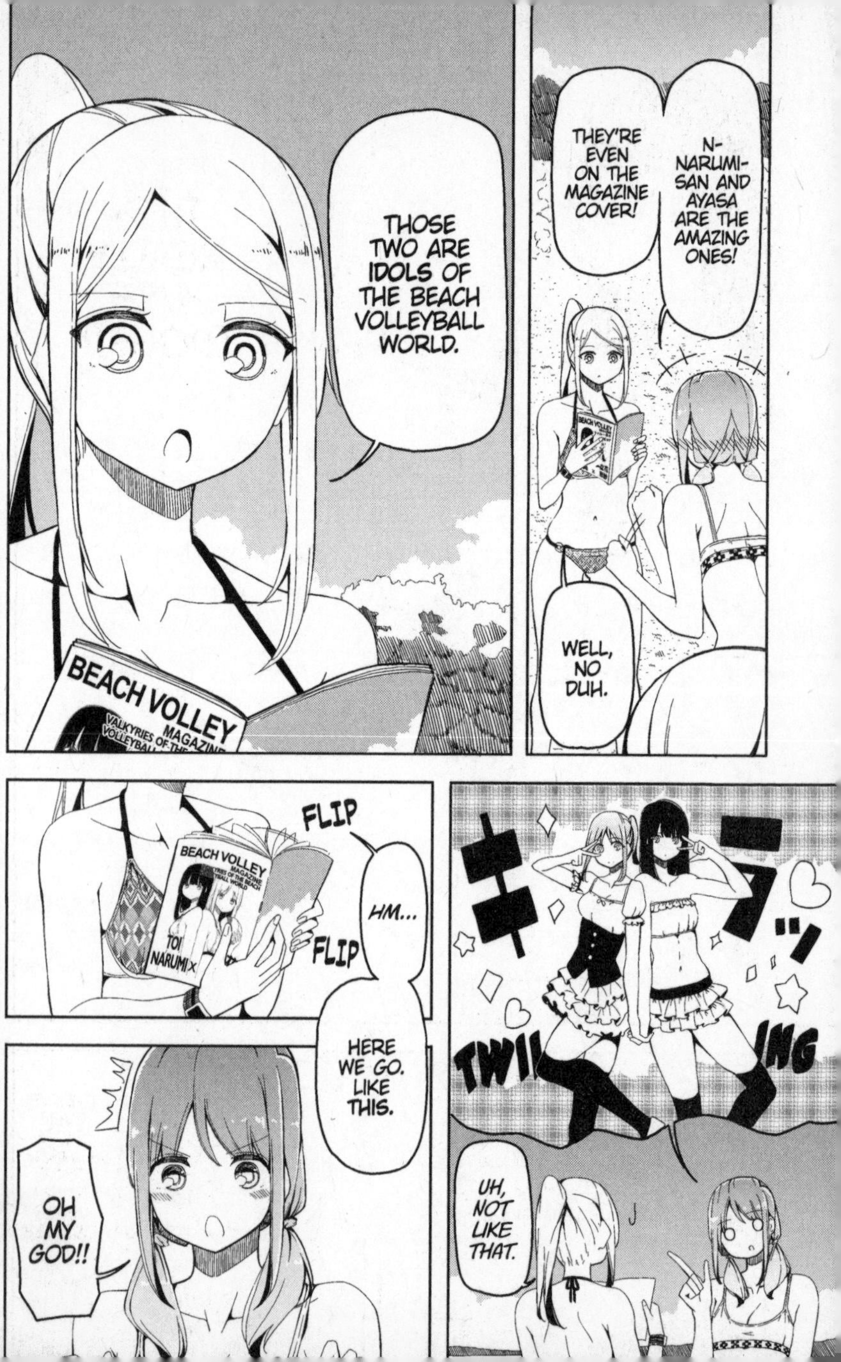
N-NARUMI-SAN AND AYASA ARE THE AMAZING ONES!
THEY'RE EVEN ON THE MAGAZINE COVER!
WELL, NO DUH.
THOSE TWO ARE IDOLS OF THE BEACH VOLLEYBALL WORLD.
BEACH VOLLEY MAGAZINE VALKYRIES OF THE VOLLEYBALL
キラッ
TWII
ING
FLIP
BEACH VOLLEY MAGAZINE VALKYRIES OF THE BEACH VOLLEYBALL WORLD
TOI NARUMI x
HM...
FLIP
HERE WE GO. LIKE THIS.
OH MY GOD!!
UH, NOT LIKE THAT.

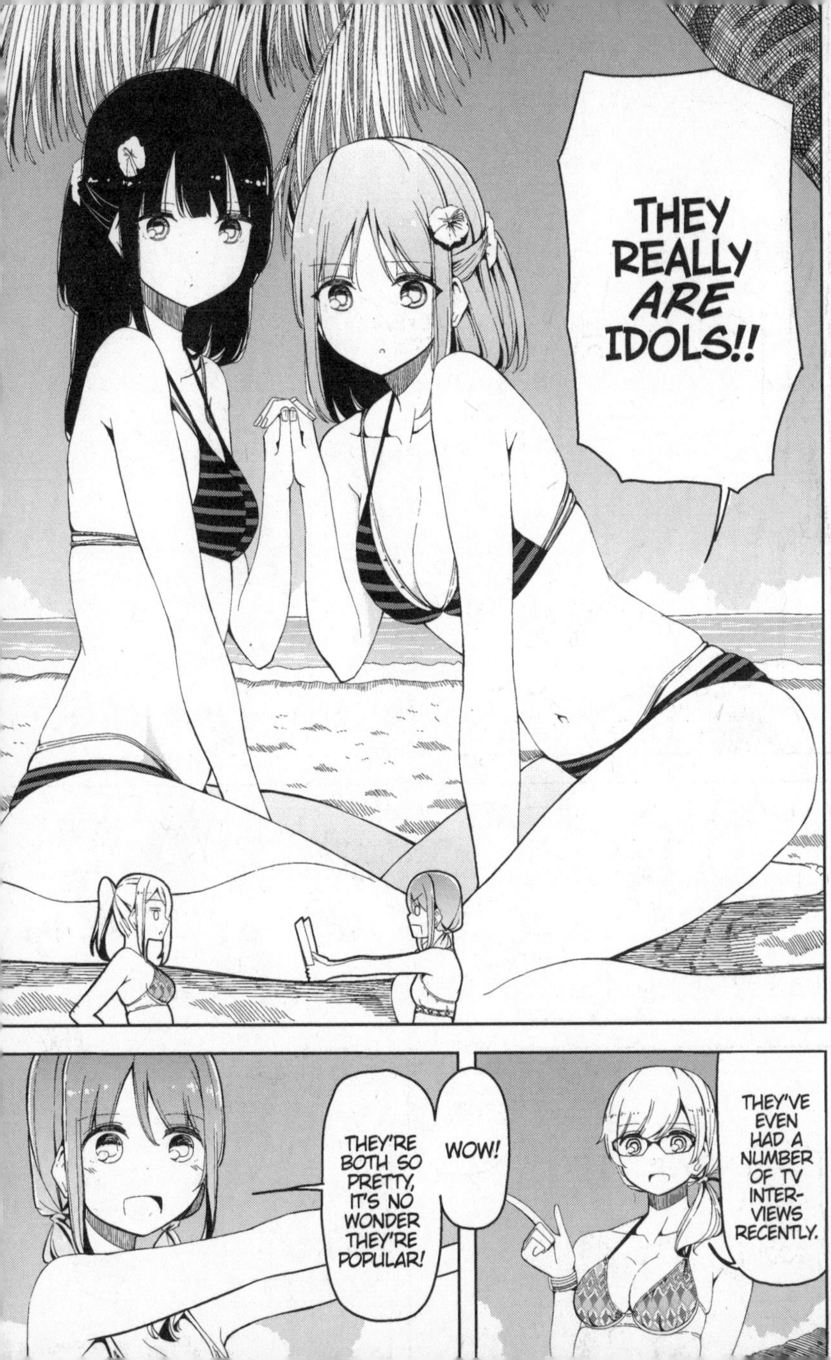
THEY REALLY *ARE* IDOLS!!
THEY'VE EVEN HAD A NUMBER OF TV INTER-VIEWS RECENTLY.
WOW!
THEY'RE BOTH SO PRETTY, IT'S NO WONDER THEY'RE POPULAR!

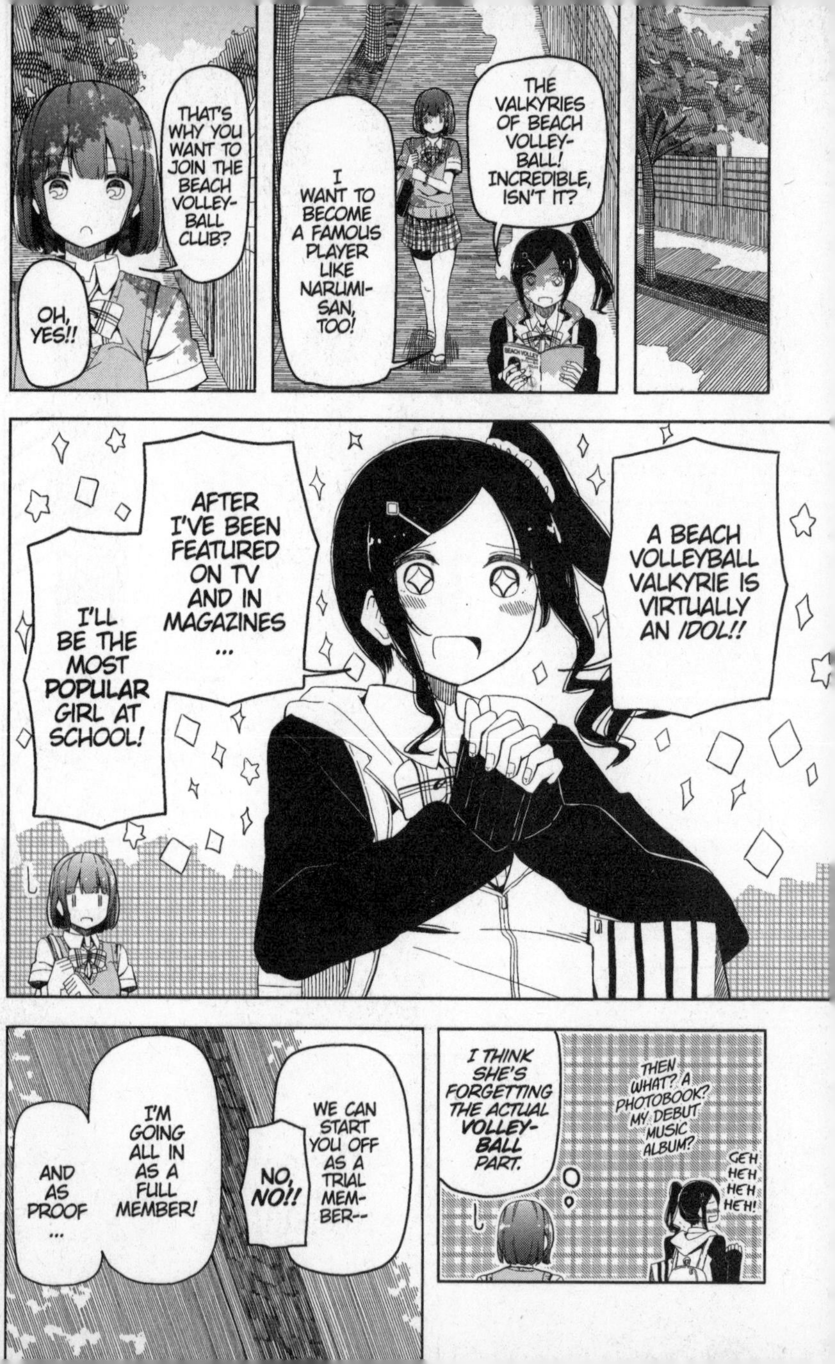
THE VALKYRIES OF BEACH VOLLEYBALL! INCREDIBLE, ISN'T IT?
I WANT TO BECOME A FAMOUS PLAYER LIKE NARUMI-SAN, TOO!
THAT'S WHY YOU WANT TO JOIN THE BEACH VOLLEYBALL CLUB?
OH, YES!!
A BEACH VOLLEYBALL VALKYRIE IS VIRTUALLY AN *IDOL!!*
AFTER I'VE BEEN FEATURED ON TV AND IN MAGAZINES...
I'LL BE THE MOST POPULAR GIRL AT SCHOOL!
THEN WHAT? A PHOTOBOOK? MY DEBUT MUSIC ALBUM?
GEH HEH HEH HEH!
I THINK SHE'S FORGETTING THE ACTUAL **VOLLEYBALL** PART.
WE CAN START YOU OFF AS A TRIAL MEMBER--
NO, **NO!!**
I'M GOING ALL IN AS A FULL MEMBER!
AND AS PROOF...

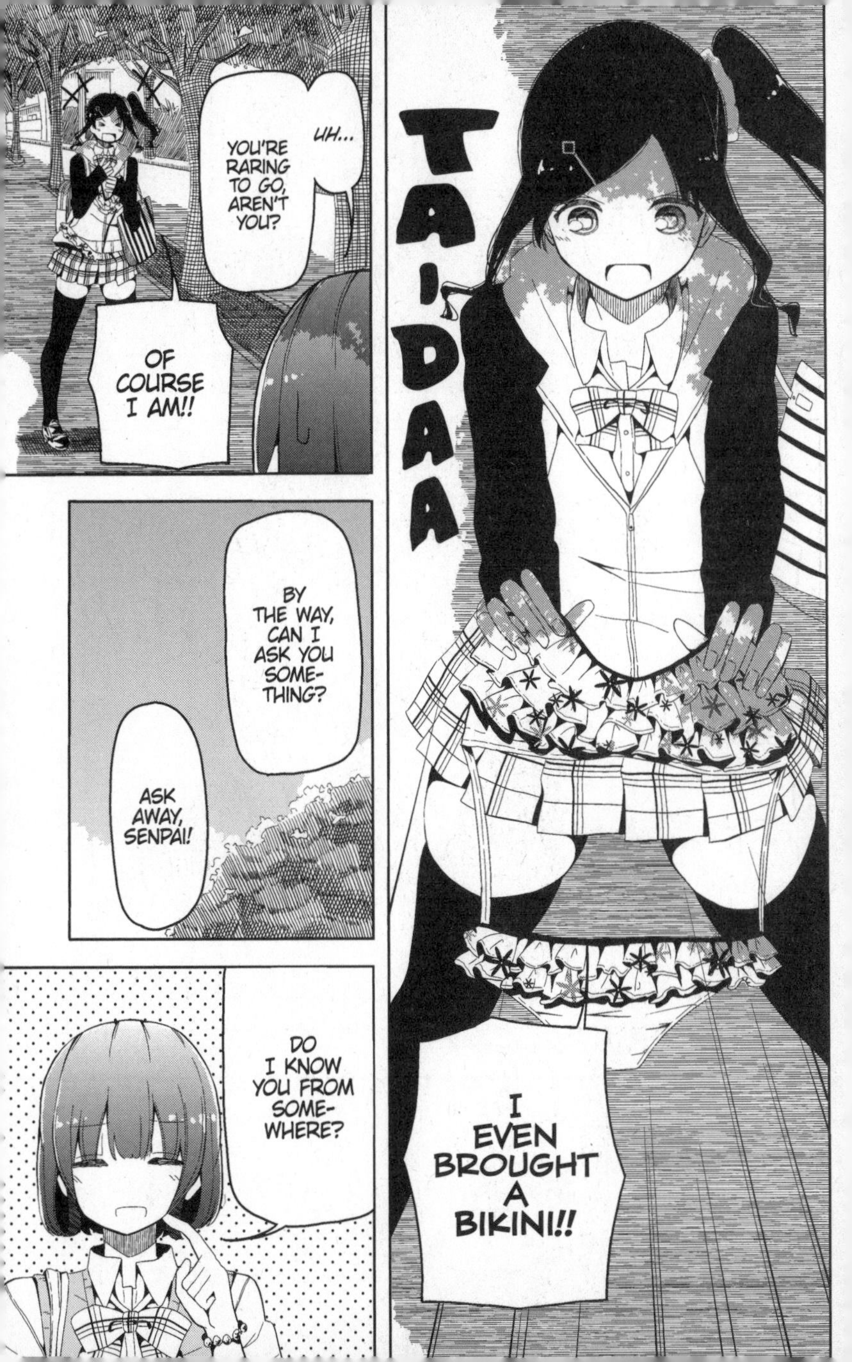
TA-DAA
I EVEN BROUGHT A BIKINI!!
UH...
YOU'RE RARING TO GO, AREN'T YOU?
OF COURSE I AM!!
BY THE WAY, CAN I ASK YOU SOME-THING?
ASK AWAY, SENPAI!
DO I KNOW YOU FROM SOME-WHERE?

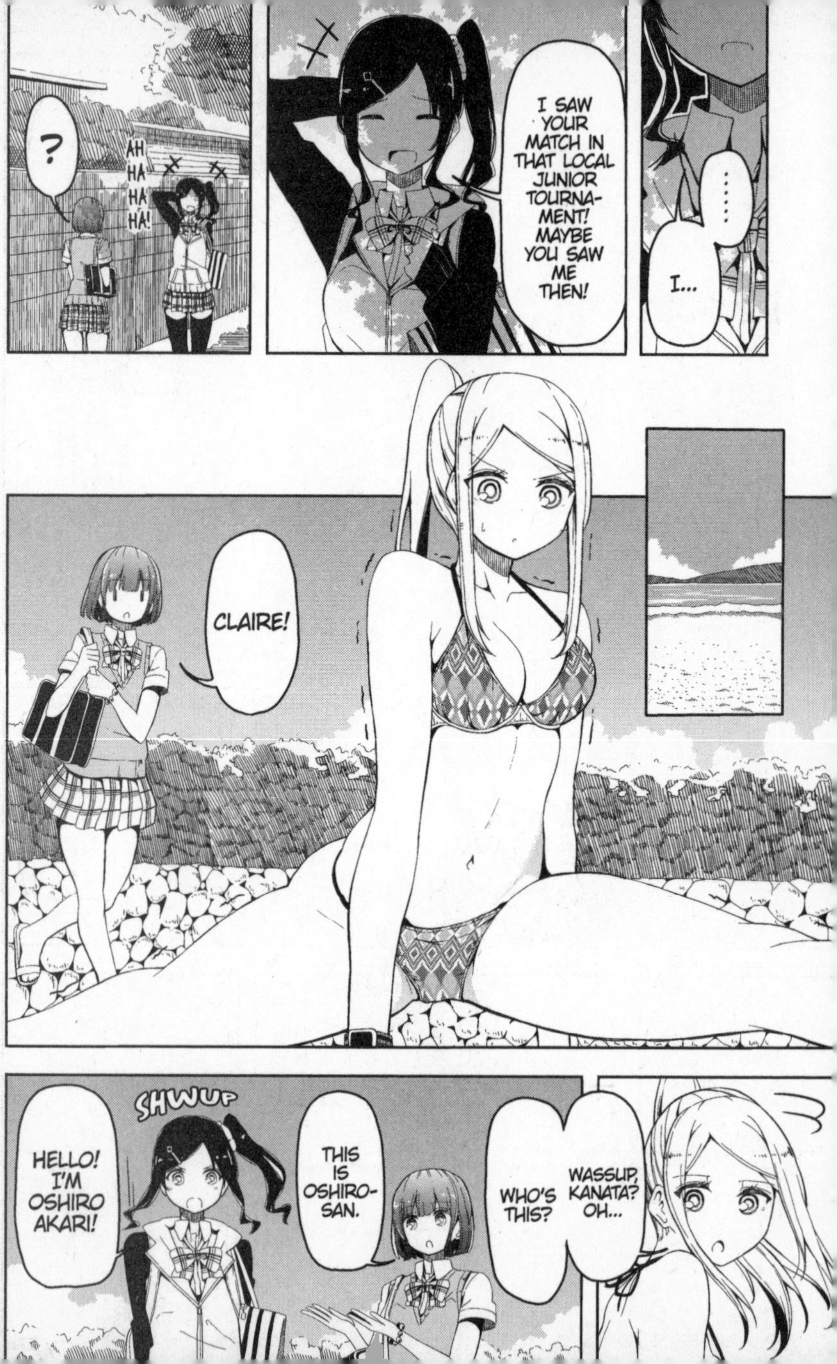
......
I...
I SAW YOUR MATCH IN THAT LOCAL JUNIOR TOURNA-MENT! MAYBE YOU SAW ME THEN!
AH HA HA HA!
?
CLAIRE!
WASSUP, KANATA? OH...
WHO'S THIS?
THIS IS OSHIRO-SAN.
SHWUP
HELLO! I'M OSHIRO AKARI!

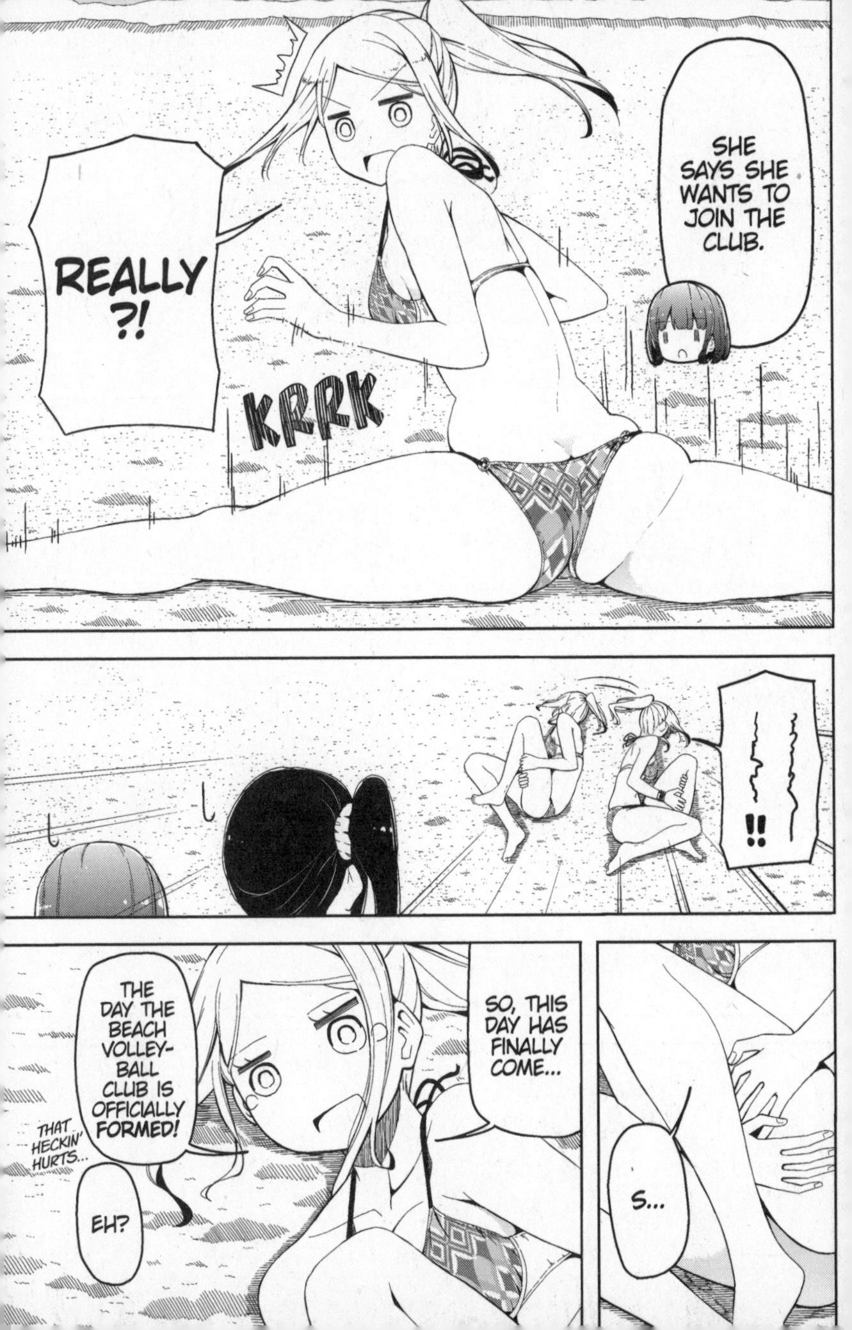
SHE SAYS SHE WANTS TO JOIN THE CLUB.
REALLY?!
KRRK
!!
S...
SO, THIS DAY HAS FINALLY COME...
THE DAY THE BEACH VOLLEY-BALL CLUB IS OFFICIALLY FORMED!
THAT HECKIN' HURTS...
EH?

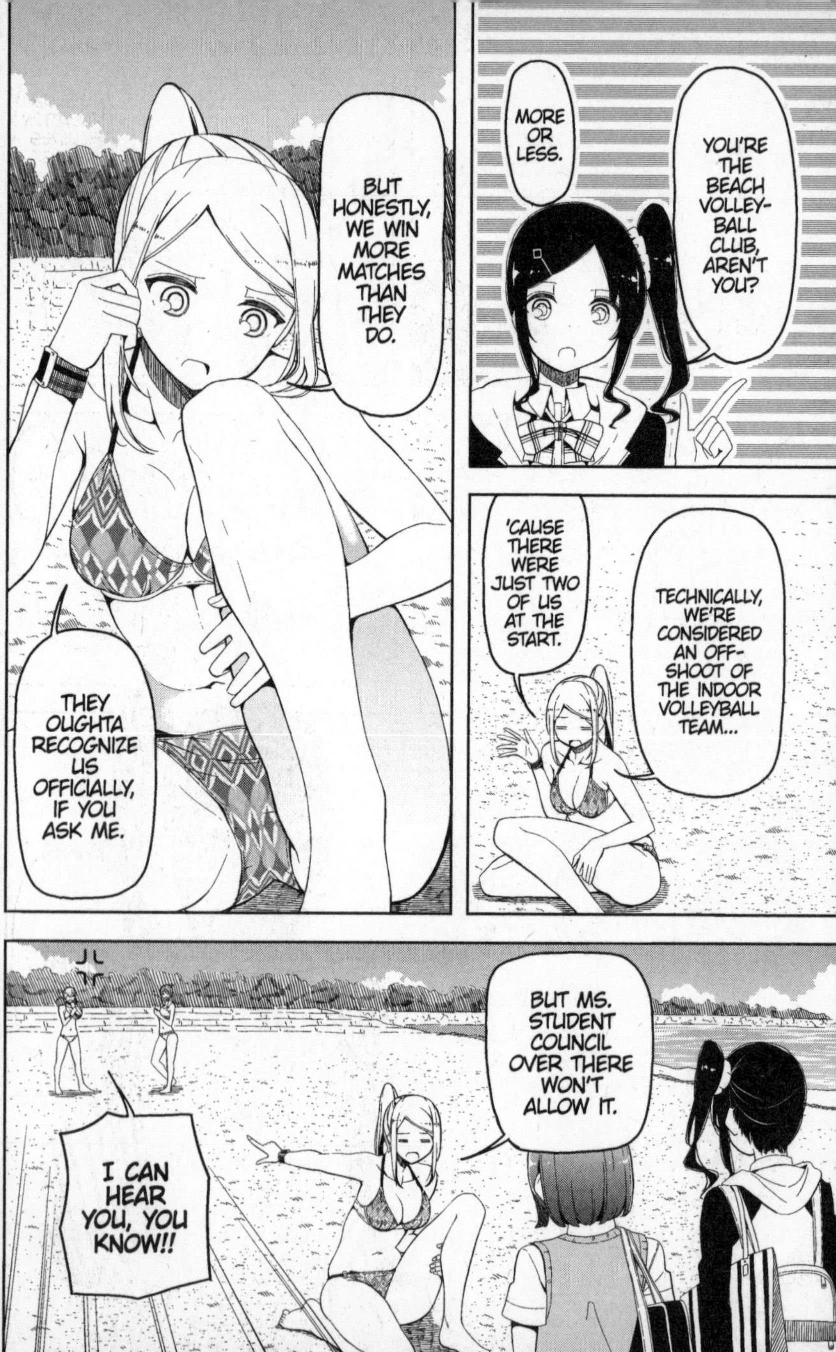
YOU'RE THE BEACH VOLLEY-BALL CLUB, AREN'T YOU?
MORE OR LESS.
TECHNICALLY, WE'RE CONSIDERED AN OFF-SHOOT OF THE INDOOR VOLLEYBALL TEAM...
'CAUSE THERE WERE JUST TWO OF US AT THE START.
BUT HONESTLY, WE WIN MORE MATCHES THAN THEY DO.
THEY OUGHTA RECOGNIZE US OFFICIALLY, IF YOU ASK ME.
BUT MS. STUDENT COUNCIL OVER THERE WON'T ALLOW IT.
I CAN HEAR YOU, YOU KNOW!!

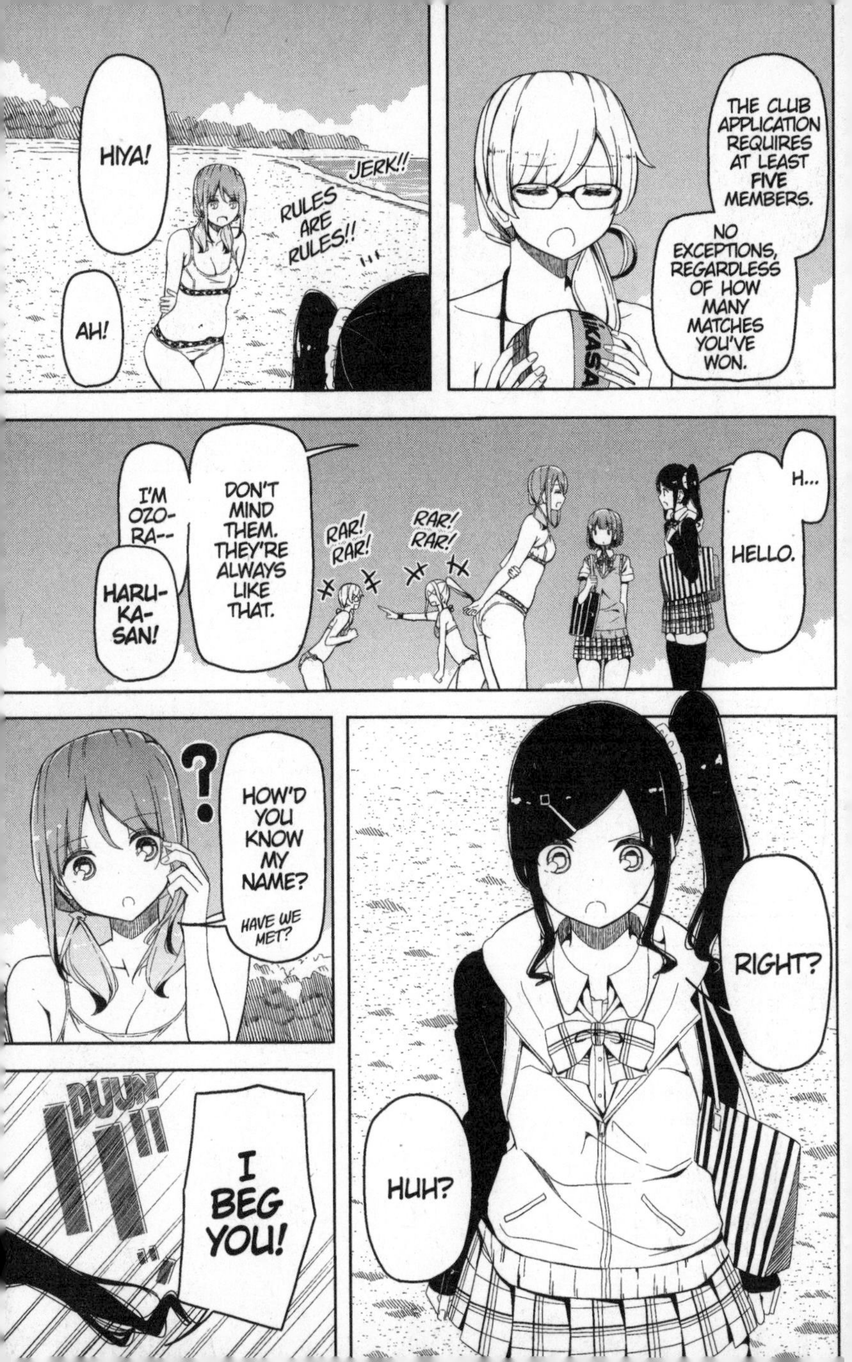
THE CLUB APPLICATION REQUIRES AT LEAST FIVE MEMBERS.
NO EXCEPTIONS, REGARDLESS OF HOW MANY MATCHES YOU'VE WON.
MIKASA
JERK!!
RULES ARE RULES!!
HIYA!
AH!
H...
HELLO.
RAR! RAR!
RAR! RAR!
DON'T MIND THEM. THEY'RE ALWAYS LIKE THAT.
I'M OZORA--
HARUKA-SAN!
RIGHT?
HUH?
HOW'D YOU KNOW MY NAME?
HAVE WE MET?
DUUN!!
I BEG YOU!

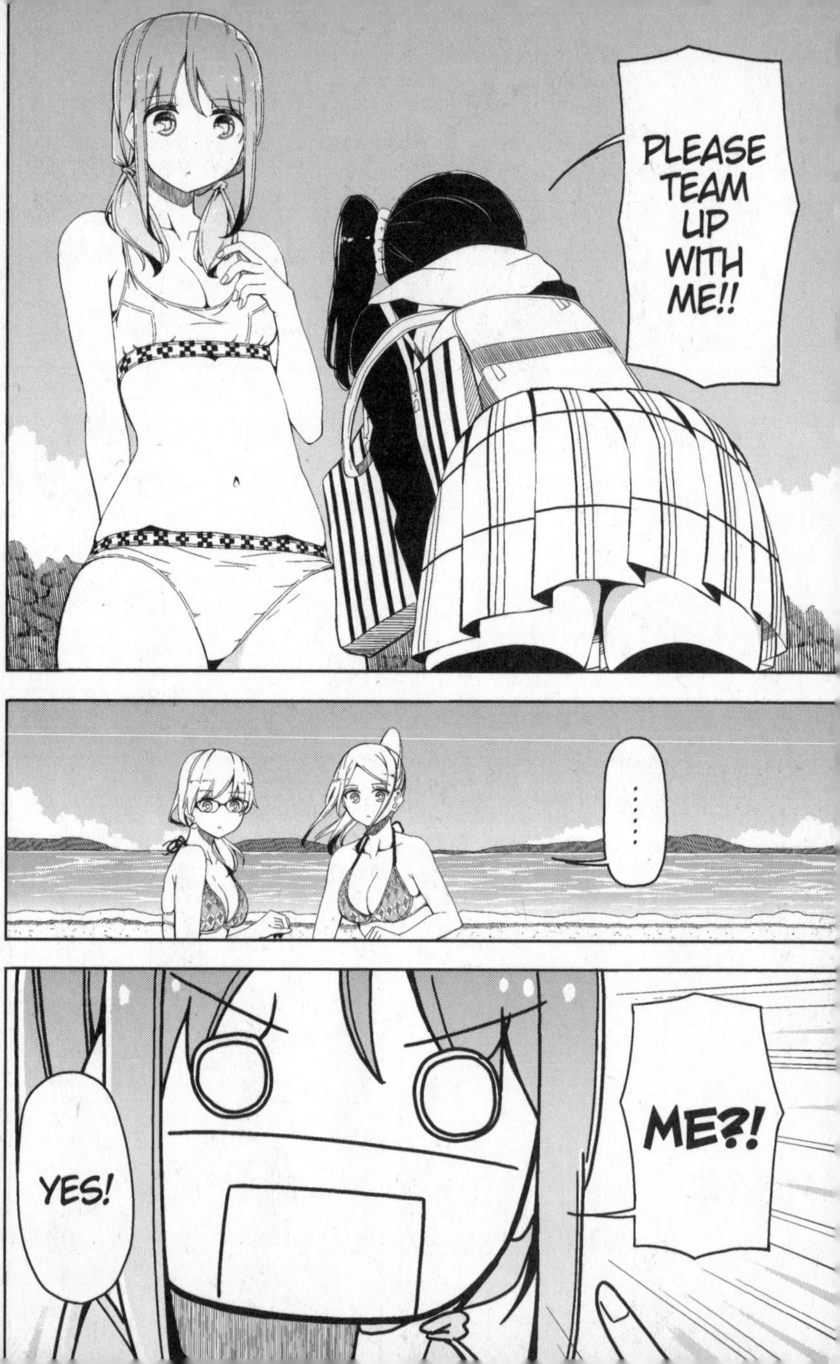
PLEASE TEAM UP WITH ME!!
......
ME?!
YES!

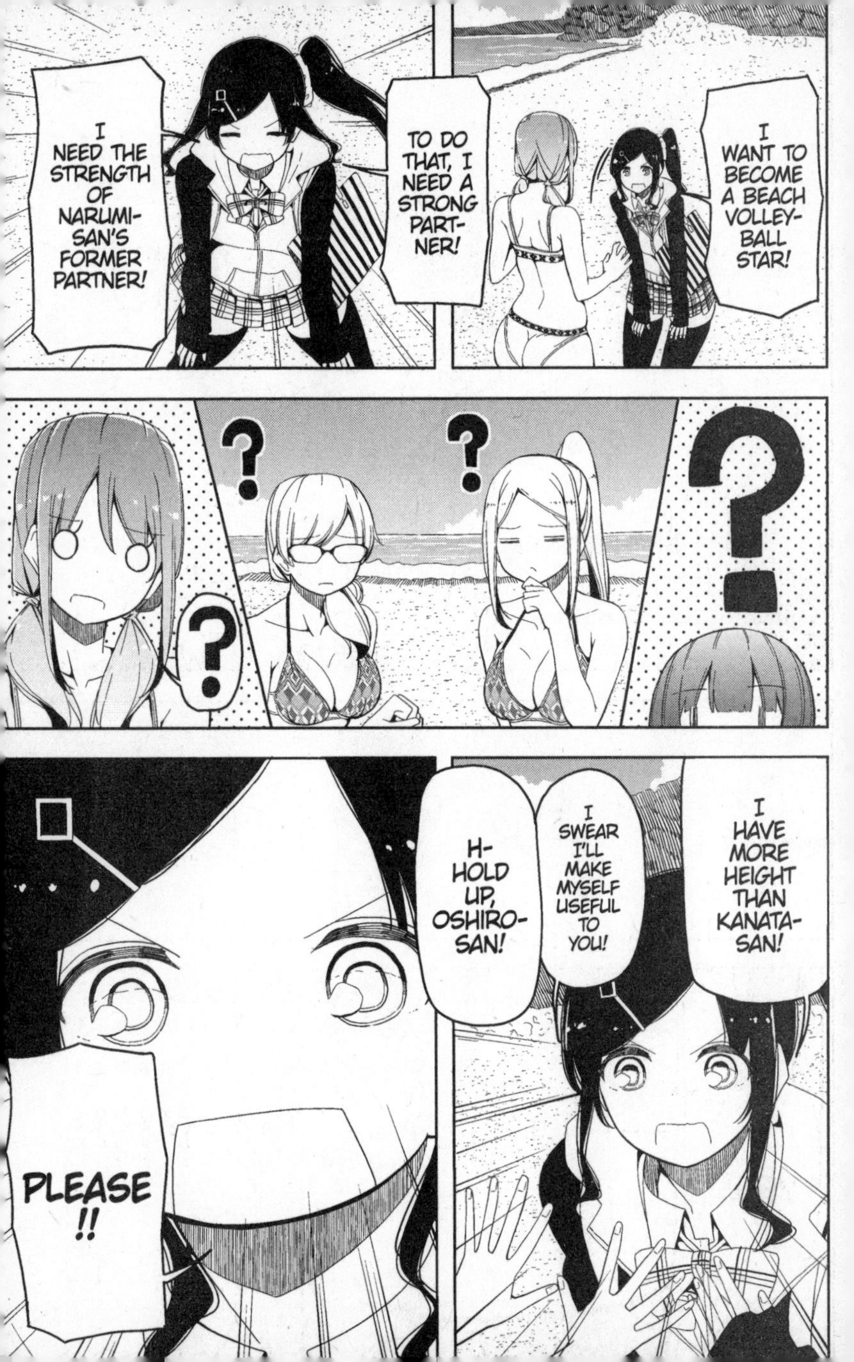
I WANT TO BECOME A BEACH VOLLEY-BALL STAR!
TO DO THAT, I NEED A STRONG PART-NER!
I NEED THE STRENGTH OF NARUMI-SAN'S FORMER PARTNER!
?!
?
?
?
I HAVE MORE HEIGHT THAN KANATA-SAN!
I SWEAR I'LL MAKE MYSELF USEFUL TO YOU!
H-HOLD UP, OSHIRO-SAN!
PLEASE!!

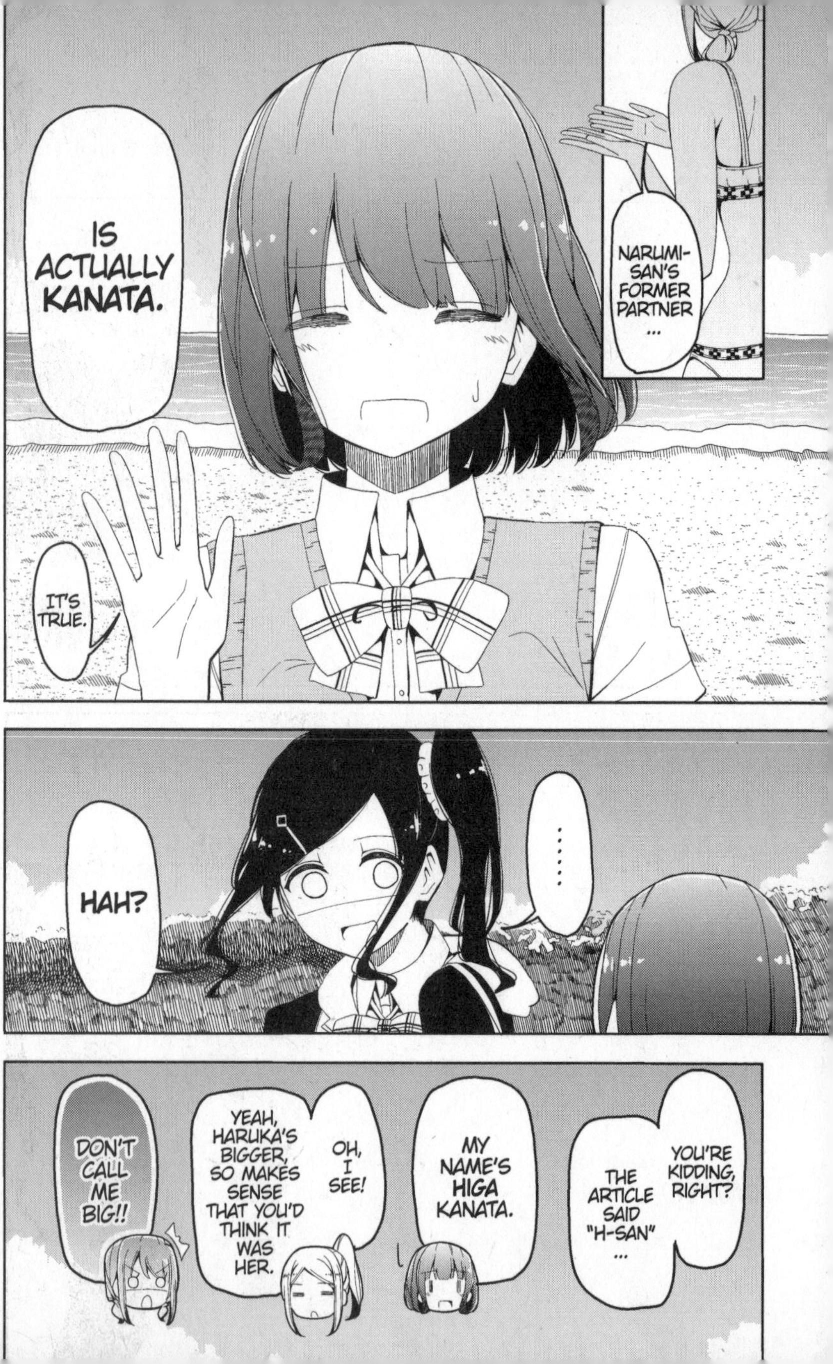
NARUMI-SAN'S FORMER PARTNER ...
IS ACTUALLY KANATA.
IT'S TRUE.
......
HAH?
YOU'RE KIDDING, RIGHT?
THE ARTICLE SAID "H-SAN" ...
MY NAME'S HIGA KANATA.
OH, I SEE!
YEAH, HARUKA'S BIGGER, SO MAKES SENSE THAT YOU'D THINK IT WAS HER.
DON'T CALL ME BIG!!

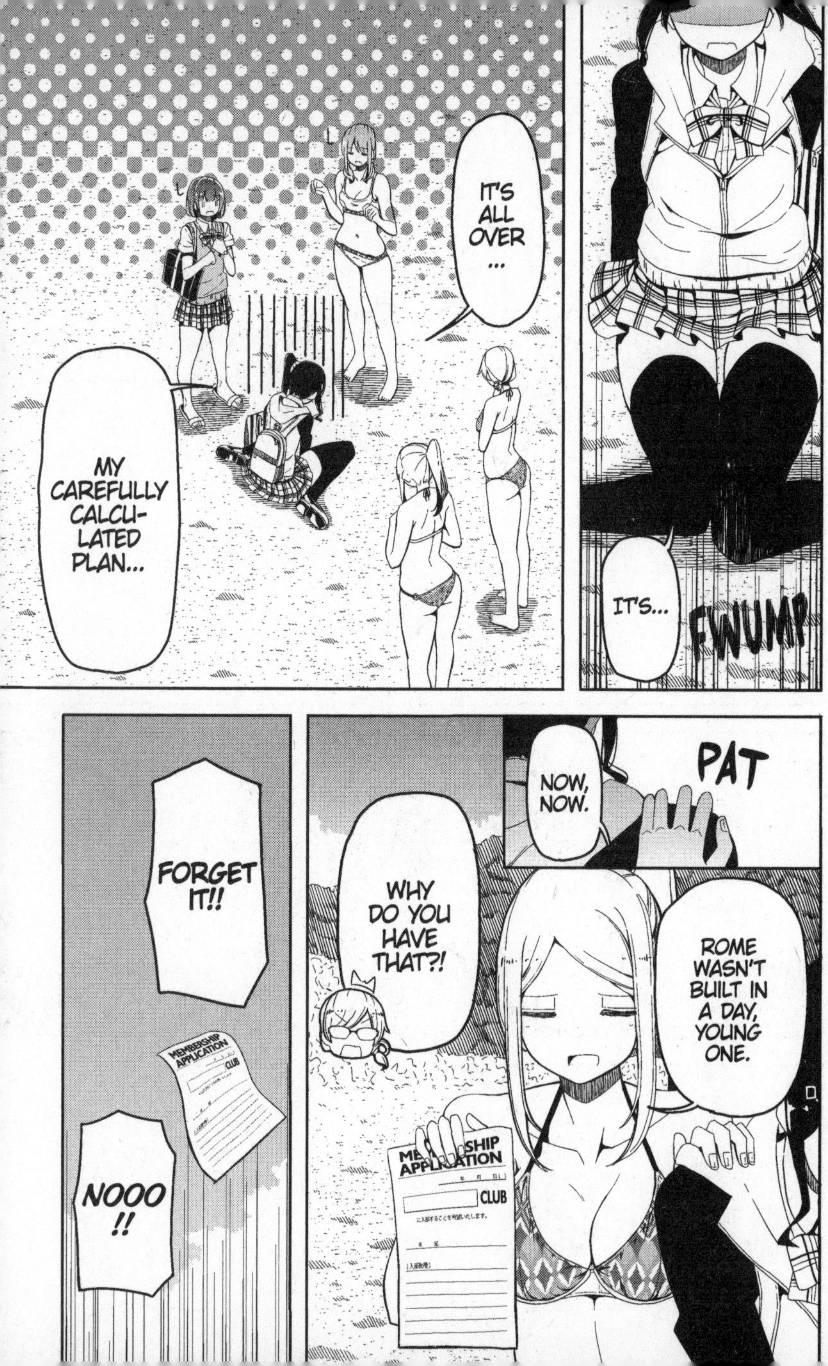
IT'S...
FWUMP
IT'S ALL OVER...
MY CAREFULLY CALCU-LATED PLAN...
NOW, NOW.
PAT
ROME WASN'T BUILT IN A DAY, YOUNG ONE.
WHY DO YOU HAVE THAT?!
CLUB
FORGET IT!!
MEMBERSHIP APPLICATION
CLUB
NOOO!!

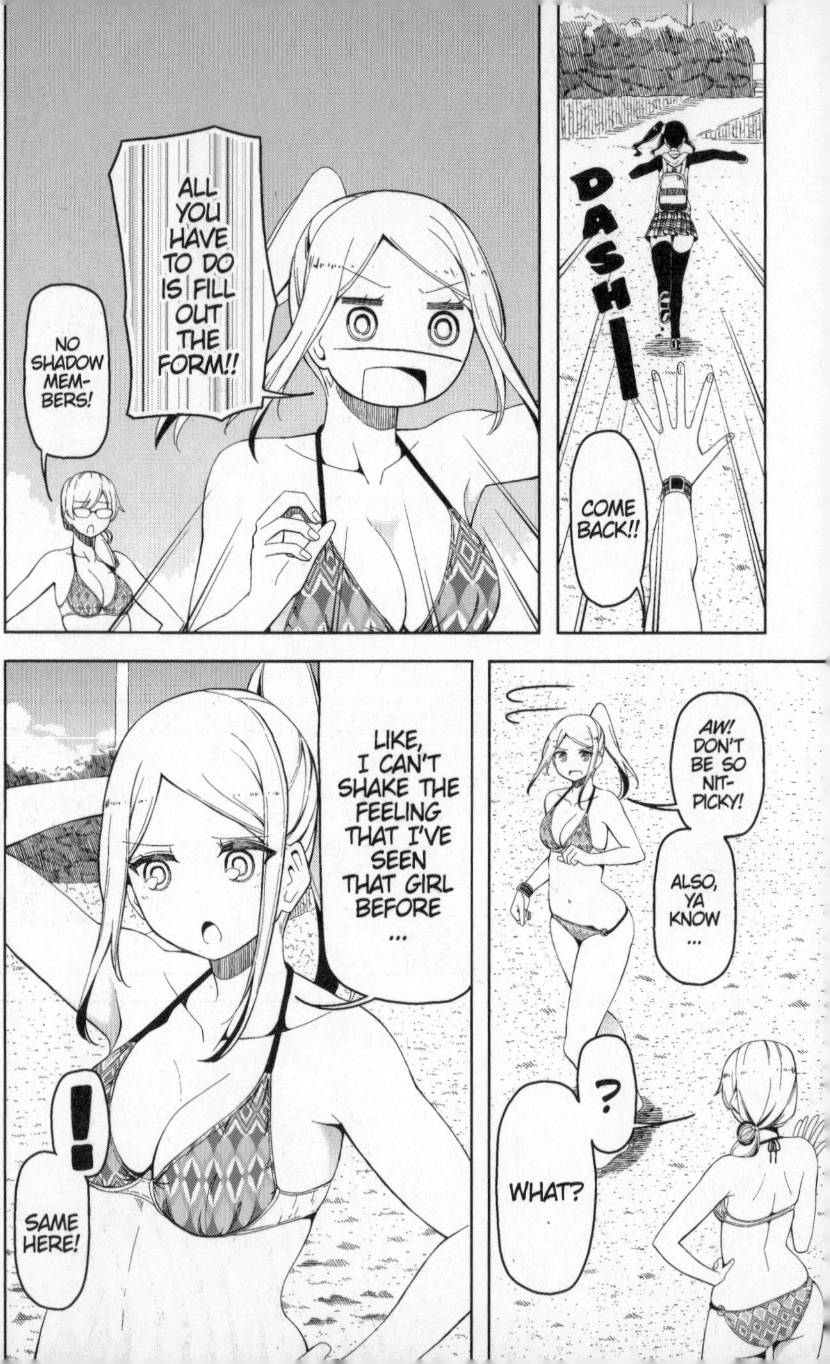
DASH
COME BACK!!
ALL YOU HAVE TO DO IS FILL OUT THE FORM!!
NO SHADOW MEM-BERS!
AW! DON'T BE SO NIT-PICKY!
ALSO, YA KNOW ...
?
WHAT?
LIKE, I CAN'T SHAKE THE FEELING THAT I'VE SEEN THAT GIRL BEFORE ...
!
SAME HERE!

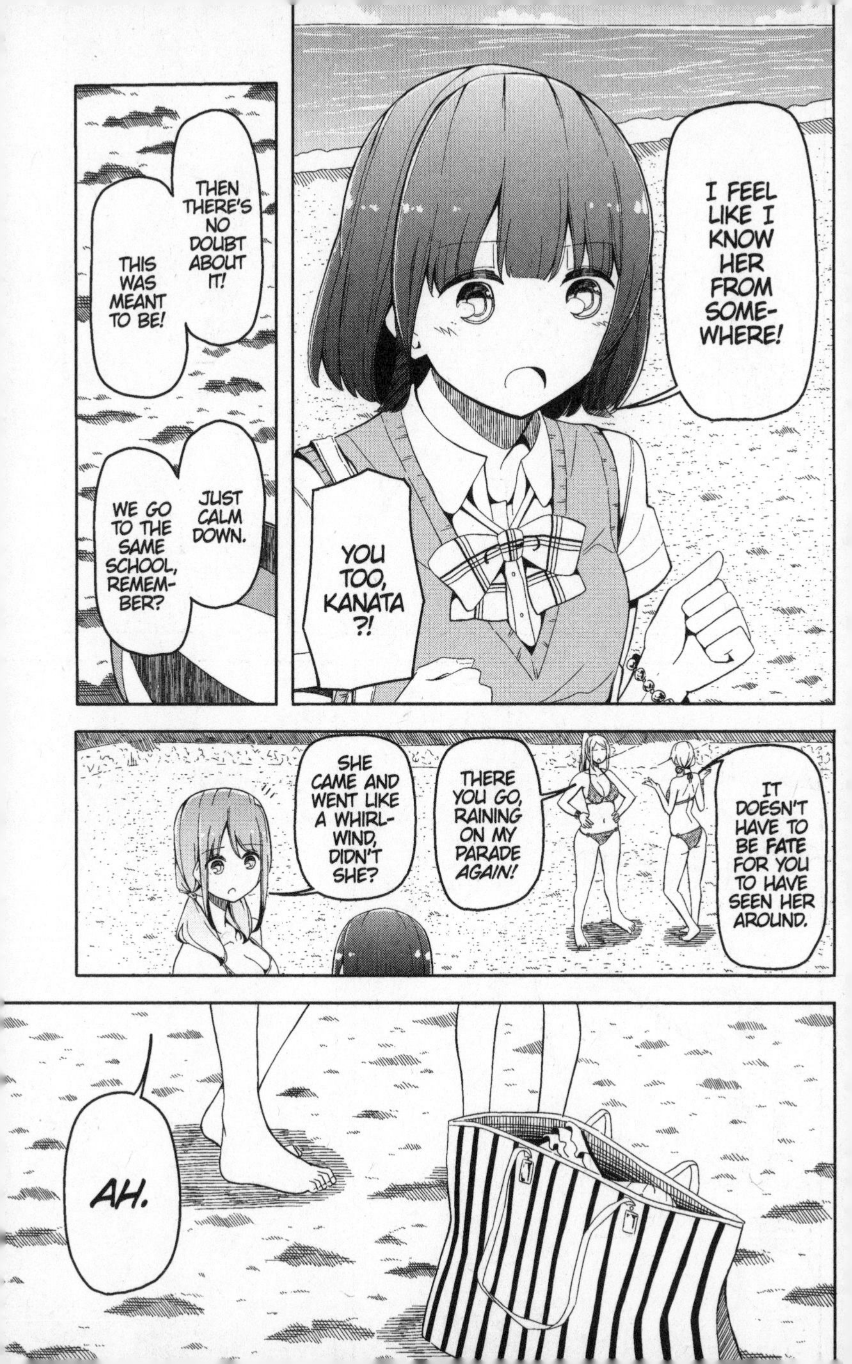
I FEEL LIKE I KNOW HER FROM SOME-WHERE!
YOU TOO, KANATA?!
THEN THERE'S NO DOUBT ABOUT IT!
THIS WAS MEANT TO BE!
JUST CALM DOWN.
WE GO TO THE SAME SCHOOL, REMEMBER?
IT DOESN'T HAVE TO BE FATE FOR YOU TO HAVE SEEN HER AROUND.
THERE YOU GO, RAINING ON MY PARADE AGAIN!
SHE CAME AND WENT LIKE A WHIRLWIND, DIDN'T SHE?
AH.

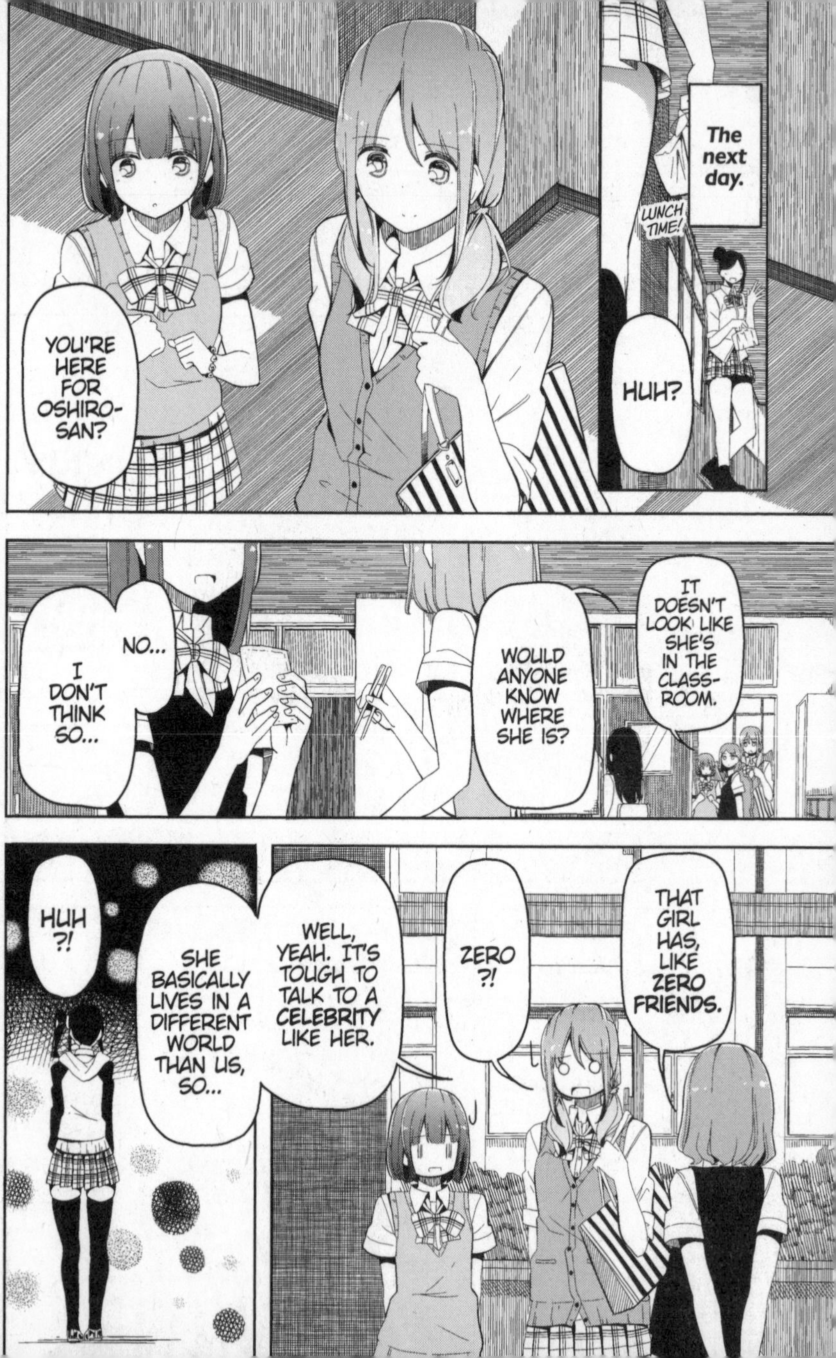
The next day.
LUNCH TIME!
HUH?
YOU'RE HERE FOR OSHIRO-SAN?
IT DOESN'T LOOK LIKE SHE'S IN THE CLASS-ROOM.
WOULD ANYONE KNOW WHERE SHE IS?
NO...
I DON'T THINK SO...
THAT GIRL HAS, LIKE ZERO FRIENDS.
ZERO?!
WELL, YEAH. IT'S TOUGH TO TALK TO A CELEBRITY LIKE HER.
SHE BASICALLY LIVES IN A DIFFERENT WORLD THAN US, SO...
HUH?!

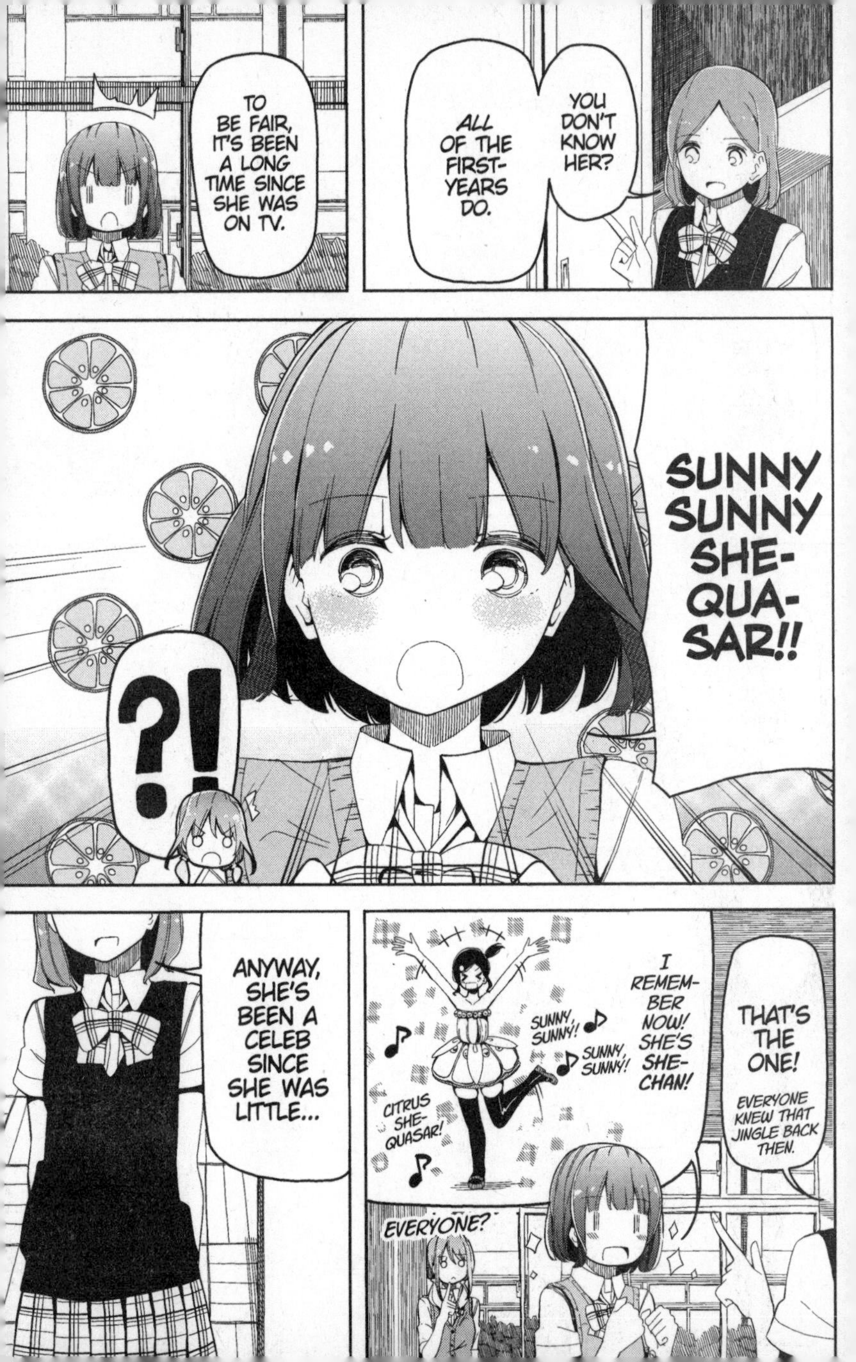
YOU DON'T KNOW HER?
ALL OF THE FIRST-YEARS DO.
TO BE FAIR, IT'S BEEN A LONG TIME SINCE SHE WAS ON TV.
SUNNY SUNNY SHE-QUA-SAR!!
?!
THAT'S THE ONE!
EVERYONE KNEW THAT JINGLE BACK THEN.
I REMEMBER NOW! SHE'S SHE-CHAN!
SUNNY, SUNNY!
SUNNY, SUNNY!
CITRUS SHE-QUASAR!
EVERYONE?
ANYWAY, SHE'S BEEN A CELEB SINCE SHE WAS LITTLE...

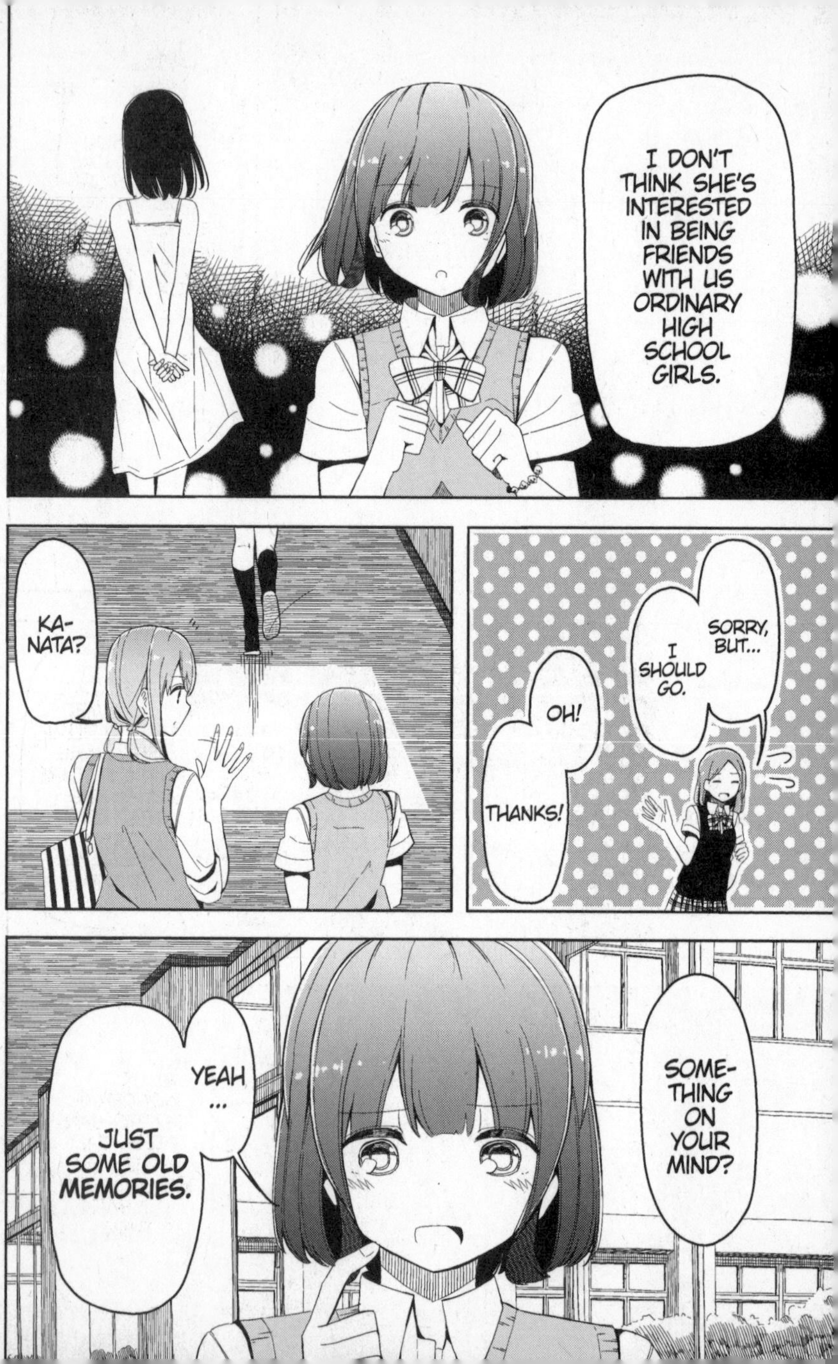
I DON'T THINK SHE'S INTERESTED IN BEING FRIENDS WITH US ORDINARY HIGH SCHOOL GIRLS.
SORRY, BUT...
I SHOULD GO.
OH!
THANKS!
KA-NATA?
SOME-THING ON YOUR MIND?
YEAH ...
JUST SOME OLD MEMORIES.

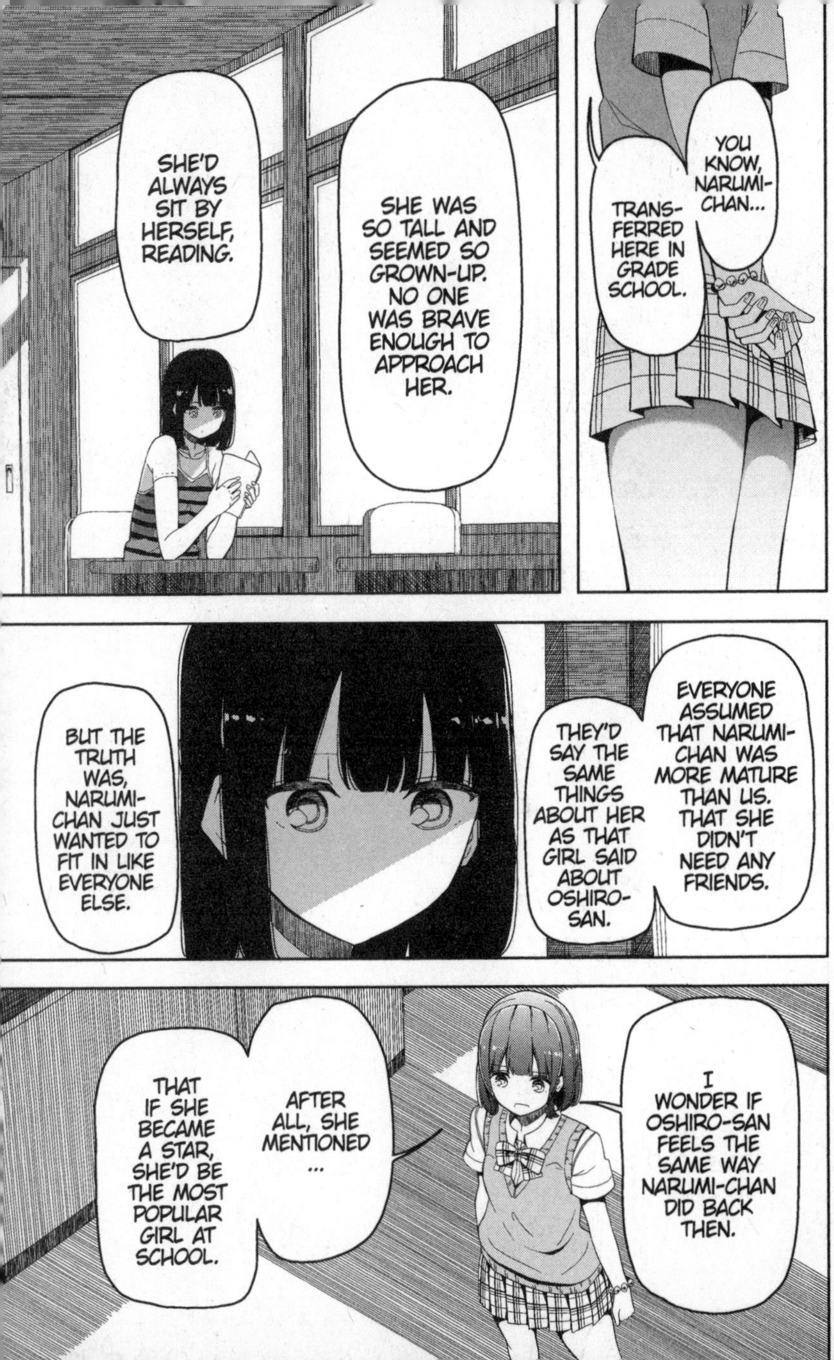
YOU KNOW, NARUMI-CHAN...
TRANS-FERRED HERE IN GRADE SCHOOL.
SHE WAS SO TALL AND SEEMED SO GROWN-UP. NO ONE WAS BRAVE ENOUGH TO APPROACH HER.
SHE'D ALWAYS SIT BY HERSELF, READING.
EVERYONE ASSUMED THAT NARUMI-CHAN WAS MORE MATURE THAN US. THAT SHE DIDN'T NEED ANY FRIENDS.
THEY'D SAY THE SAME THINGS ABOUT HER AS THAT GIRL SAID ABOUT OSHIRO-SAN.
BUT THE TRUTH WAS, NARUMI-CHAN JUST WANTED TO FIT IN LIKE EVERYONE ELSE.
I WONDER IF OSHIRO-SAN FEELS THE SAME WAY NARUMI-CHAN DID BACK THEN.
AFTER ALL, SHE MENTIONED...
THAT IF SHE BECAME A STAR, SHE'D BE THE MOST POPULAR GIRL AT SCHOOL.

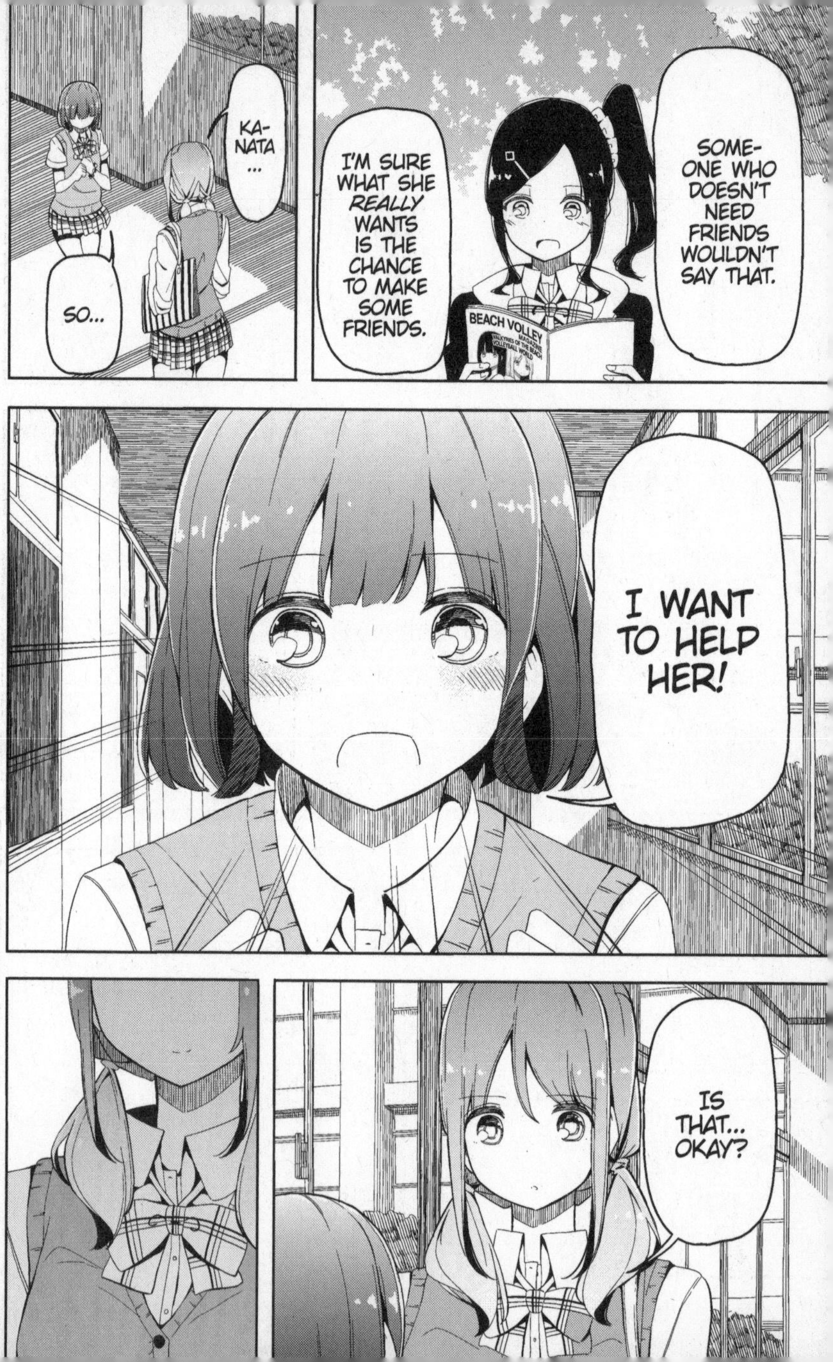
SOME-ONE WHO DOESN'T NEED FRIENDS WOULDN'T SAY THAT.
I'M SURE WHAT SHE *REALLY* WANTS IS THE CHANCE TO MAKE SOME FRIENDS.
BEACH VOLLEY
MAGAZINE
VALKYRIES OF THE BEACH
VOLLEYBALL WORLD
KA-NATA...
SO...
I WANT TO HELP HER!
IS THAT... OKAY?

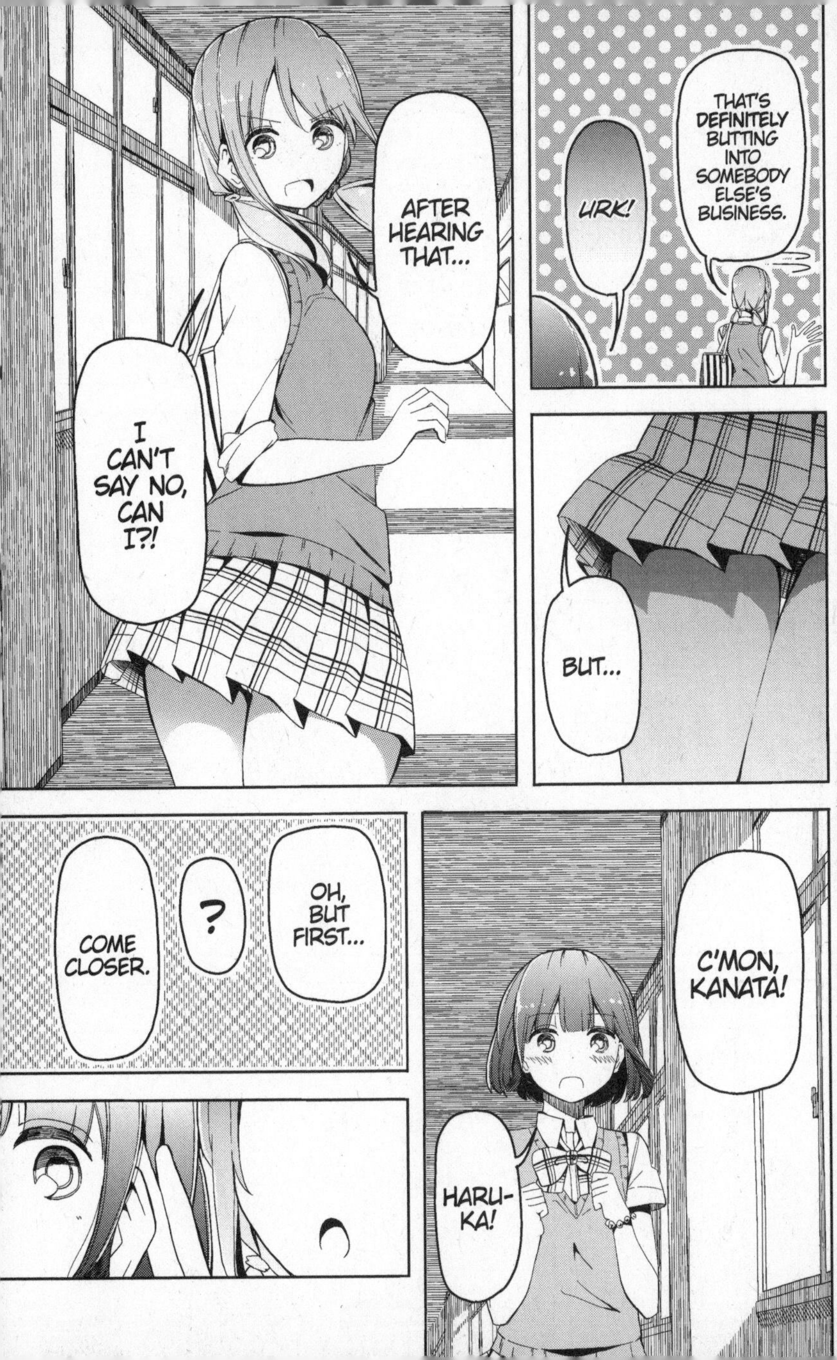
THAT'S DEFINITELY BUTTING INTO SOMEBODY ELSE'S BUSINESS.
URK!
BUT...
AFTER HEARING THAT...
I CAN'T SAY NO, CAN I?!
C'MON, KANATA!
HARU-KA!
OH, BUT FIRST...
?
COME CLOSER.

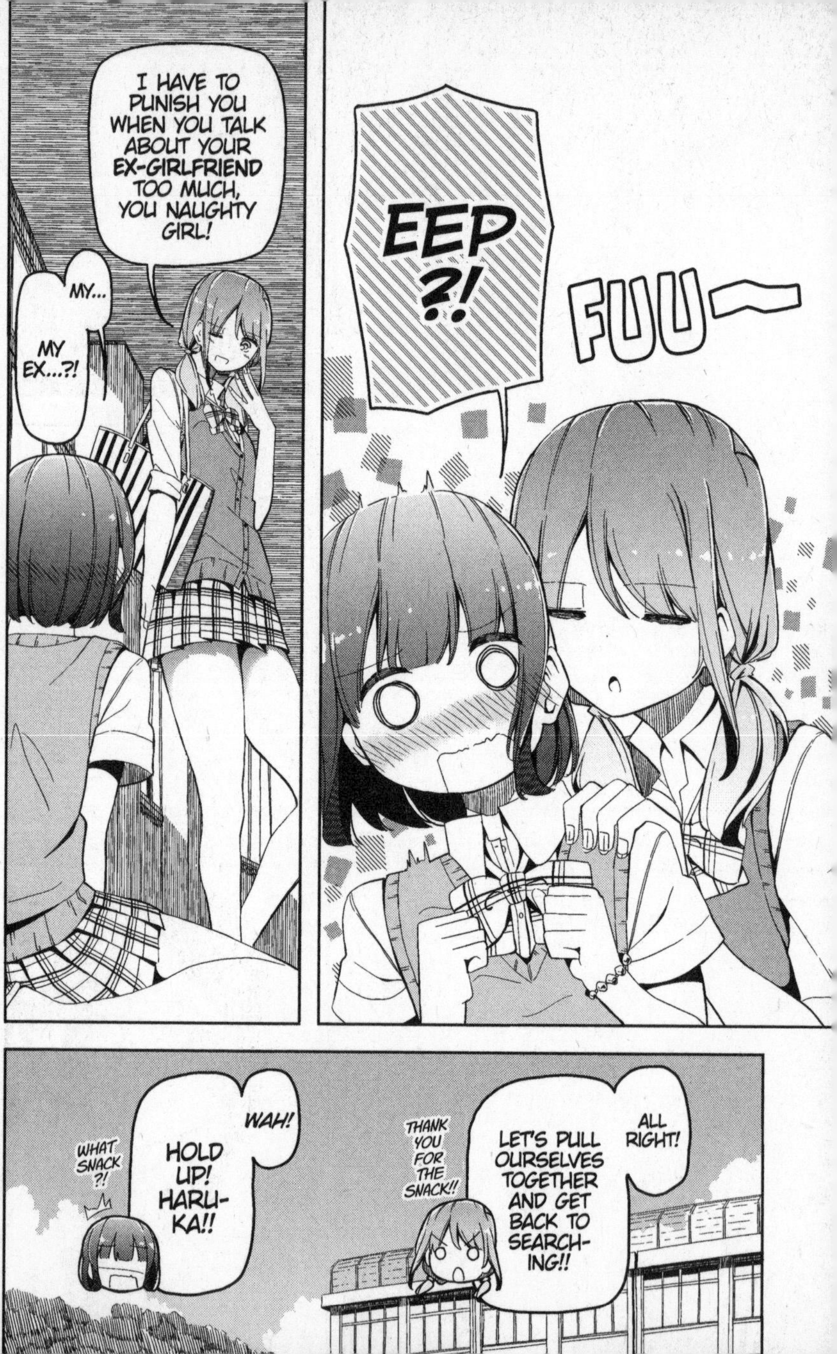
EEP ?!
FUU~
I HAVE TO PUNISH YOU WHEN YOU TALK ABOUT YOUR EX-GIRLFRIEND TOO MUCH, YOU NAUGHTY GIRL!
MY...
MY EX...?!
ALL RIGHT!
LET'S PULL OURSELVES TOGETHER AND GET BACK TO SEARCH-ING!!
THANK YOU FOR THE SNACK!!
WAH!
HOLD UP! HARU-KA!!
WHAT SNACK ?!

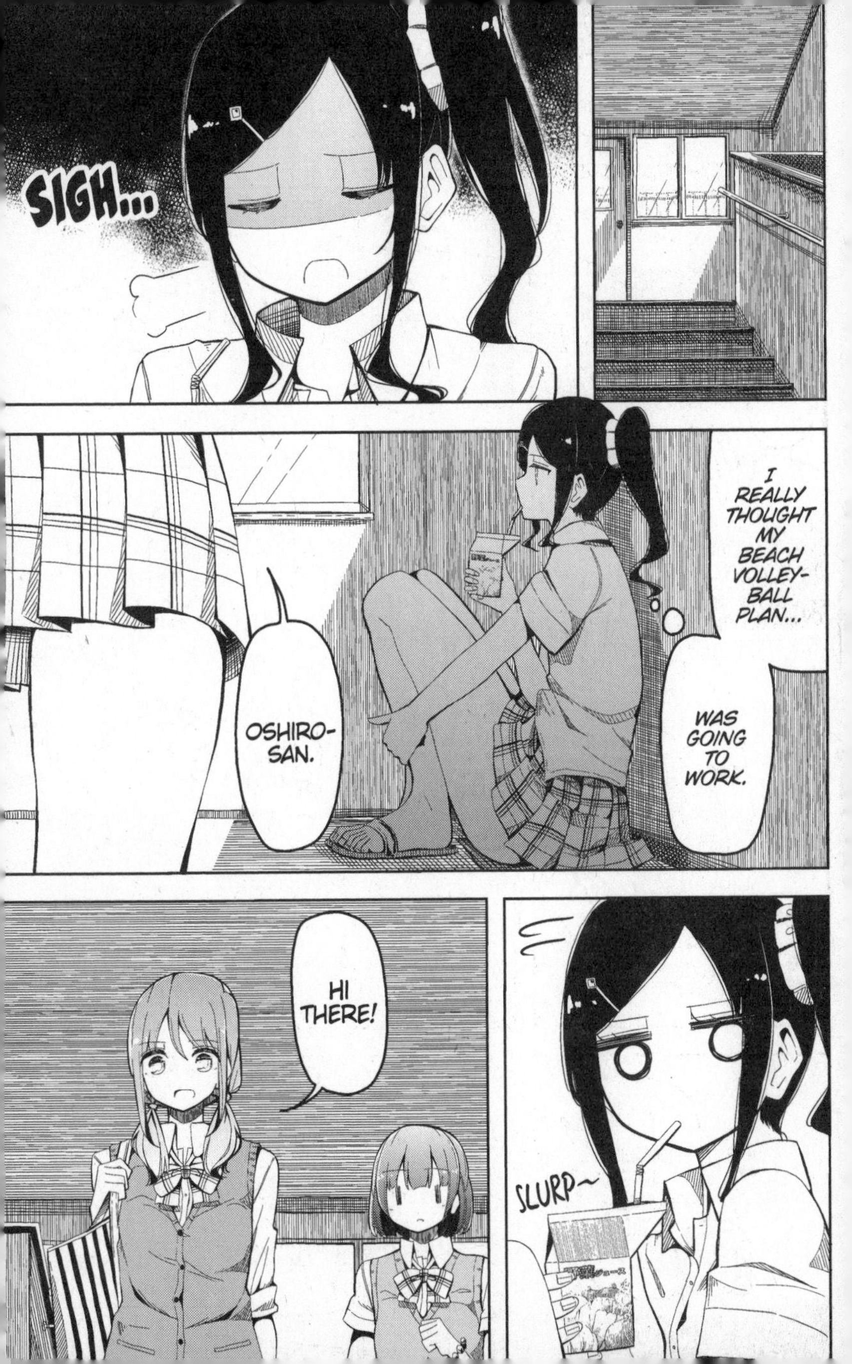
SIGH...
I REALLY THOUGHT MY BEACH VOLLEY-BALL PLAN...
WAS GOING TO WORK.
OSHIRO-SAN.
SLURP~
HI THERE!

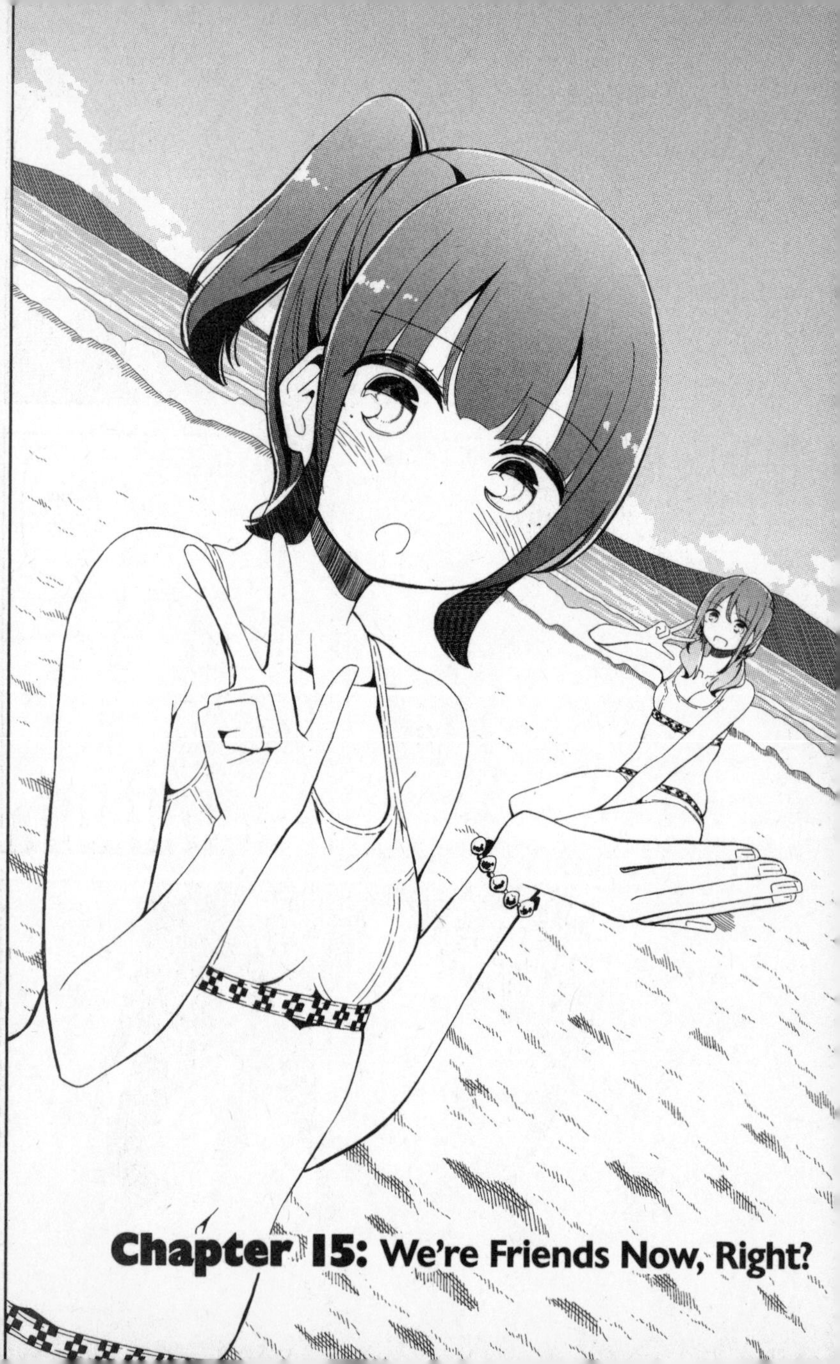

Chapter 15: We're Friends Now, Right?

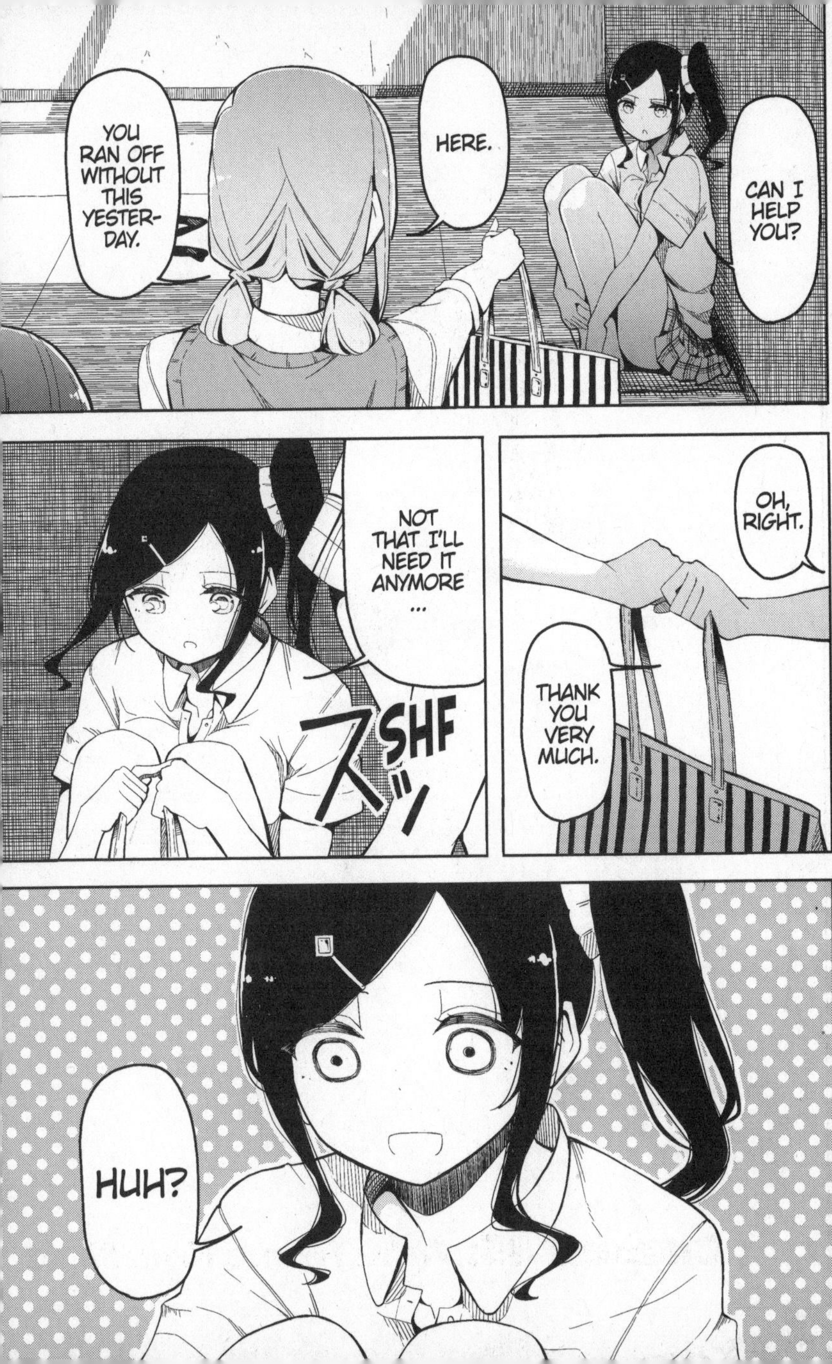
CAN I HELP YOU?
HERE.
YOU RAN OFF WITHOUT THIS YESTER-DAY.
OH, RIGHT.
THANK YOU VERY MUCH.
NOT THAT I'LL NEED IT ANYMORE ...
スッ
SHF
HUH?

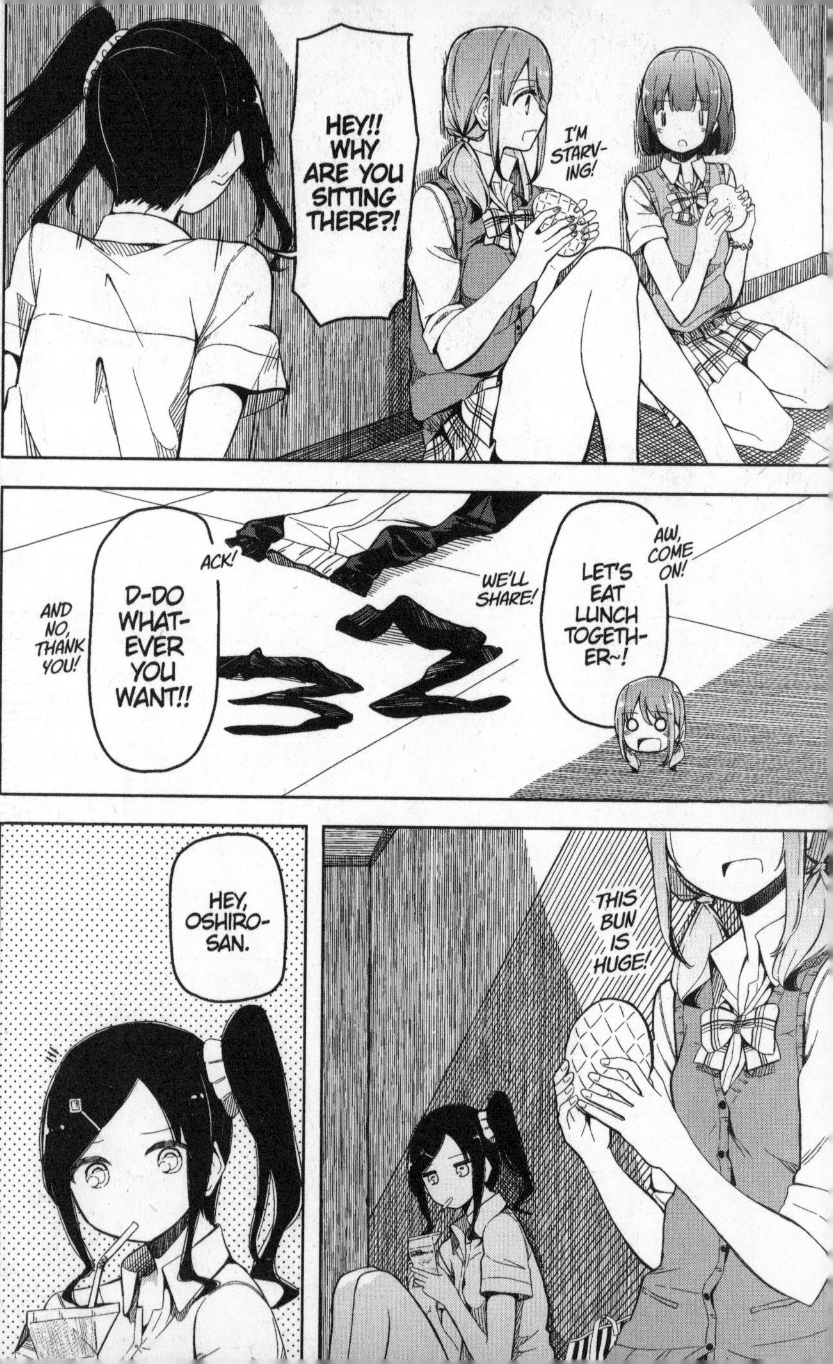
I'M STARV-ING!
HEY!! WHY ARE YOU SITTING THERE?!
AW, COME ON!
LET'S EAT LUNCH TOGETH-ER~!
WE'LL SHARE!
ACK!
D-DO WHAT-EVER YOU WANT!!
AND NO, THANK YOU!
THIS BUN IS HUGE!
HEY, OSHIRO-SAN.

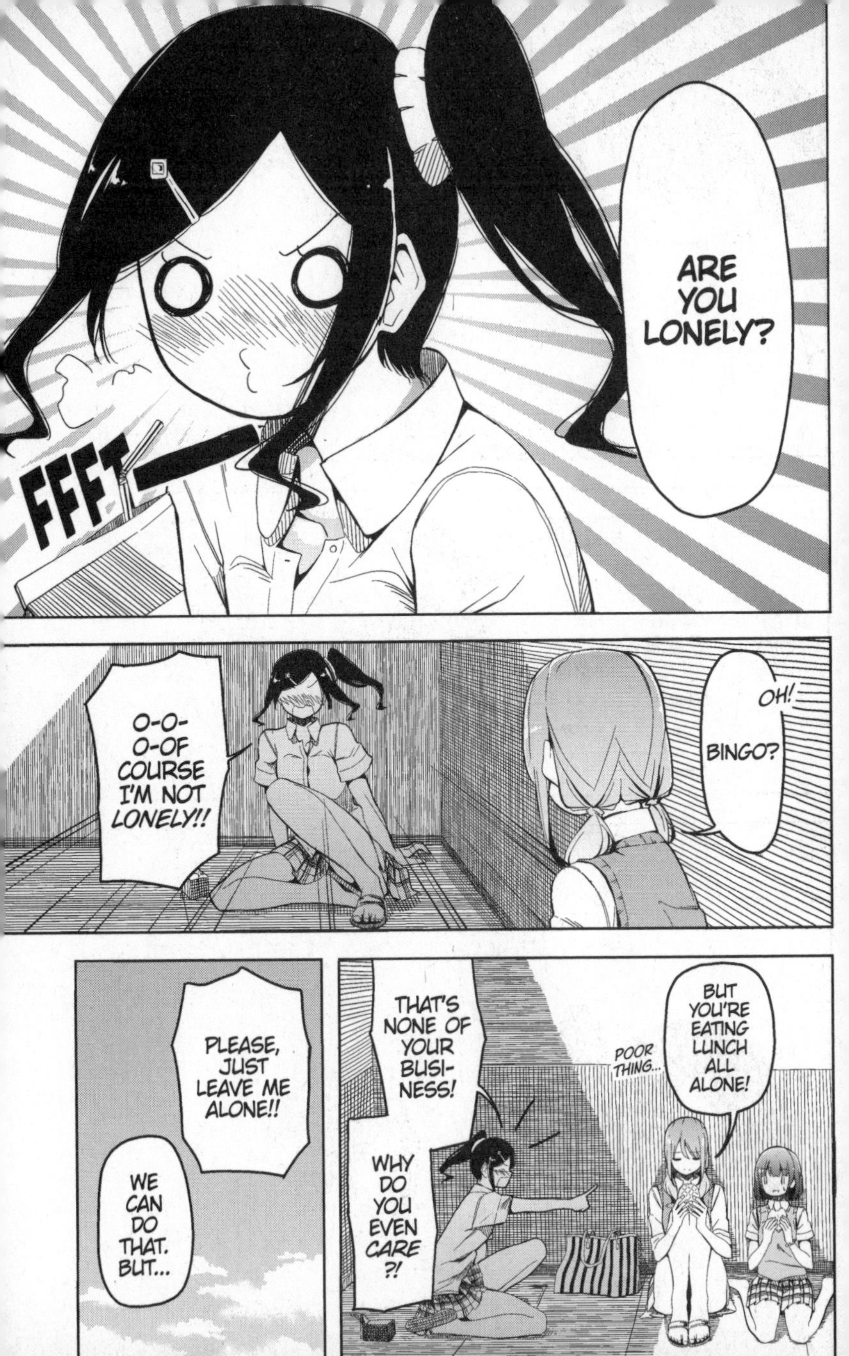
ARE YOU LONELY?
FFFT
OH!
BINGO?
O-O-O-OF COURSE I'M NOT LONELY!!
BUT YOU'RE EATING LUNCH ALL ALONE!
POOR THING...
THAT'S NONE OF YOUR BUSI-NESS!
WHY DO YOU EVEN CARE?!
PLEASE, JUST LEAVE ME ALONE!!
WE CAN DO THAT. BUT...

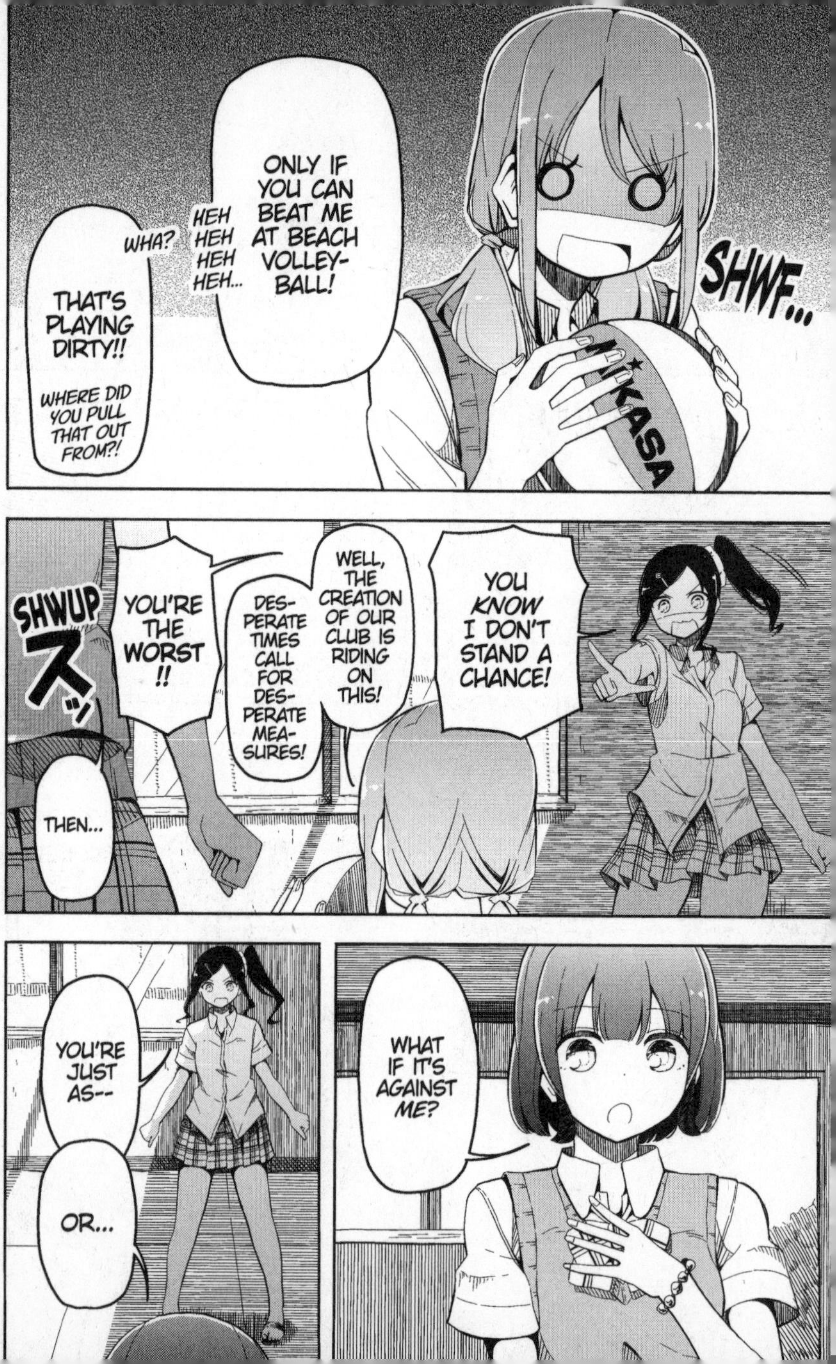
SHWF...
ONLY IF YOU CAN BEAT ME AT BEACH VOLLEY-BALL!
HEH HEH HEH HEH...
MIKASA
WHA?
THAT'S PLAYING DIRTY!!
WHERE DID YOU PULL THAT OUT FROM?!
YOU KNOW I DON'T STAND A CHANCE!
WELL, THE CREATION OF OUR CLUB IS RIDING ON THIS!
DES-PERATE TIMES CALL FOR DES-PERATE MEA-SURES!
YOU'RE THE WORST!!
SHWUP
スッ
THEN...
WHAT IF IT'S AGAINST ME?
YOU'RE JUST AS--
OR...

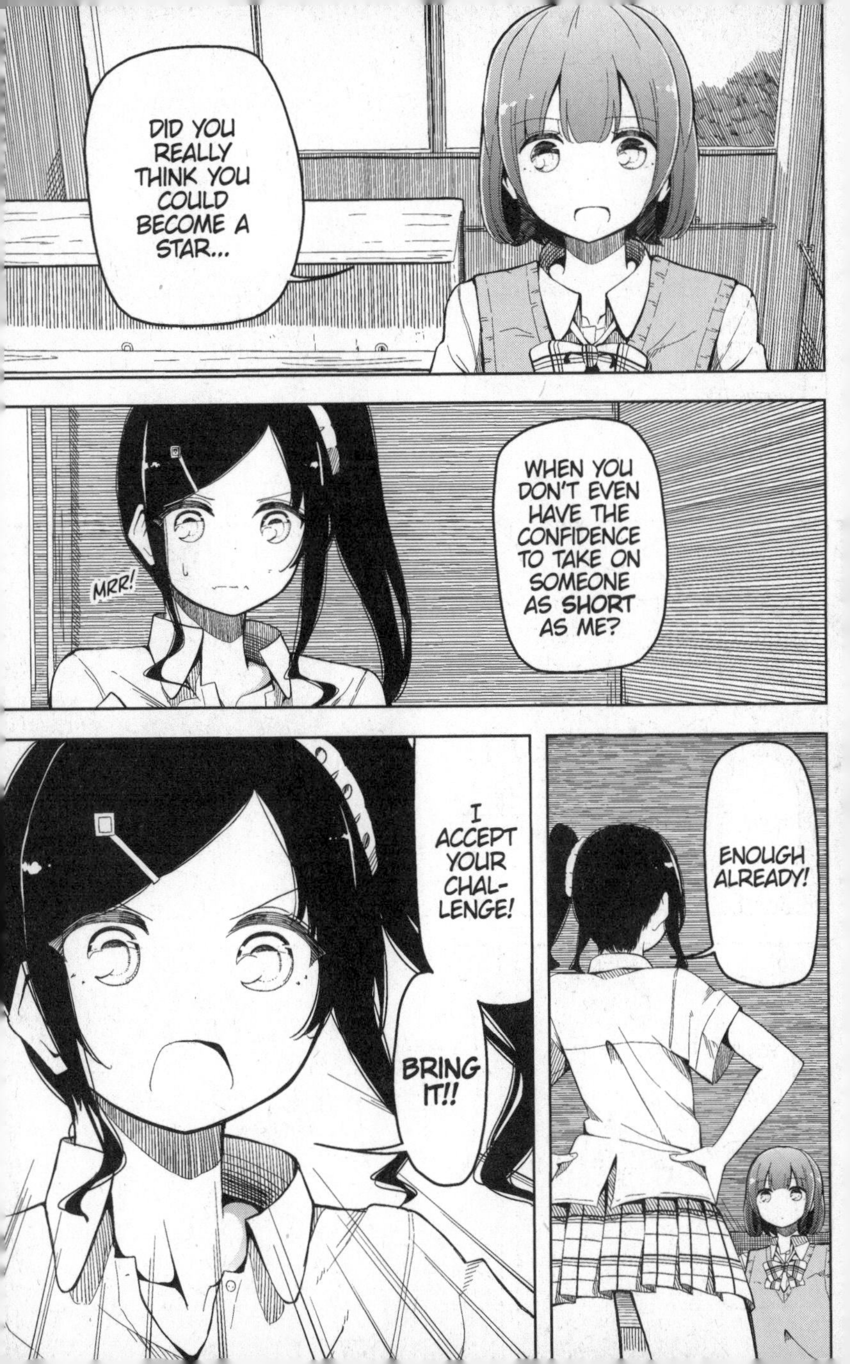
DID YOU REALLY THINK YOU COULD BECOME A STAR...
WHEN YOU DON'T EVEN HAVE THE CONFIDENCE TO TAKE ON SOMEONE AS SHORT AS ME?
MRR!
ENOUGH ALREADY!
I ACCEPT YOUR CHAL-LENGE!
BRING IT!!

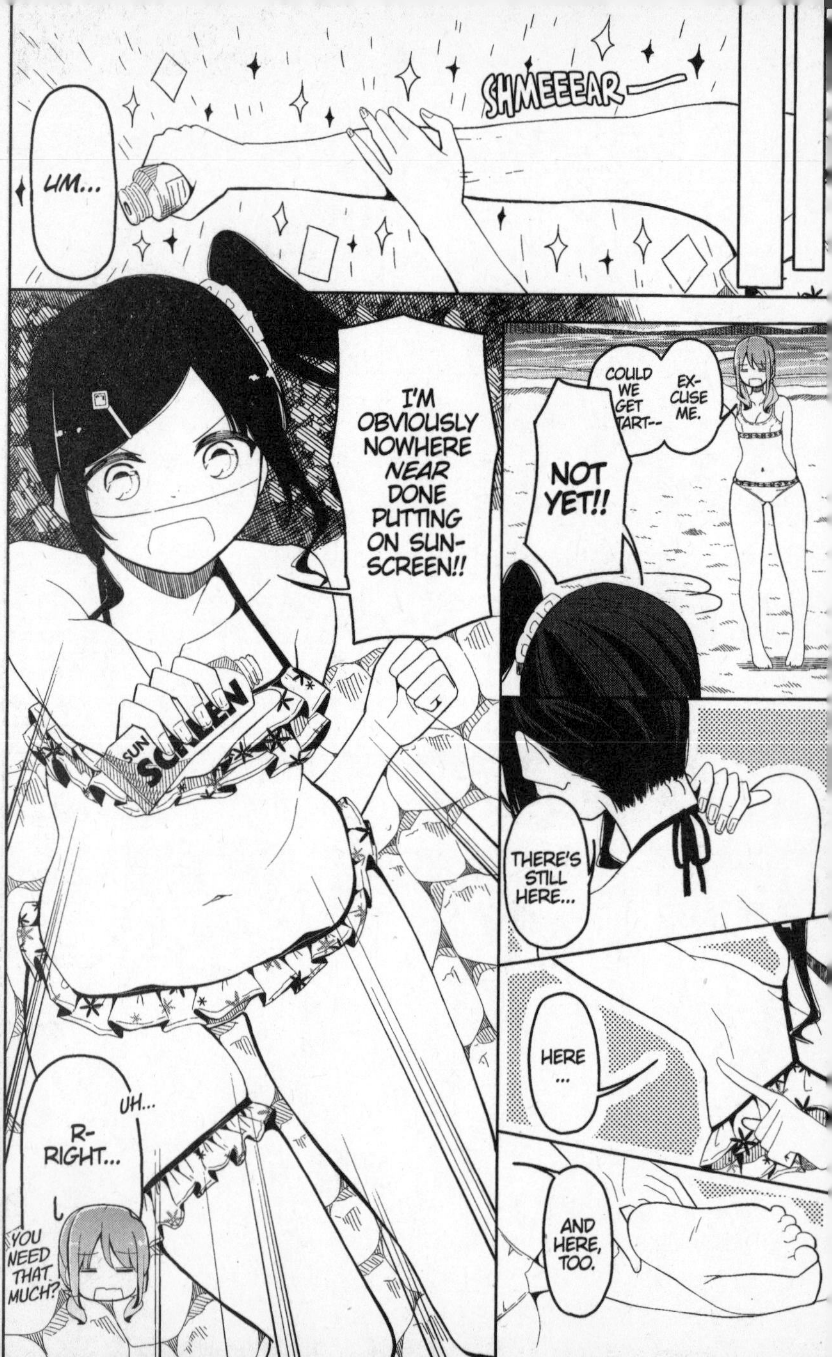

SHMEEEAR
UM...
EX-CUSE ME.
COULD WE GET START--
NOT YET!!
THERE'S STILL HERE...
HERE ...
AND HERE, TOO.
I'M OBVIOUSLY NOWHERE *NEAR* DONE PUTTING ON SUN-SCREEN!!
SUN SCREEN
UH...
R-RIGHT...
YOU NEED THAT MUCH?

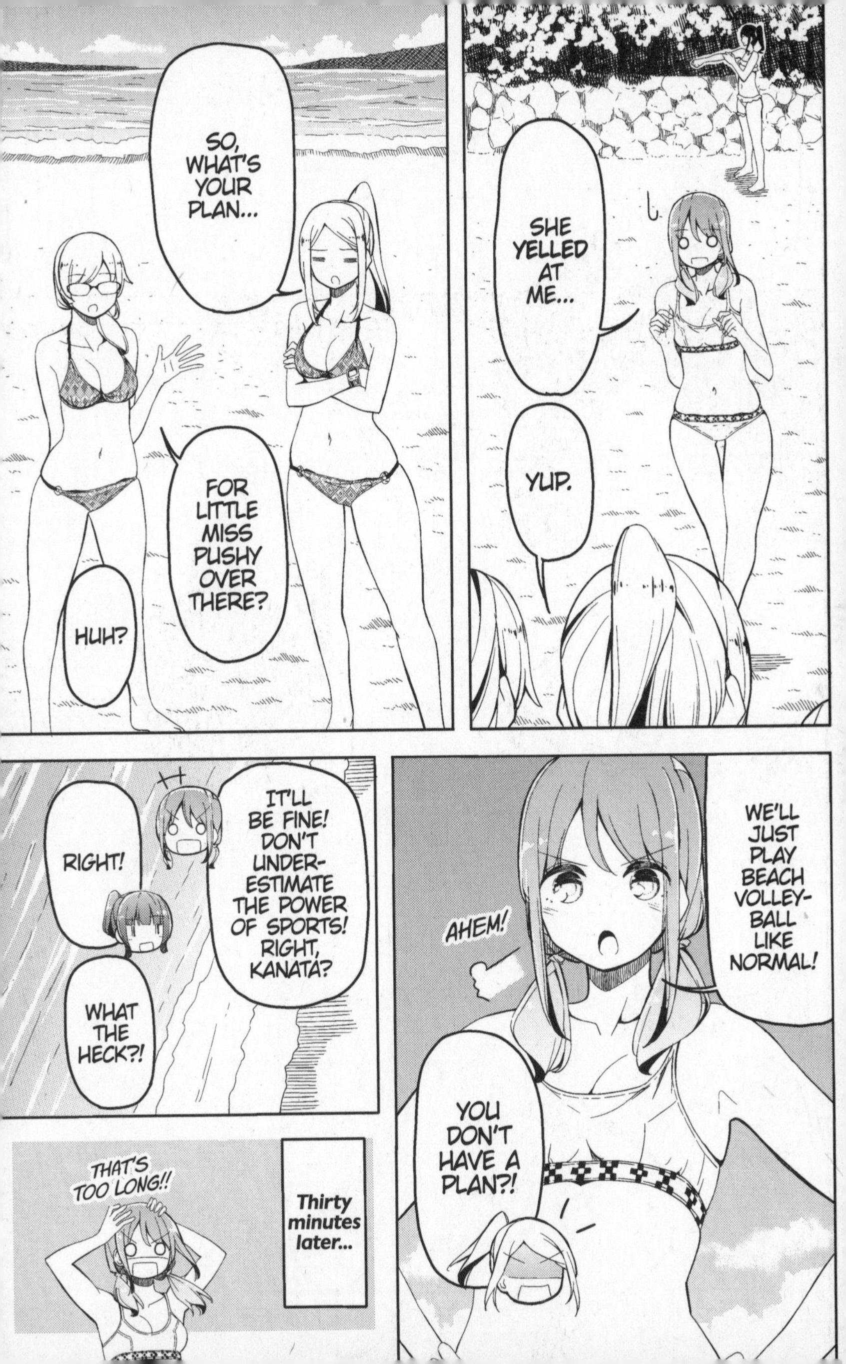
SHE YELLED AT ME...
YUP.
SO, WHAT'S YOUR PLAN...
FOR LITTLE MISS PUSHY OVER THERE?
HUH?
WE'LL JUST PLAY BEACH VOLLEY-BALL LIKE NORMAL!
AHEM!
YOU DON'T HAVE A PLAN?!
IT'LL BE FINE! DON'T UNDER-ESTIMATE THE POWER OF SPORTS! RIGHT, KANATA?
RIGHT!
WHAT THE HECK?!
Thirty minutes later...
THAT'S TOO LONG!!

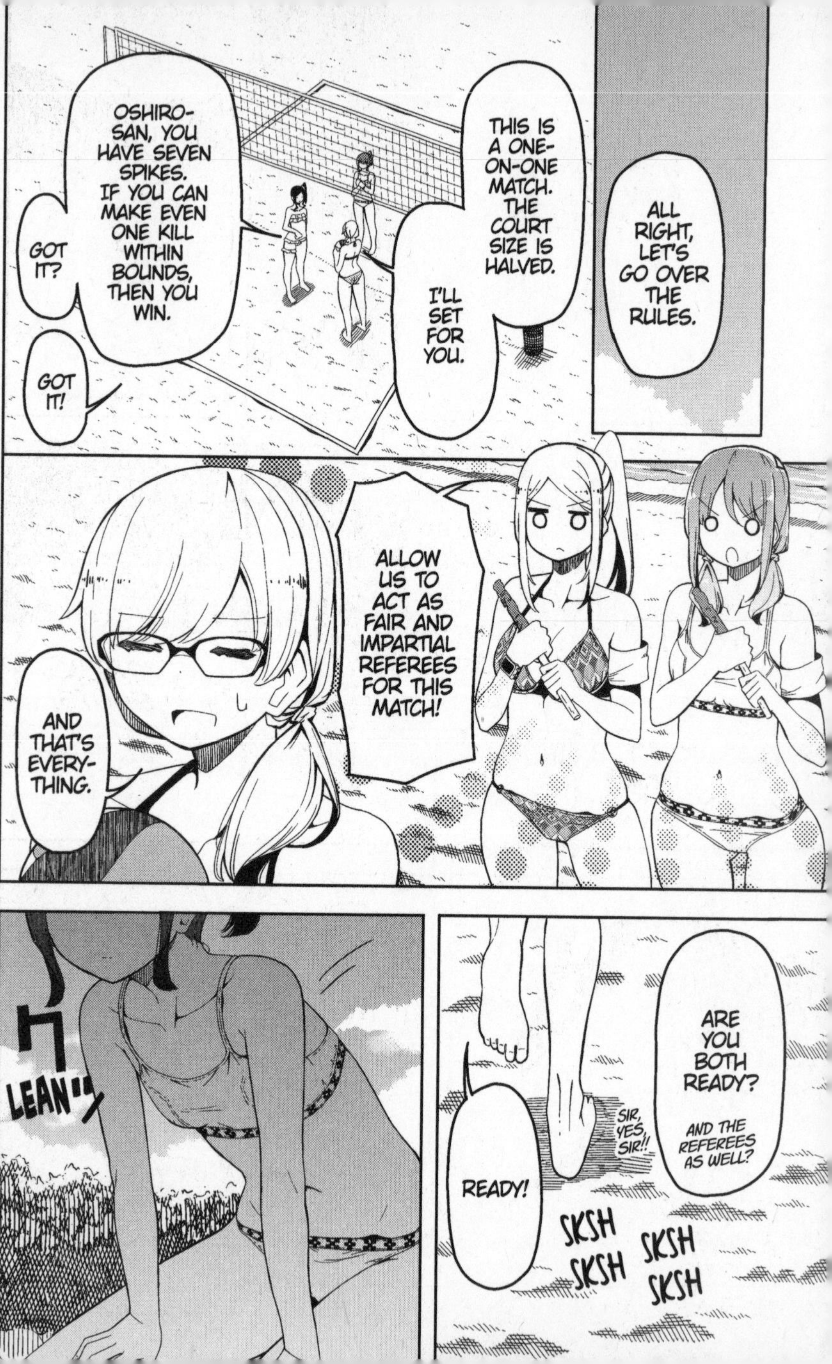
ALL RIGHT, LET'S GO OVER THE RULES.
THIS IS A ONE-ON-ONE MATCH. THE COURT SIZE IS HALVED.
I'LL SET FOR YOU.
OSHIRO-SAN, YOU HAVE SEVEN SPIKES. IF YOU CAN MAKE EVEN ONE KILL WITHIN BOUNDS, THEN YOU WIN.
GOT IT?
GOT IT!
ALLOW US TO ACT AS FAIR AND IMPARTIAL REFEREES FOR THIS MATCH!
AND THAT'S EVERY-THING.
ARE YOU BOTH READY?
AND THE REFEREES AS WELL?
SIR, YES, SIR!!
READY!
SKSH SKSH
SKSH SKSH
LEAN

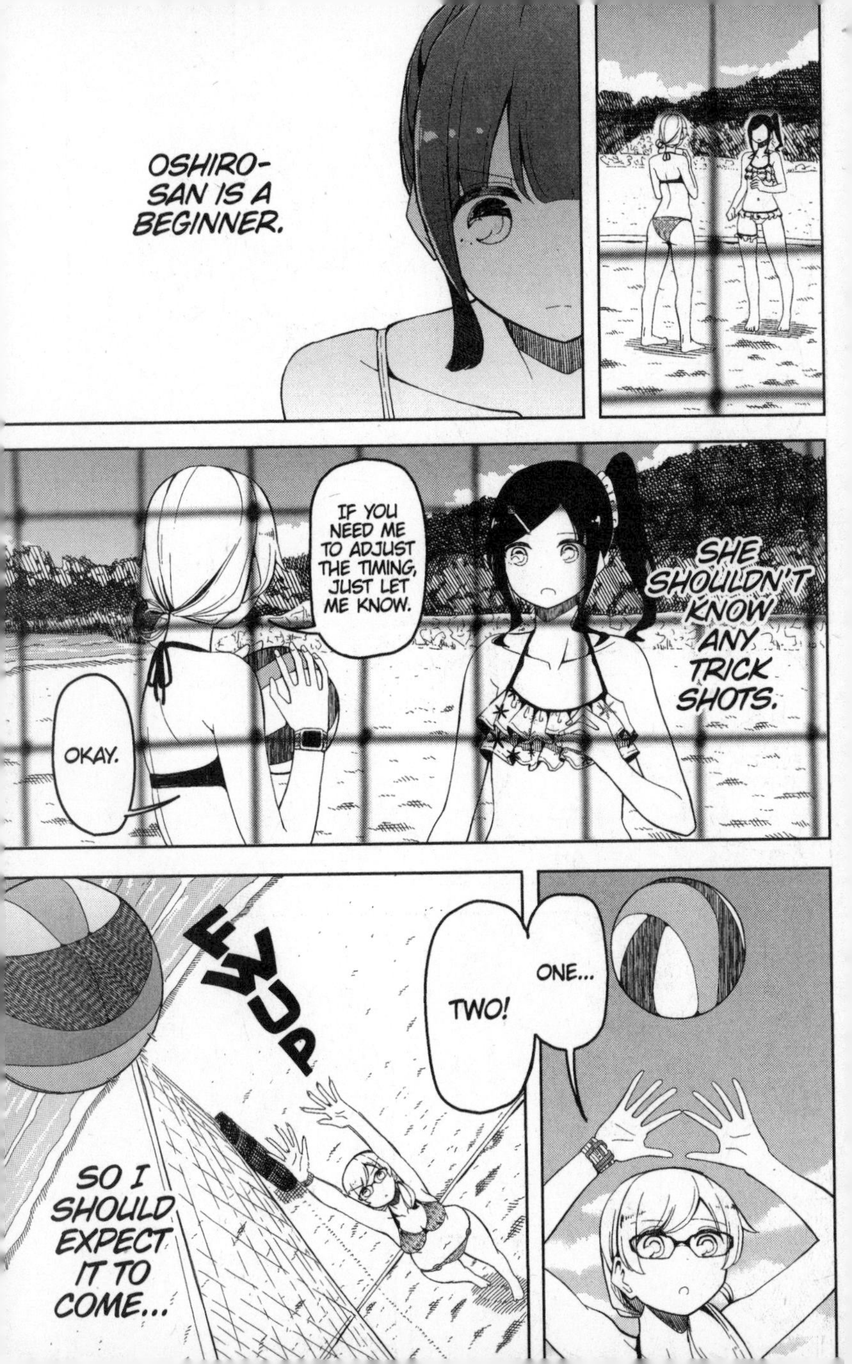
OSHIRO-SAN IS A BEGINNER.
SHE SHOULDN'T KNOW ANY TRICK SHOTS.
IF YOU NEED ME TO ADJUST THE TIMING, JUST LET ME KNOW.
OKAY.
ONE...
TWO!
FWUP
SO I SHOULD EXPECT IT TO COME...

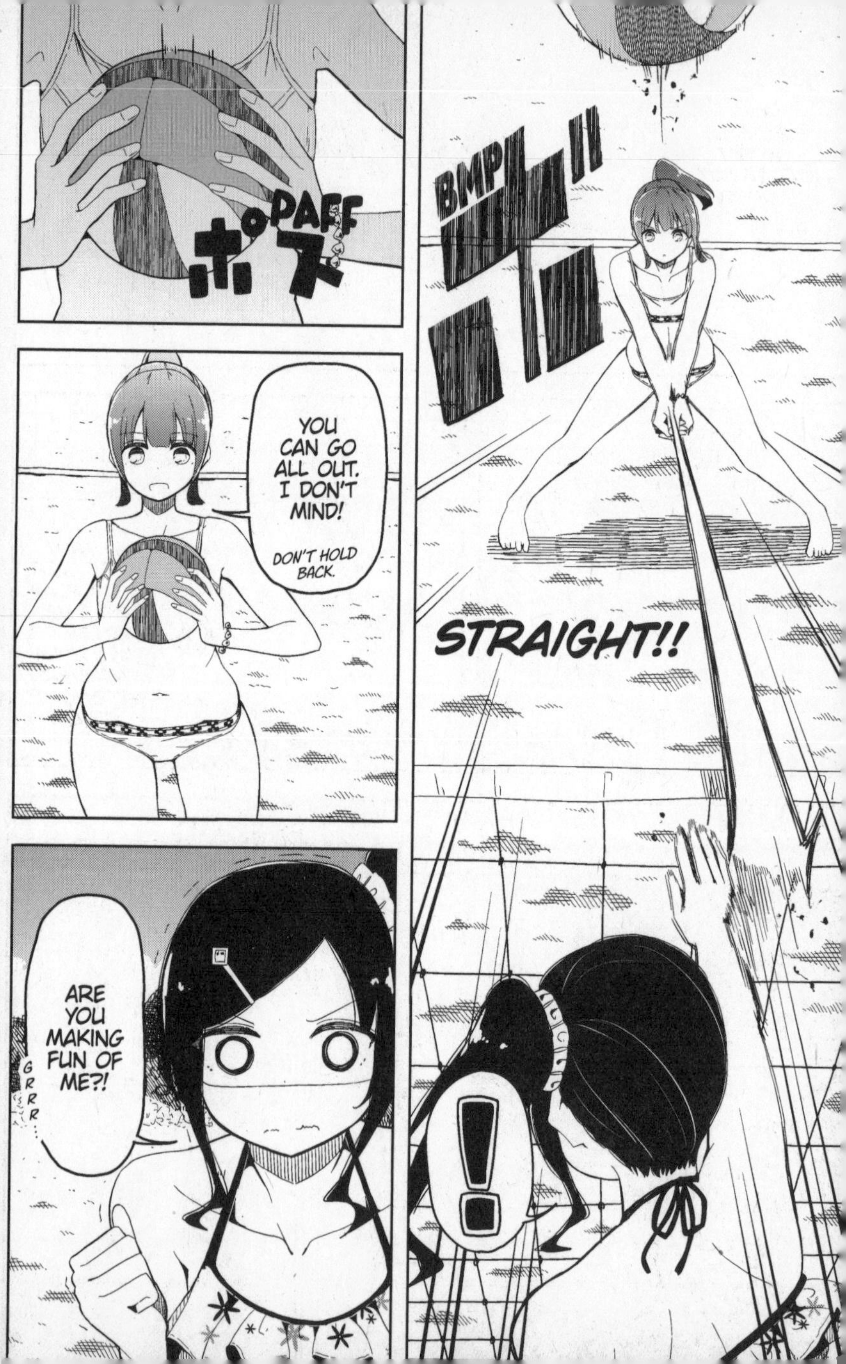
BMP!!
STRAIGHT!!
!
PAFF
YOU CAN GO ALL OUT. I DON'T MIND!
DON'T HOLD BACK.
ARE YOU MAKING FUN OF ME?!
GRRR...

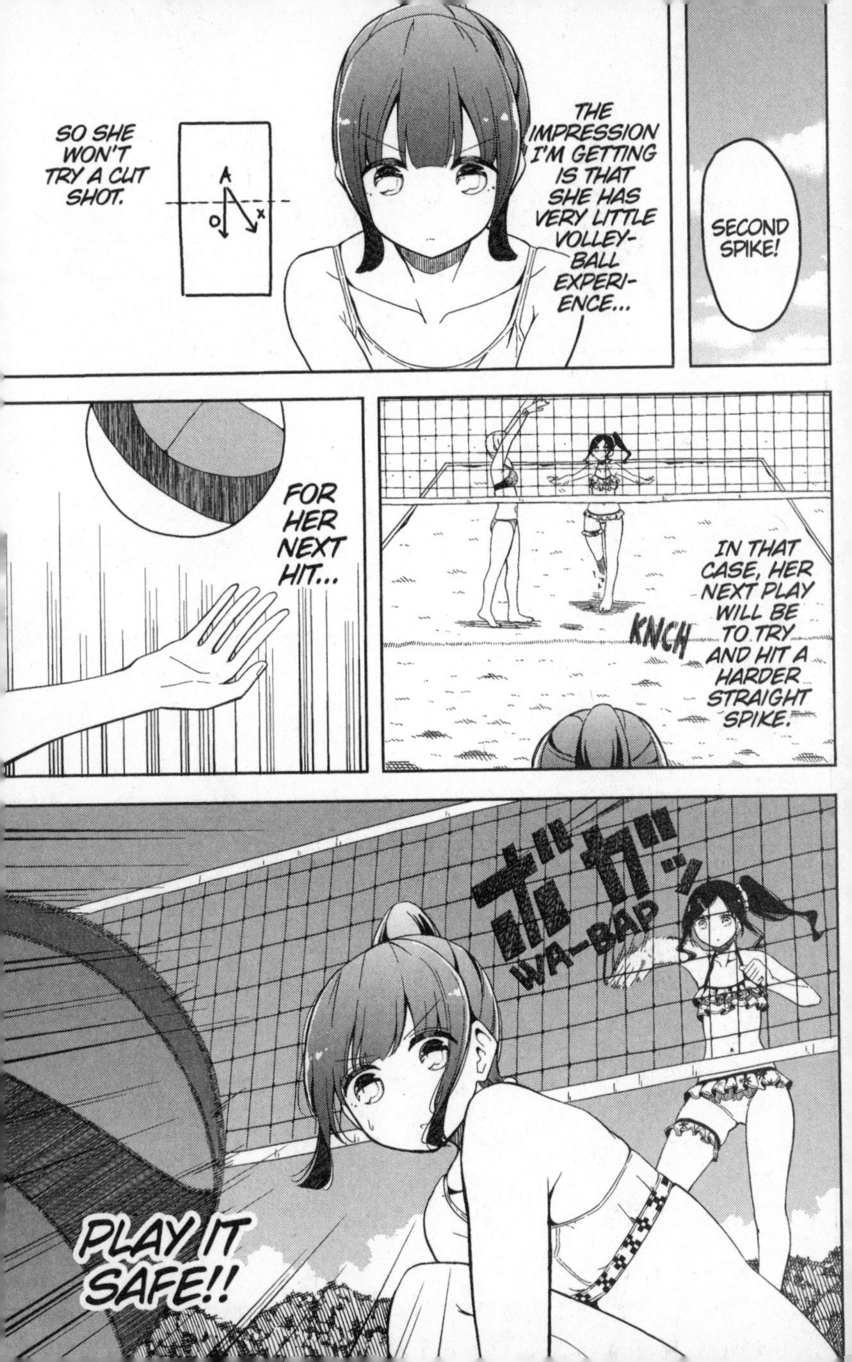
SECOND SPIKE!
THE IMPRESSION I'M GETTING IS THAT SHE HAS VERY LITTLE VOLLEY-BALL EXPERI-ENCE...
SO SHE WON'T TRY A CUT SHOT.
A
O
X
IN THAT CASE, HER NEXT PLAY WILL BE TO TRY AND HIT A HARDER STRAIGHT SPIKE.
KNCH
FOR HER NEXT HIT...
WA-BAP
PLAY IT SAFE!!

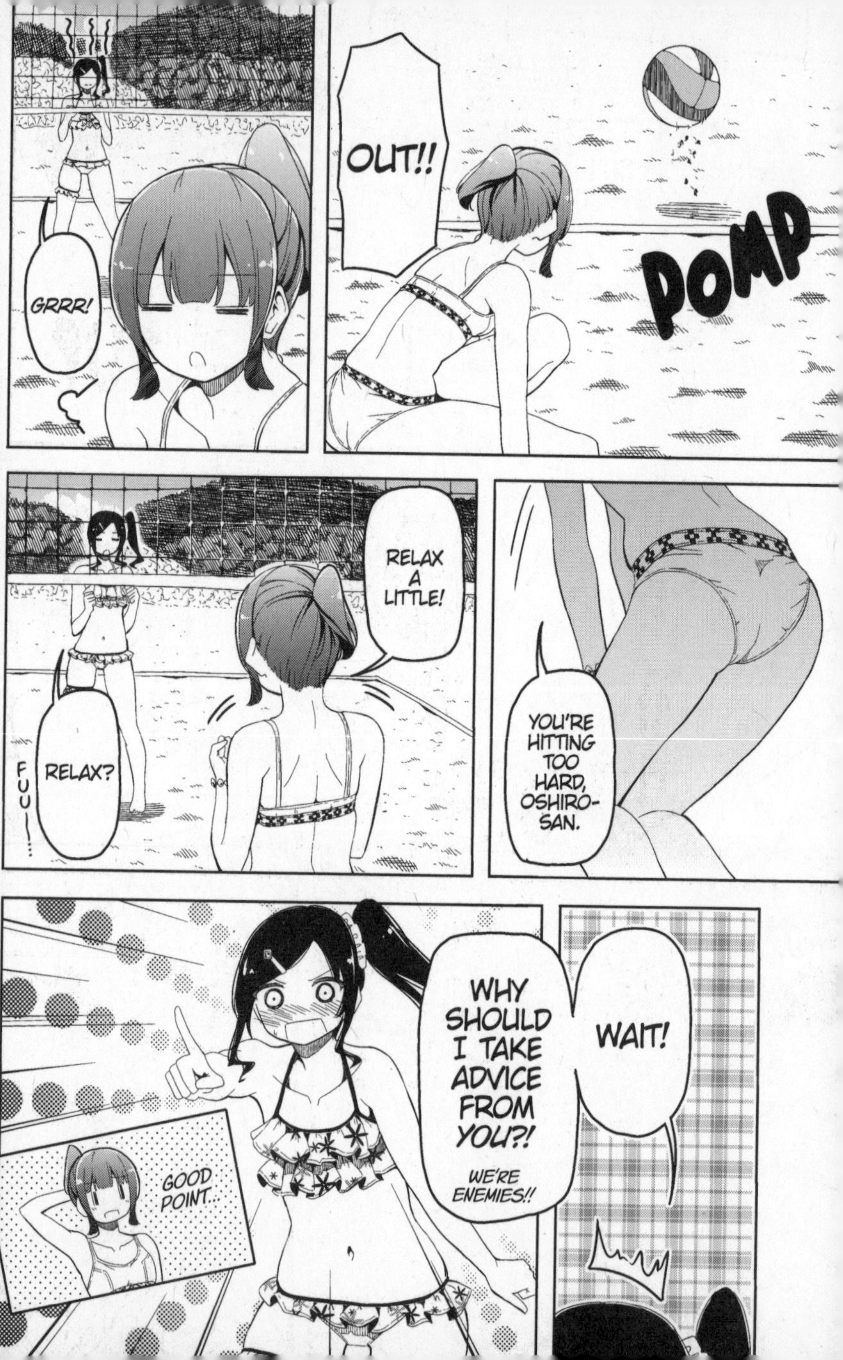
OUT!!
POMP
GRRR!
YOU'RE HITTING TOO HARD, OSHIRO-SAN.
RELAX A LITTLE!
RELAX?
FUU—...
WAIT!
WHY SHOULD I TAKE ADVICE FROM YOU?!
WE'RE ENEMIES!!
GOOD POINT...

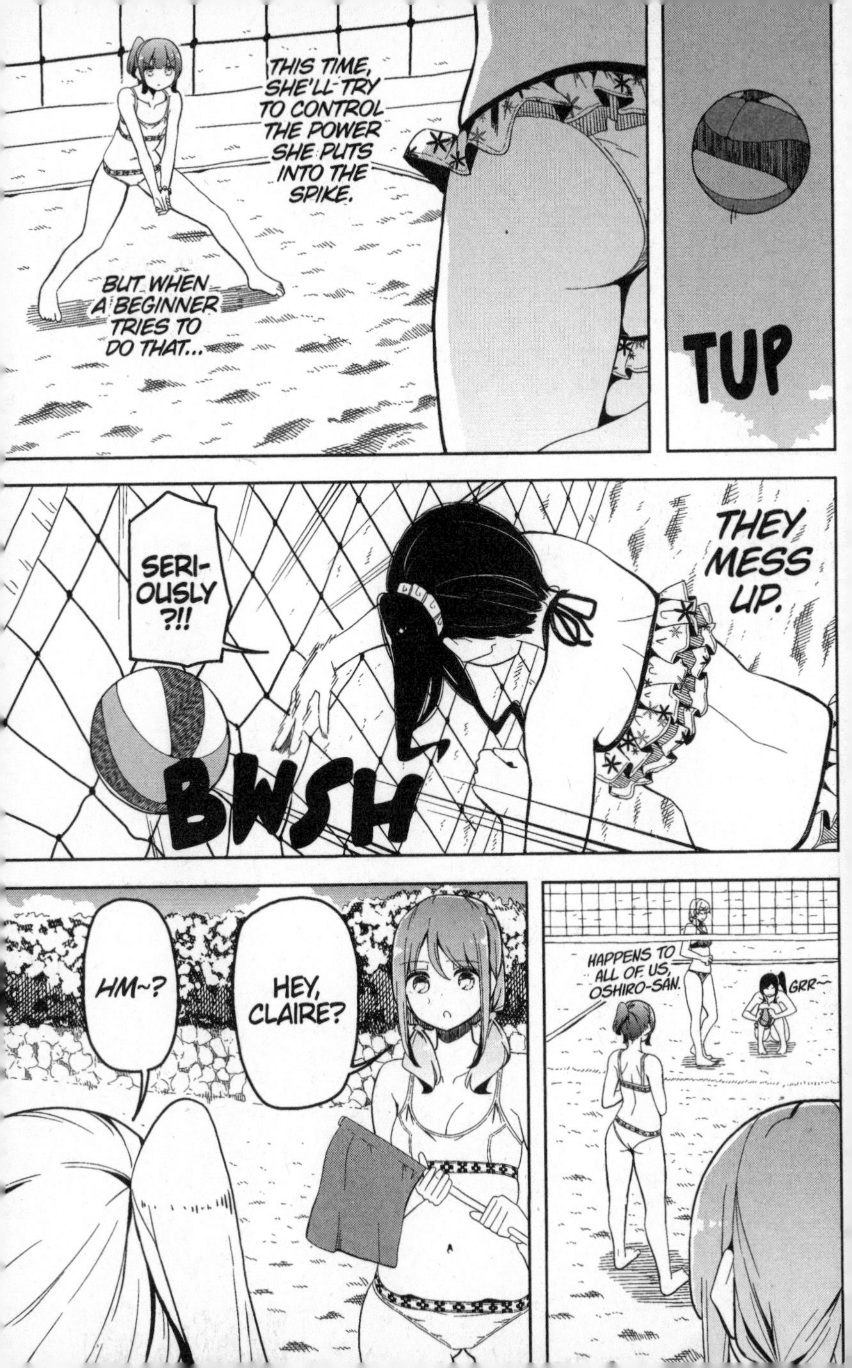
TUP
THIS TIME, SHE'LL TRY TO CONTROL THE POWER SHE PUTS INTO THE SPIKE.
BUT WHEN A BEGINNER TRIES TO DO THAT...
THEY MESS UP.
SERI-OUSLY ?!!
BWSH
GRR~
HAPPENS TO ALL OF US, OSHIRO-SAN.
HEY, CLAIRE?
HM~?

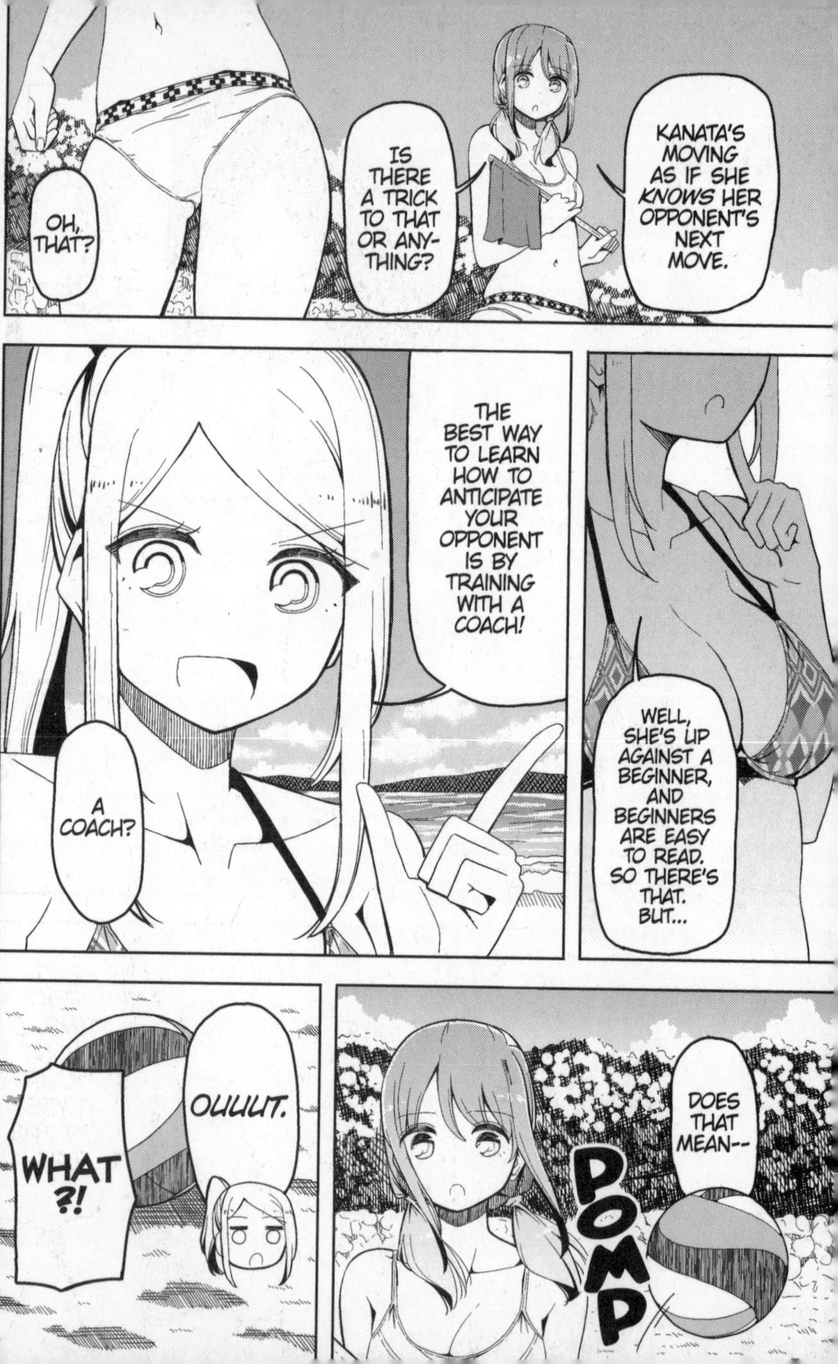

KANATA'S MOVING AS IF SHE *KNOWS* HER OPPONENT'S NEXT MOVE.
IS THERE A TRICK TO THAT OR ANY-THING?
OH, THAT?
WELL, SHE'S UP AGAINST A BEGINNER, AND BEGINNERS ARE EASY TO READ. SO THERE'S THAT. BUT...
THE BEST WAY TO LEARN HOW TO ANTICIPATE YOUR OPPONENT IS BY TRAINING WITH A COACH!
A COACH?
DOES THAT MEAN--
POMP
OUUUT.
WHAT ?!

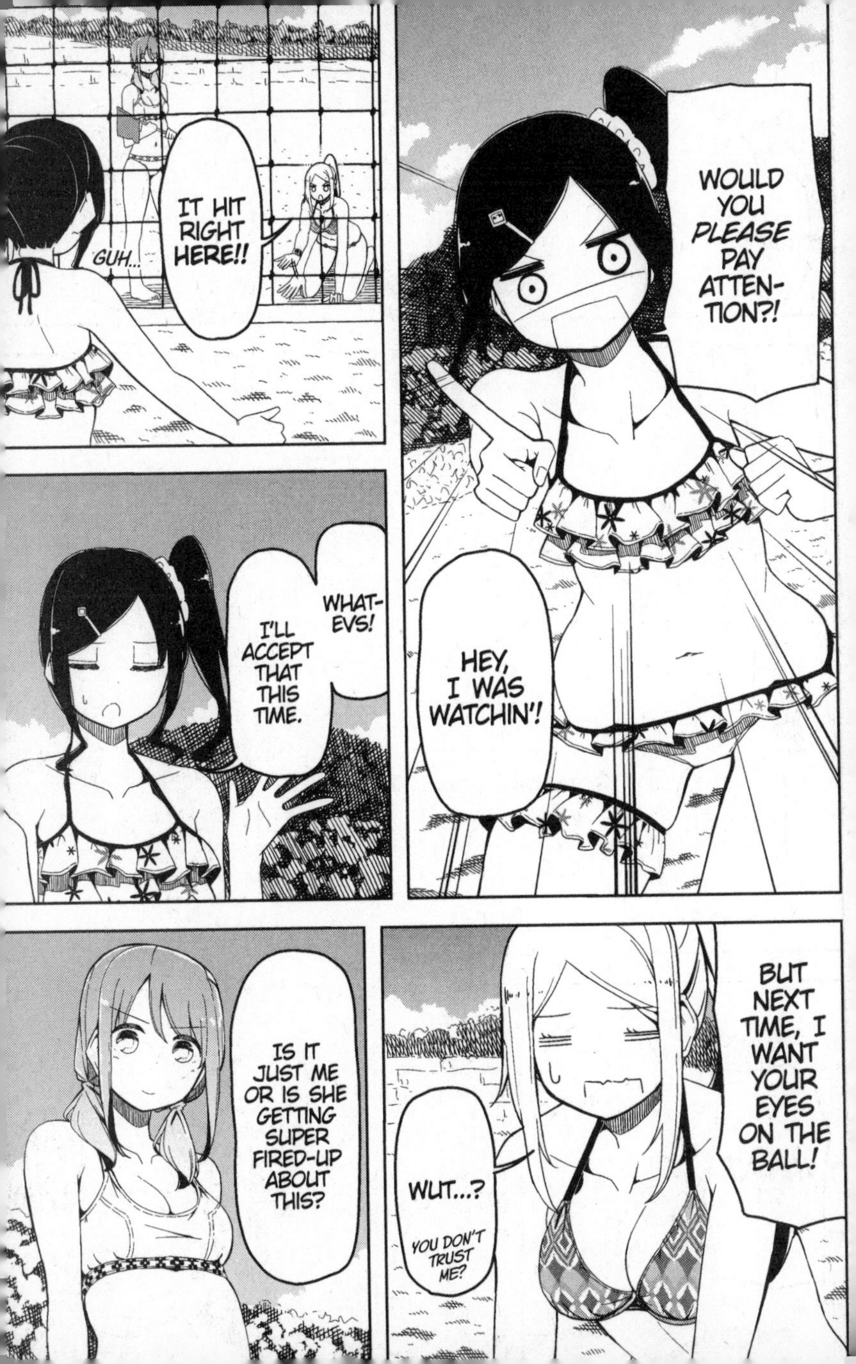
WOULD YOU PLEASE PAY ATTENTION?!
HEY, I WAS WATCHIN'!
IT HIT RIGHT HERE!!
GUH...
WHAT-EVS!
I'LL ACCEPT THAT THIS TIME.
BUT NEXT TIME, I WANT YOUR EYES ON THE BALL!
WUT...?
YOU DON'T TRUST ME?
IS IT JUST ME OR IS SHE GETTING SUPER FIRED-UP ABOUT THIS?

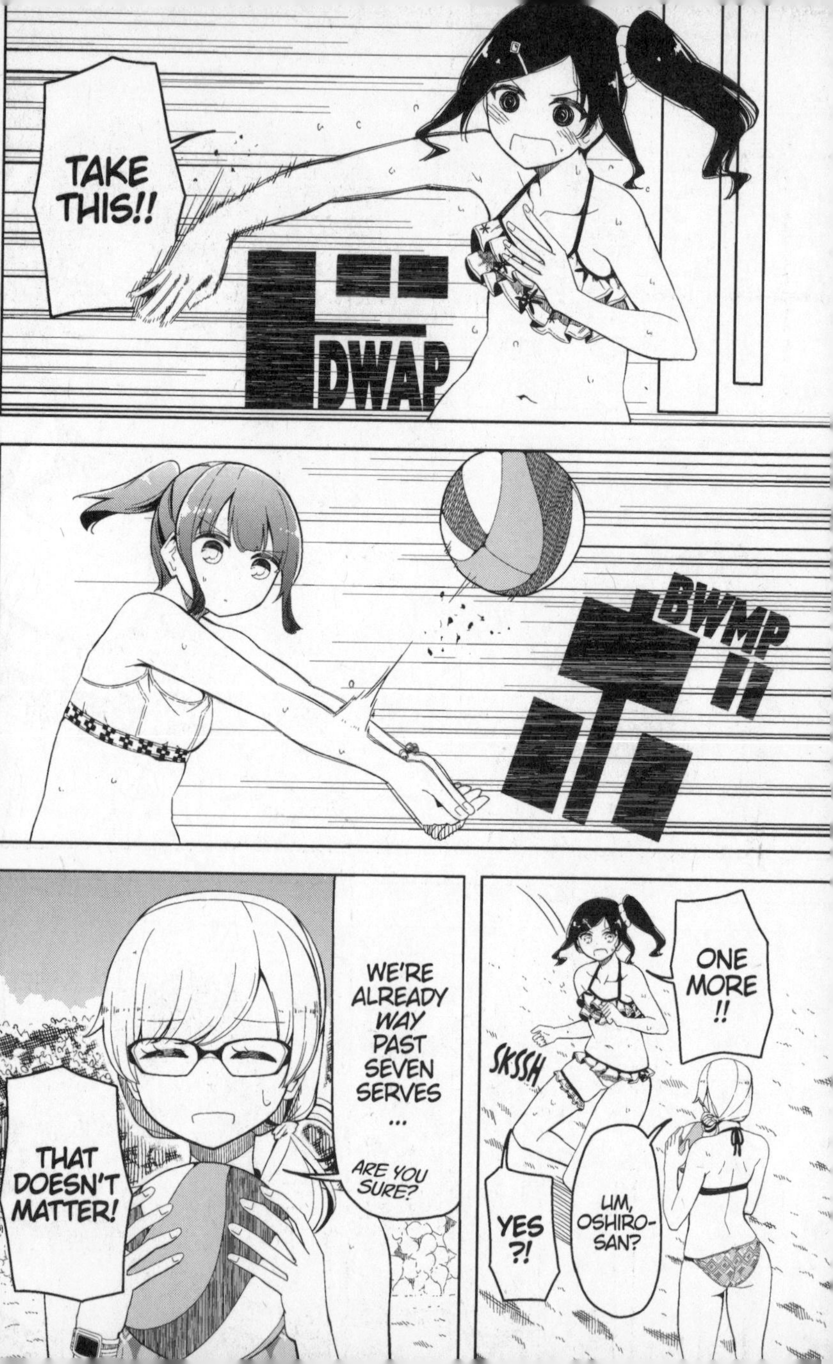
TAKE THIS!!
DWAP
BWMP!!
ONE MORE!!
SKSSH
UM, OSHIRO-SAN?
YES?!
WE'RE ALREADY WAY PAST SEVEN SERVES...
ARE YOU SURE?
THAT DOESN'T MATTER!

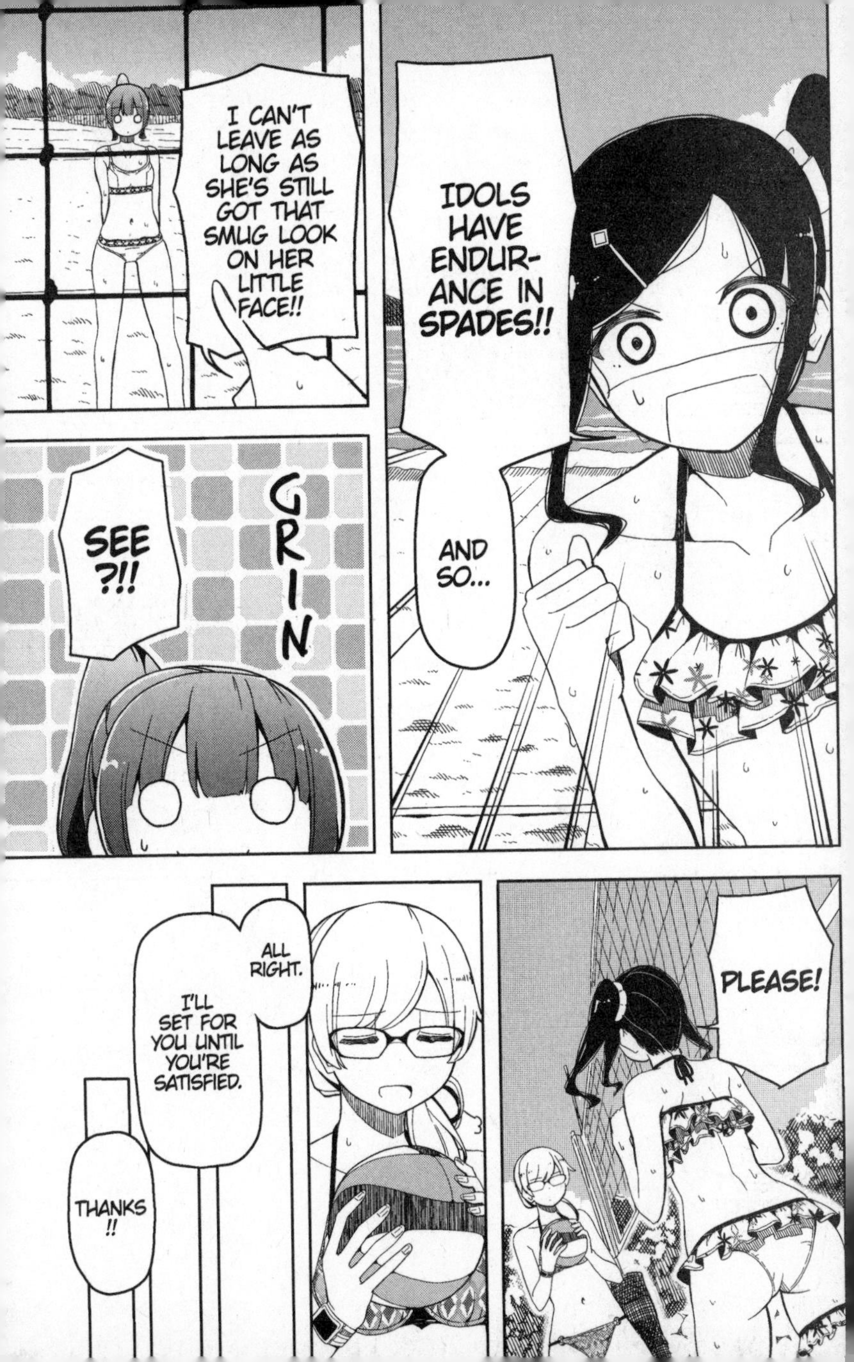
IDOLS HAVE ENDUR-ANCE IN SPADES!!
AND SO...
I CAN'T LEAVE AS LONG AS SHE'S STILL GOT THAT SMUG LOOK ON HER LITTLE FACE!!
SEE?!!
GRIN
PLEASE!
ALL RIGHT.
I'LL SET FOR YOU UNTIL YOU'RE SATISFIED.
THANKS!!

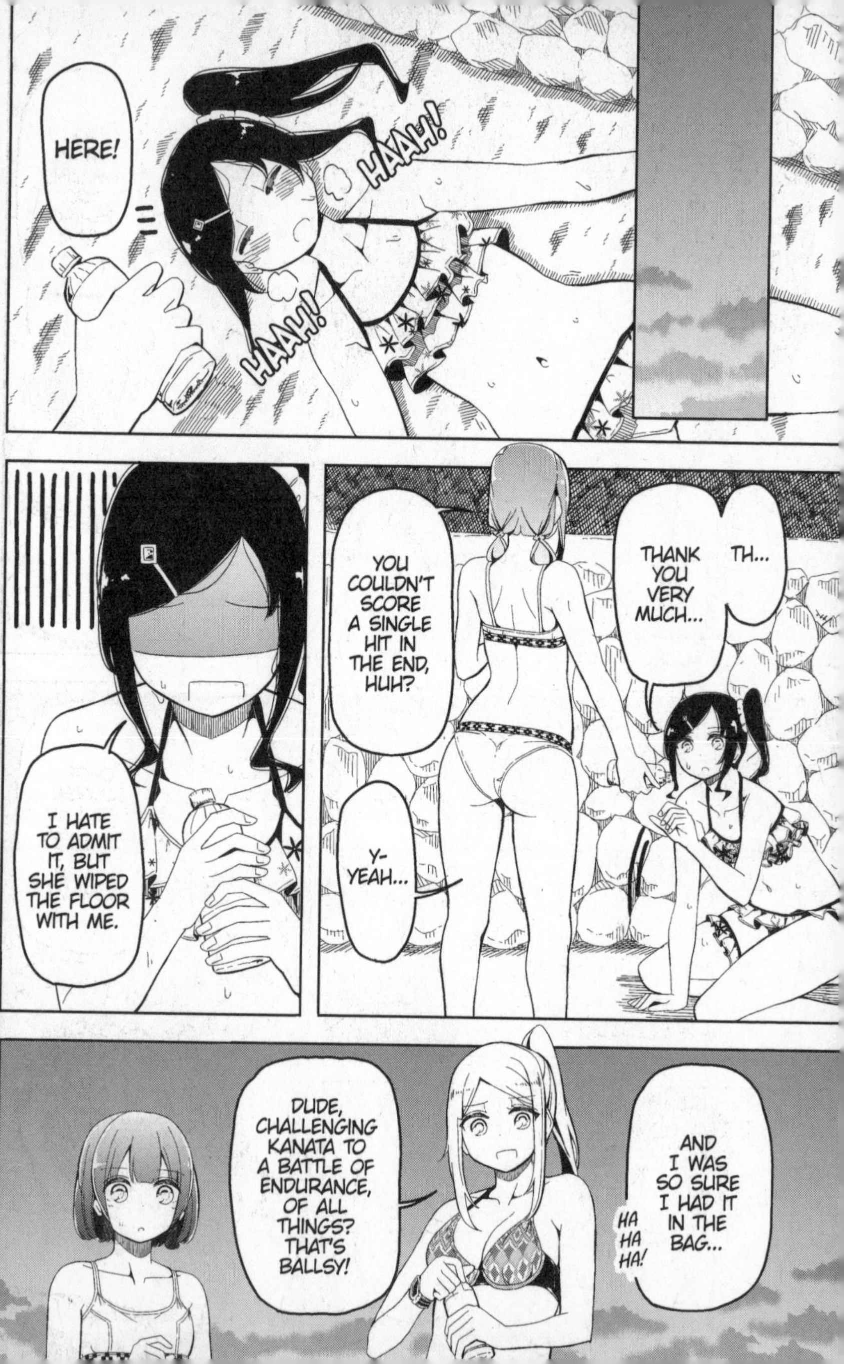
HAAAH!
HERE!
HAAAH!
TH...
THANK YOU VERY MUCH...
YOU COULDN'T SCORE A SINGLE HIT IN THE END, HUH?
Y-YEAH...
I HATE TO ADMIT IT, BUT SHE WIPED THE FLOOR WITH ME.
AND I WAS SO SURE I HAD IT IN THE BAG...
HA HA HA!
DUDE, CHALLENGING KANATA TO A BATTLE OF ENDURANCE, OF ALL THINGS? THAT'S BALLSY!

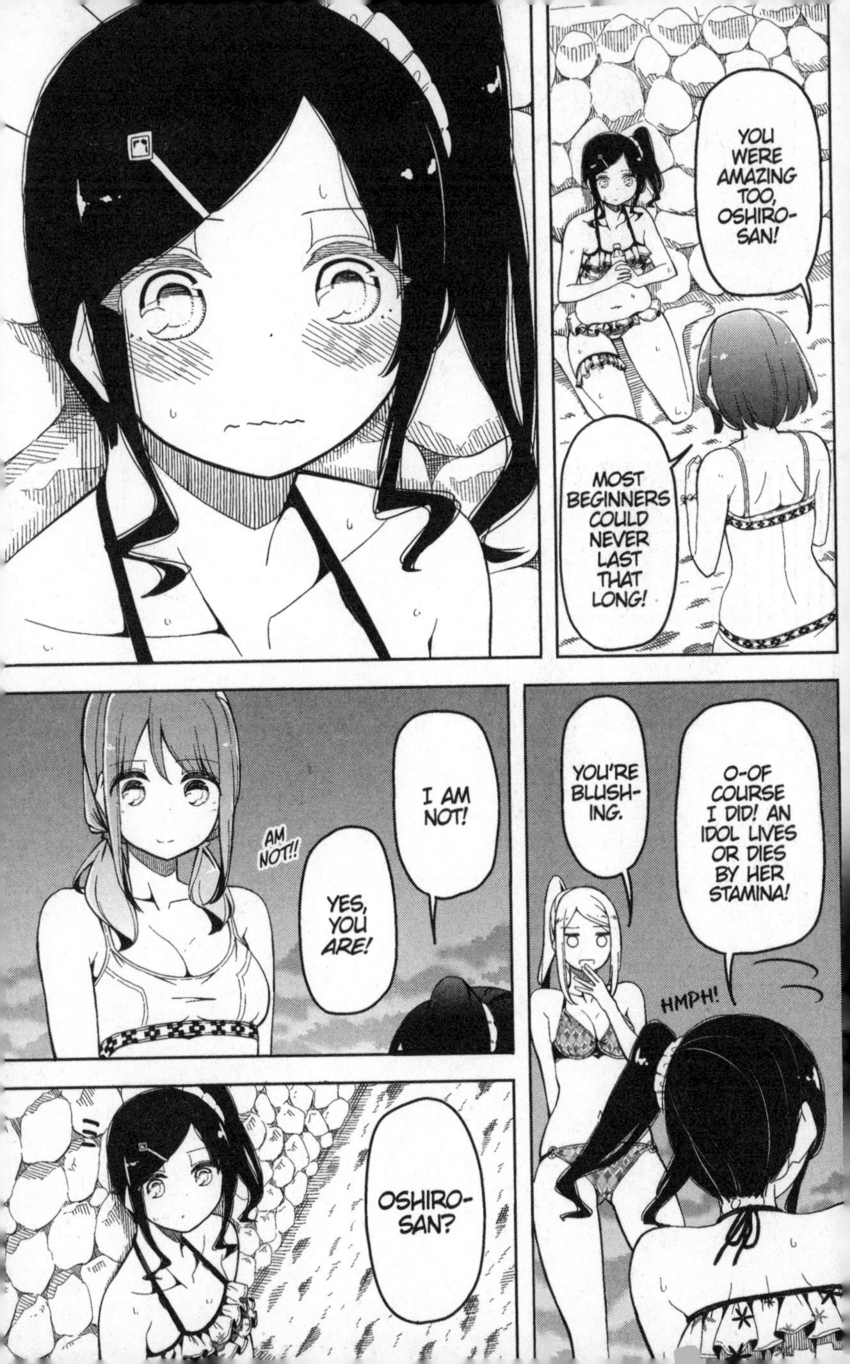
YOU WERE AMAZING TOO, OSHIRO-SAN!
MOST BEGINNERS COULD NEVER LAST THAT LONG!
O-OF COURSE I DID! AN IDOL LIVES OR DIES BY HER STAMINA!
YOU'RE BLUSH-ING.
HMPH!
I AM NOT!
YES, YOU ARE!
AM NOT!!
OSHIRO-SAN?

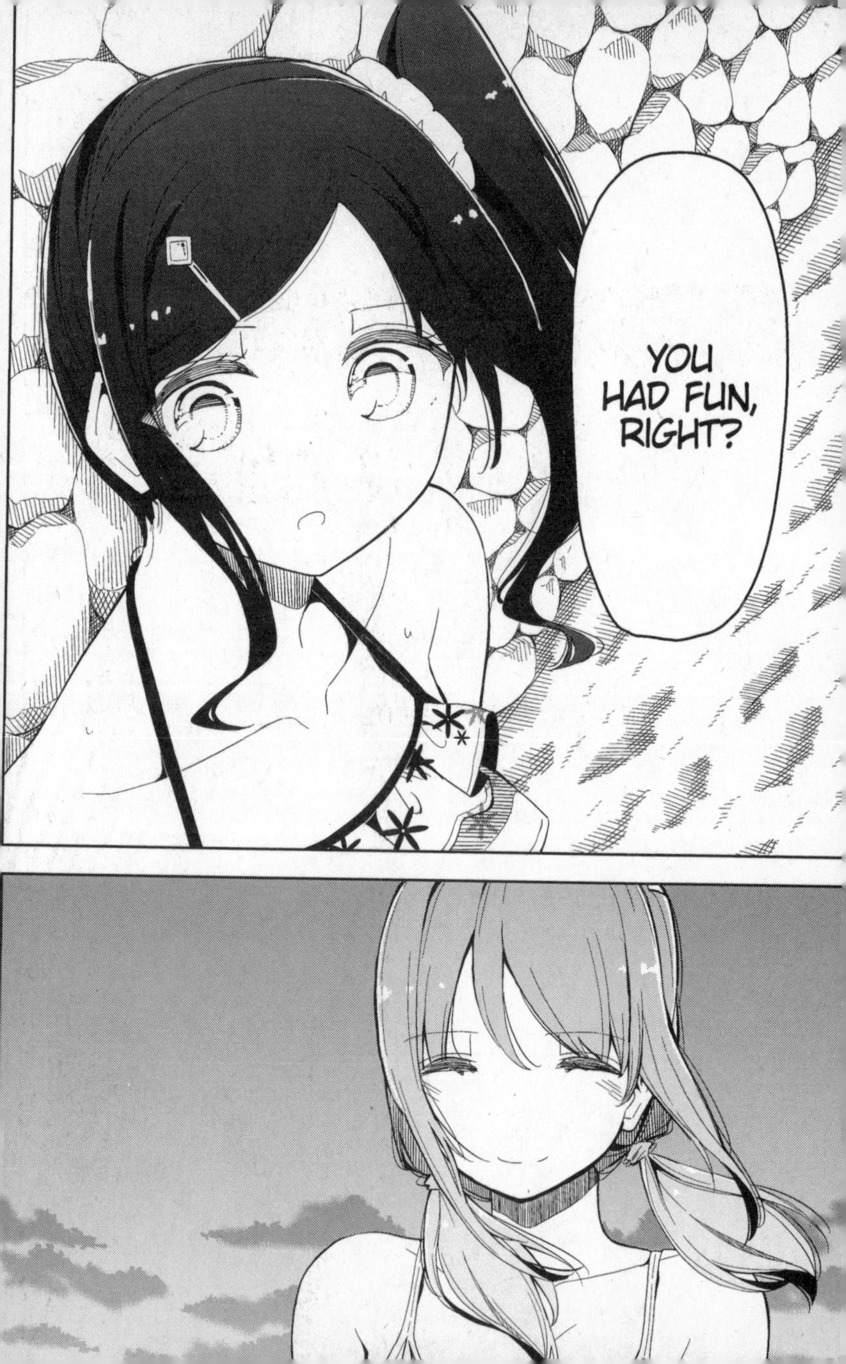
YOU HAD FUN, RIGHT?

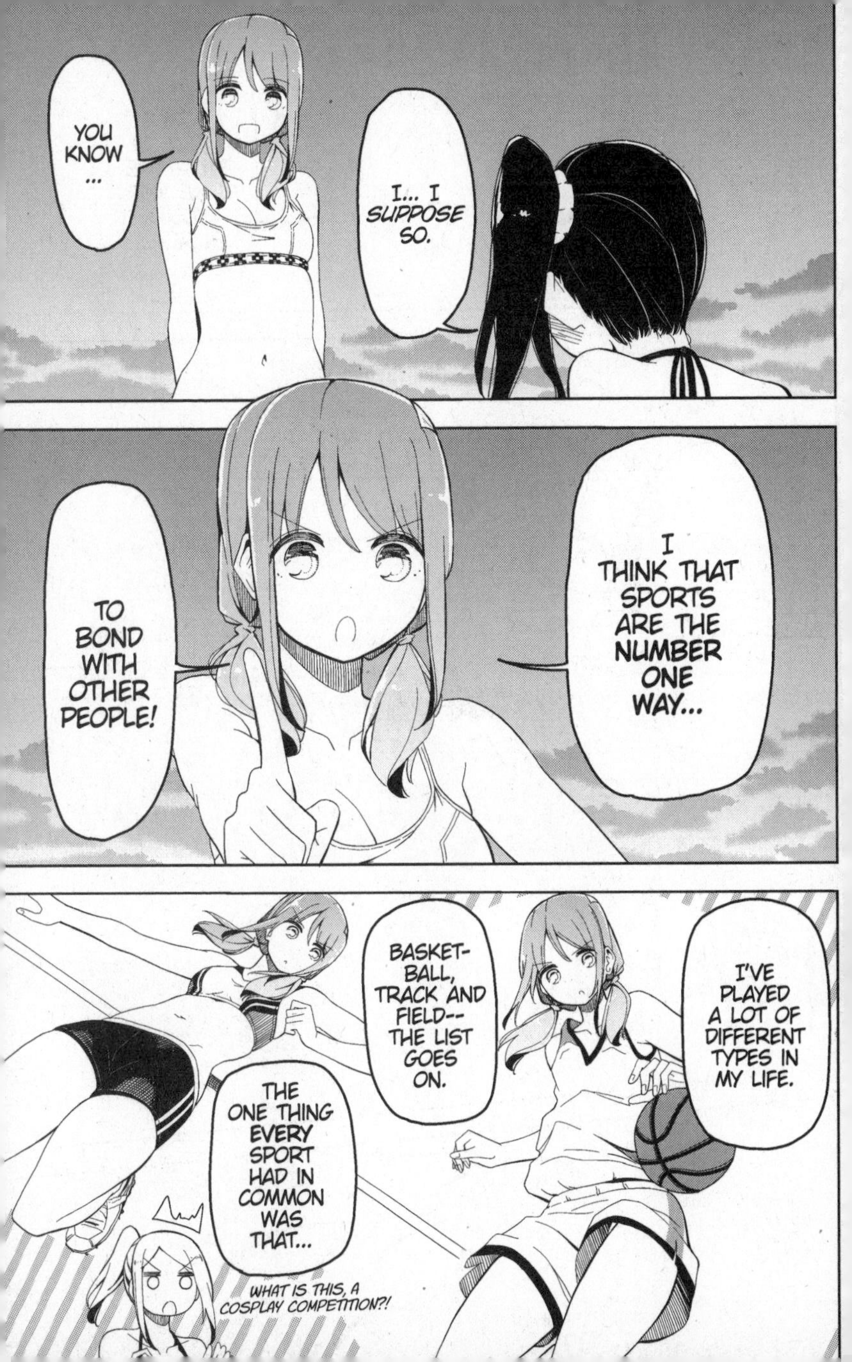
I... I SUPPOSE SO.
YOU KNOW ...
I THINK THAT SPORTS ARE THE NUMBER ONE WAY...
TO BOND WITH OTHER PEOPLE!
I'VE PLAYED A LOT OF DIFFERENT TYPES IN MY LIFE.
BASKET-BALL, TRACK AND FIELD-- THE LIST GOES ON.
THE ONE THING EVERY SPORT HAD IN COMMON WAS THAT...
WHAT IS THIS, A COSPLAY COMPETITION?!

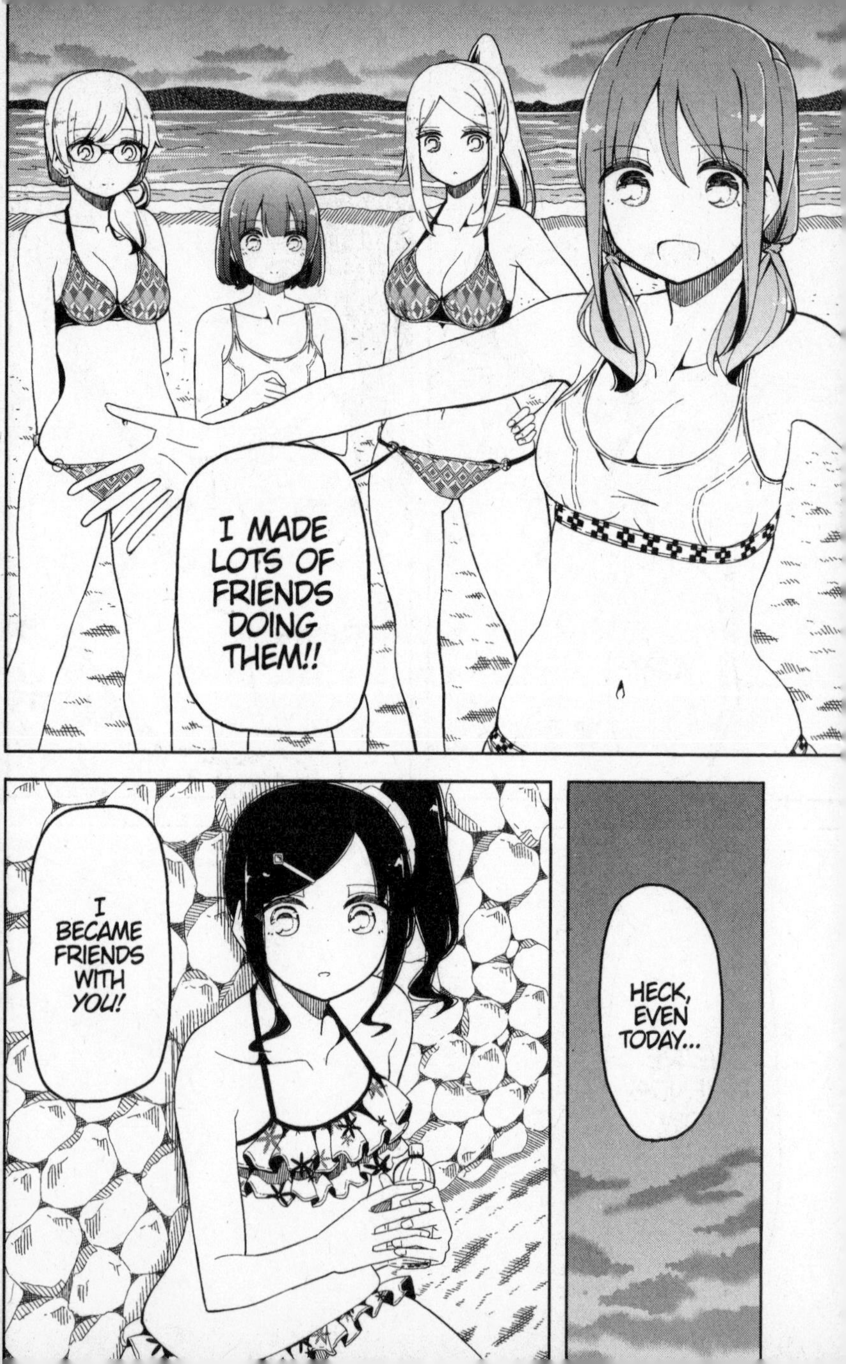
I MADE LOTS OF FRIENDS DOING THEM!!
HECK, EVEN TODAY...
I BECAME FRIENDS WITH YOU!

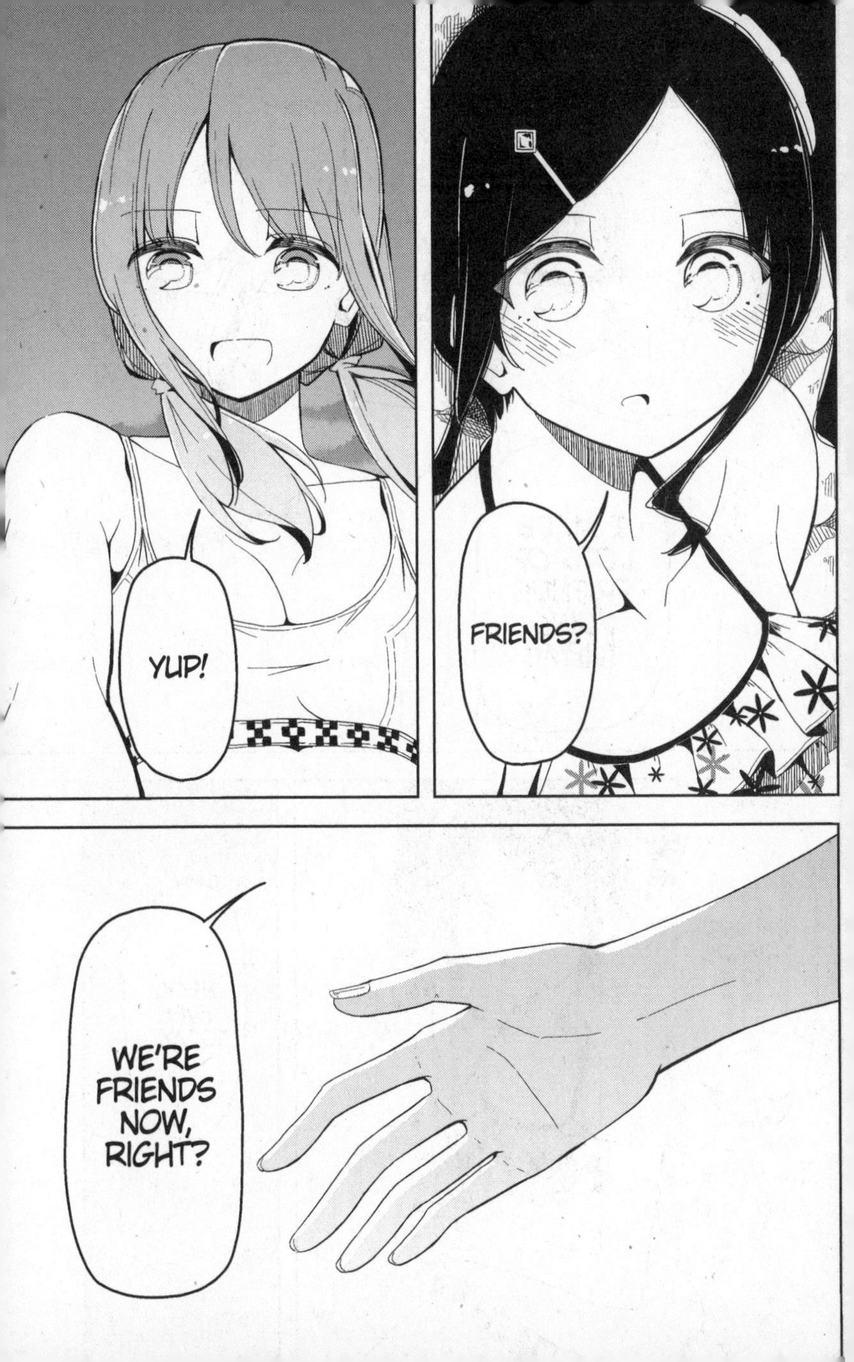
FRIENDS?
YUP!
WE'RE FRIENDS NOW, RIGHT?

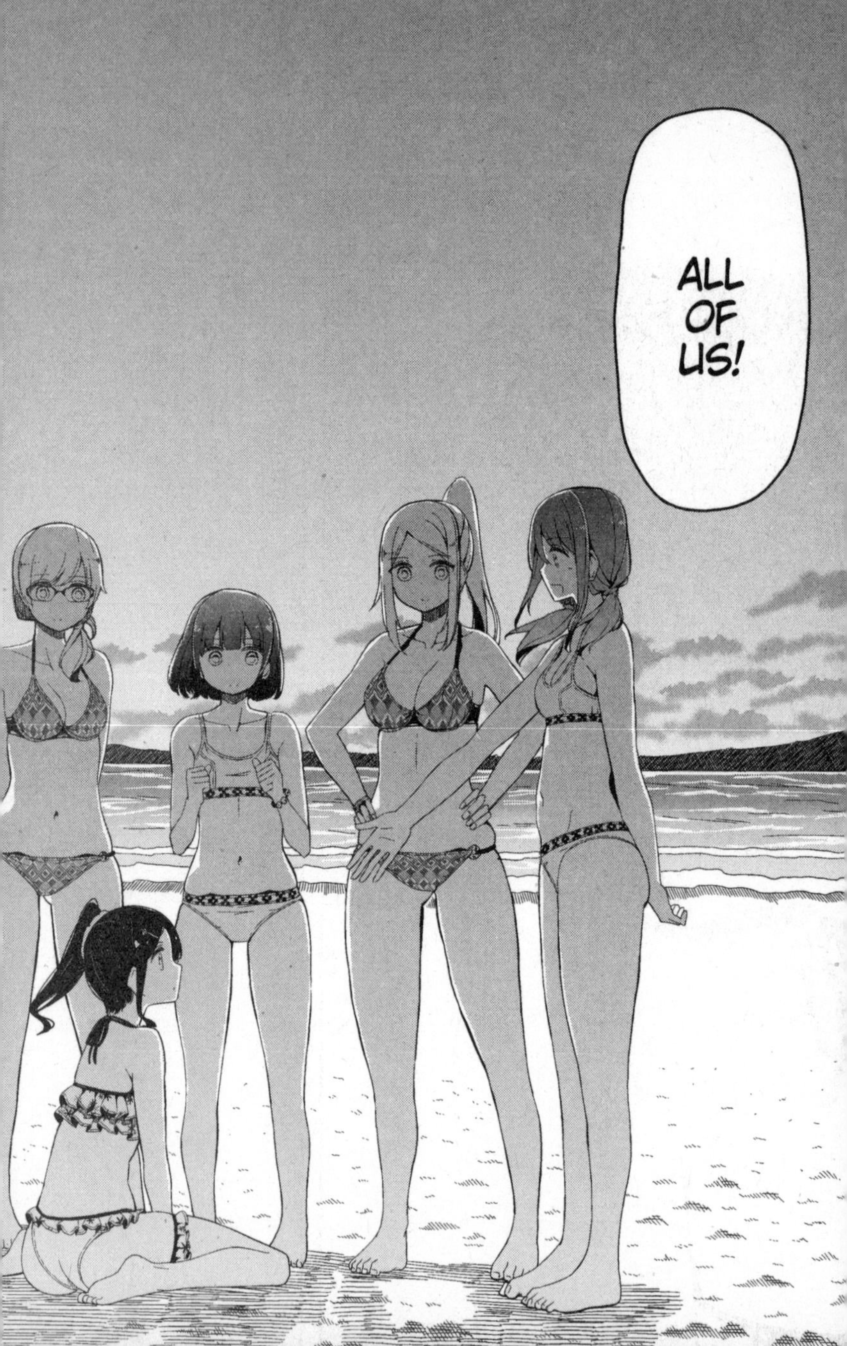
ALL OF US!

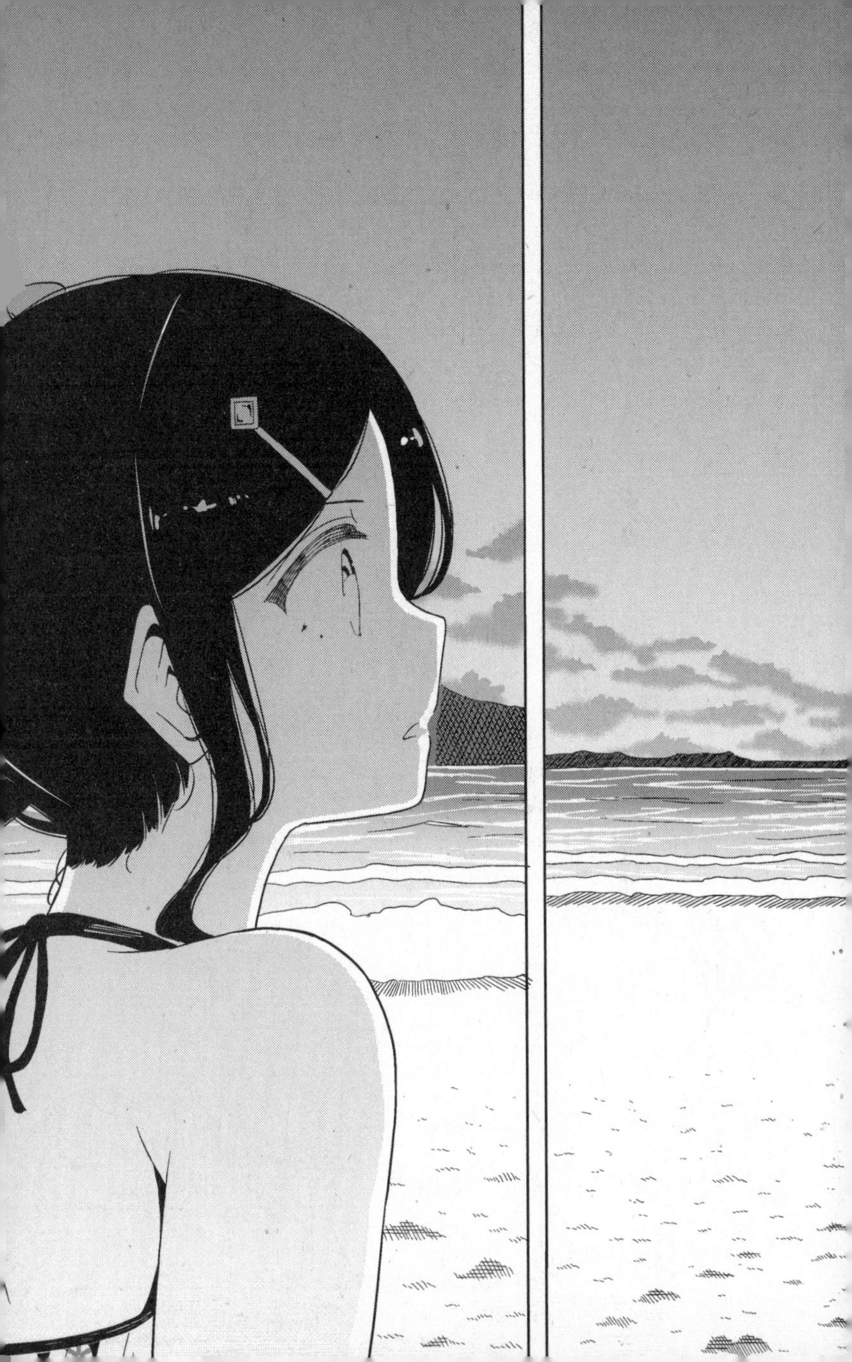

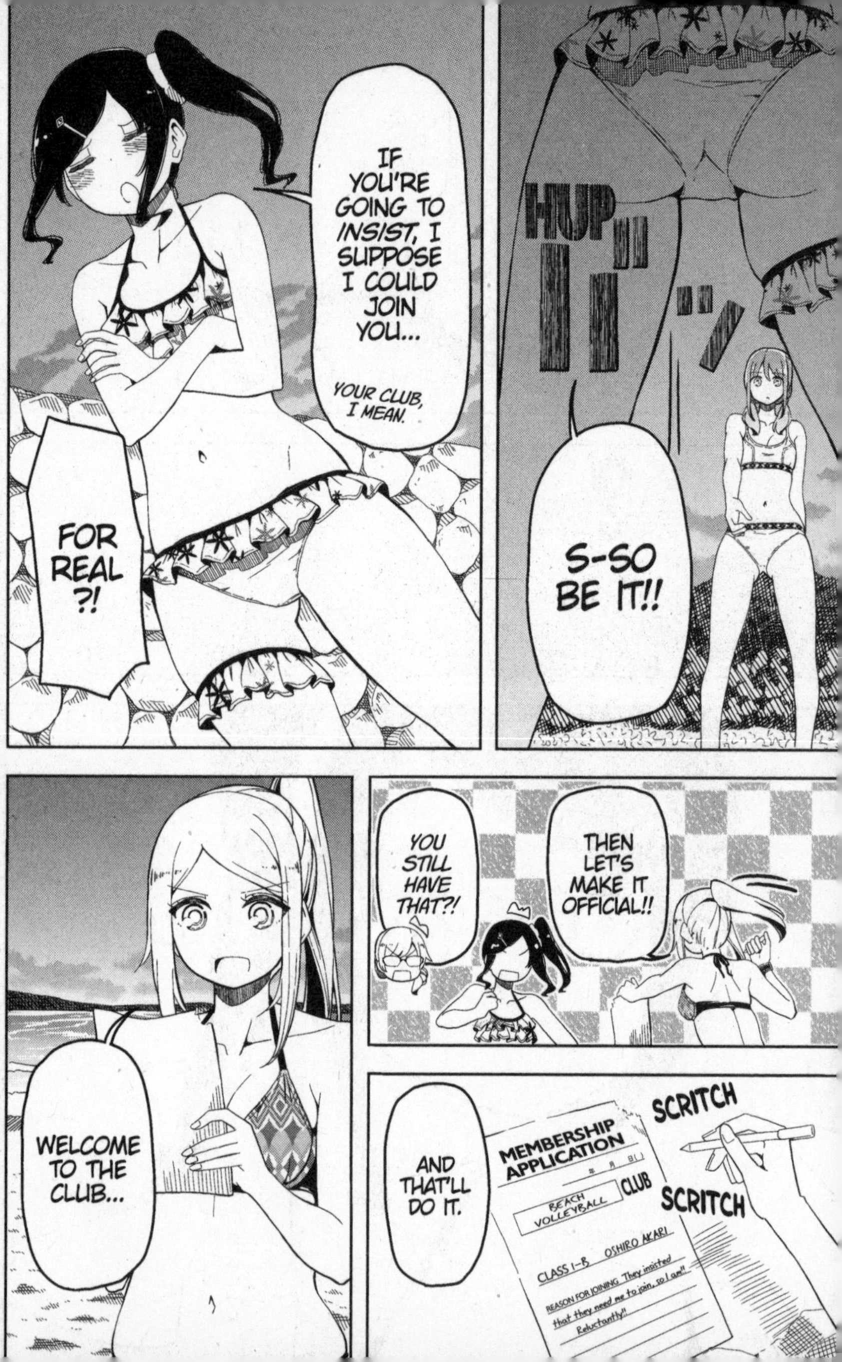
HUP
S-SO BE IT!!
IF YOU'RE GOING TO *INSIST*, I SUPPOSE I COULD JOIN YOU...
YOUR CLUB, I MEAN.
FOR REAL?!
THEN LET'S MAKE IT OFFICIAL!!
YOU STILL HAVE THAT?!
SCRITCH
SCRITCH
MEMBERSHIP APPLICATION
年 月 日( )
BEACH VOLLEYBALL CLUB
CLASS 1-B OSHIRO AKARI
REASON FOR JOINING They insisted that they need me to join, so I am!! Reluctantly!!
AND THAT'LL DO IT.
WELCOME TO THE CLUB...

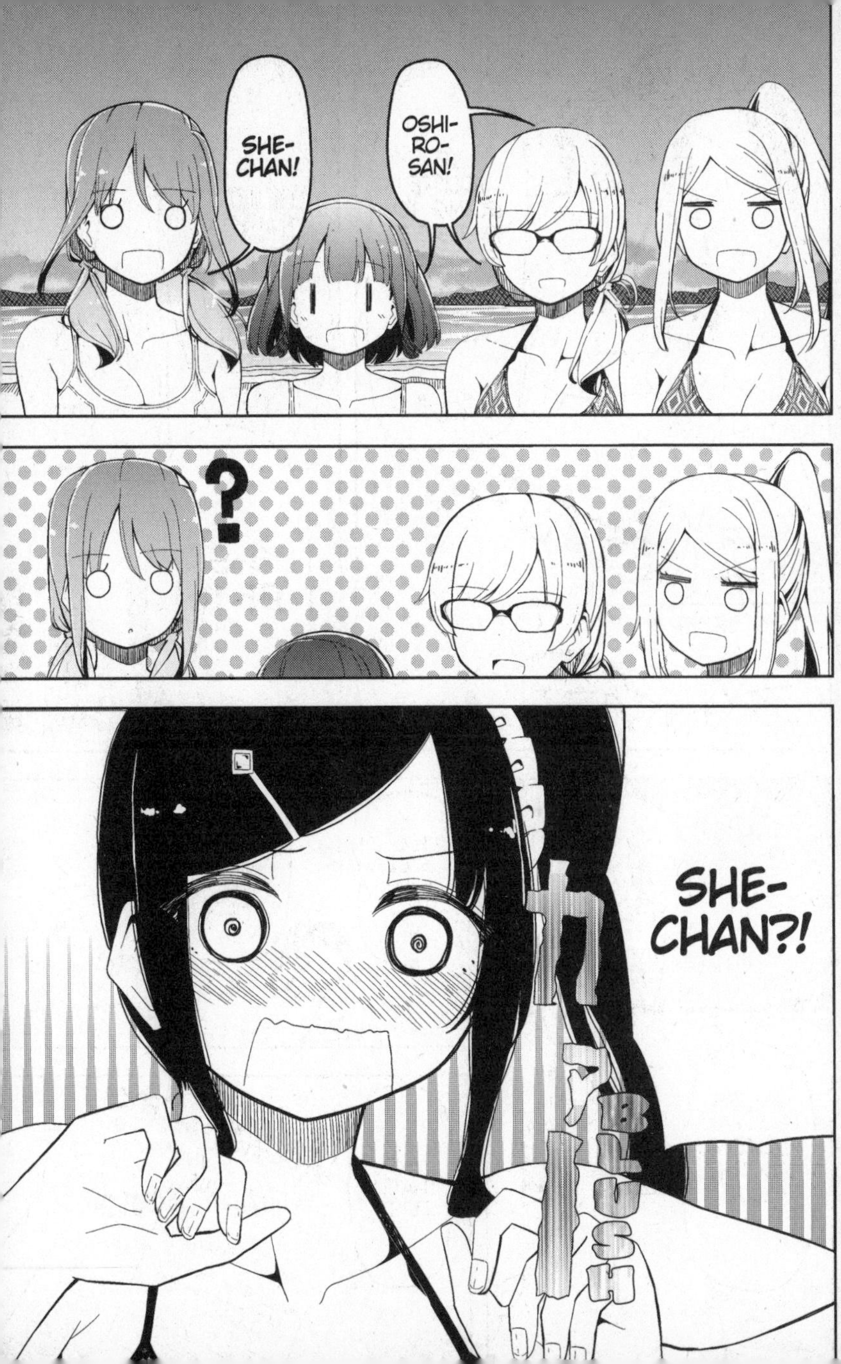
OSHI-RO-SAN!
SHE-CHAN!
?
SHE-CHAN?!
BLUSH

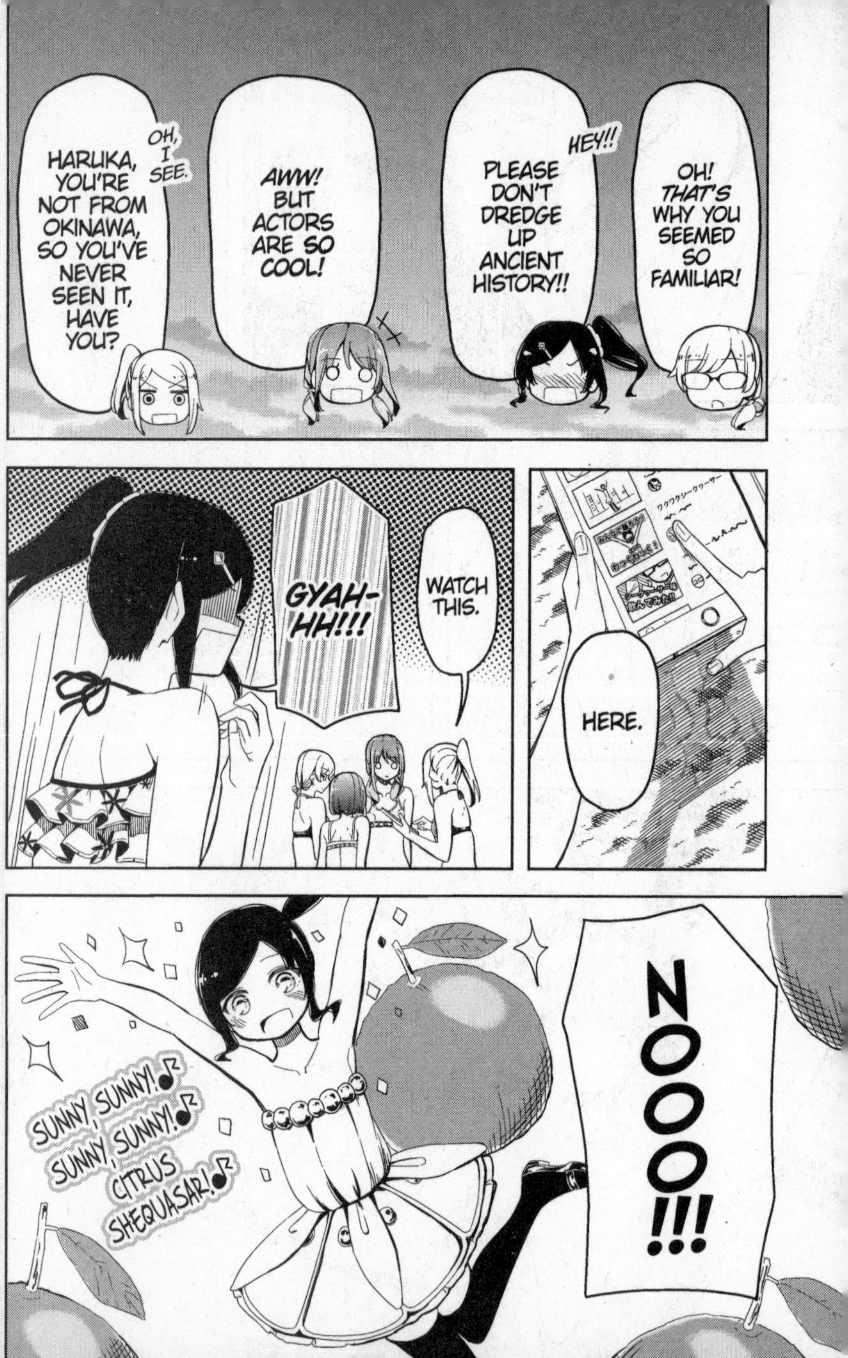
OH! THAT'S WHY YOU SEEMED SO FAMILIAR!
HEY!!
PLEASE DON'T DREDGE UP ANCIENT HISTORY!!
AWW! BUT ACTORS ARE SO COOL!
OH, I SEE.
HARUKA, YOU'RE NOT FROM OKINAWA, SO YOU'VE NEVER SEEN IT, HAVE YOU?
HERE.
WATCH THIS.
GYAH-HH!!!
NOOOO!!!
SUNNY, SUNNY!♪ SUNNY, SUNNY!♪ CITRUS SHEQUASAR!♪

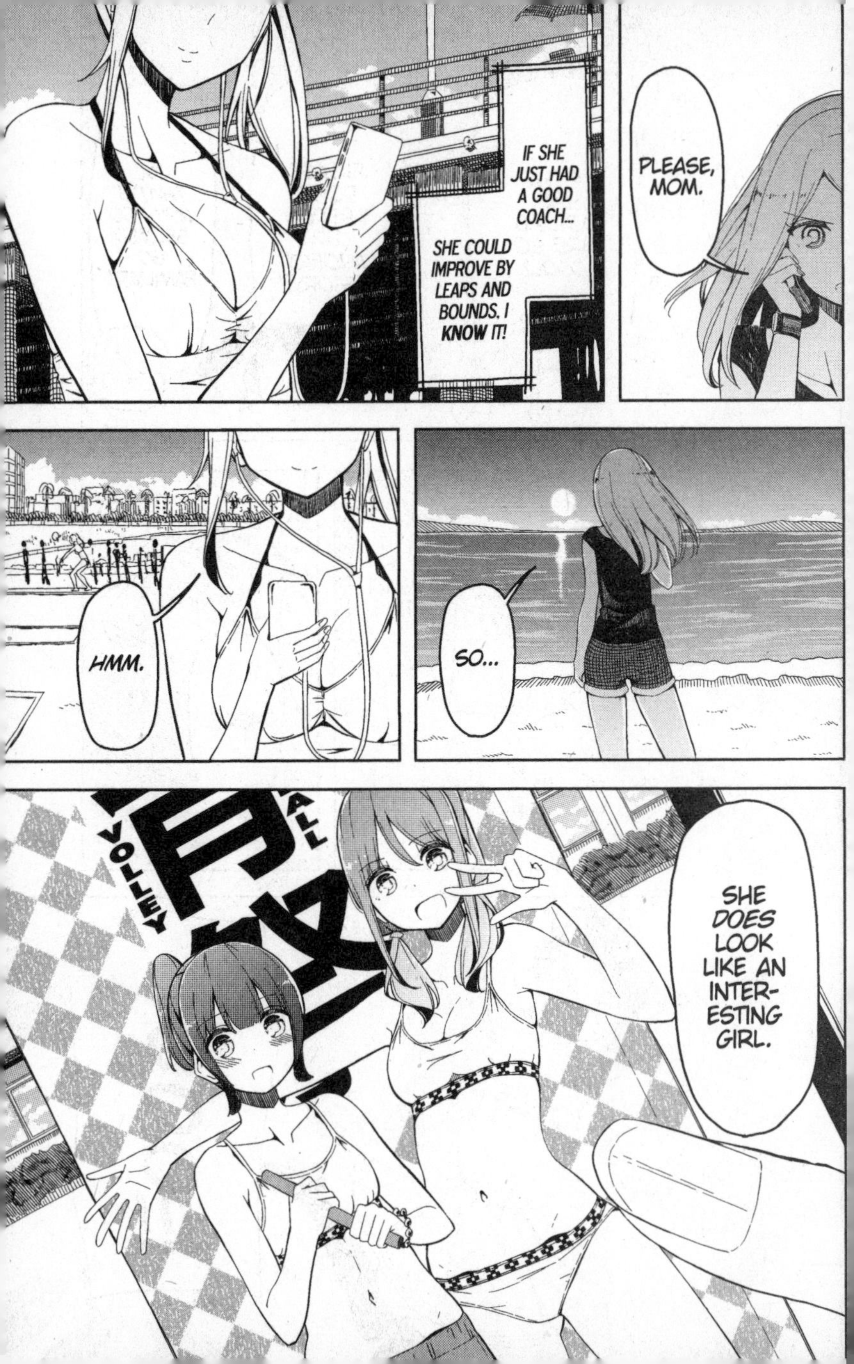
PLEASE, MOM.
IF SHE JUST HAD A GOOD COACH...
SHE COULD IMPROVE BY LEAPS AND BOUNDS. I KNOW IT!
SO...
HMM.
SHE DOES LOOK LIKE AN INTER-ESTING GIRL.
VOLLEY
ALL

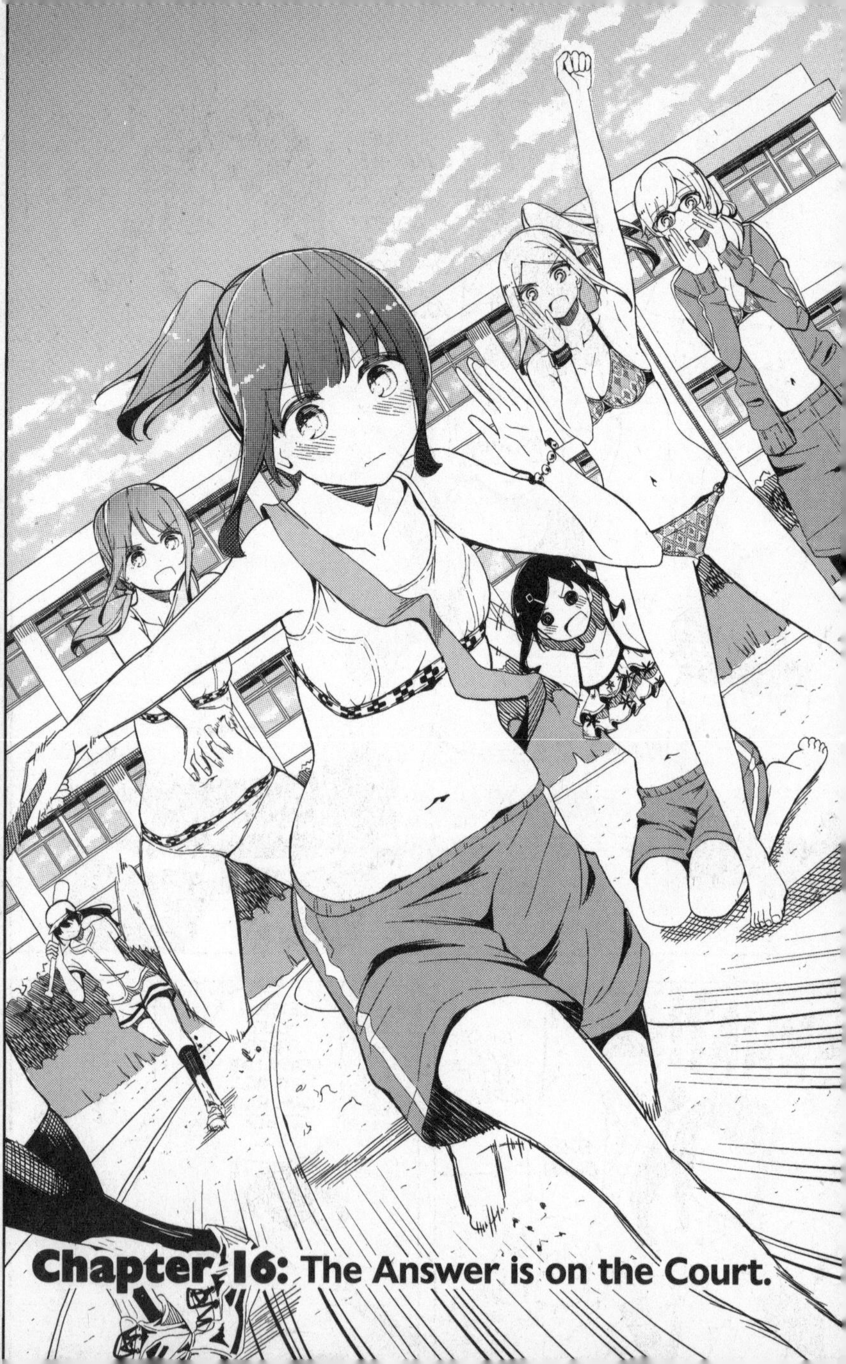
Chapter 16: The Answer is on the Court.

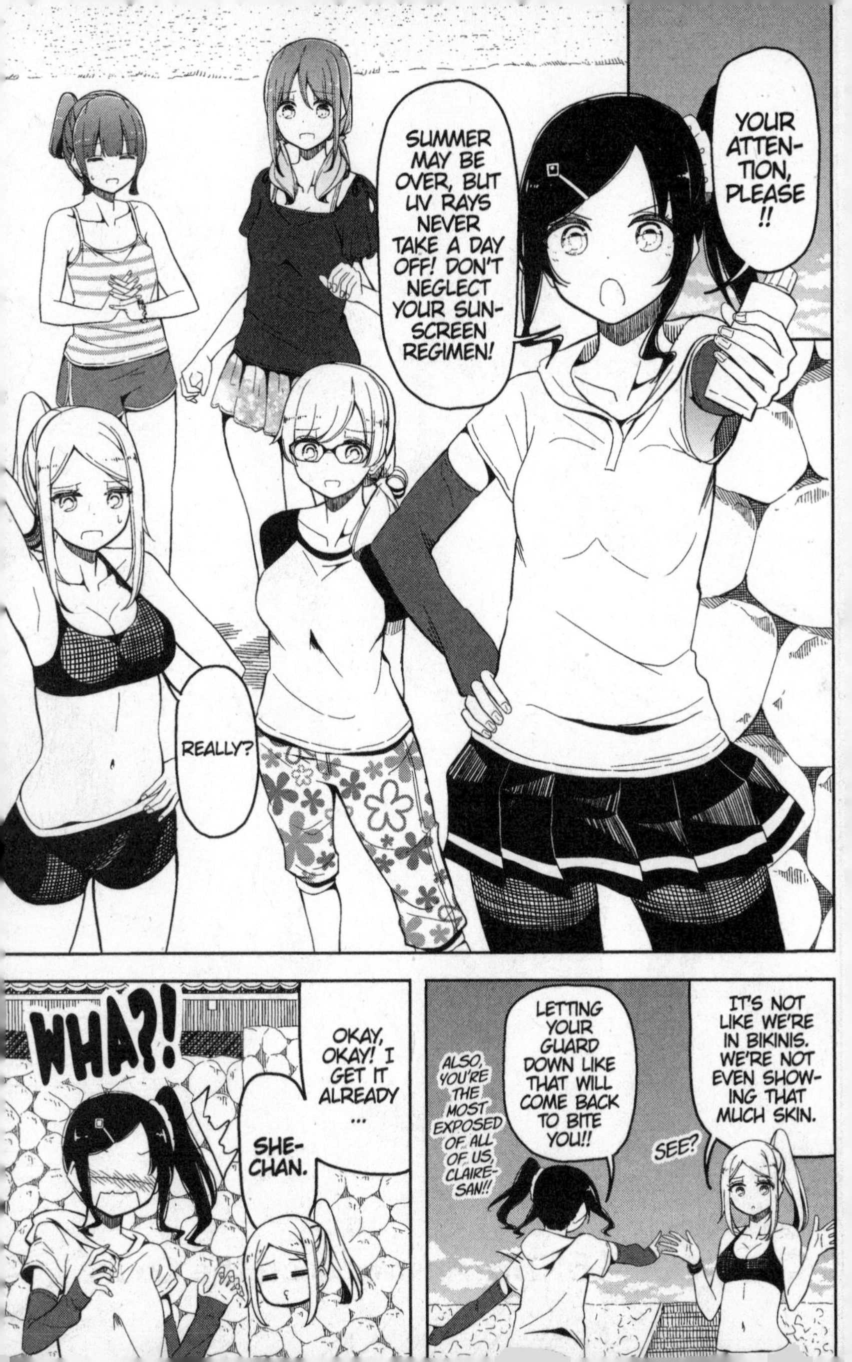
YOUR ATTEN-TION, PLEASE!!
SUMMER MAY BE OVER, BUT UV RAYS NEVER TAKE A DAY OFF! DON'T NEGLECT YOUR SUN-SCREEN REGIMEN!
REALLY?
IT'S NOT LIKE WE'RE IN BIKINIS. WE'RE NOT EVEN SHOW-ING THAT MUCH SKIN.
SEE?
LETTING YOUR GUARD DOWN LIKE THAT WILL COME BACK TO BITE YOU!!
ALSO, YOU'RE THE MOST EXPOSED OF ALL OF US, CLAIRE-SAN!!
OKAY, OKAY! I GET IT ALREADY...
SHE-CHAN.
WHA?!

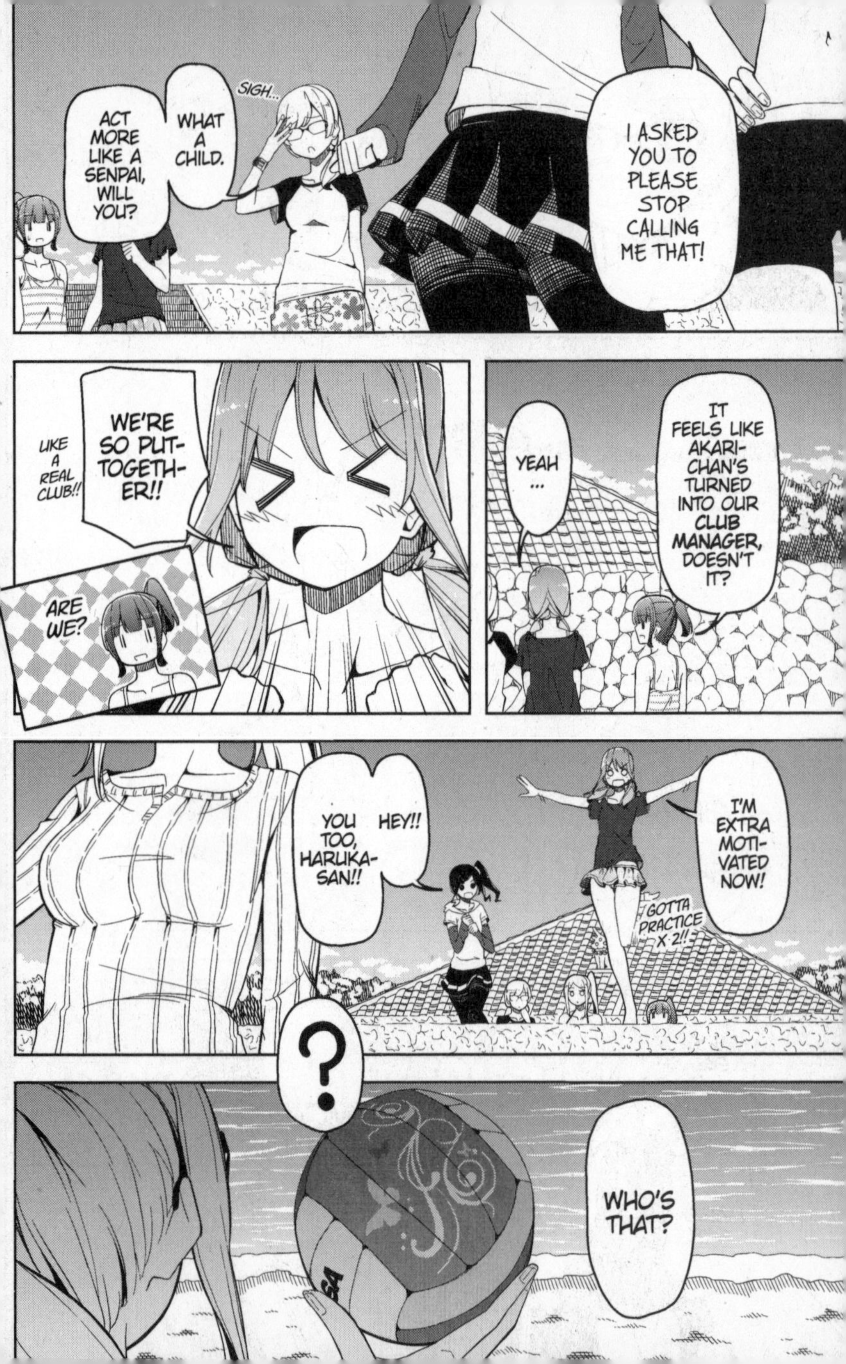
I ASKED YOU TO PLEASE STOP CALLING ME THAT!
SIGH...
WHAT A CHILD.
ACT MORE LIKE A SENPAI, WILL YOU?
IT FEELS LIKE AKARI-CHAN'S TURNED INTO OUR CLUB MANAGER, DOESN'T IT?
YEAH ...
WE'RE SO PUT-TOGETHER!!
LIKE A REAL CLUB!!
ARE WE?
I'M EXTRA MOTI-VATED NOW!
GOTTA PRACTICE X 2!!
HEY!!
YOU TOO, HARUKA-SAN!!
?
WHO'S THAT?

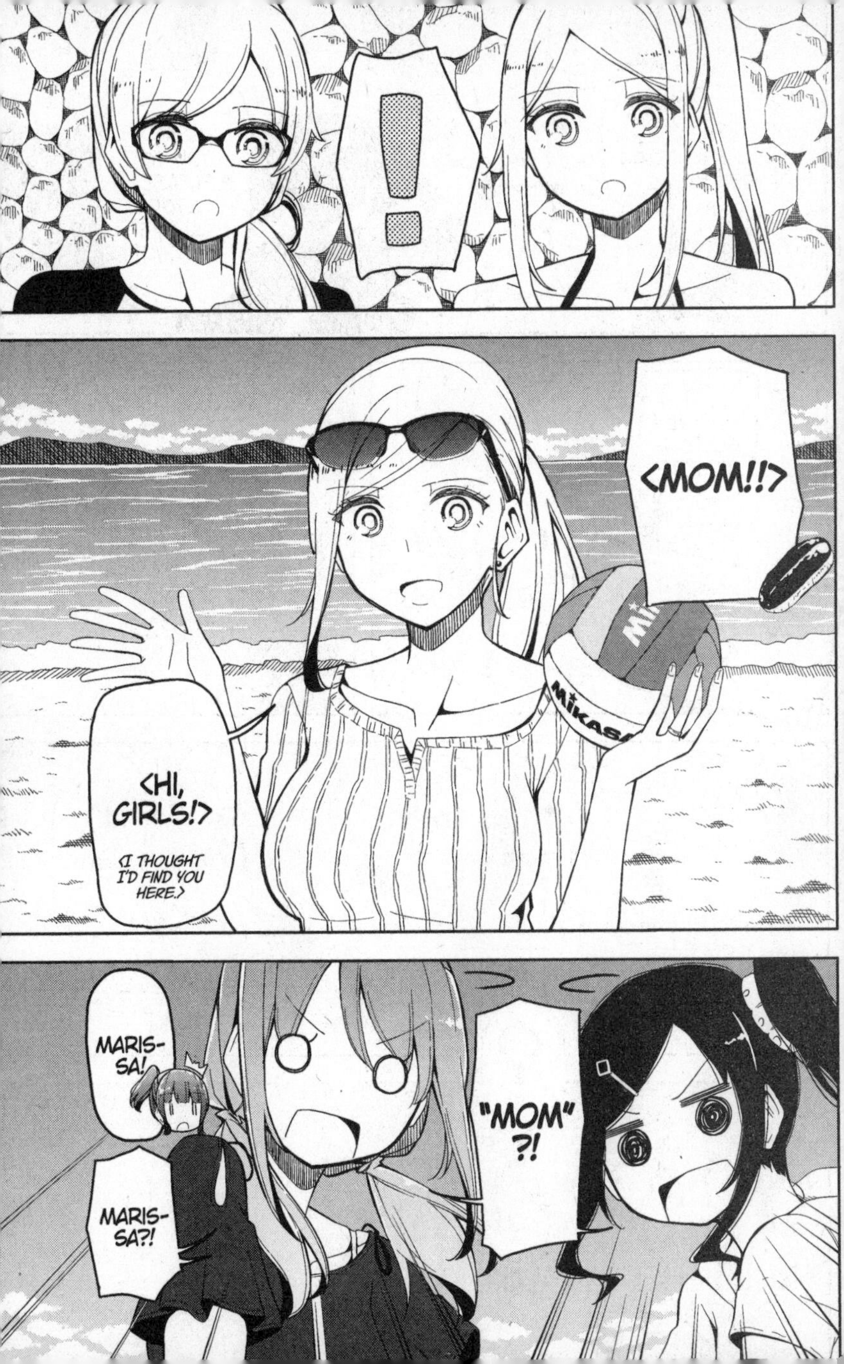
!
<MOM!!>
<HI, GIRLS!>
<I THOUGHT I'D FIND YOU HERE.>
"MOM" ?!
MARIS-SA!
MARIS-SA?!

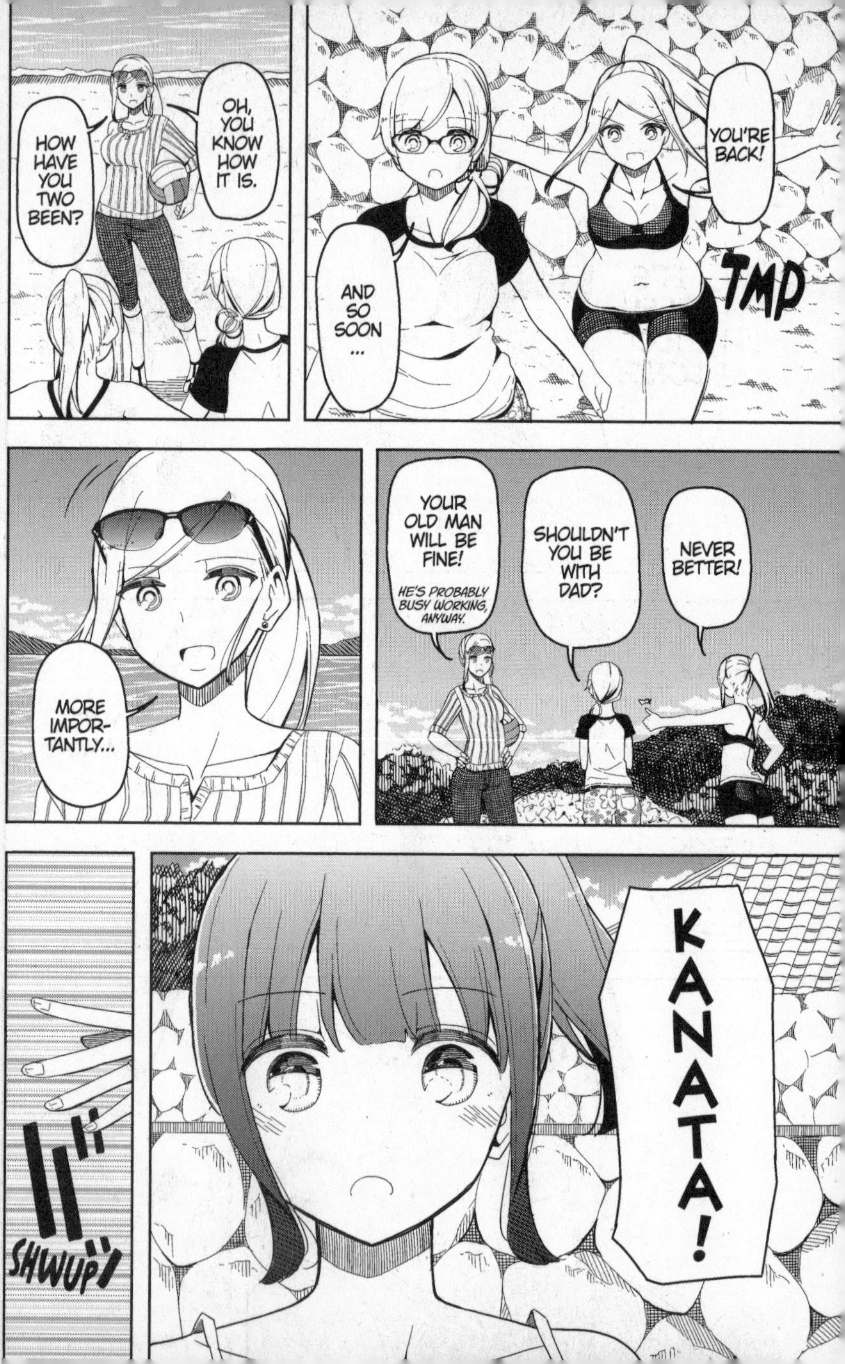
YOU'RE BACK!
TMP
AND SO SOON ...
OH, YOU KNOW HOW IT IS.
HOW HAVE YOU TWO BEEN?
NEVER BETTER!
SHOULDN'T YOU BE WITH DAD?
YOUR OLD MAN WILL BE FINE!
HE'S PROBABLY BUSY WORKING, ANYWAY.
MORE IMPOR-TANTLY...
KANATA!
SHWUP

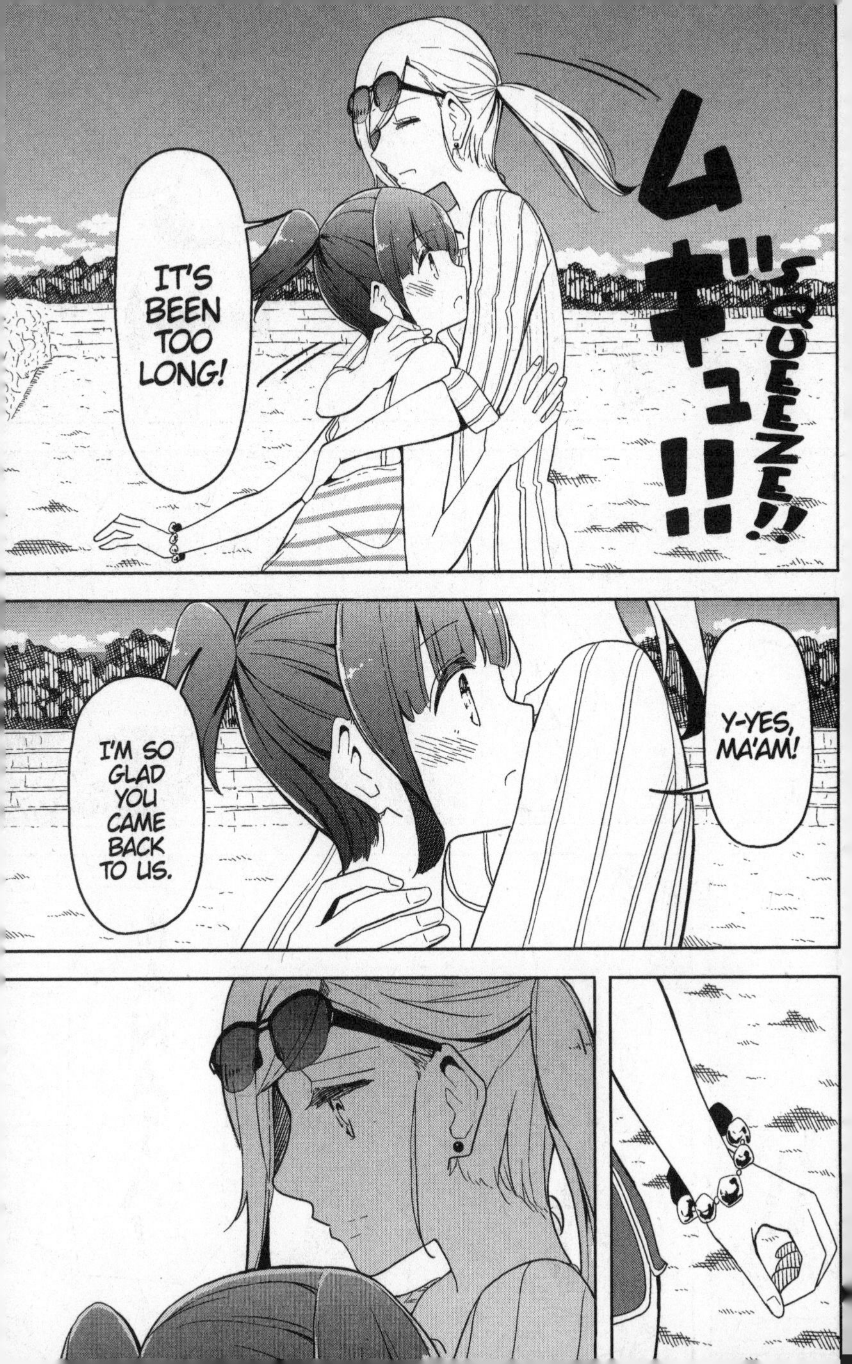
ムギュ!!
SQUEEZE!!
IT'S BEEN TOO LONG!
Y-YES, MA'AM!
I'M SO GLAD YOU CAME BACK TO US.

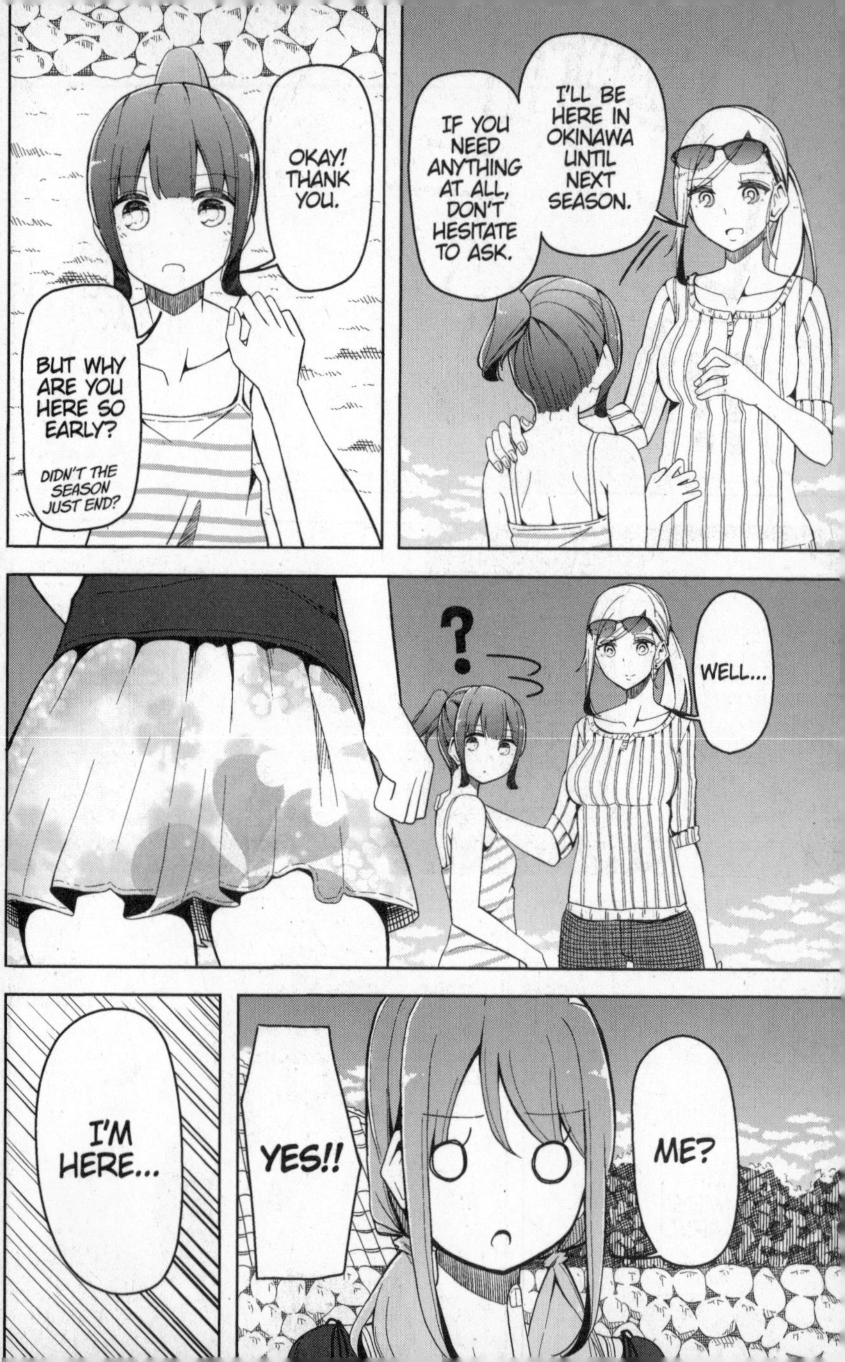
I'LL BE HERE IN OKINAWA UNTIL NEXT SEASON.
IF YOU NEED ANYTHING AT ALL, DON'T HESITATE TO ASK.
OKAY! THANK YOU.
BUT WHY ARE YOU HERE SO EARLY?
DIDN'T THE SEASON JUST END?
?
WELL...
ME?
YES!!
I'M HERE...

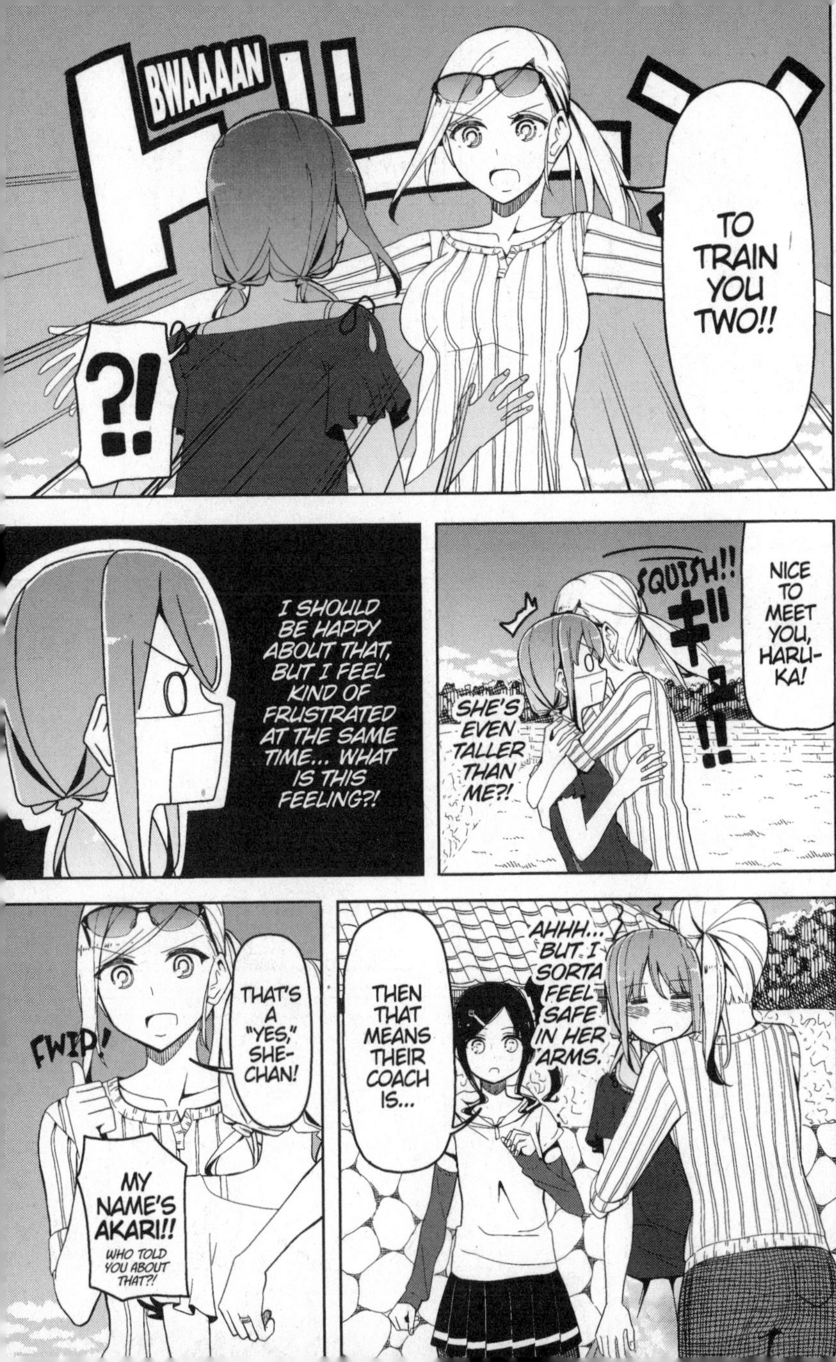
TO TRAIN YOU TWO!!
BWAAAAN
?!
NICE TO MEET YOU, HARU-KA!
SQUISH!!
SHE'S EVEN TALLER THAN ME?!
I SHOULD BE HAPPY ABOUT THAT, BUT I FEEL KIND OF FRUSTRATED AT THE SAME TIME... WHAT IS THIS FEELING?!
AHHH... BUT I SORTA FEEL SAFE IN HER ARMS.
THEN THAT MEANS THEIR COACH IS...
THAT'S A "YES," SHE-CHAN!
FWIP!
MY NAME'S AKARI!!
WHO TOLD YOU ABOUT THAT?!

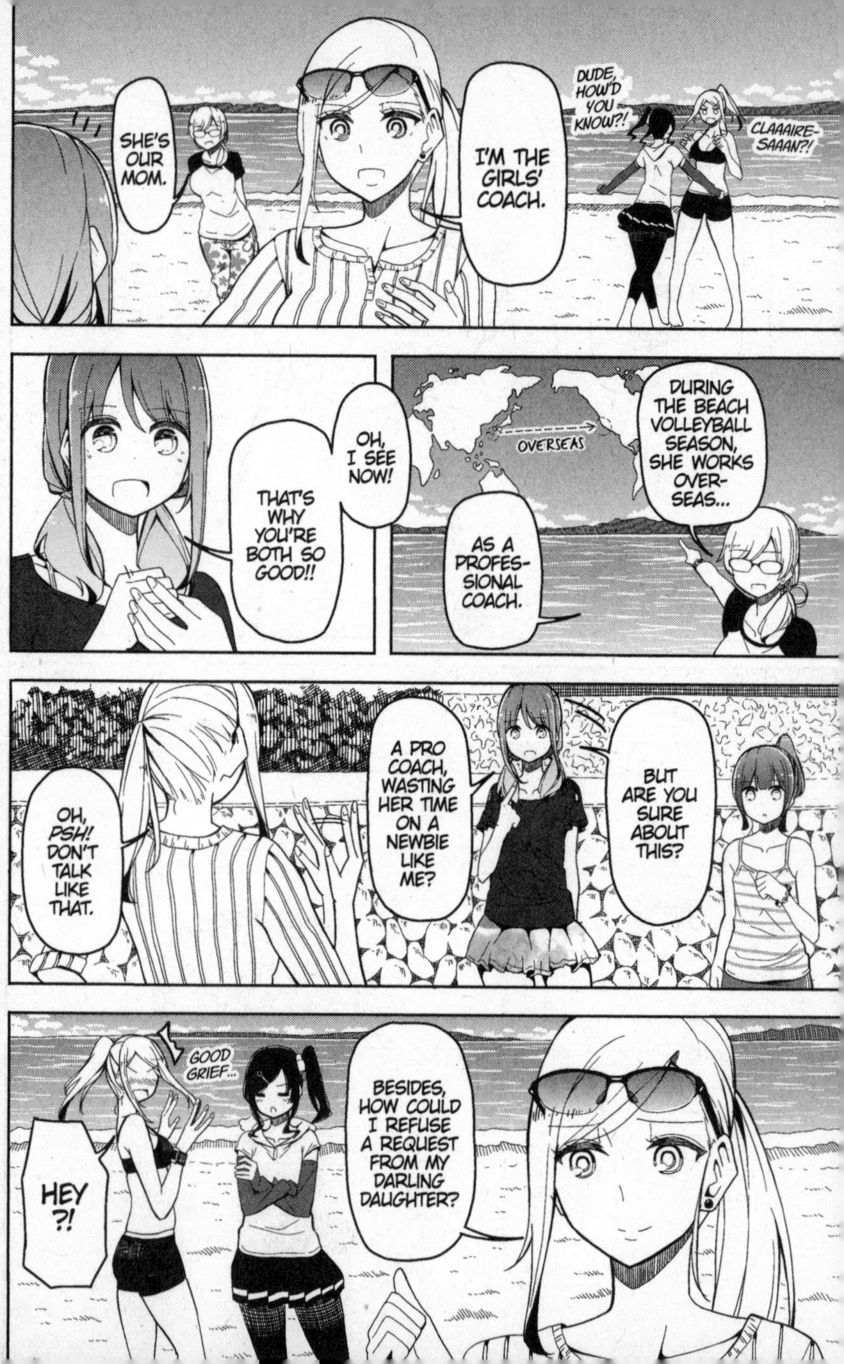
CLAAAIRE-SAAAN?!
DUDE, HOW'D YOU KNOW?!
I'M THE GIRLS' COACH.
SHE'S OUR MOM.
DURING THE BEACH VOLLEYBALL SEASON, SHE WORKS OVER-SEAS...
OVERSEAS
AS A PROFES-SIONAL COACH.
OH, I SEE NOW!
THAT'S WHY YOU'RE BOTH SO GOOD!!
BUT ARE YOU SURE ABOUT THIS?
A PRO COACH, WASTING HER TIME ON A NEWBIE LIKE ME?
OH, *PSH!* DON'T TALK LIKE THAT.
BESIDES, HOW COULD I REFUSE A REQUEST FROM MY DARLING DAUGHTER?
GOOD GRIEF...
HEY ?!

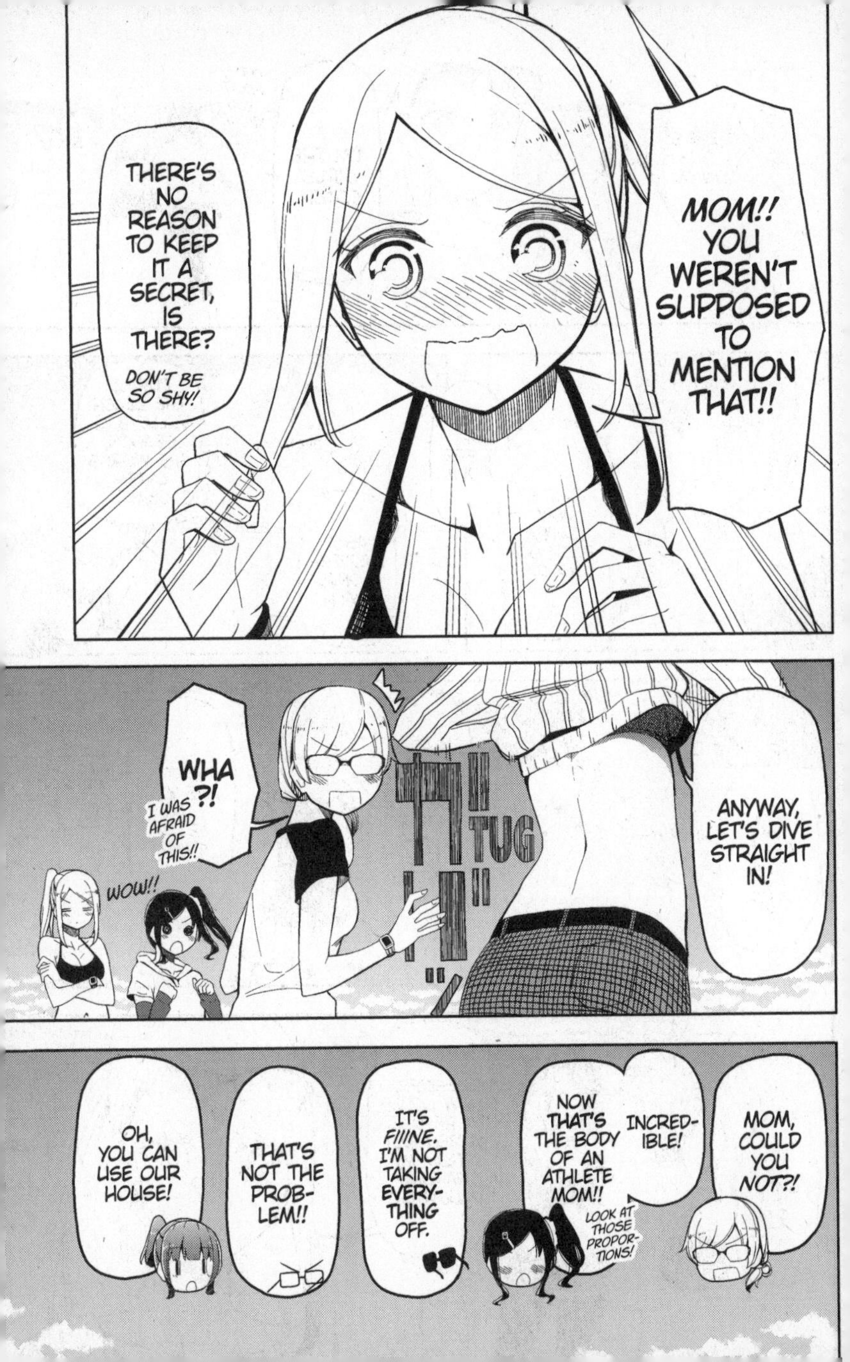
MOM!! YOU WEREN'T SUPPOSED TO MENTION THAT!!
THERE'S NO REASON TO KEEP IT A SECRET, IS THERE?
DON'T BE SO SHY!
ANYWAY, LET'S DIVE STRAIGHT IN!
TUG
WHA?!
I WAS AFRAID OF THIS!!
WOW!!
MOM, COULD YOU NOT?!
INCREDIBLE!
NOW THAT'S THE BODY OF AN ATHLETE MOM!!
LOOK AT THOSE PROPORTIONS!
IT'S FIIINE. I'M NOT TAKING EVERYTHING OFF.
THAT'S NOT THE PROBLEM!!
OH, YOU CAN USE OUR HOUSE!

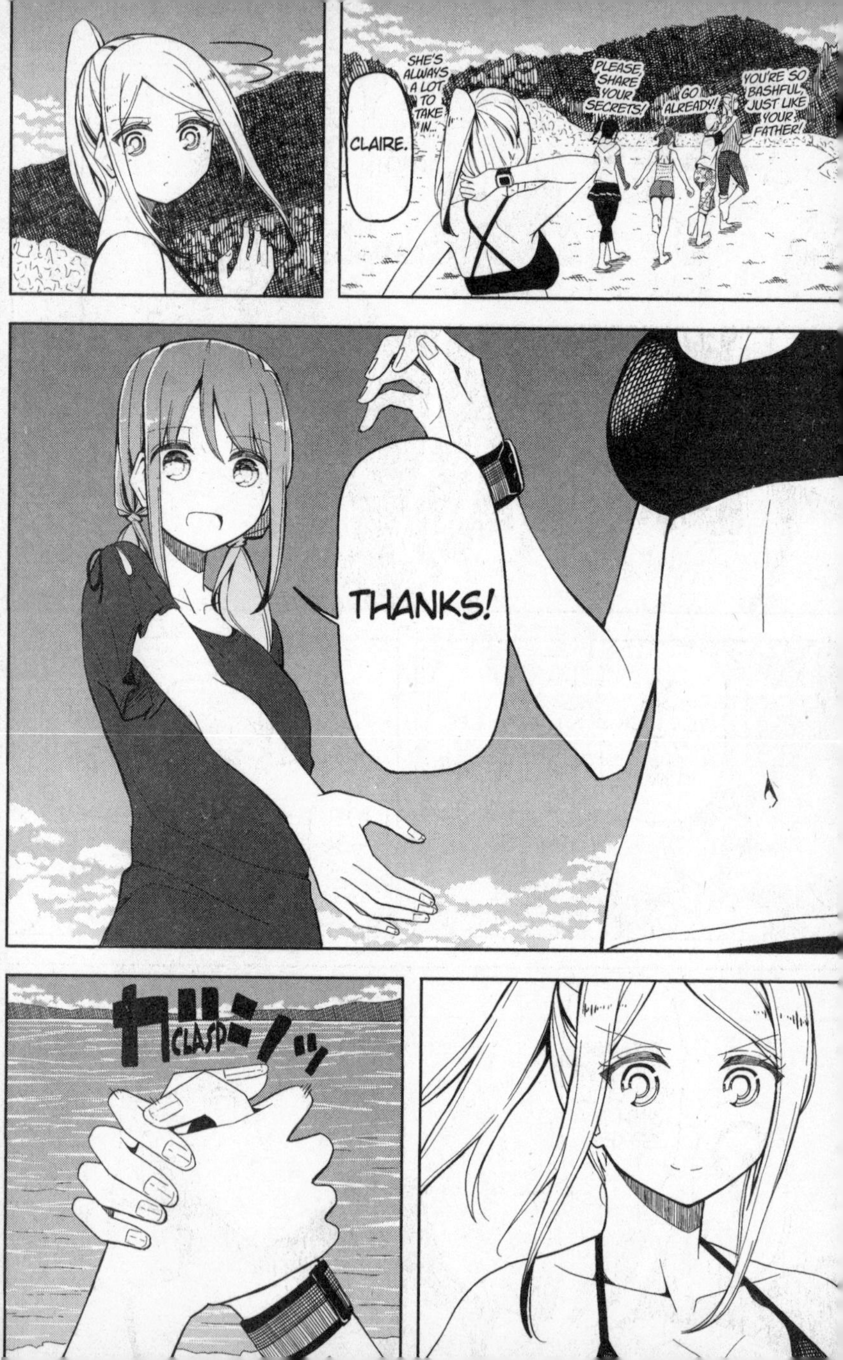
YOU'RE SO BASHFUL, JUST LIKE YOUR FATHER!
GO ALREADY!!
PLEASE, SHARE YOUR SECRETS!
SHE'S ALWAYS A LOT TO TAKE IN...
CLAIRE.
THANKS!
CLASP

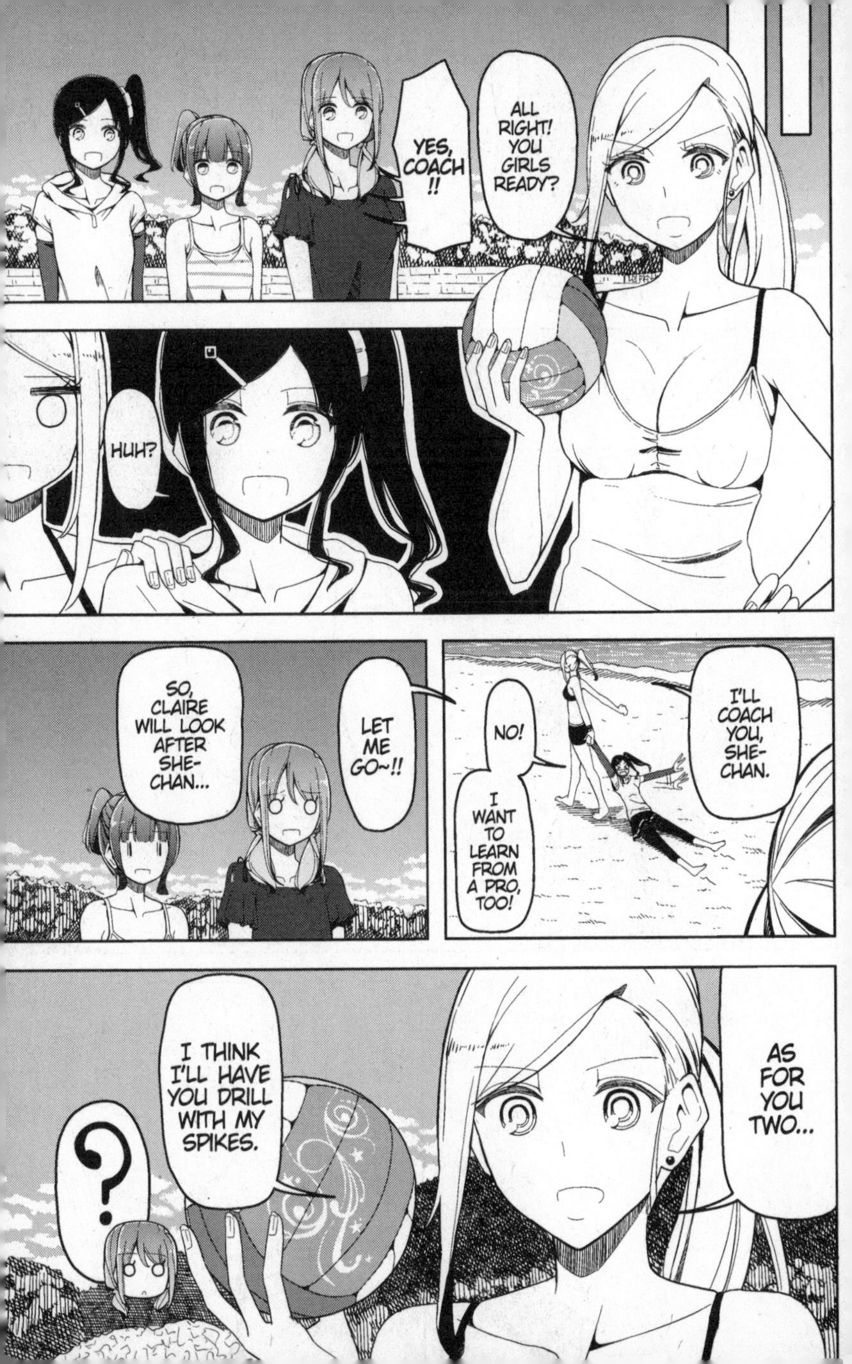
ALL RIGHT! YOU GIRLS READY?
YES, COACH!!
HUH?
I'LL COACH YOU, SHE-CHAN.
NO!
I WANT TO LEARN FROM A PRO, TOO!
LET ME GO~!!
SO, CLAIRE WILL LOOK AFTER SHE-CHAN...
AS FOR YOU TWO...
I THINK I'LL HAVE YOU DRILL WITH MY SPIKES.
?

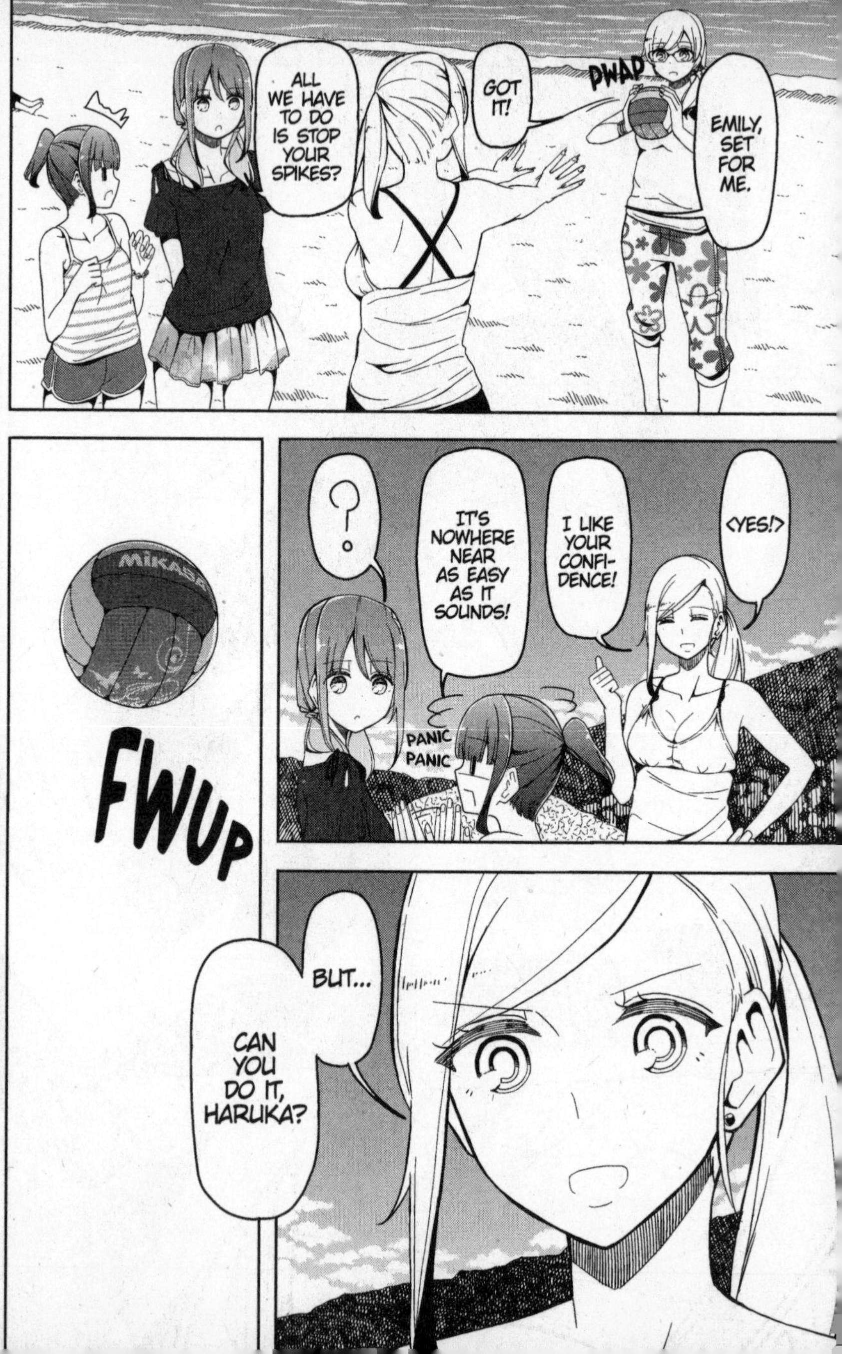
EMILY, SET FOR ME.
PWAP
GOT IT!
ALL WE HAVE TO DO IS STOP YOUR SPIKES?
<YES!>
I LIKE YOUR CONFIDENCE!
IT'S NOWHERE NEAR AS EASY AS IT SOUNDS!
PANIC PANIC
?
BUT...
CAN YOU DO IT, HARUKA?
MIKASA
FWUP

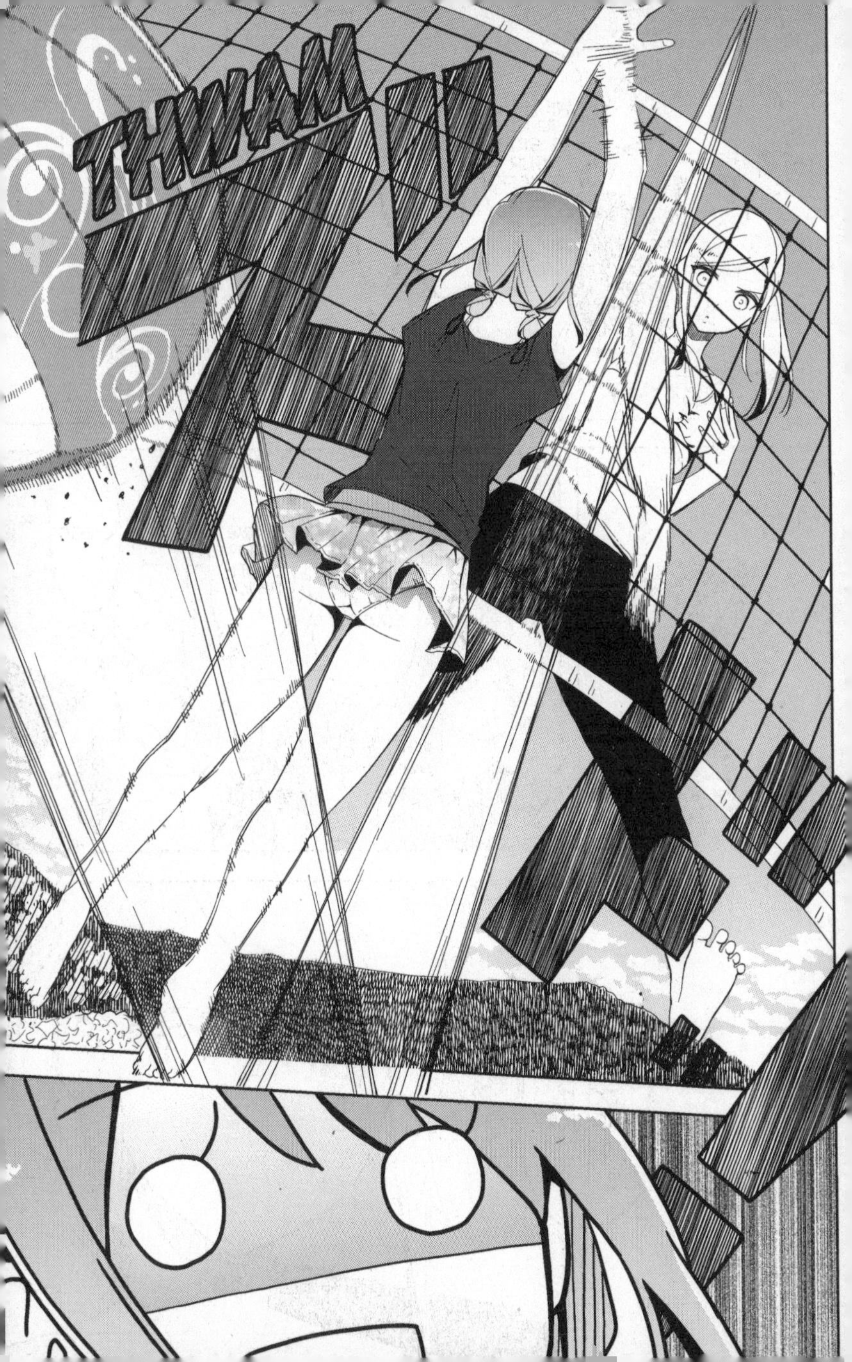
THWAM

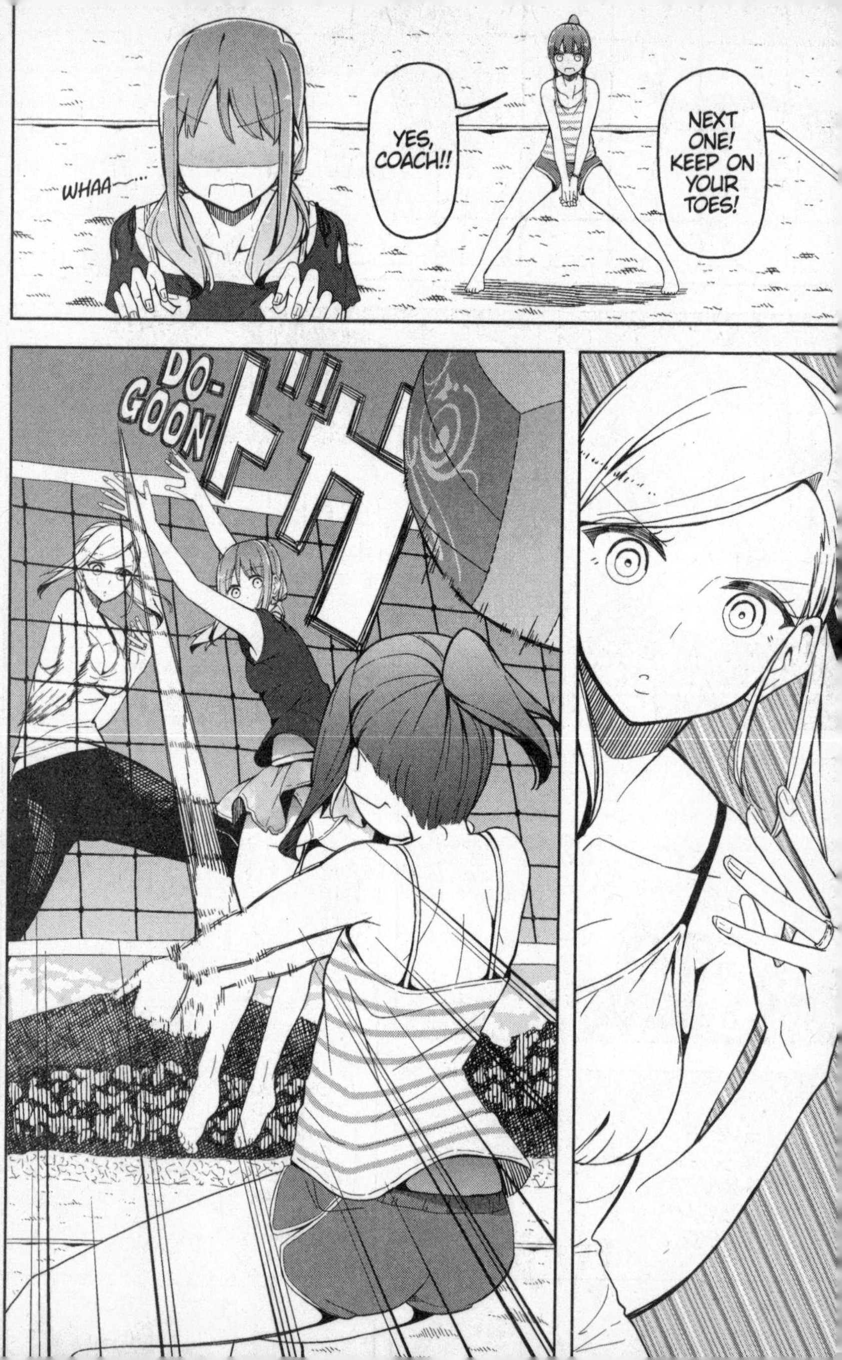
NEXT ONE! KEEP ON YOUR TOES!
YES, COACH!!
WHAA~...
DO-GOON

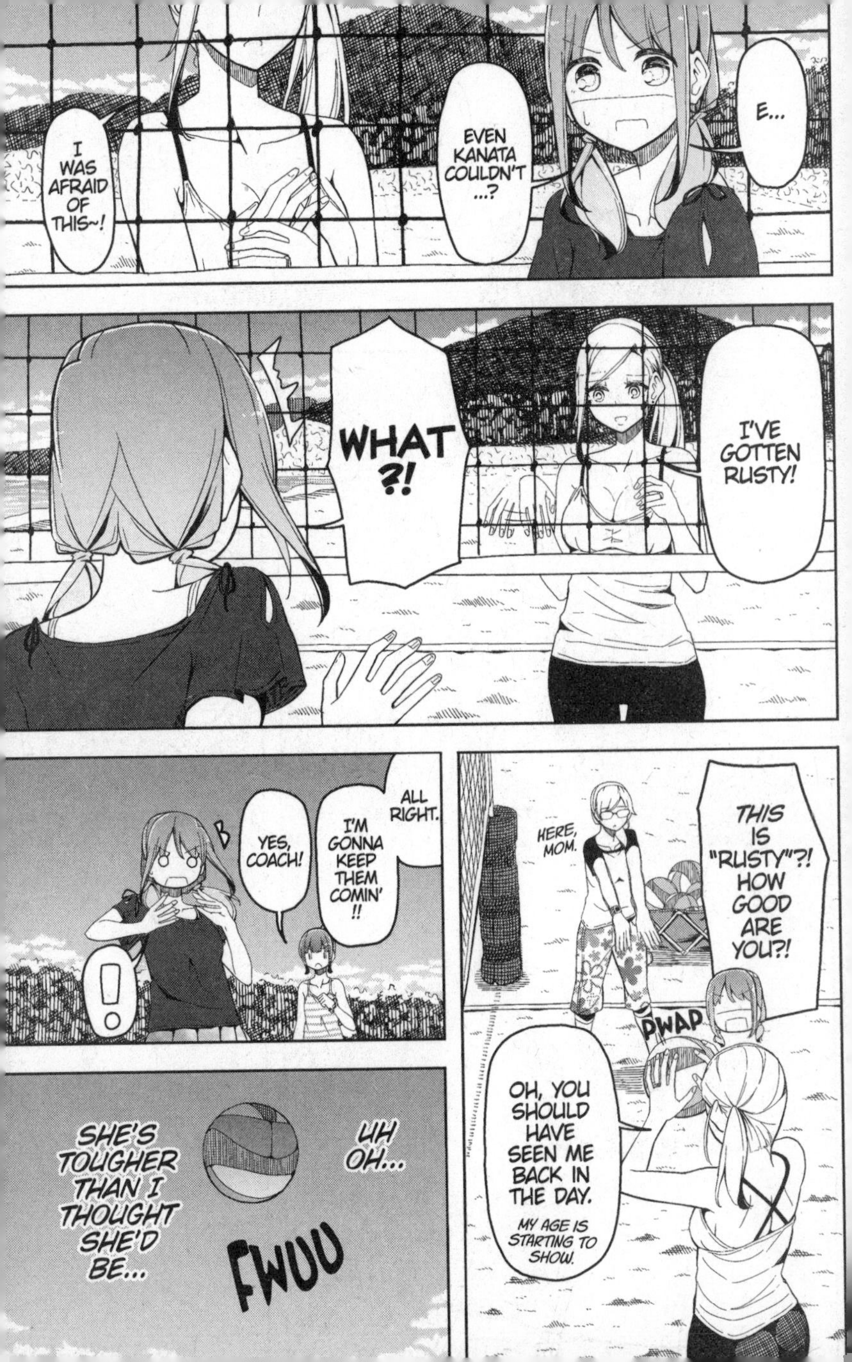
E...
EVEN KANATA COULDN'T ...?
I WAS AFRAID OF THIS~!
I'VE GOTTEN RUSTY!
WHAT?!
THIS IS "RUSTY"?! HOW GOOD ARE YOU?!
HERE, MOM.
PWAP
OH, YOU SHOULD HAVE SEEN ME BACK IN THE DAY.
MY AGE IS STARTING TO SHOW.
ALL RIGHT. I'M GONNA KEEP THEM COMIN'!!
YES, COACH!
!
UH OH...
SHE'S TOUGHER THAN I THOUGHT SHE'D BE...
FWUU

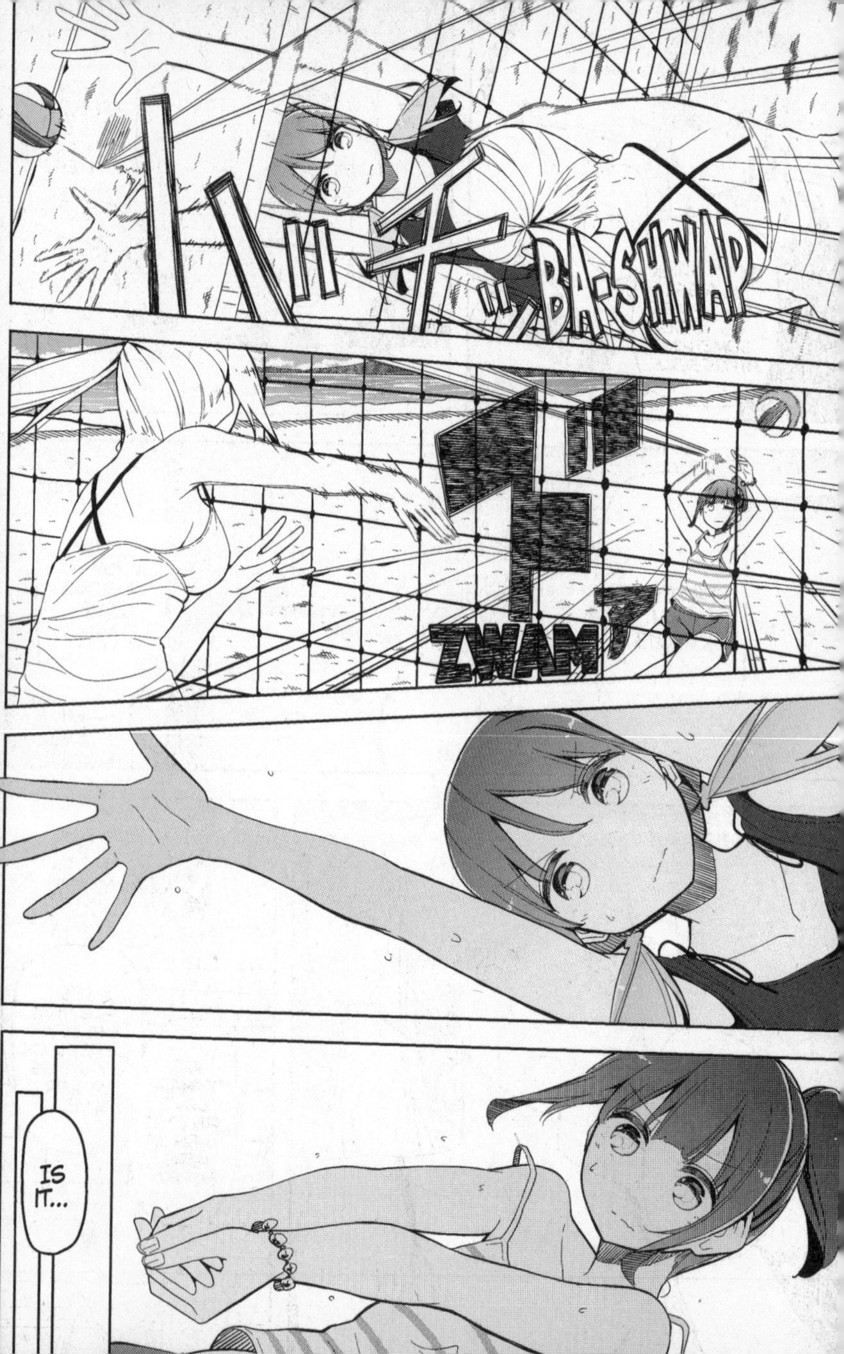
BA-SHWAP
ZWAM
IS IT...

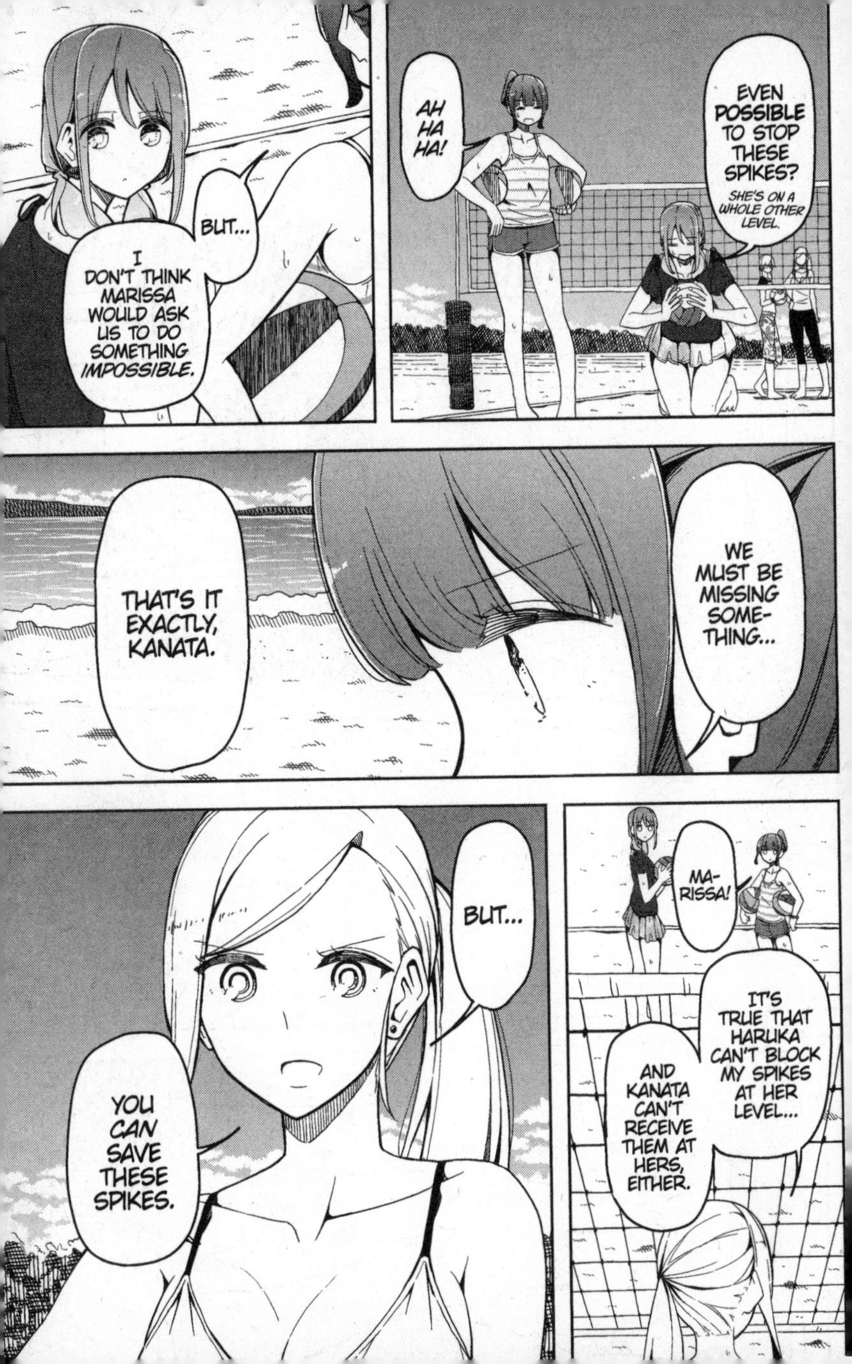
EVEN POSSIBLE TO STOP THESE SPIKES?
SHE'S ON A WHOLE OTHER LEVEL.
AH HA HA!
BUT...
I DON'T THINK MARISSA WOULD ASK US TO DO SOMETHING *IMPOSSIBLE*.
WE MUST BE MISSING SOME-THING...
THAT'S IT EXACTLY, KANATA.
MA-RISSA!
IT'S TRUE THAT HARUKA CAN'T BLOCK MY SPIKES AT HER LEVEL...
AND KANATA CAN'T RECEIVE THEM AT HERS, EITHER.
BUT...
YOU CAN SAVE THESE SPIKES.

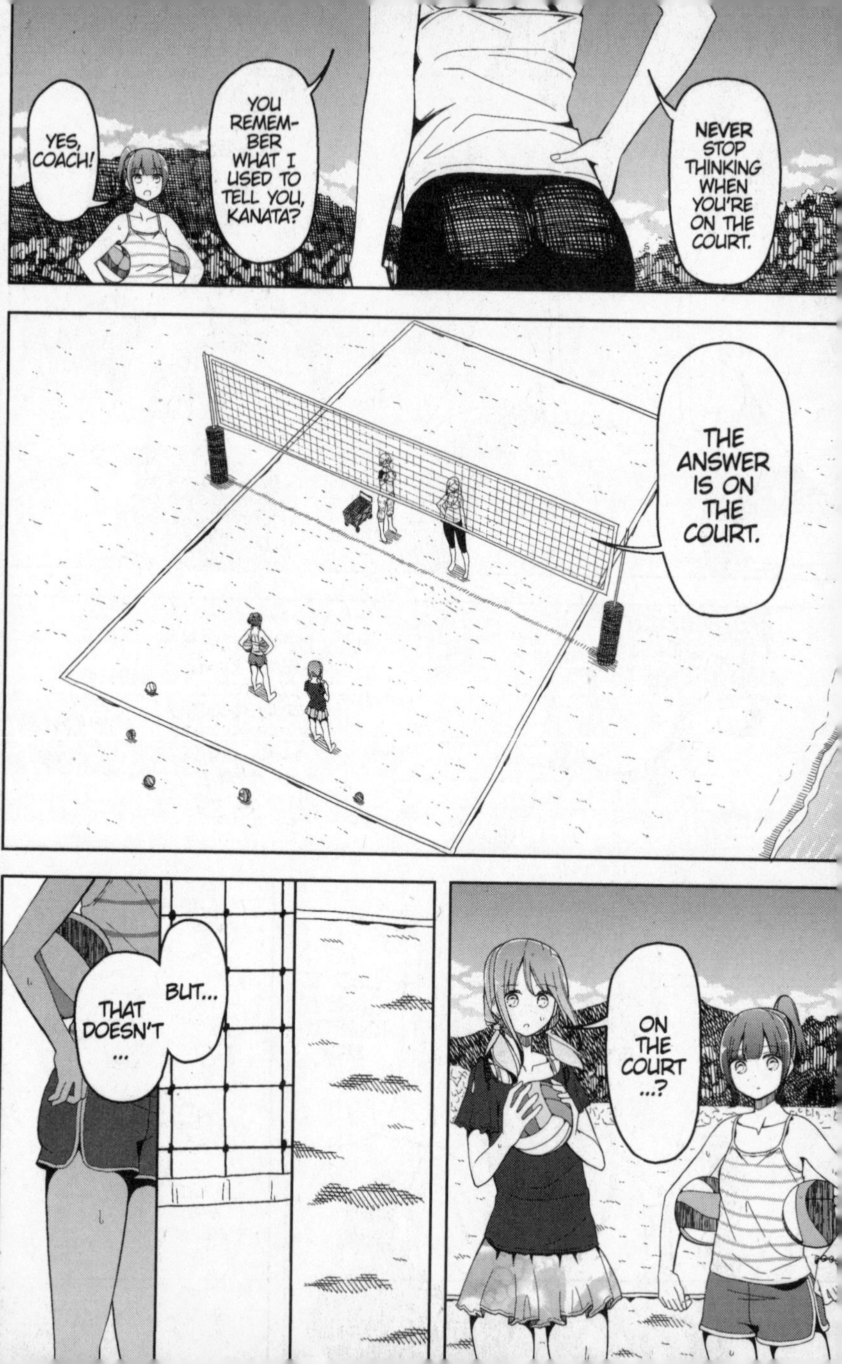
NEVER STOP THINKING WHEN YOU'RE ON THE COURT.
YOU REMEMBER WHAT I USED TO TELL YOU, KANATA?
YES, COACH!
THE ANSWER IS ON THE COURT.
ON THE COURT ...?
BUT...
THAT DOESN'T ...

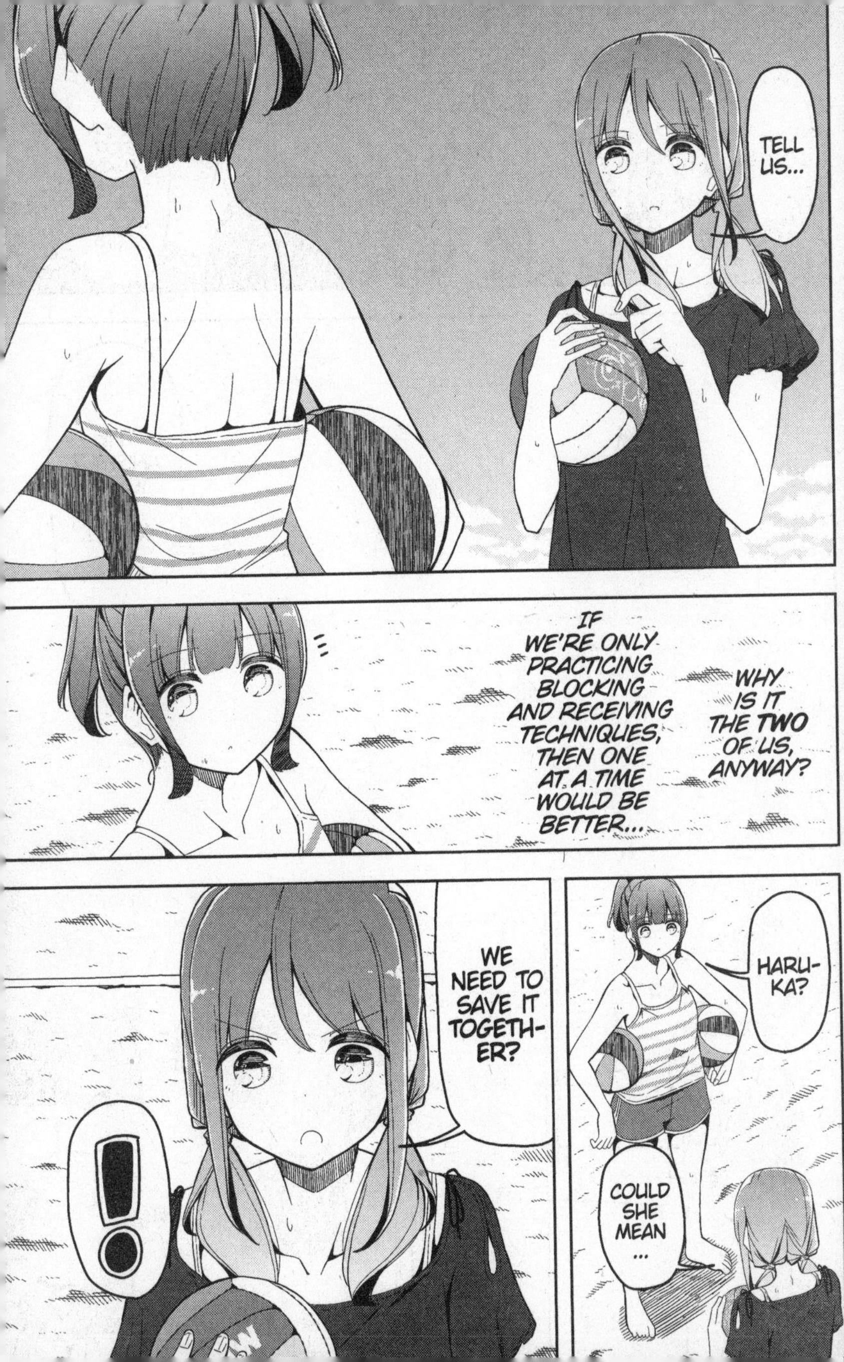
TELL US...
WHY IS IT THE TWO OF US, ANYWAY?
IF WE'RE ONLY PRACTICING BLOCKING AND RECEIVING TECHNIQUES, THEN ONE AT A TIME WOULD BE BETTER...
HARU-KA?
COULD SHE MEAN ...
WE NEED TO SAVE IT TOGETH-ER?
!

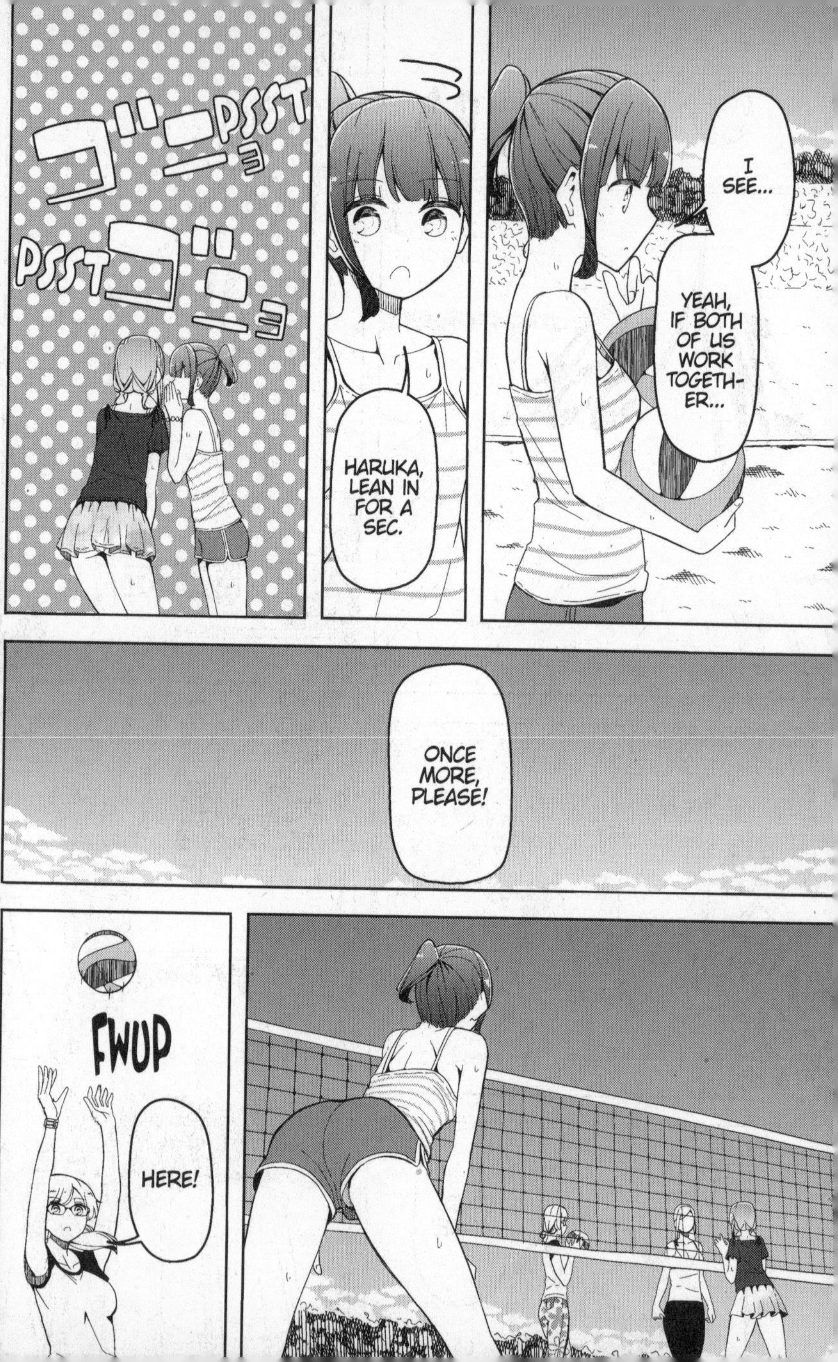
I SEE...
YEAH, IF BOTH OF US WORK TOGETHER...
HARUKA, LEAN IN FOR A SEC.
PSSST
PSSST
ONCE MORE, PLEASE!
FWUP
HERE!

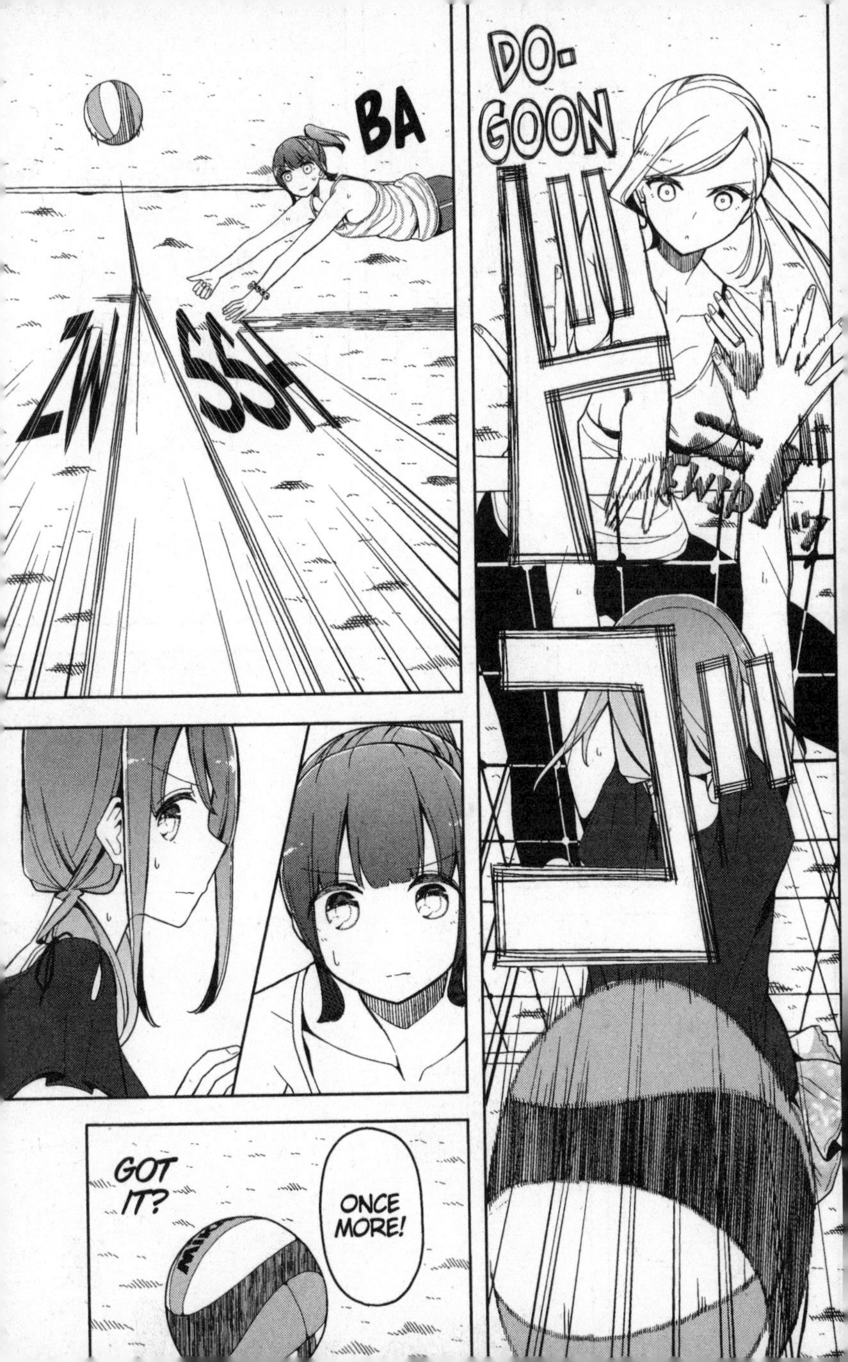
DO-GOON
BA
ZWSSH
ONCE MORE!
GOT IT?

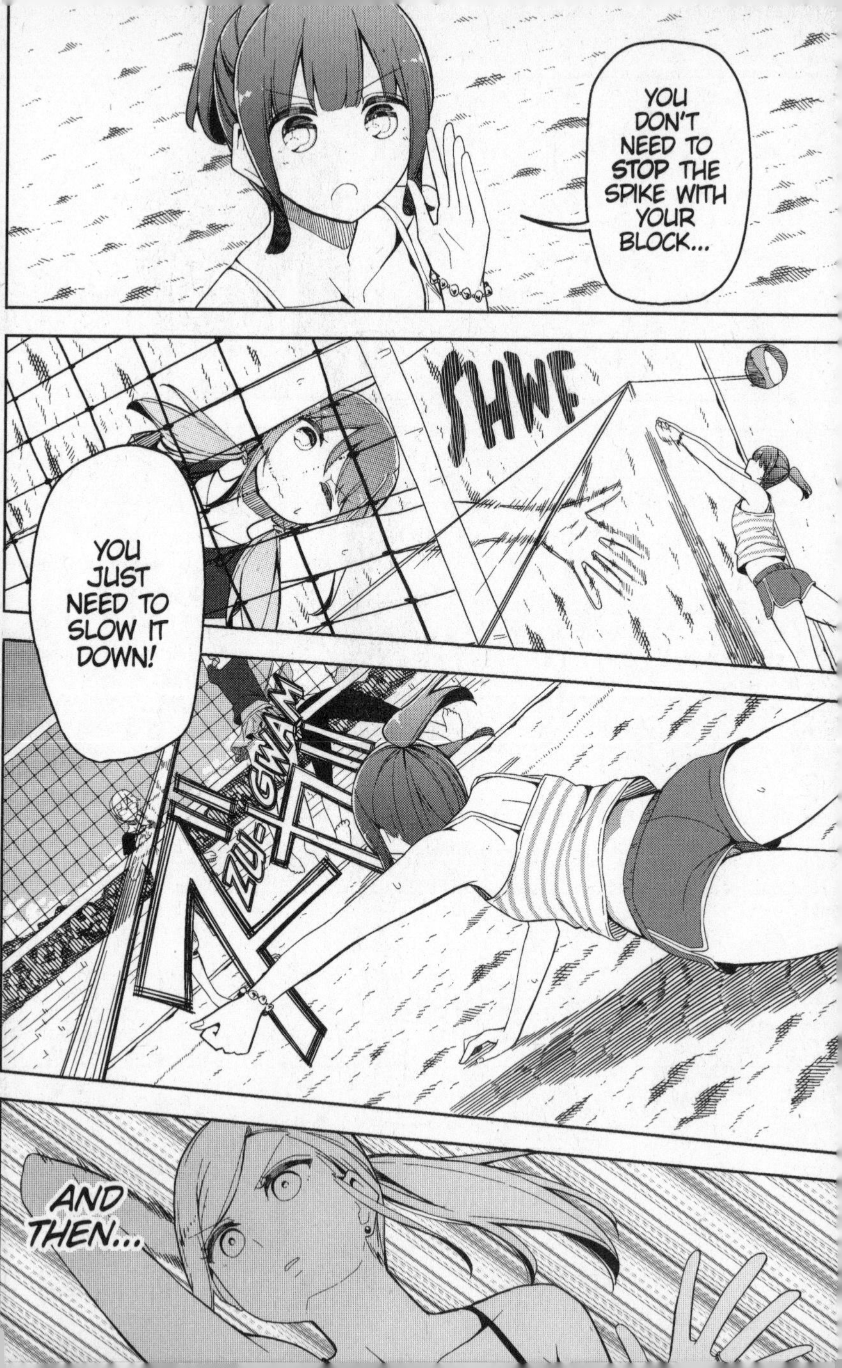
YOU DON'T NEED TO STOP THE SPIKE WITH YOUR BLOCK...
SHWF
YOU JUST NEED TO SLOW IT DOWN!
ZU-GWAM
AND THEN...

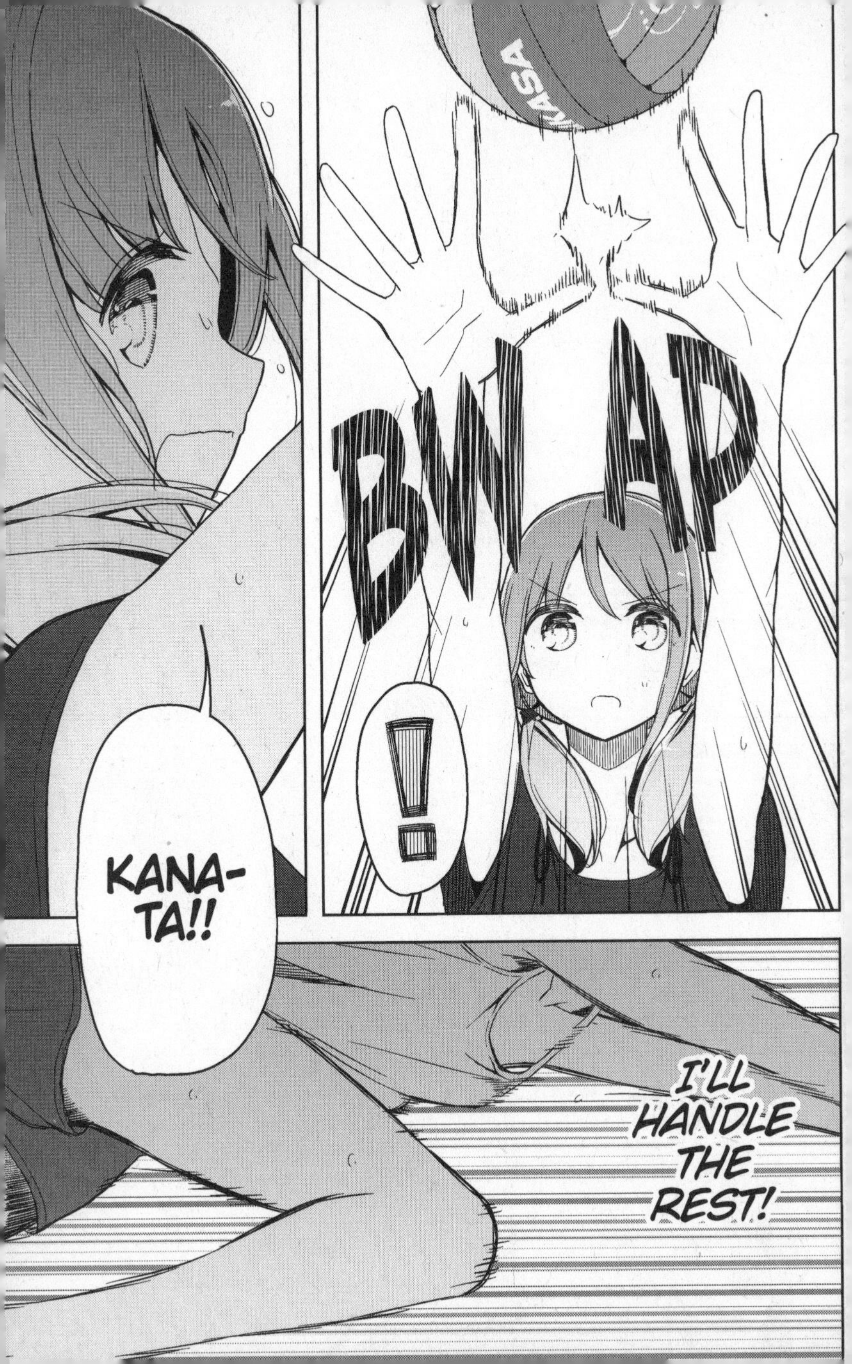
BWAP
!
KANA-TA!!
I'LL HANDLE THE REST!

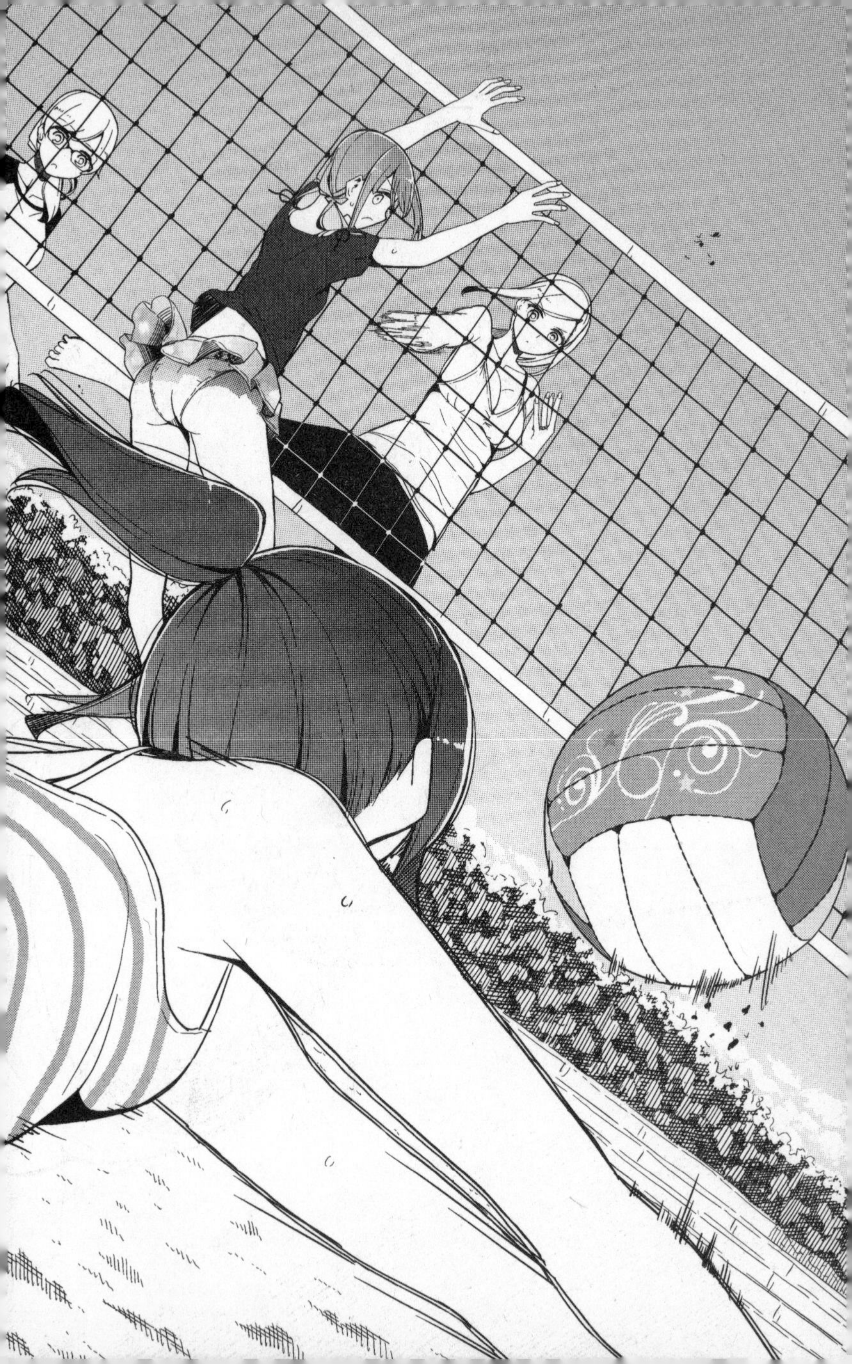

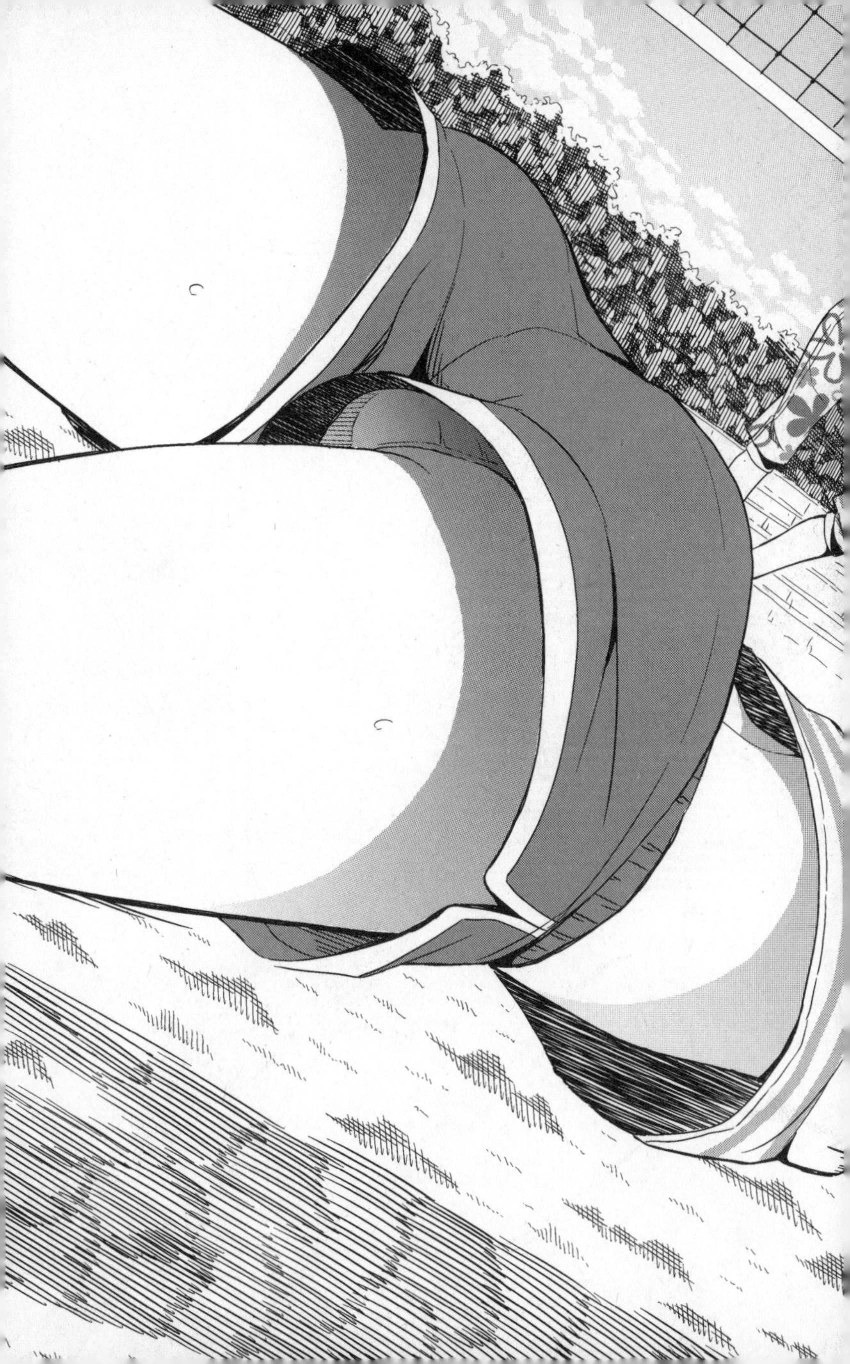

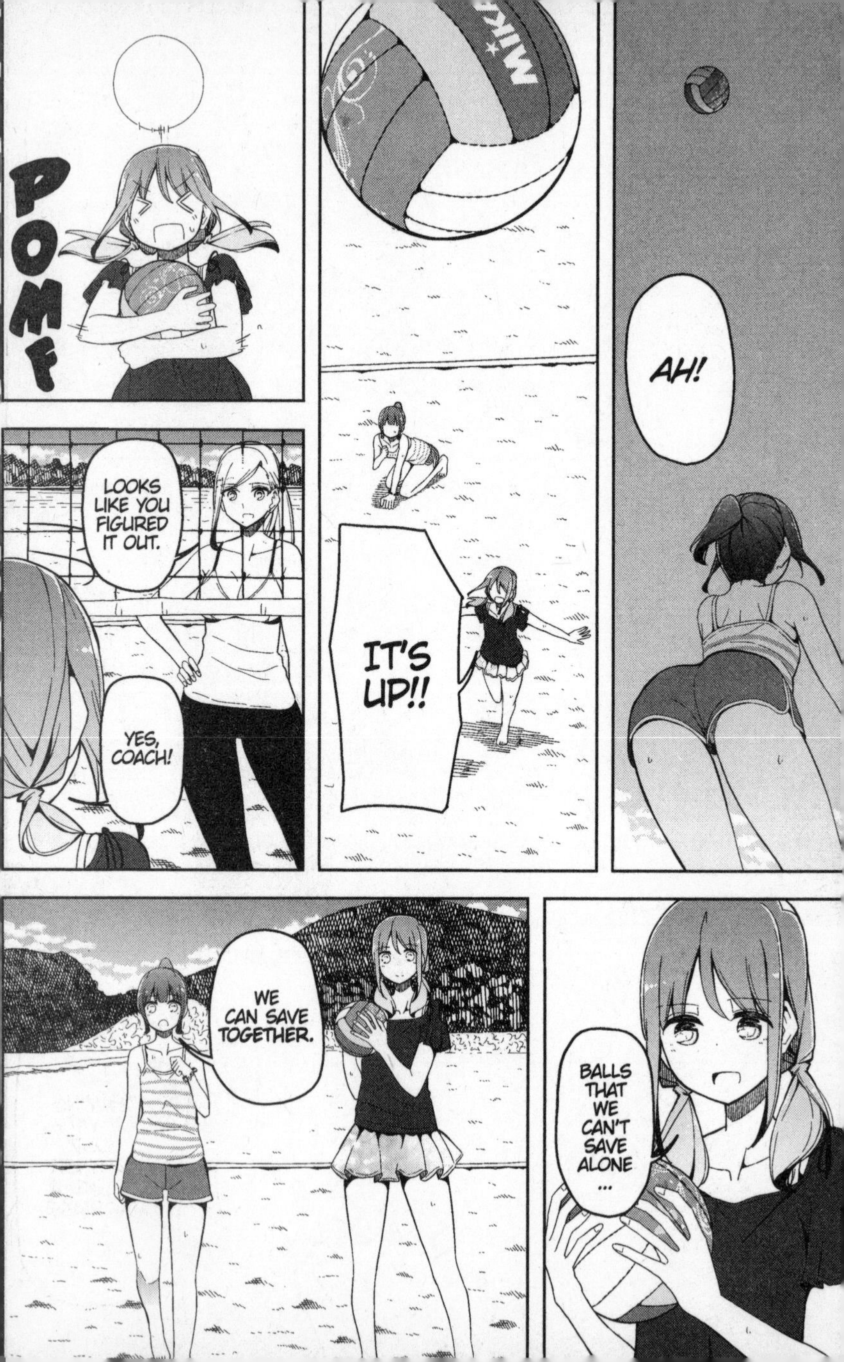
AH!
IT'S UP!!
POMF
LOOKS LIKE YOU FIGURED IT OUT.
YES, COACH!
BALLS THAT WE CAN'T SAVE ALONE ...
WE CAN SAVE TOGETHER.

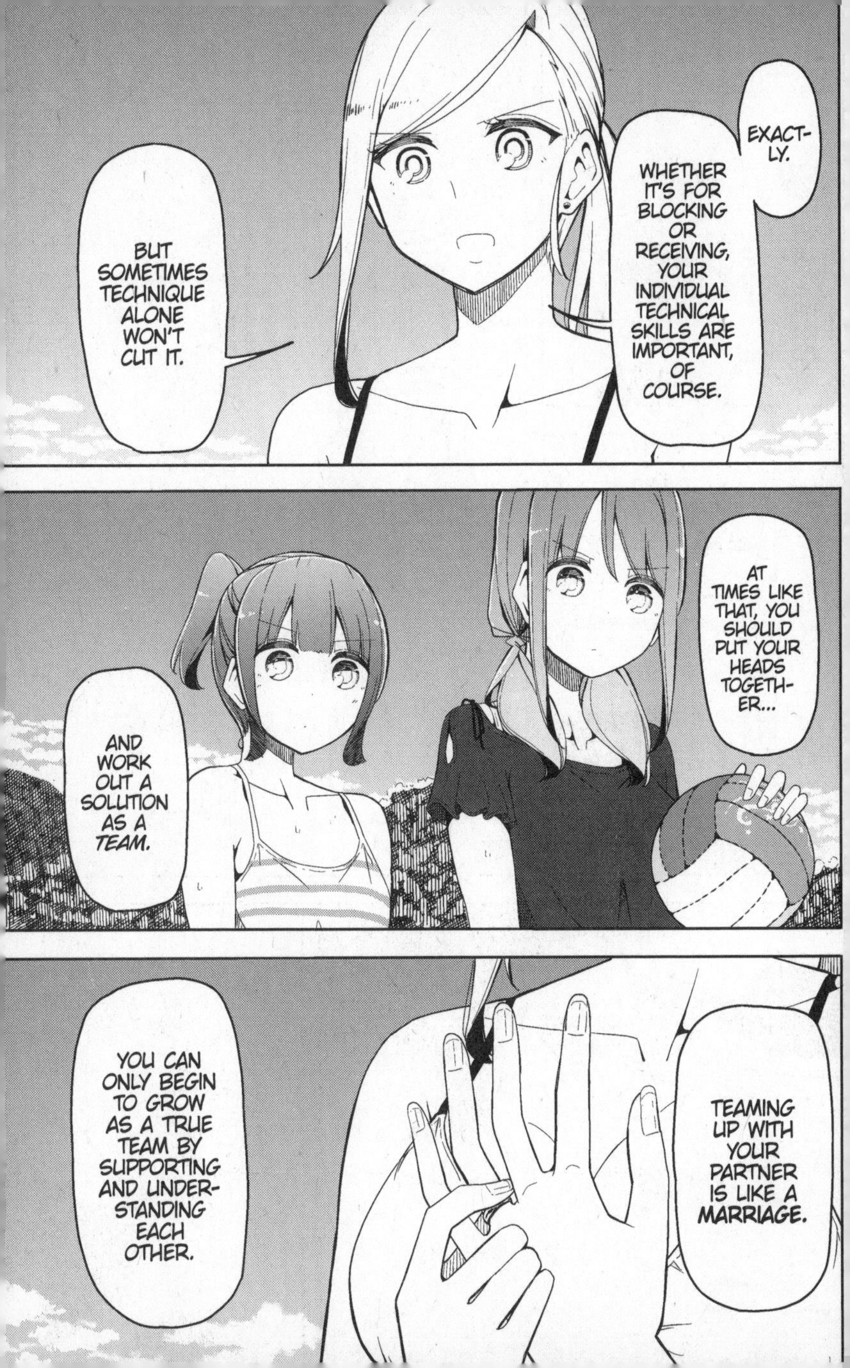
EXACT-LY.
WHETHER IT'S FOR BLOCKING OR RECEIVING, YOUR INDIVIDUAL TECHNICAL SKILLS ARE IMPORTANT, OF COURSE.
BUT SOMETIMES TECHNIQUE ALONE WON'T CUT IT.
AT TIMES LIKE THAT, YOU SHOULD PUT YOUR HEADS TOGETH-ER...
AND WORK OUT A SOLUTION AS A *TEAM.*
TEAMING UP WITH YOUR PARTNER IS LIKE A MARRIAGE.
YOU CAN ONLY BEGIN TO GROW AS A TRUE TEAM BY SUPPORTING AND UNDER-STANDING EACH OTHER.

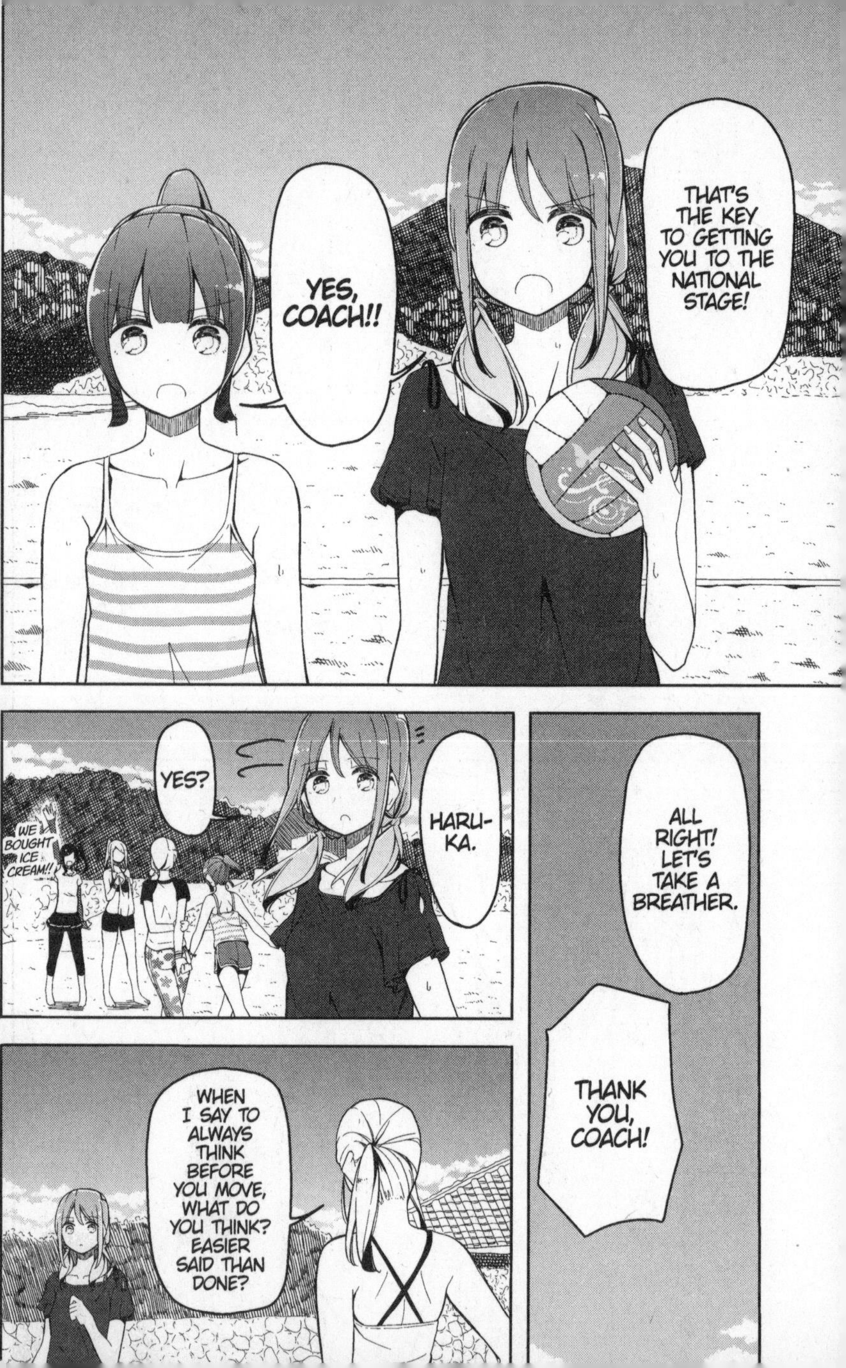
THAT'S THE KEY TO GETTING YOU TO THE NATIONAL STAGE!
YES, COACH!!
ALL RIGHT! LET'S TAKE A BREATHER.
THANK YOU, COACH!
HARU-KA.
YES?
WE BOUGHT ICE CREAM!!
WHEN I SAY TO ALWAYS THINK BEFORE YOU MOVE, WHAT DO YOU THINK? EASIER SAID THAN DONE?

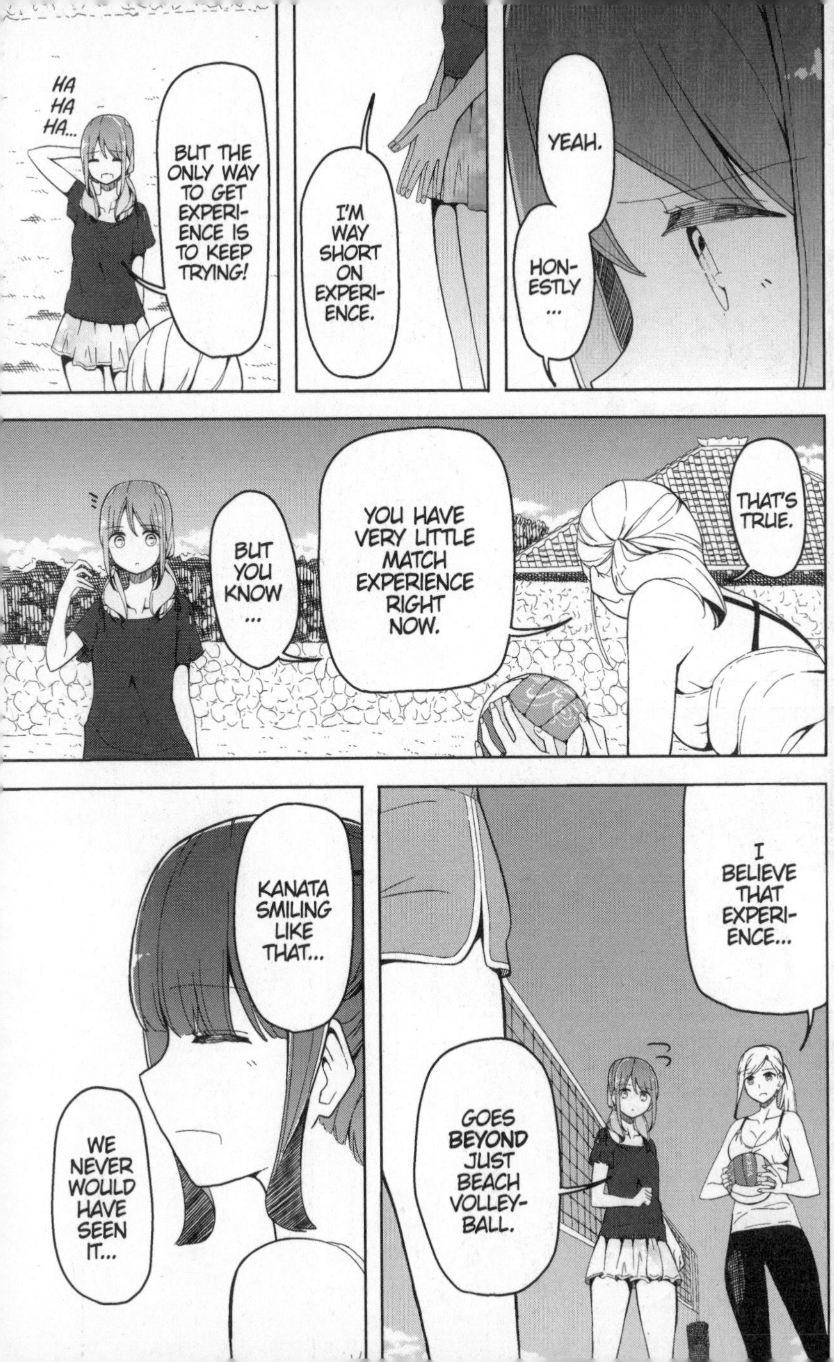
YEAH.
HON-ESTLY ...
I'M WAY SHORT ON EXPERI-ENCE.
HA HA HA...
BUT THE ONLY WAY TO GET EXPERI-ENCE IS TO KEEP TRYING!
THAT'S TRUE.
YOU HAVE VERY LITTLE MATCH EXPERIENCE RIGHT NOW.
BUT YOU KNOW ...
I BELIEVE THAT EXPERI-ENCE...
GOES BEYOND JUST BEACH VOLLEY-BALL.
KANATA SMILING LIKE THAT...
WE NEVER WOULD HAVE SEEN IT...

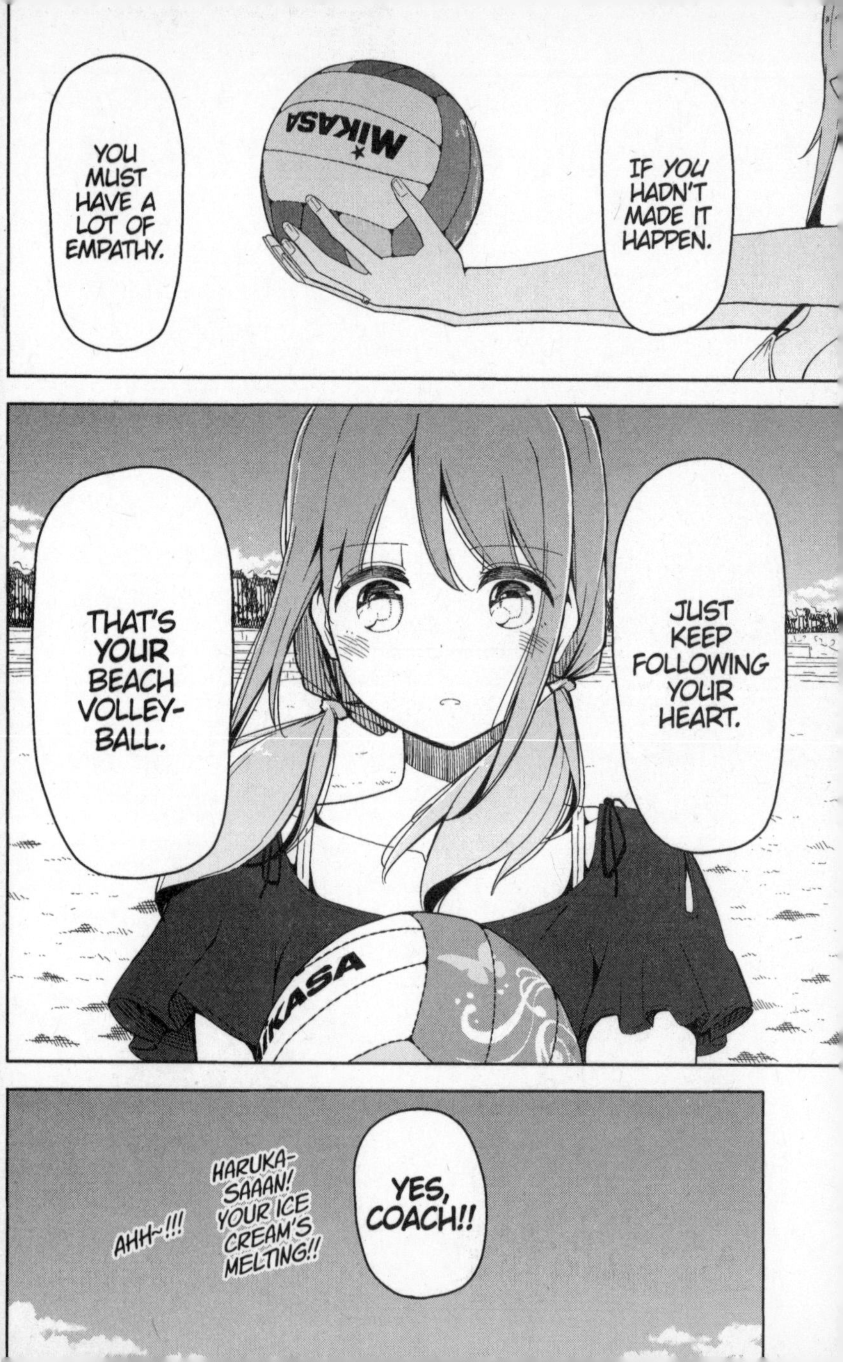
IF YOU HADN'T MADE IT HAPPEN.
YOU MUST HAVE A LOT OF EMPATHY.
JUST KEEP FOLLOWING YOUR HEART.
THAT'S YOUR BEACH VOLLEY-BALL.
YES, COACH!!
HARUKA-SAAAN! YOUR ICE CREAM'S MELTING!!
AHH~!!!

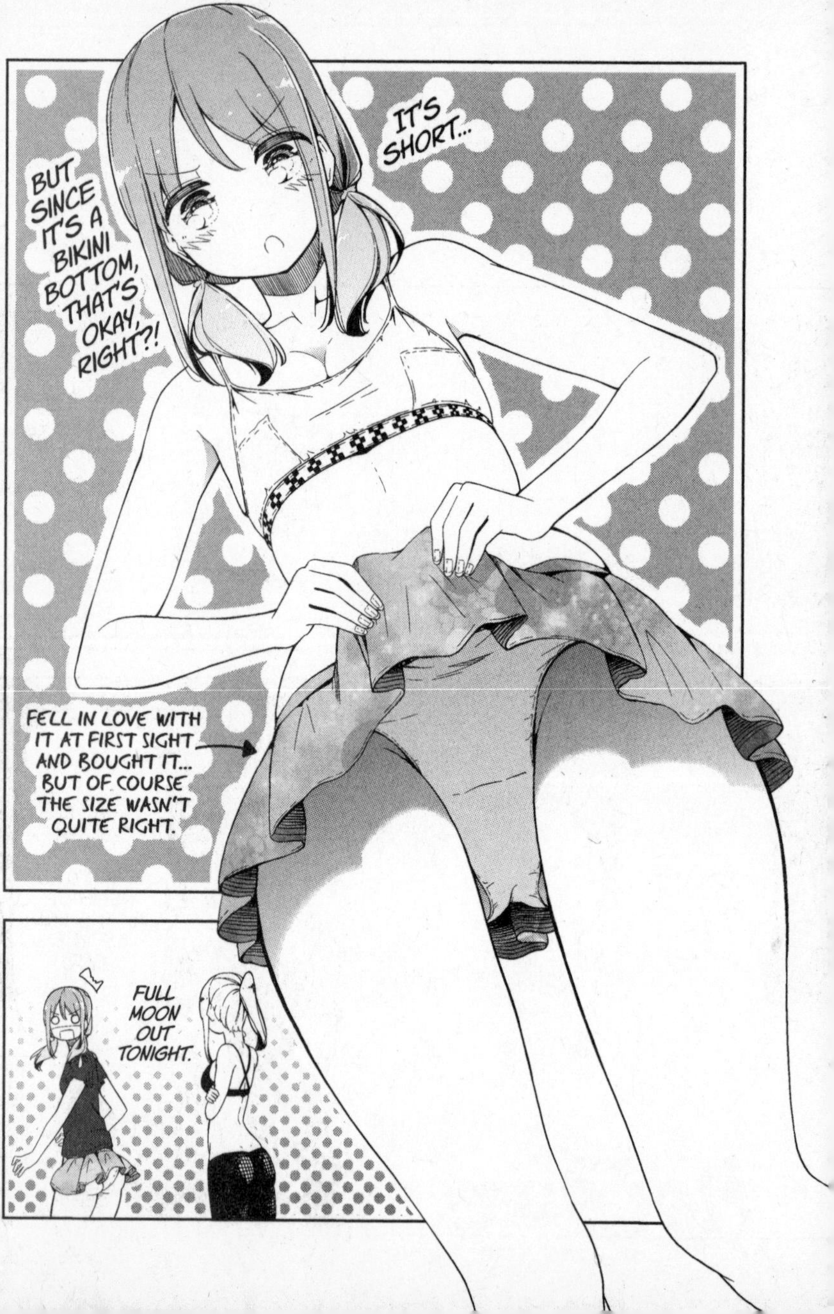
IT'S SHORT...
BUT SINCE IT'S A BIKINI BOTTOM, THAT'S OKAY, RIGHT?!
FELL IN LOVE WITH IT AT FIRST SIGHT AND BOUGHT IT... BUT OF COURSE THE SIZE WASN'T QUITE RIGHT.
FULL MOON OUT TONIGHT.

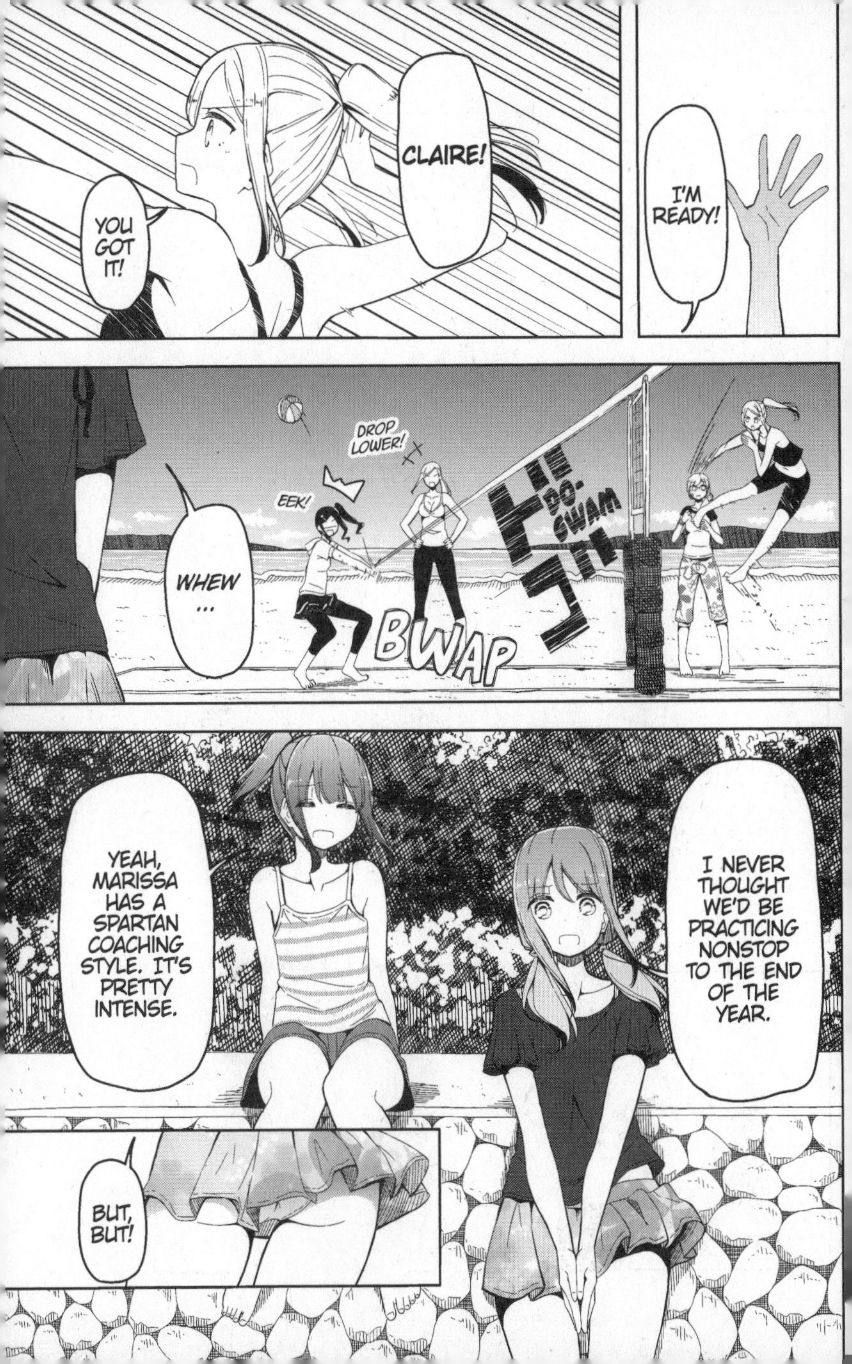
I'M READY!
CLAIRE!
YOU GOT IT!
DO-SWAM
DROP LOWER!
EEK!
BWAP
WHEW ...
I NEVER THOUGHT WE'D BE PRACTICING NONSTOP TO THE END OF THE YEAR.
YEAH, MARISSA HAS A SPARTAN COACHING STYLE. IT'S PRETTY INTENSE.
BUT, BUT!

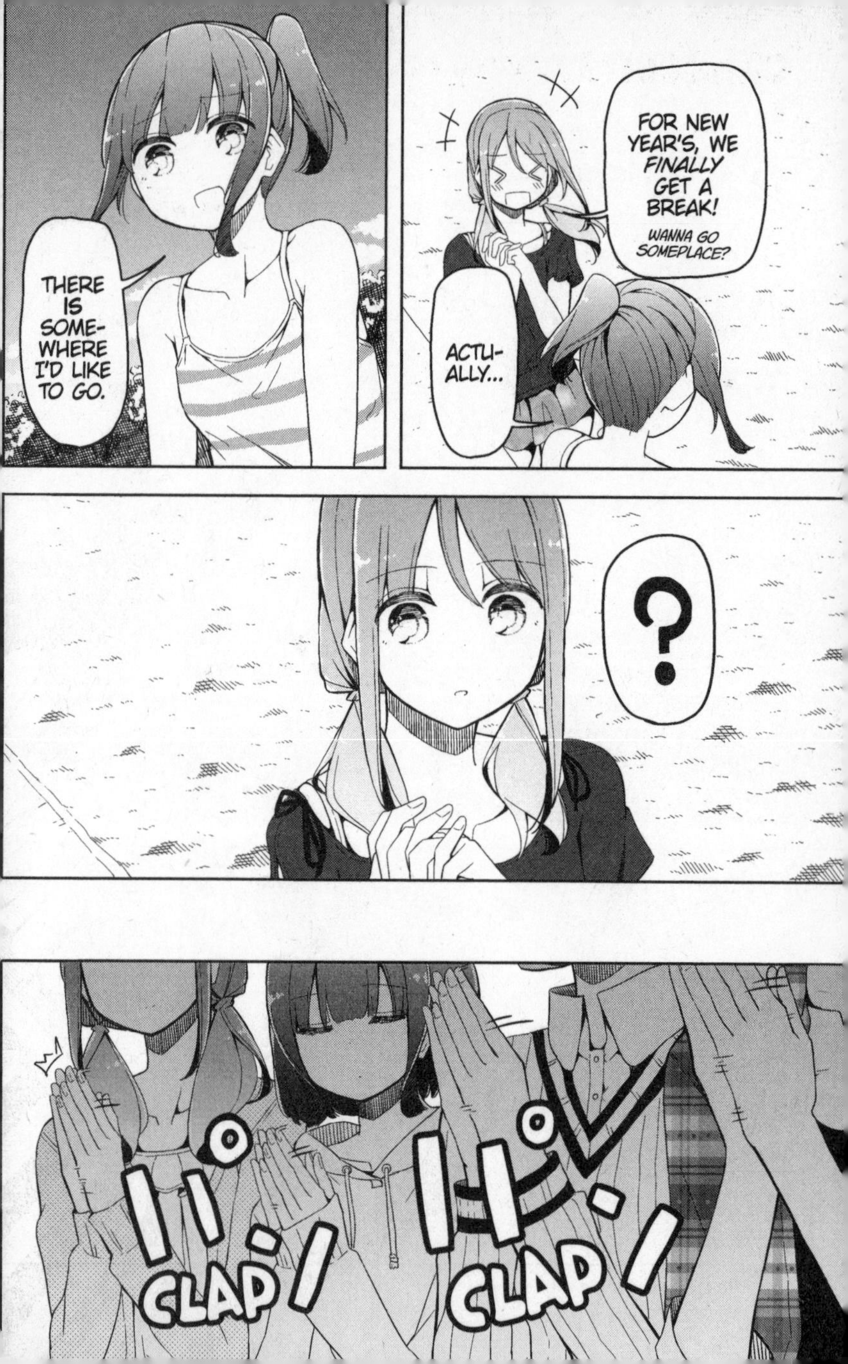
FOR NEW YEAR'S, WE *FINALLY* GET A BREAK!
WANNA GO SOMEPLACE?
ACTUALLY...
THERE IS SOMEWHERE I'D LIKE TO GO.
?
CLAP
CLAP

Chapter 17: Why Me?

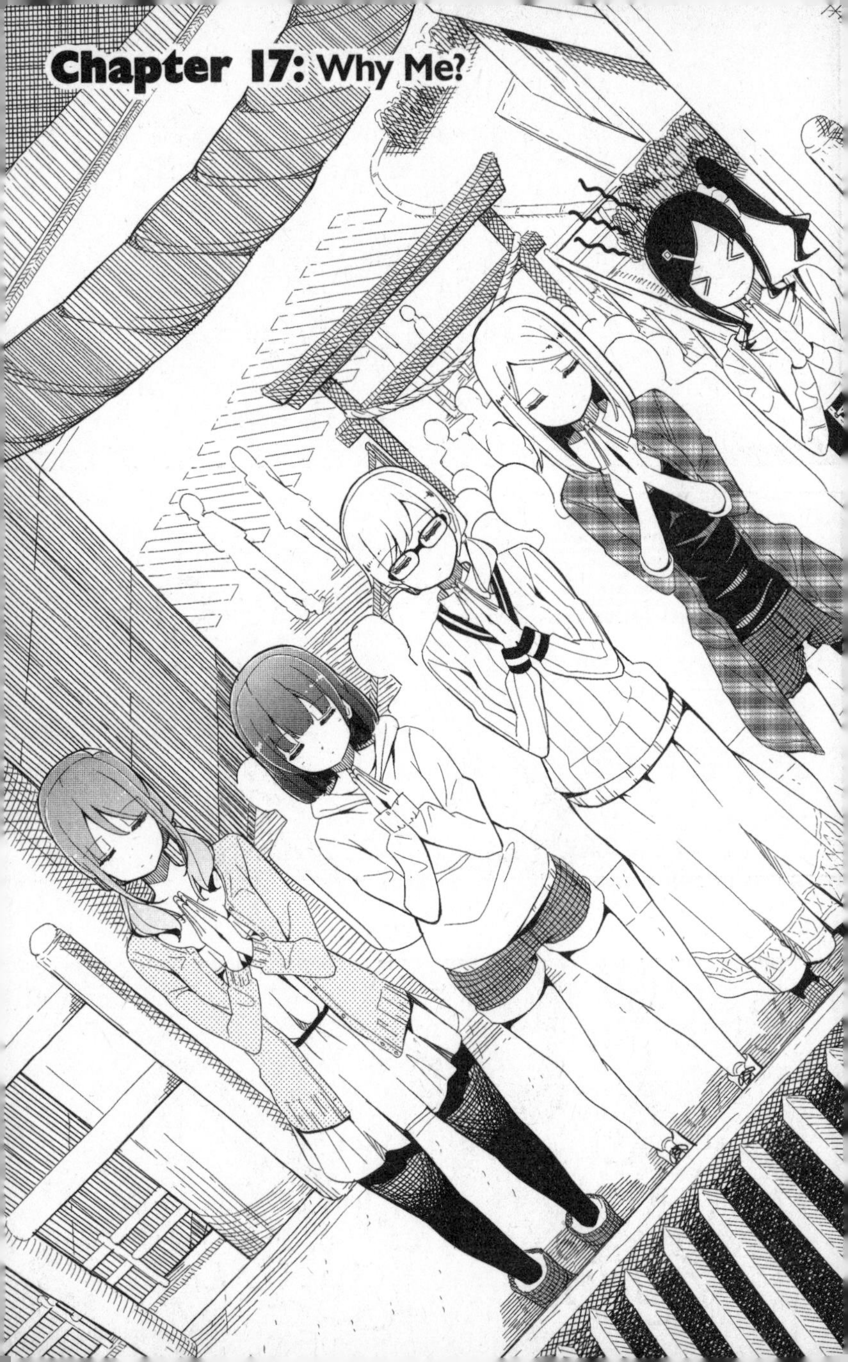

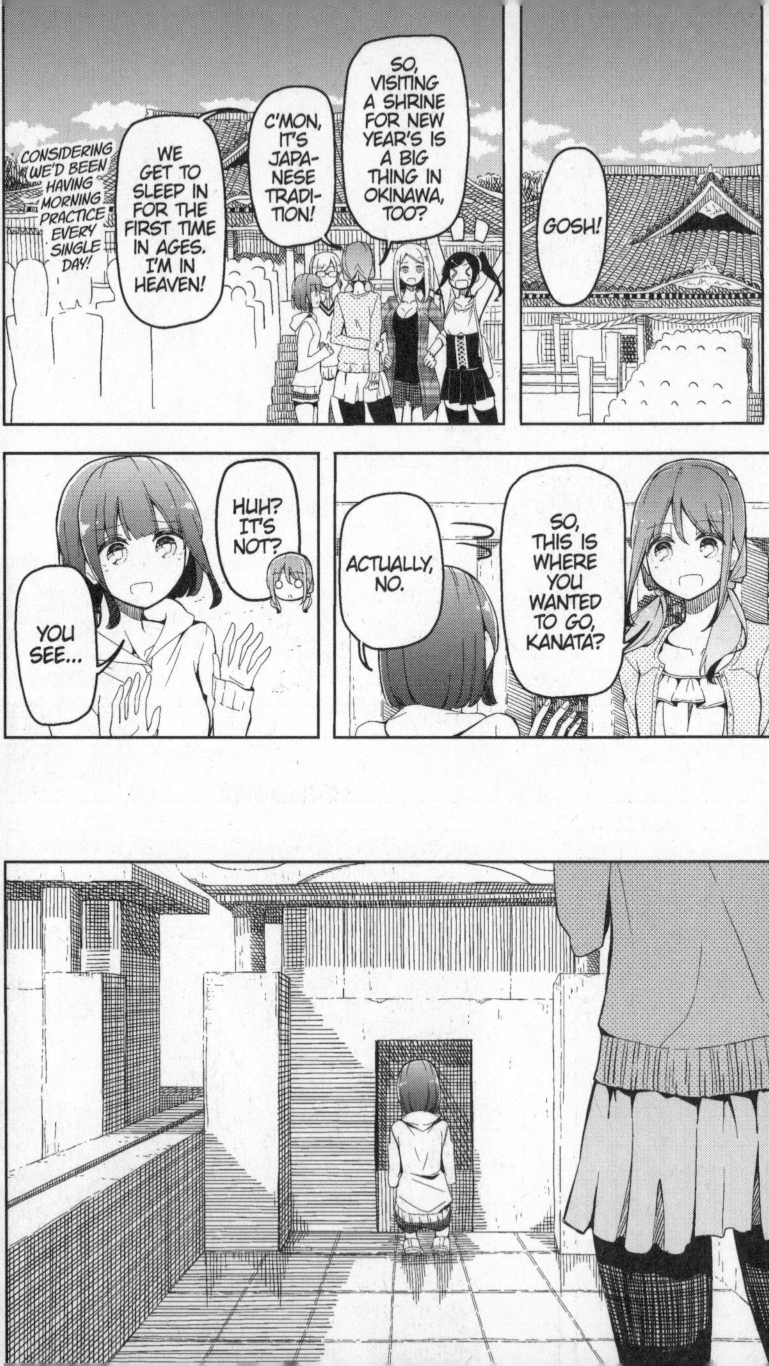
GOSH!
SO, VISITING A SHRINE FOR NEW YEAR'S IS A BIG THING IN OKINAWA, TOO?
C'MON, IT'S JAPANESE TRADITION!
WE GET TO SLEEP IN FOR THE FIRST TIME IN AGES. I'M IN HEAVEN!
CONSIDERING WE'D BEEN HAVING MORNING PRACTICE EVERY SINGLE DAY!
SO, THIS IS WHERE YOU WANTED TO GO, KANATA?
ACTUALLY, NO.
HUH? IT'S NOT?
YOU SEE...

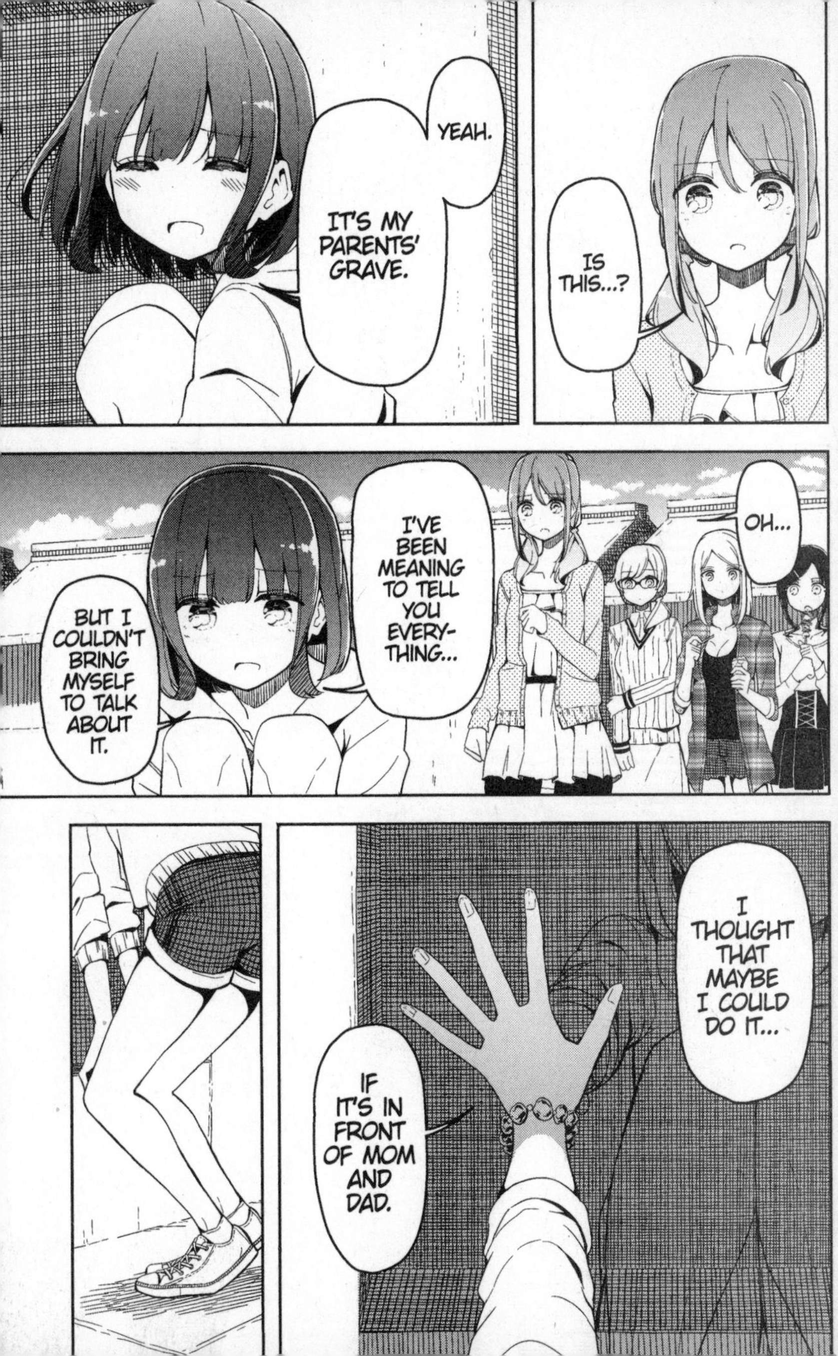
IS THIS...?
YEAH.
IT'S MY PARENTS' GRAVE.
OH...
I'VE BEEN MEANING TO TELL YOU EVERYTHING...
BUT I COULDN'T BRING MYSELF TO TALK ABOUT IT.
I THOUGHT THAT MAYBE I COULD DO IT...
IF IT'S IN FRONT OF MOM AND DAD.

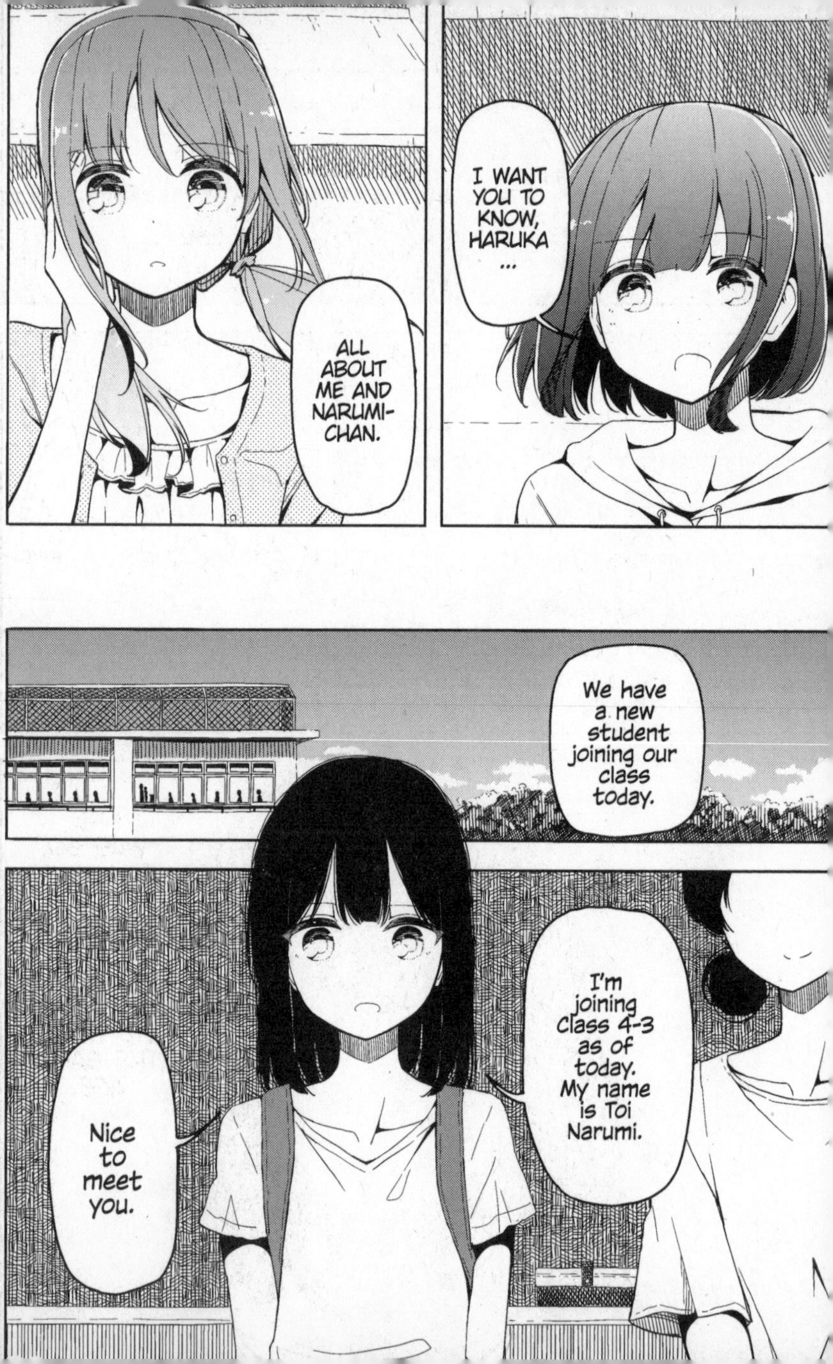
I WANT YOU TO KNOW, HARUKA ...
ALL ABOUT ME AND NARUMI-CHAN.
We have a new student joining our class today.
I'm joining Class 4-3 as of today. My name is Toi Narumi.
Nice to meet you.

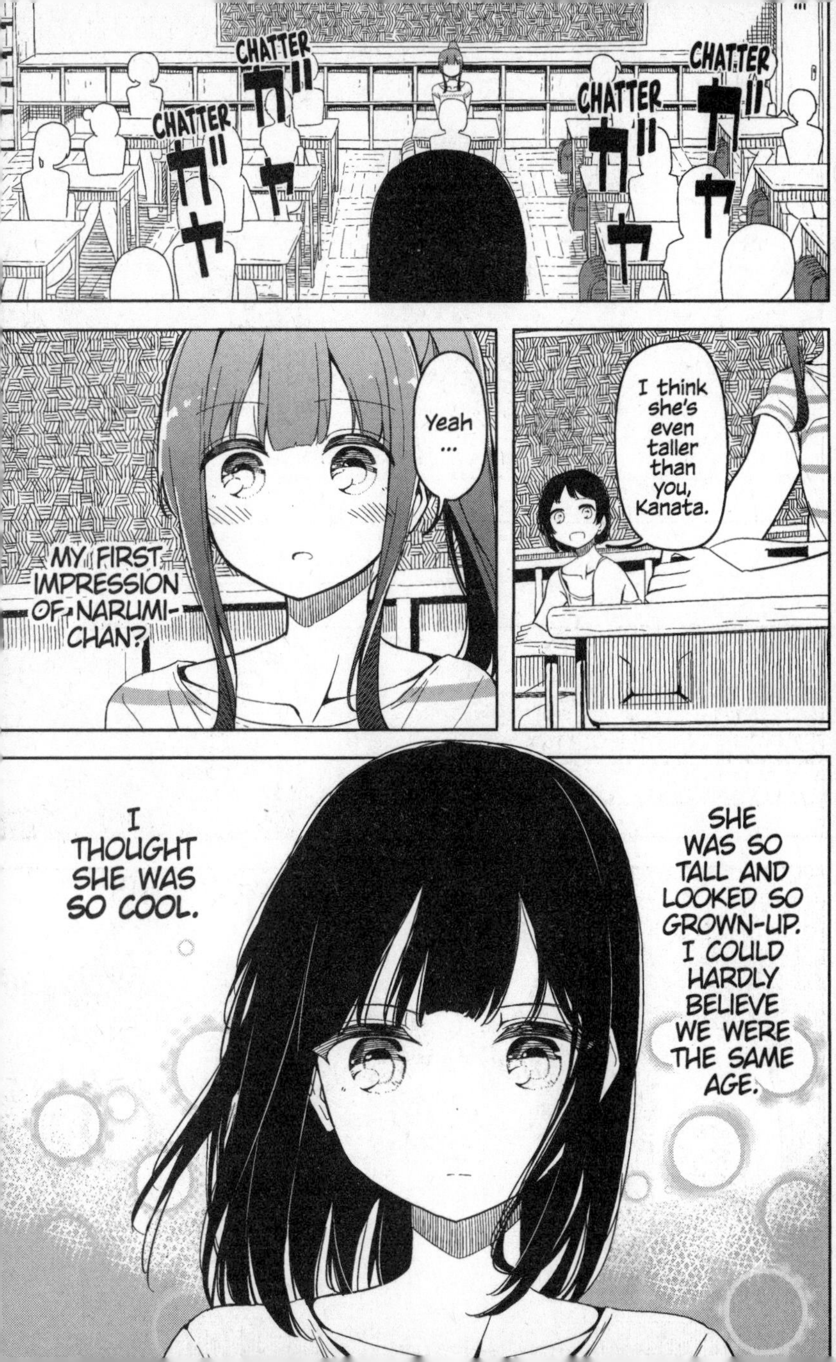

CHATTER ガヤ
CHATTER ガヤ
CHATTER ガヤ
CHATTER ガヤ
I think she's even taller than you, Kanata.
Yeah ...
MY FIRST IMPRESSION OF NARUMI-CHAN?
SHE WAS SO TALL AND LOOKED SO GROWN-UP. I COULD HARDLY BELIEVE WE WERE THE SAME AGE.
I THOUGHT SHE WAS SO COOL.

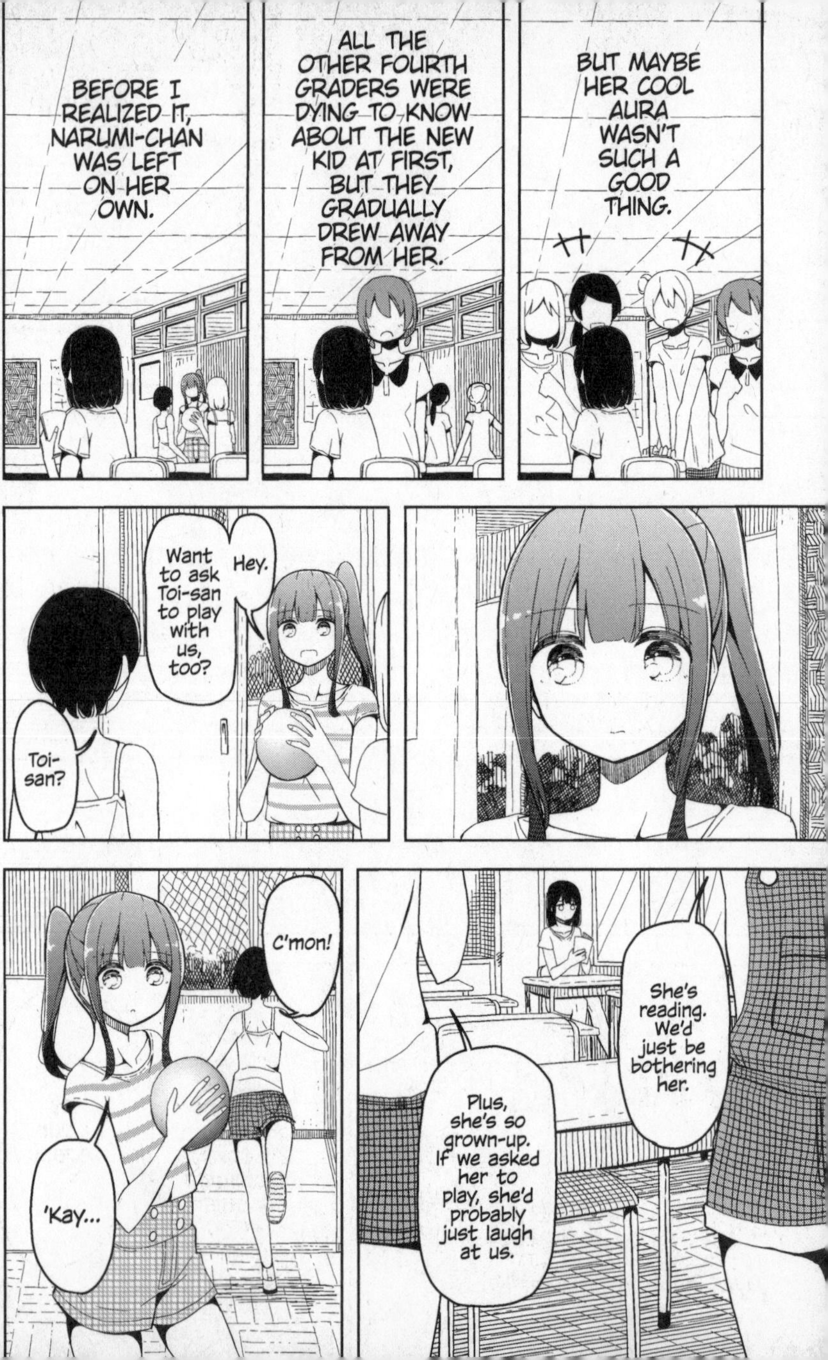

BUT MAYBE HER COOL AURA WASN'T SUCH A GOOD THING.
ALL THE OTHER FOURTH GRADERS WERE DYING TO KNOW ABOUT THE NEW KID AT FIRST, BUT THEY GRADUALLY DREW AWAY FROM HER.
BEFORE I REALIZED IT, NARUMI-CHAN WAS LEFT ON HER OWN.
Hey.
Want to ask Toi-san to play with us, too?
Toi-san?
She's reading. We'd just be bothering her.
Plus, she's so grown-up. If we asked her to play, she'd probably just laugh at us.
C'mon!
'Kay...

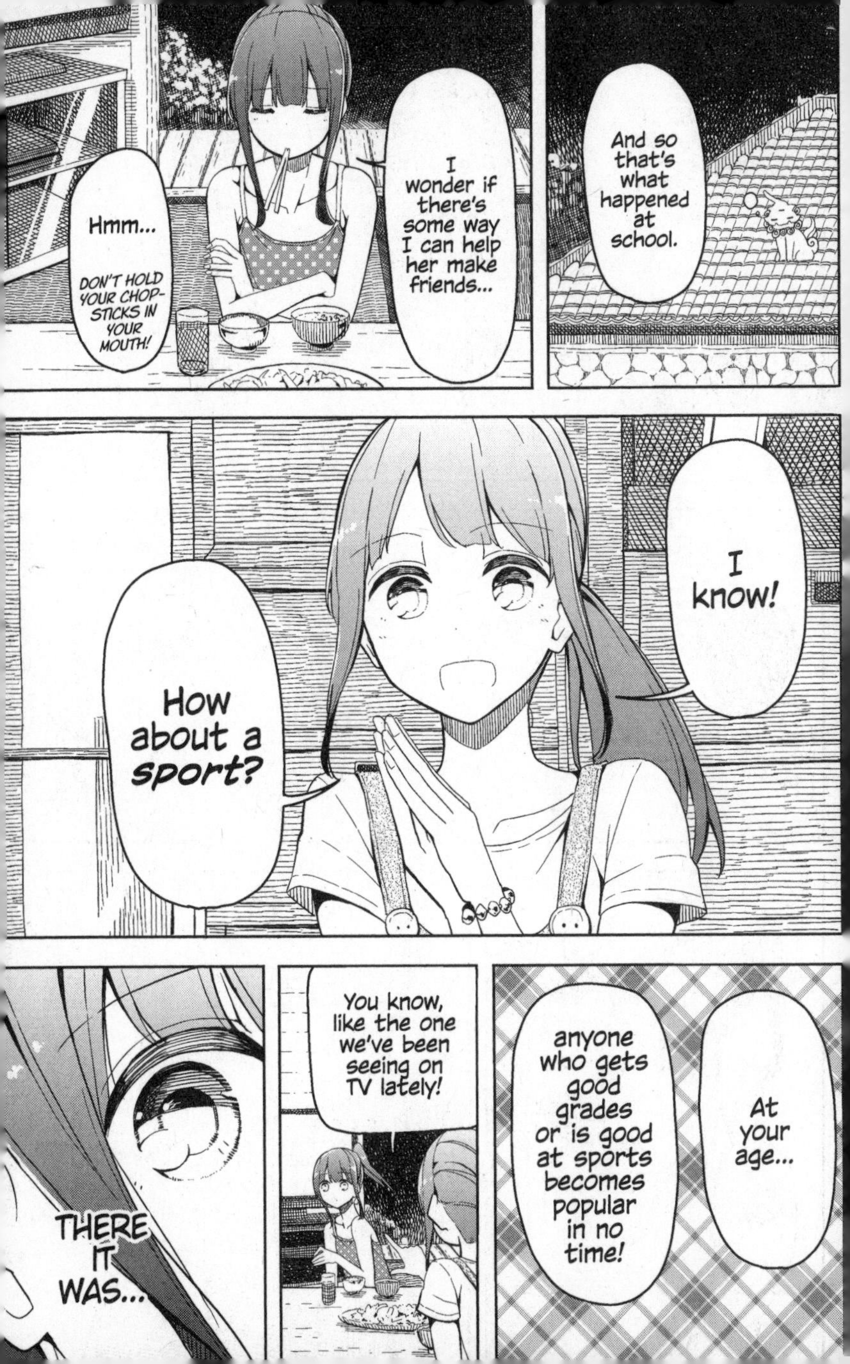
And so that's what happened at school.
I wonder if there's some way I can help her make friends...
Hmm...
DON'T HOLD YOUR CHOPSTICKS IN YOUR MOUTH!
I know!
How about a *sport?*
At your age...
anyone who gets good grades or is good at sports becomes popular in no time!
You know, like the one we've been seeing on TV lately!
THERE IT WAS...

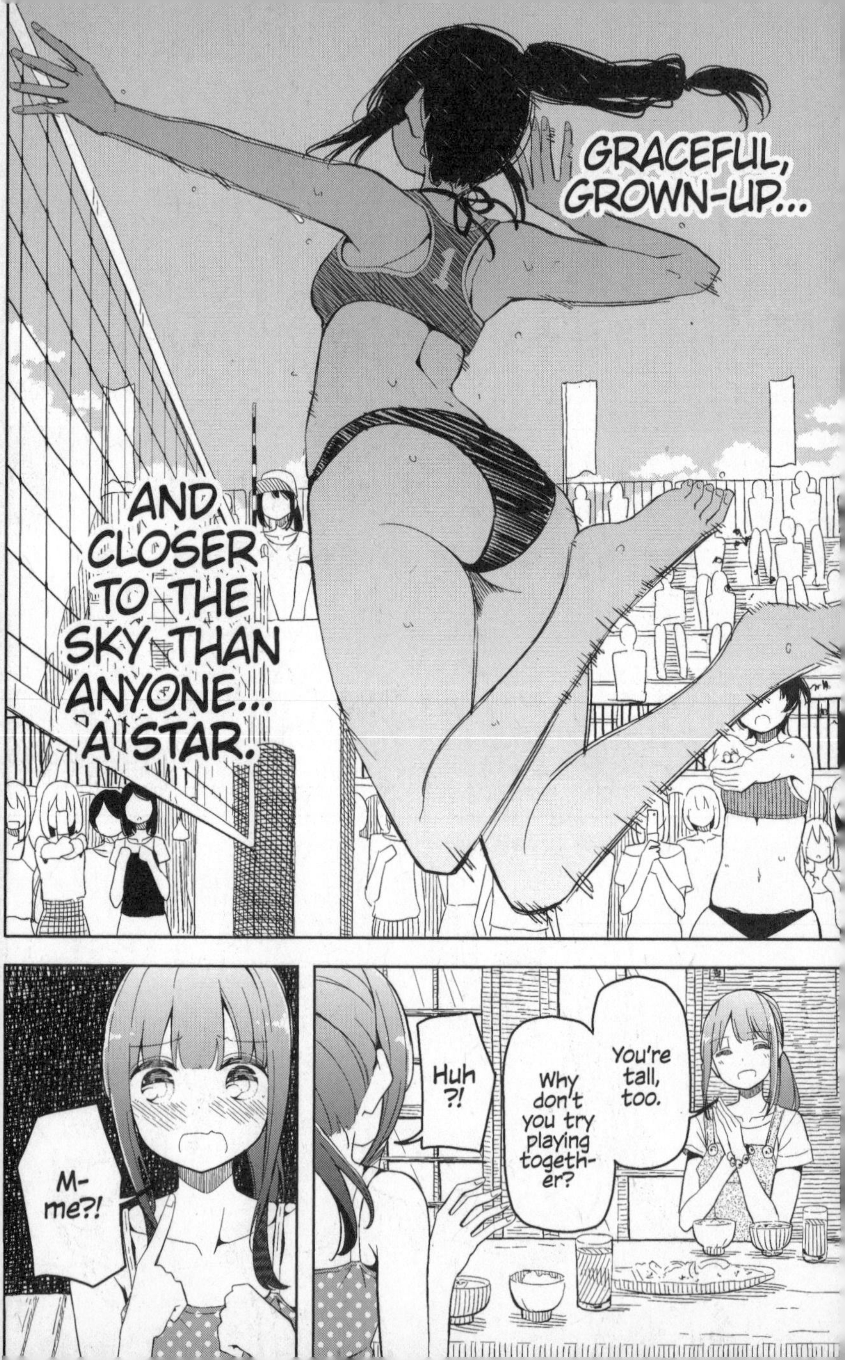
GRACEFUL, GROWN-UP...
AND CLOSER TO THE SKY THAN ANYONE... A STAR.
You're tall, too.
Why don't you try playing togeth-er?
Huh?!
M-me?!

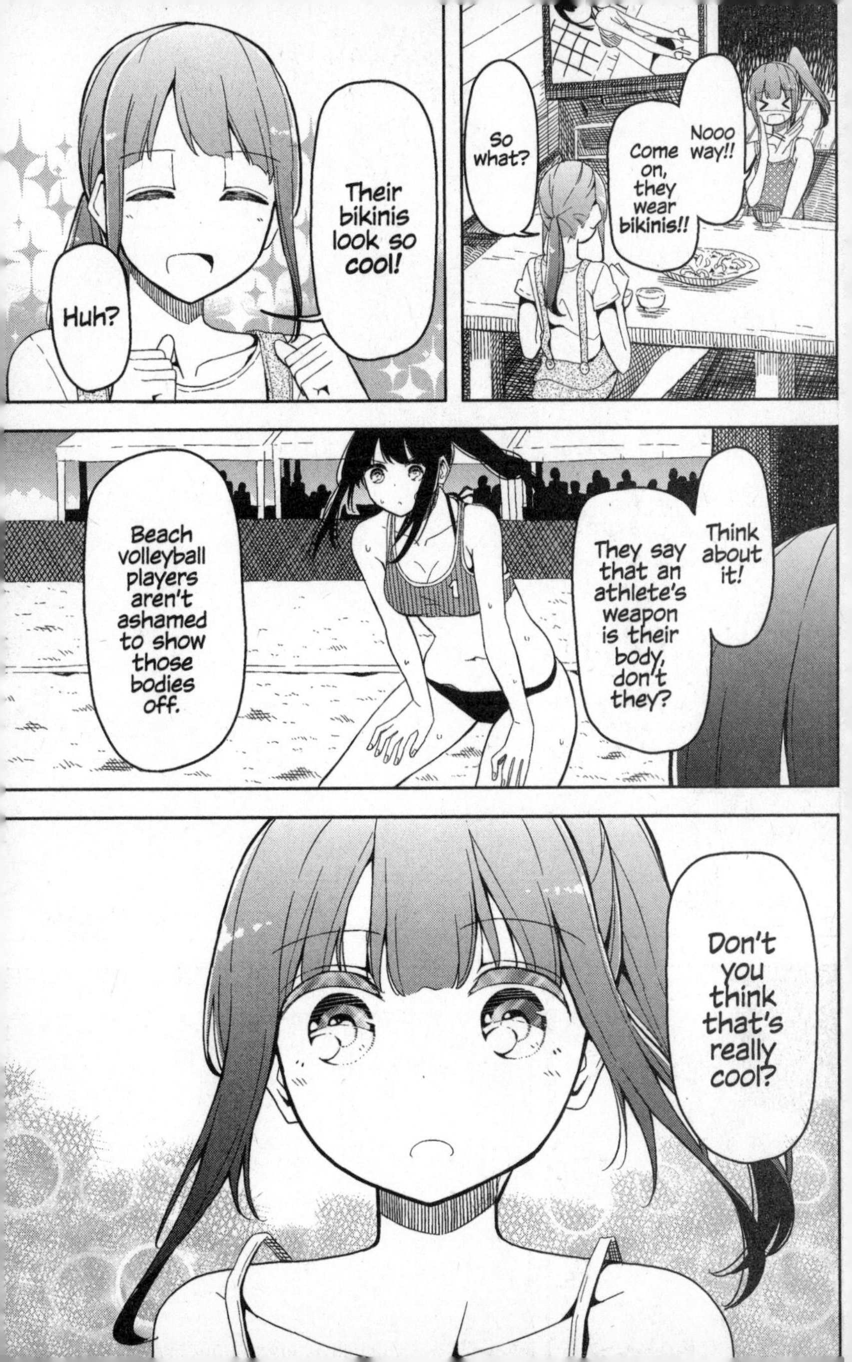
Nooo way!!
Come on, they wear bikinis!!
So what?
Their bikinis look so cool!
Huh?
Think about it!
They say that an athlete's weapon is their body, don't they?
Beach volleyball players aren't ashamed to show those bodies off.
Don't you think that's really cool?

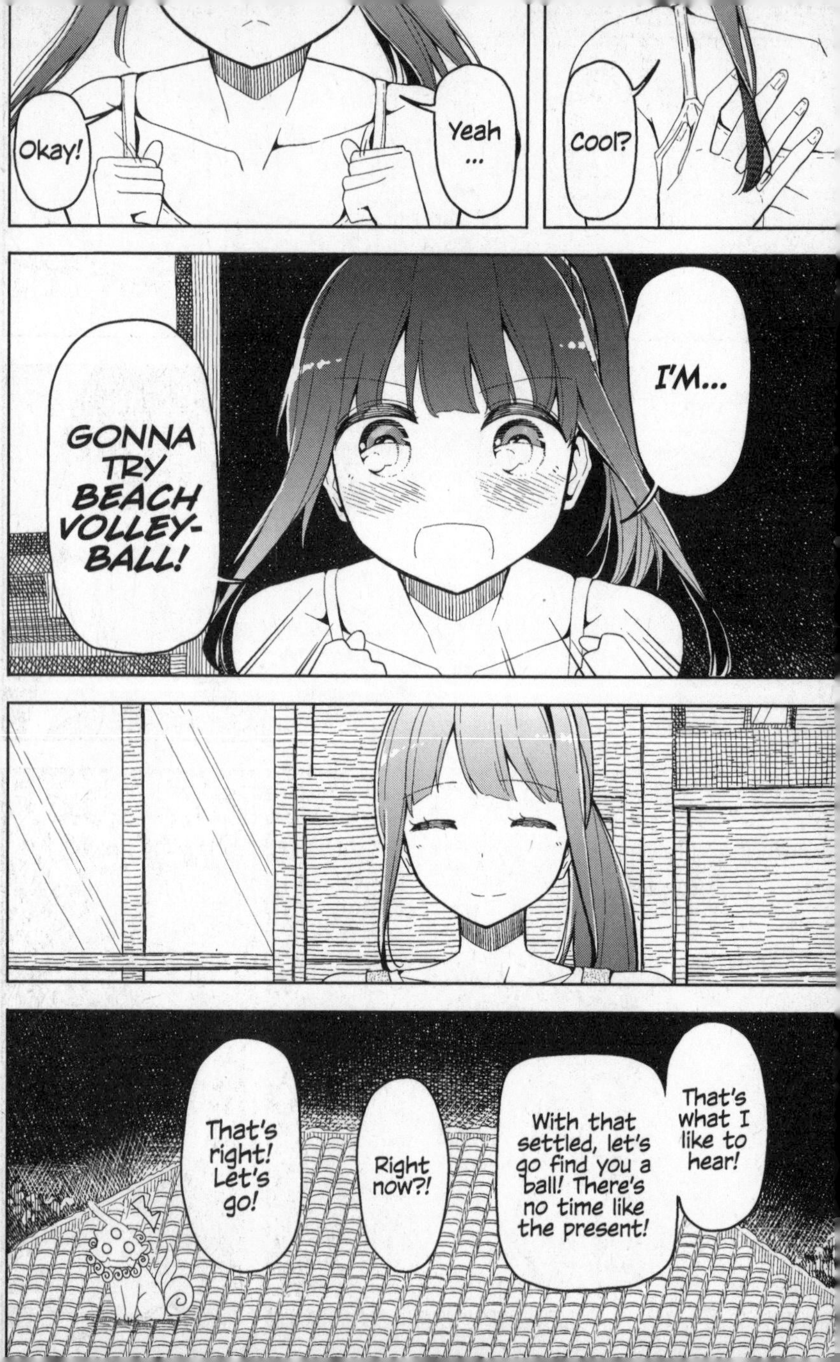
Cool?
Yeah ...
Okay!
I'M...
GONNA TRY BEACH VOLLEY-BALL!
That's what I like to hear!
With that settled, let's go find you a ball! There's no time like the present!
Right now?!
That's right! Let's go!

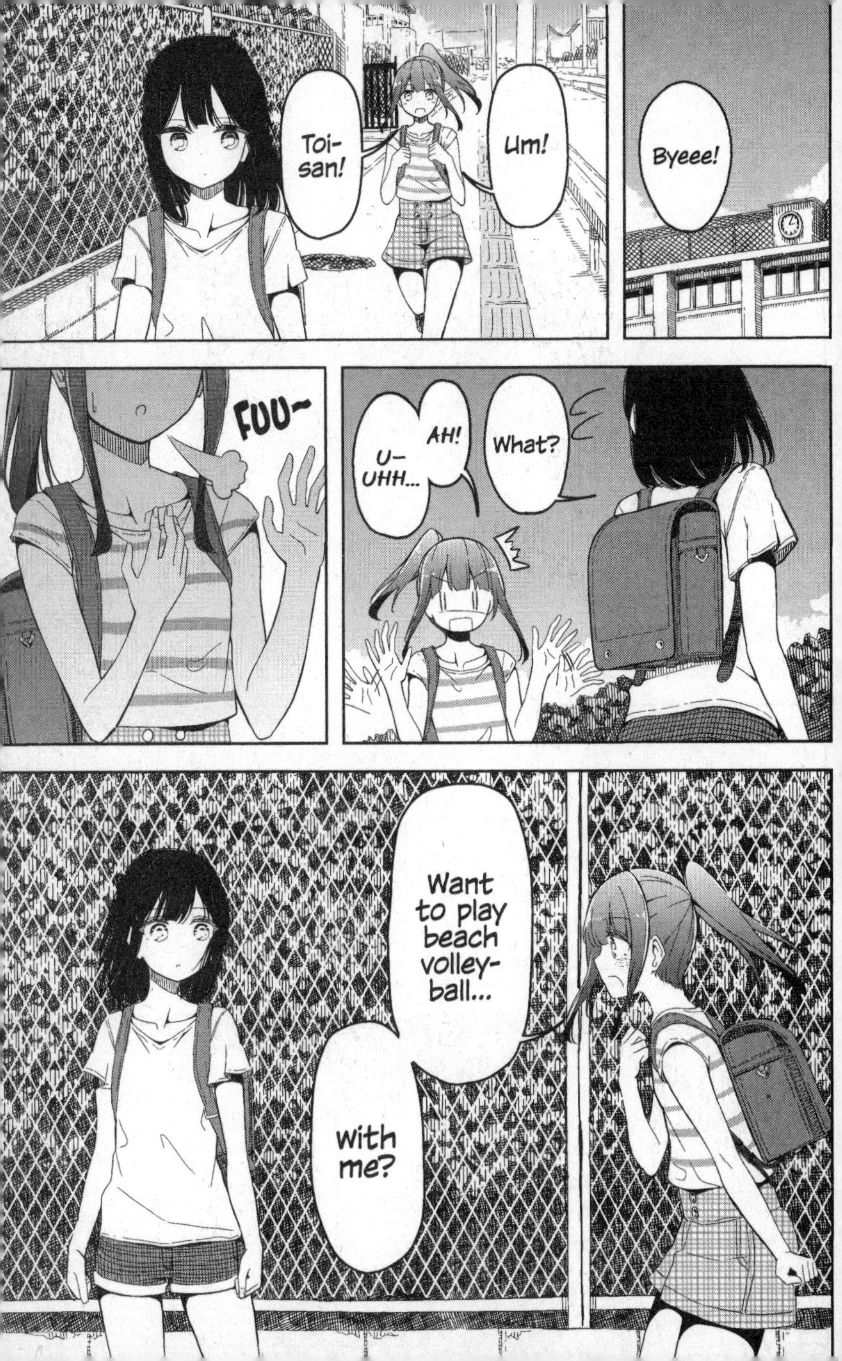
Byeee!
Um!
Toi-san!
What?
AH! U-UHH...
FUU-
Want to play beach volley-ball...
with me?

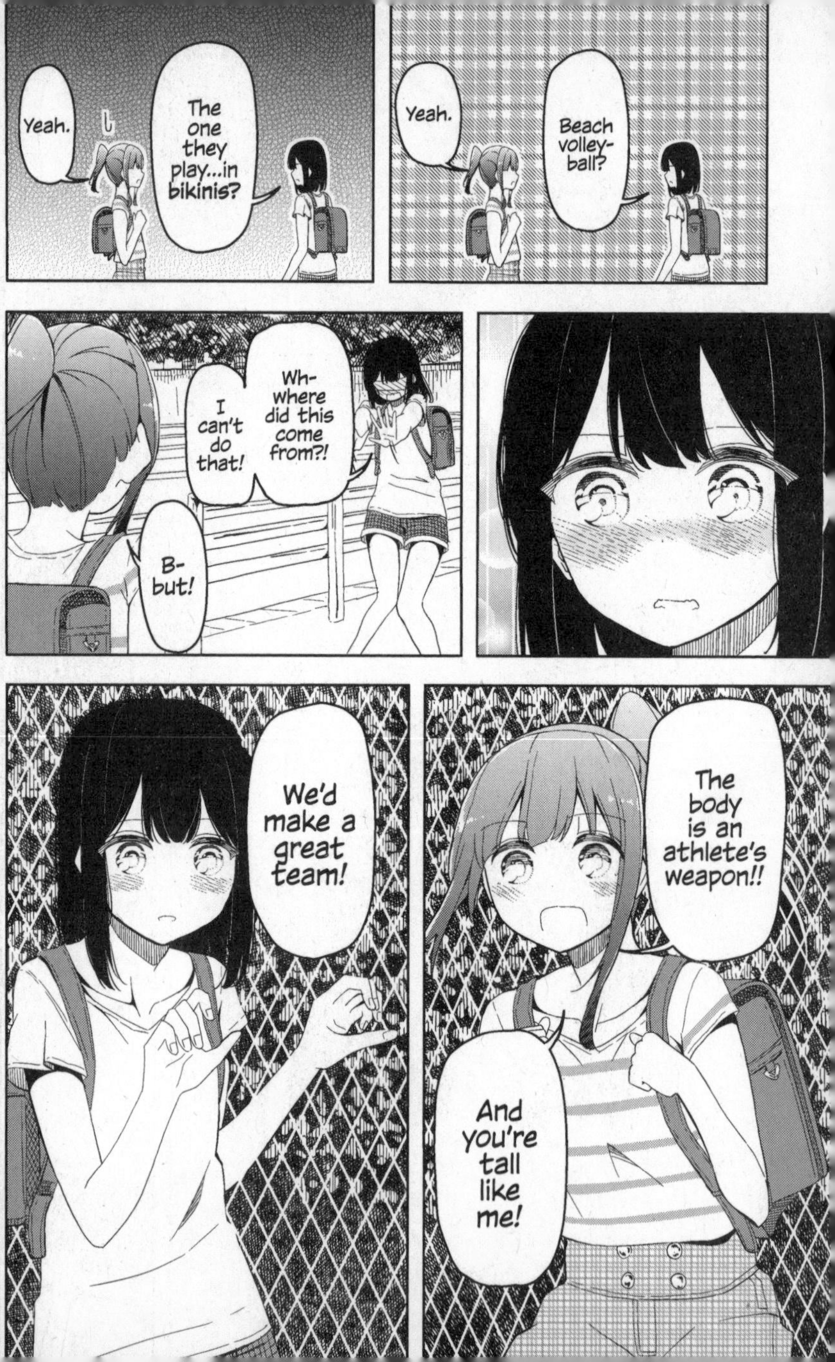
Beach volley-ball?
Yeah.
The one they play...in bikinis?
Yeah.
Wh-where did this come from?!
I can't do that!
B-but!
The body is an athlete's weapon!!
And you're tall like me!
We'd make a great team!

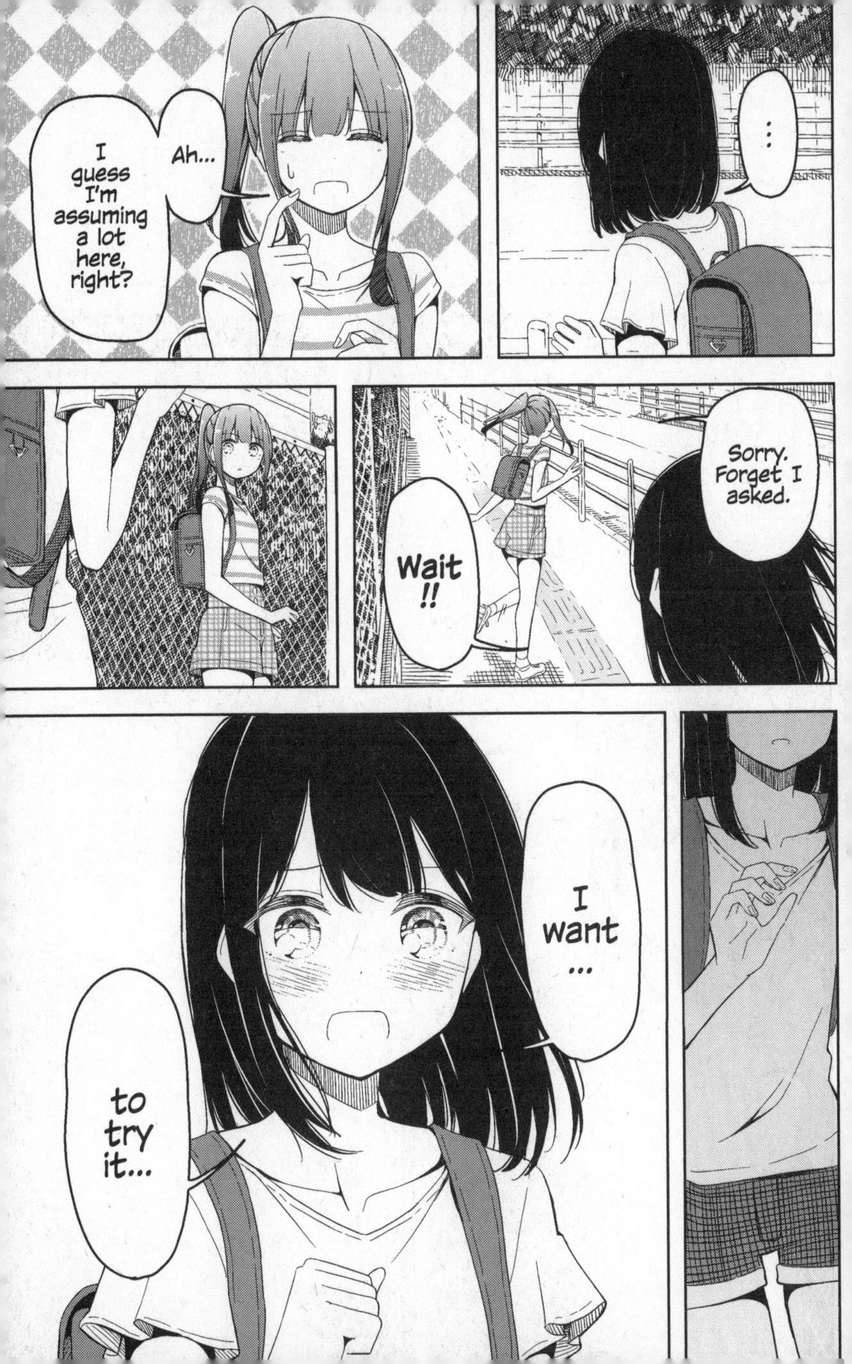
...
Ah...
I guess I'm assuming a lot here, right?
Sorry. Forget I asked.
Wait!!
I want...
to try it...

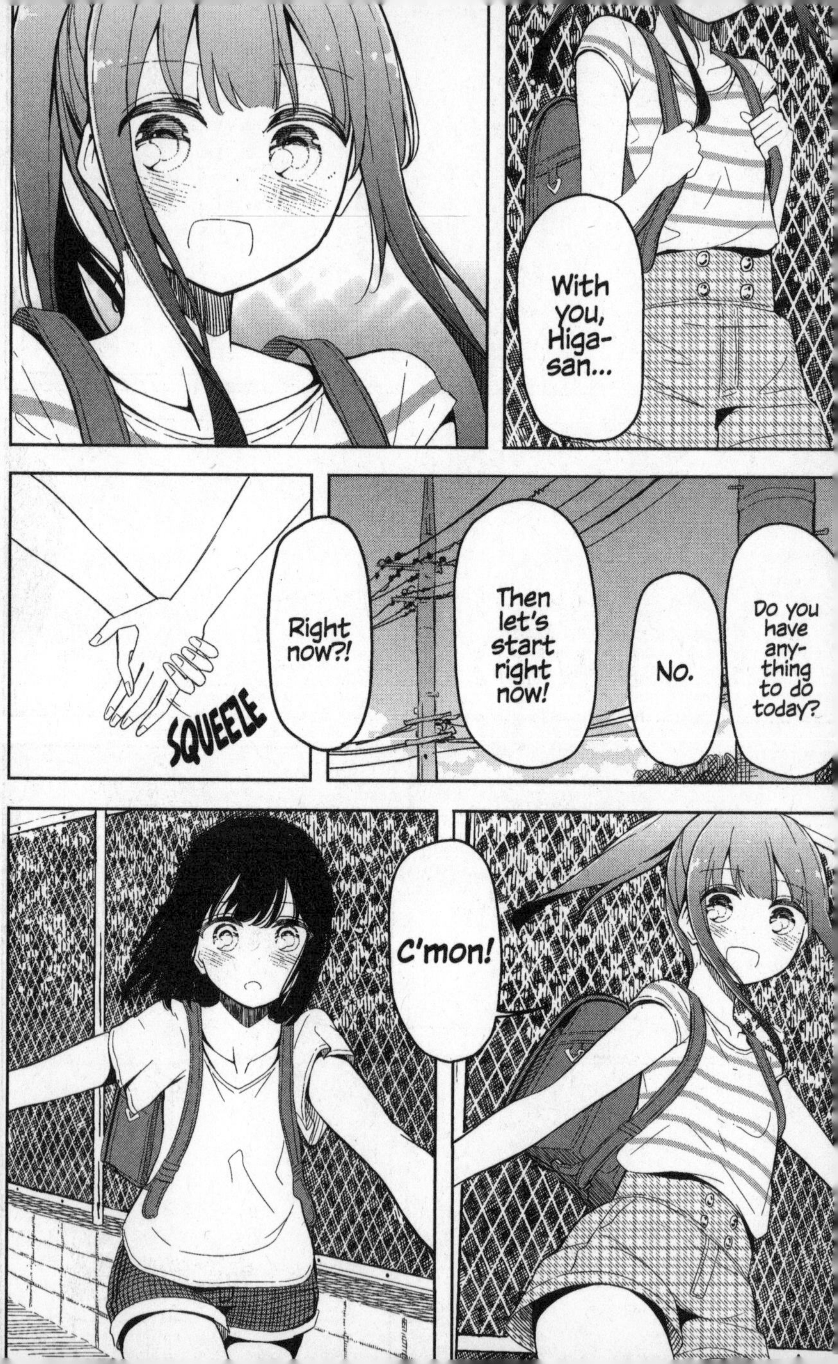
With you, Higa-san...
Do you have anything to do today?
No.
Then let's start right now!
Right now?!
SQUEEZE
C'mon!

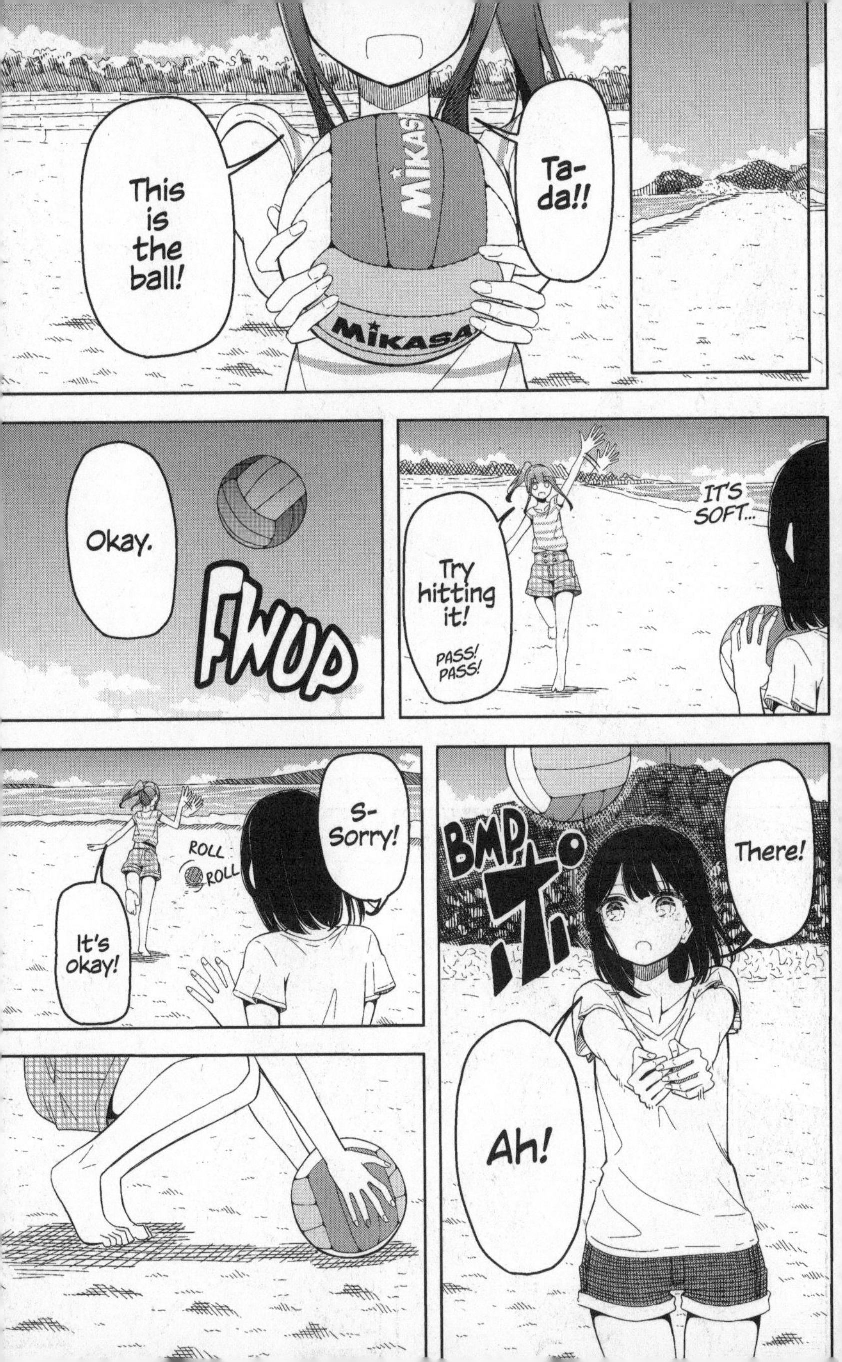
Ta-da!!
MIKASA
This is the ball!
IT'S SOFT...
Try hitting it!
PASS! PASS!
Okay.
FWUP
There!
BMP
Ah!
S-Sorry!
ROLL ROLL
It's okay!

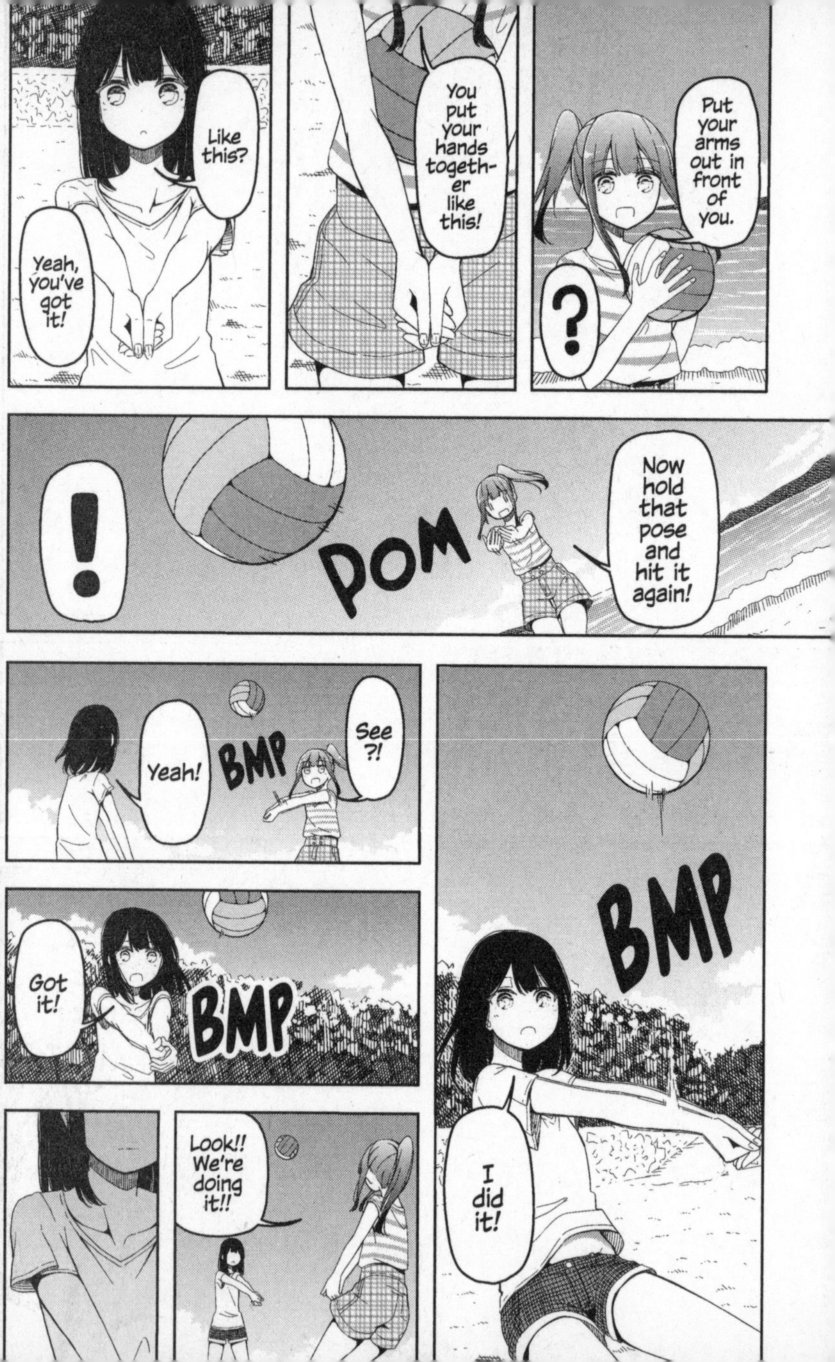
Put your arms out in front of you.
?
You put your hands together like this!
Like this?
Yeah, you've got it!
Now hold that pose and hit it again!
POM
!
BMP
I did it!
See?!
BMP
Yeah!
BMP
Got it!
Look!! We're doing it!!

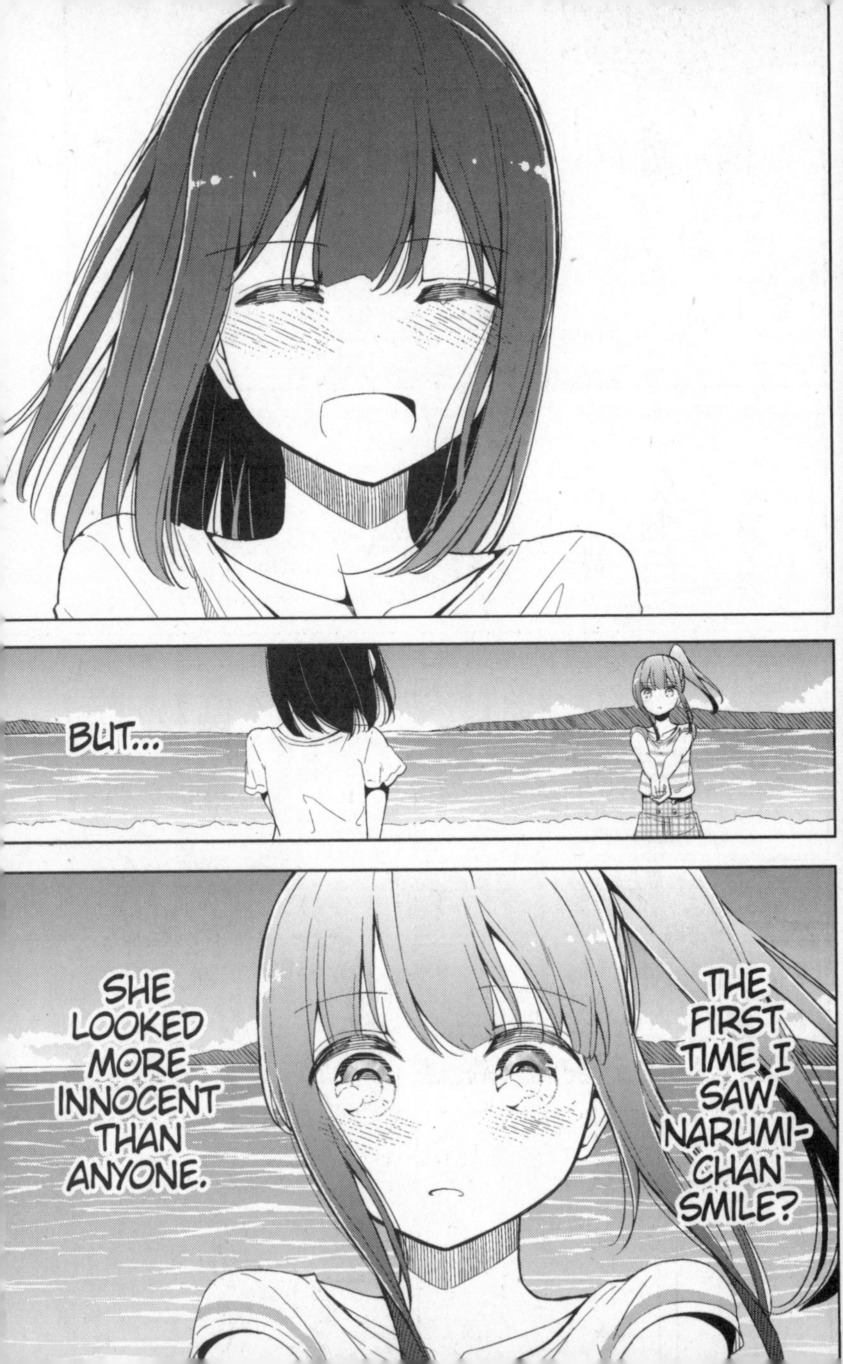
BUT...
THE FIRST TIME I SAW NARUMI-CHAN SMILE?
SHE LOOKED MORE INNOCENT THAN ANYONE.

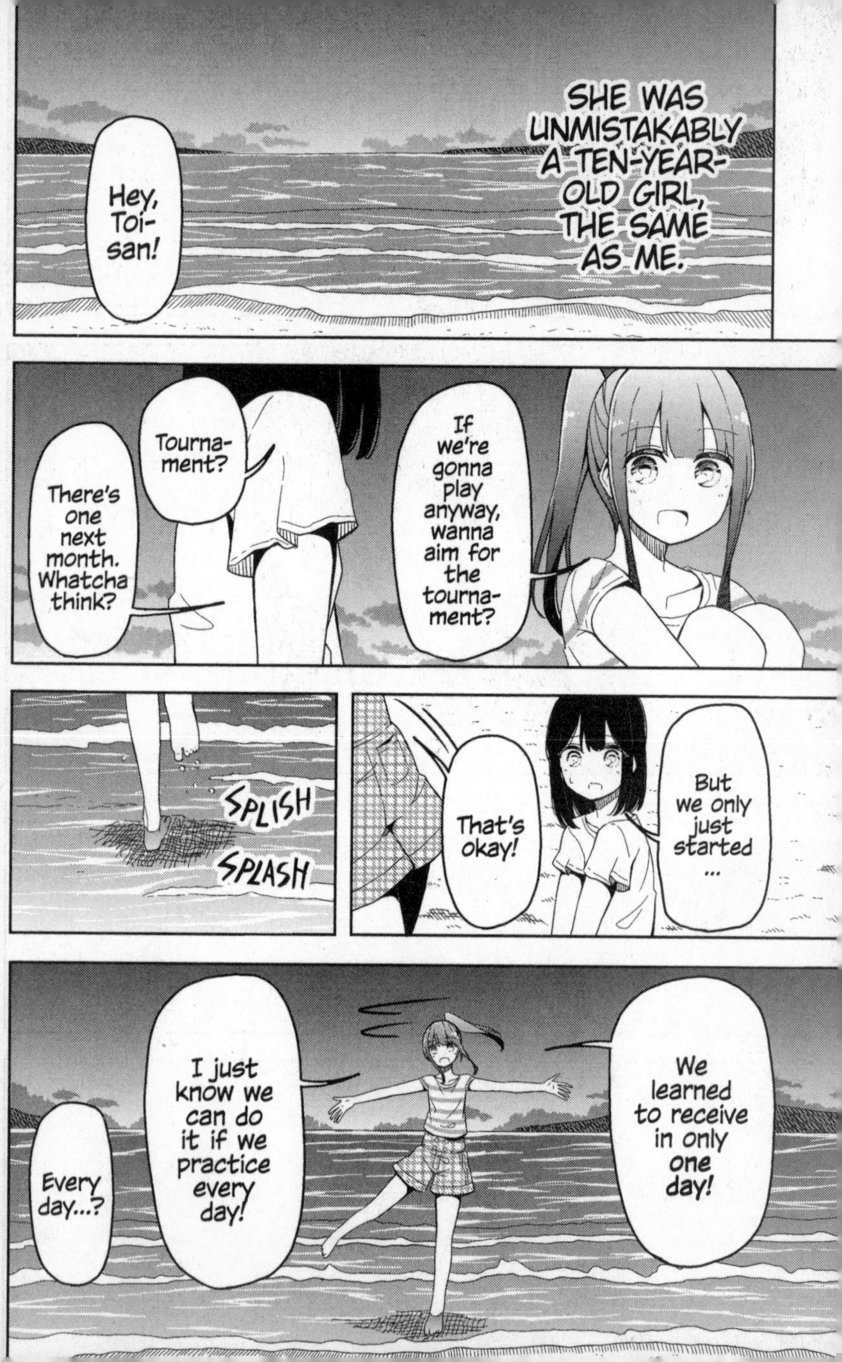
SHE WAS UNMISTAKABLY A TEN-YEAR-OLD GIRL, THE SAME AS ME.
Hey, Toi-san!
If we're gonna play anyway, wanna aim for the tournament?
Tournament?
There's one next month. Whatcha think?
But we only just started...
That's okay!
SPLISH
SPLASH
We learned to receive in only one day!
I just know we can do it if we practice every day!
Every day...?

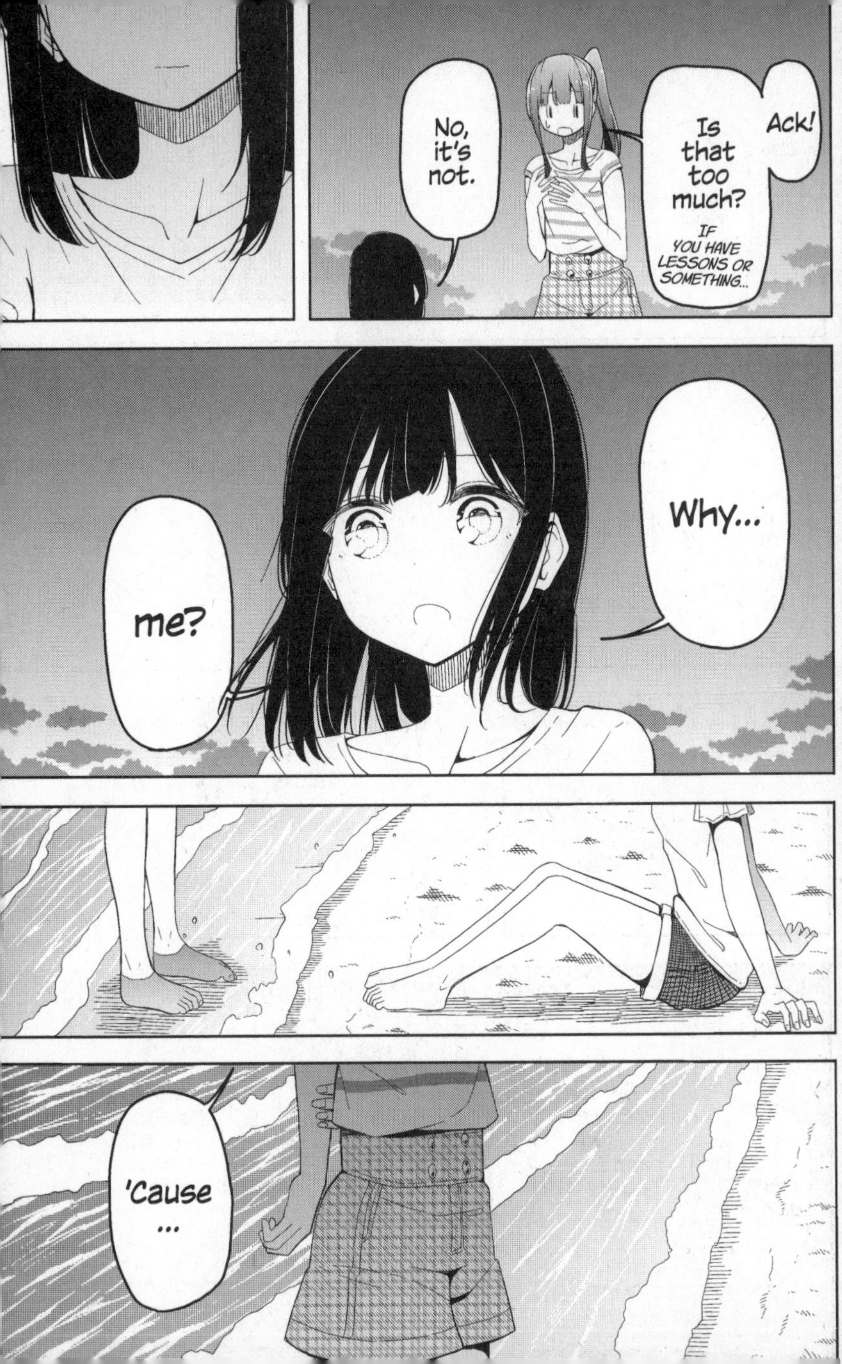
Ack! Is that too much?
IF YOU HAVE LESSONS OR SOMETHING...
No, it's not.
Why...
me?
'Cause ...

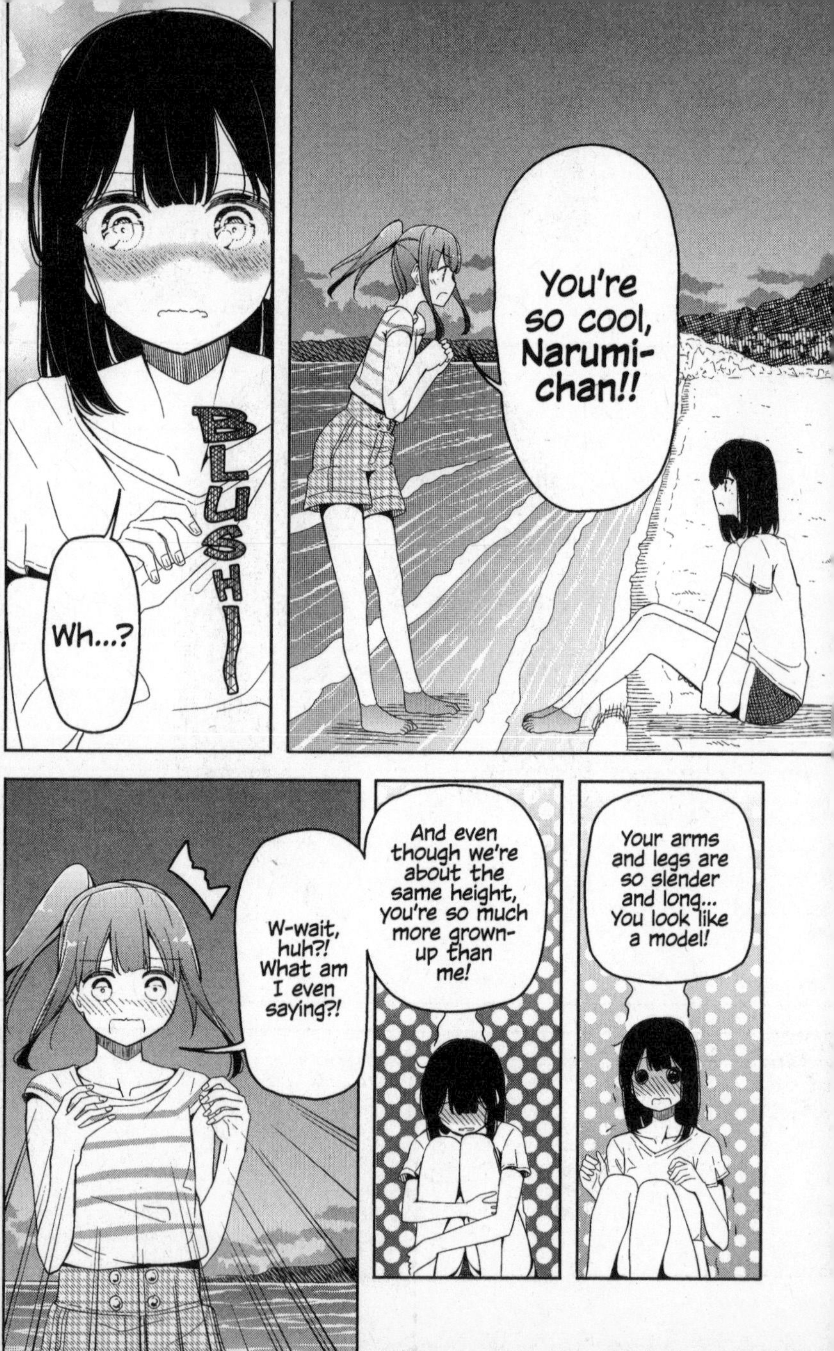
You're so cool, Narumi-chan!!
BLUSH!
Wh...?
Your arms and legs are so slender and long... You look like a model!
And even though we're about the same height, you're so much more grown-up than me!
W-wait, huh?! What am I even saying?!

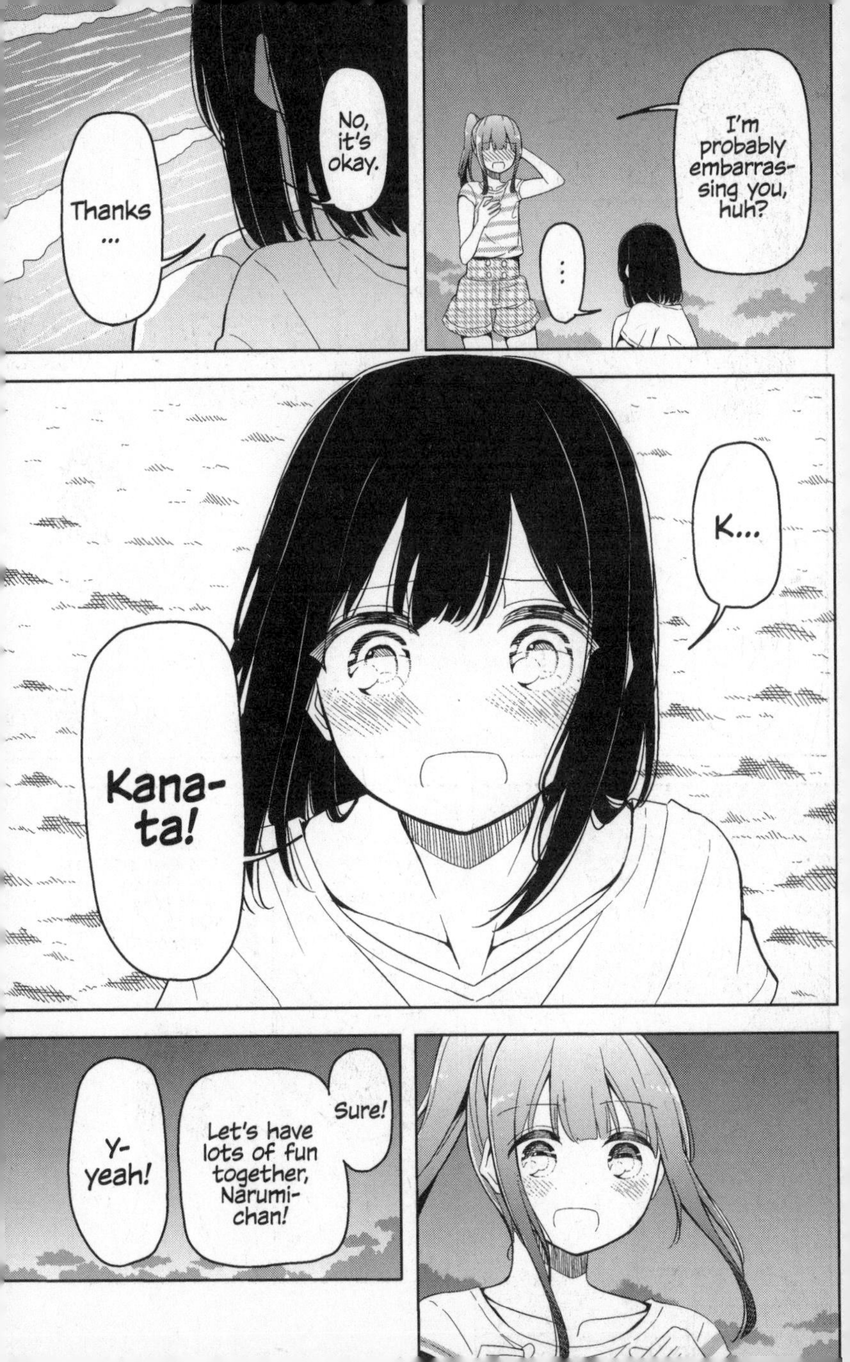
I'm probably embarras-sing you, huh?
...
No, it's okay.
Thanks...
K...
Kana-ta!
Sure!
Let's have lots of fun together, Narumi-chan!
Y-yeah!

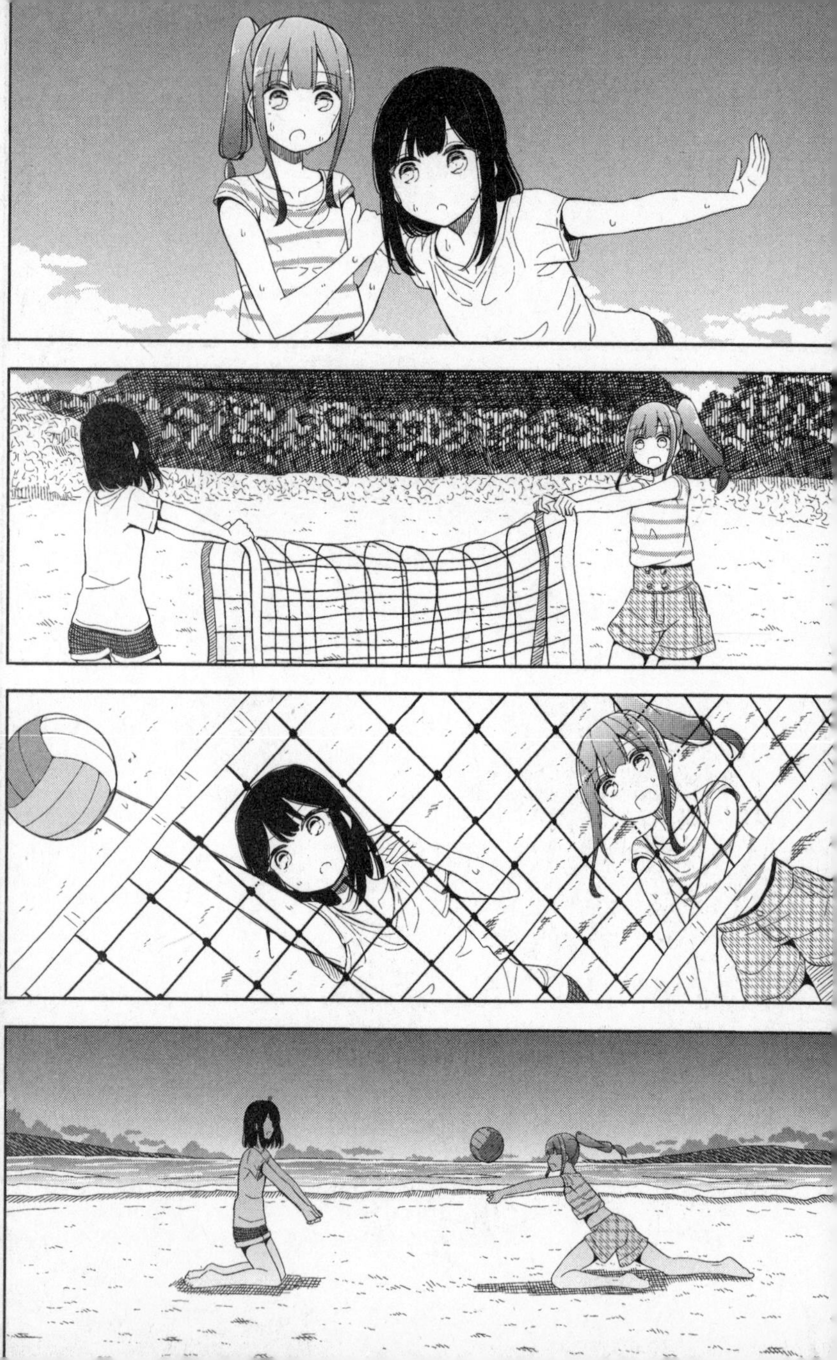

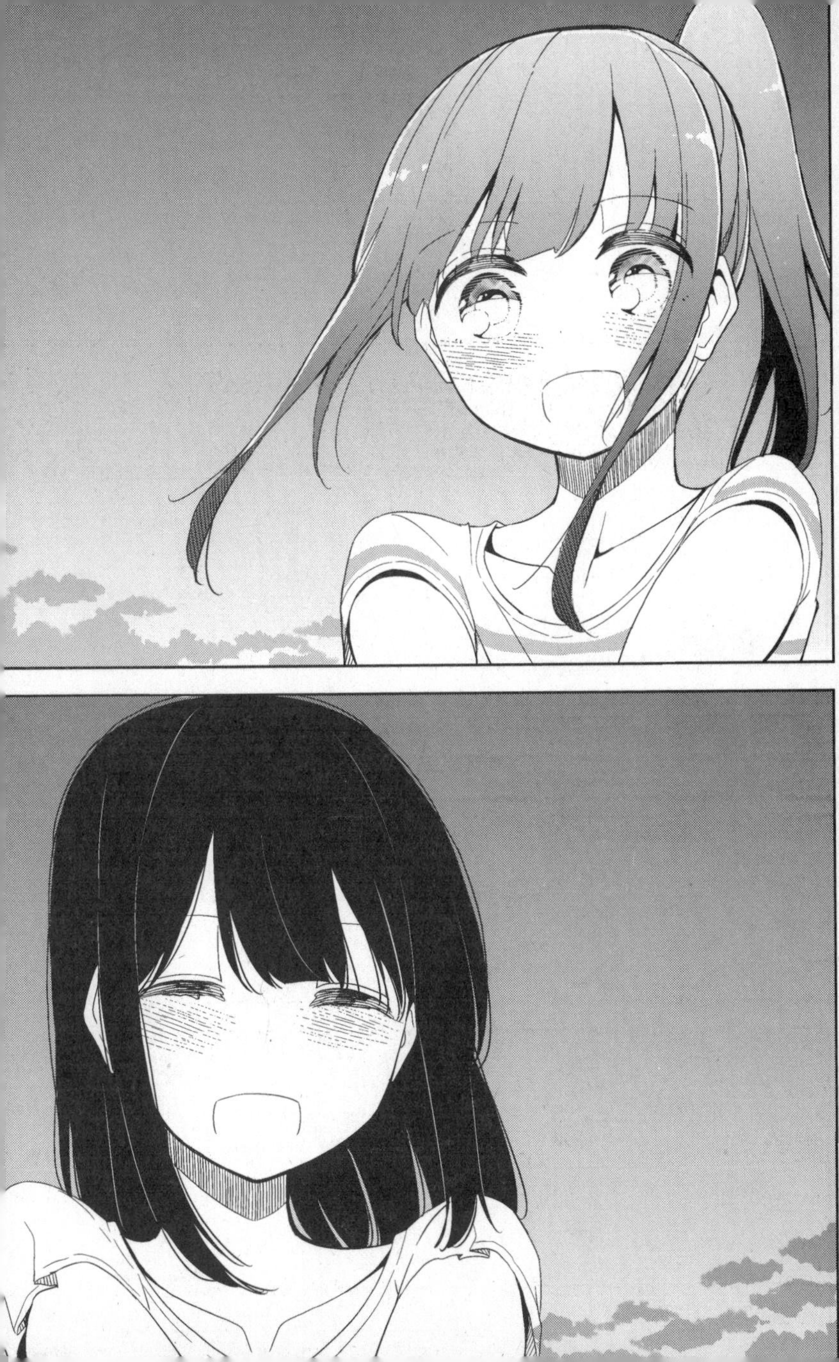

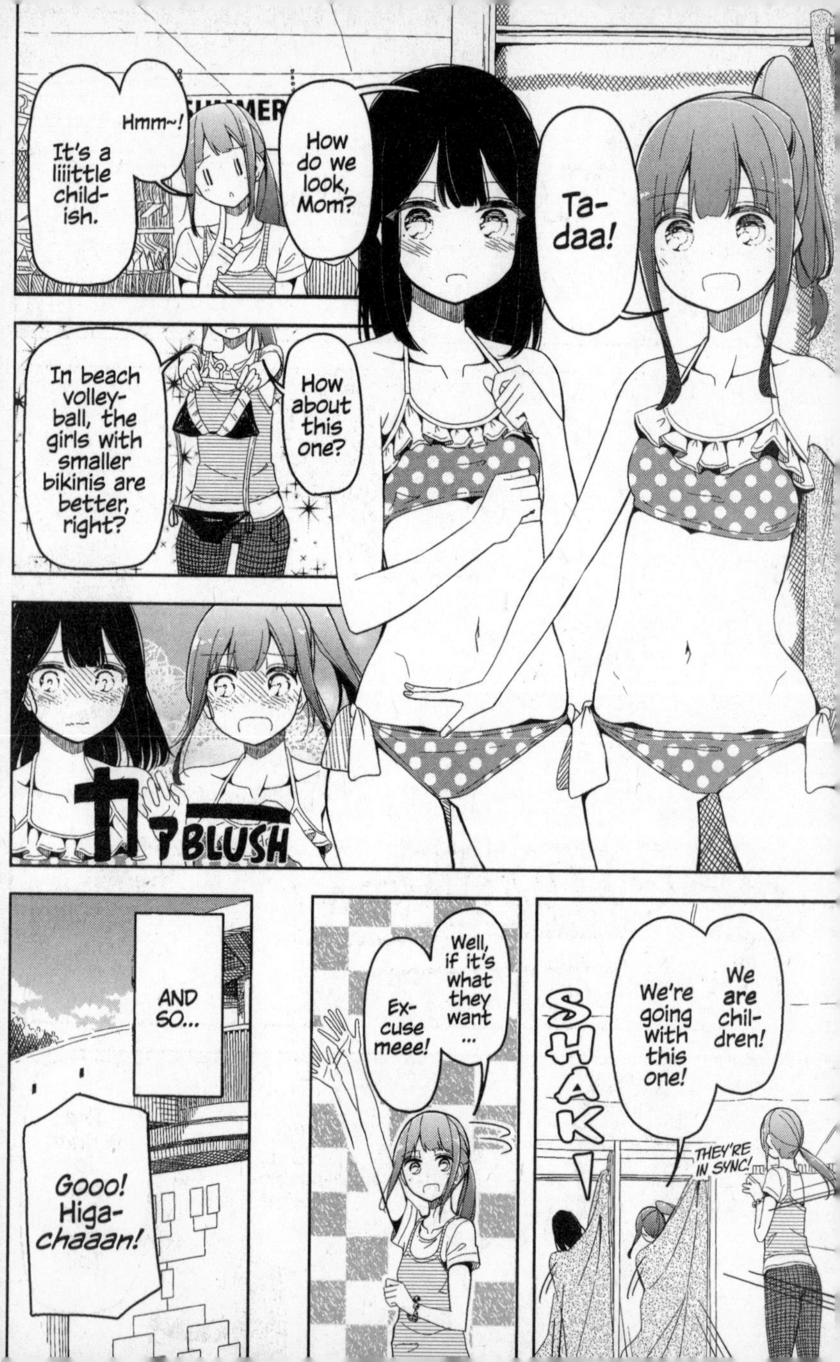

Ta-daa!
How do we look, Mom?
Hmm~!
It's a liiittle child-ish.
How about this one?
In beach volley-ball, the girls with smaller bikinis are better, right?
BLUSH
We are chil-dren!
We're going with this one!
SHAK!
THEY'RE IN SYNC!
Well, if it's what they want...
Ex-cuse meee!
AND SO...
Gooo! Higa-chaaan!

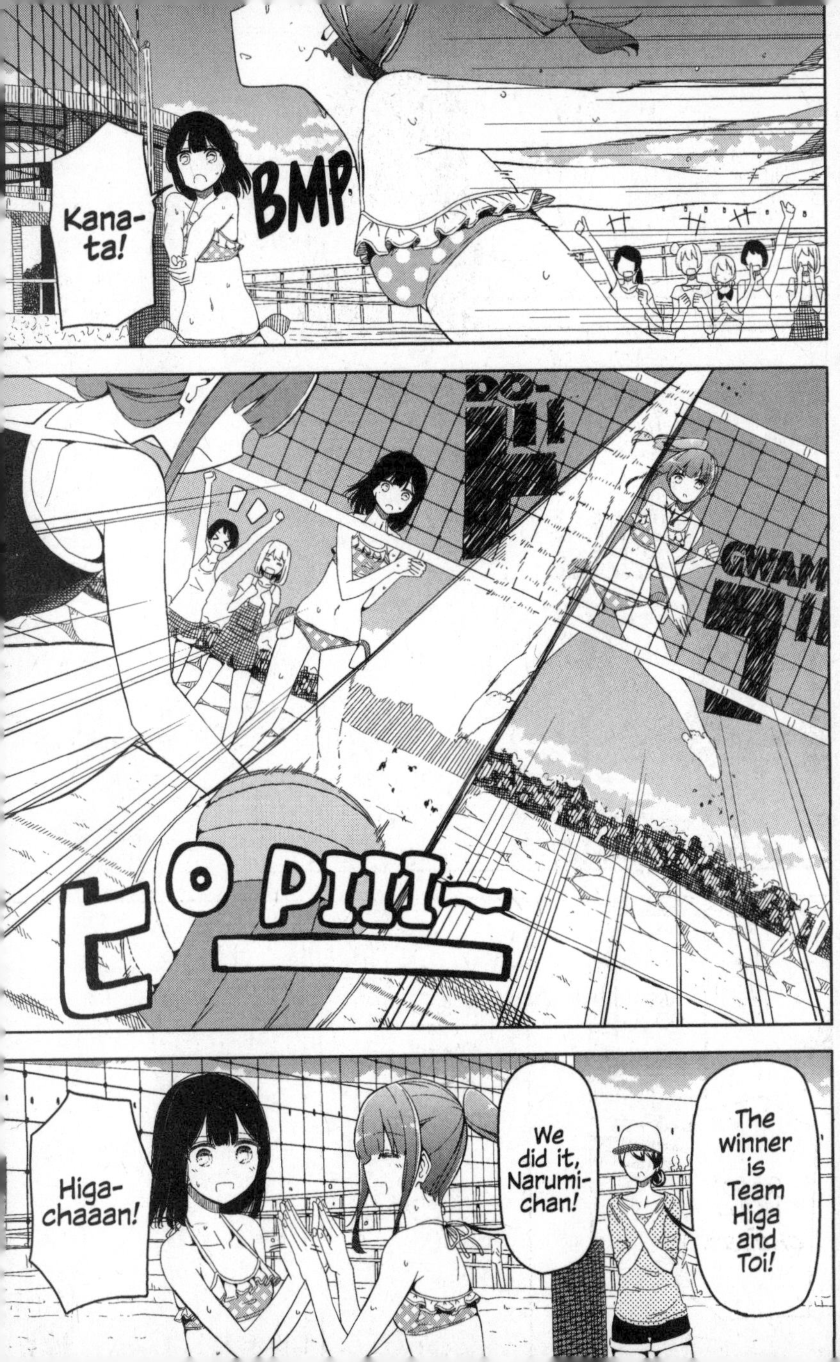
BMP
Kana-ta!
DO-
PIII~
The winner is Team Higa and Toi!
We did it, Narumi-chan!
Higa-chaaan!

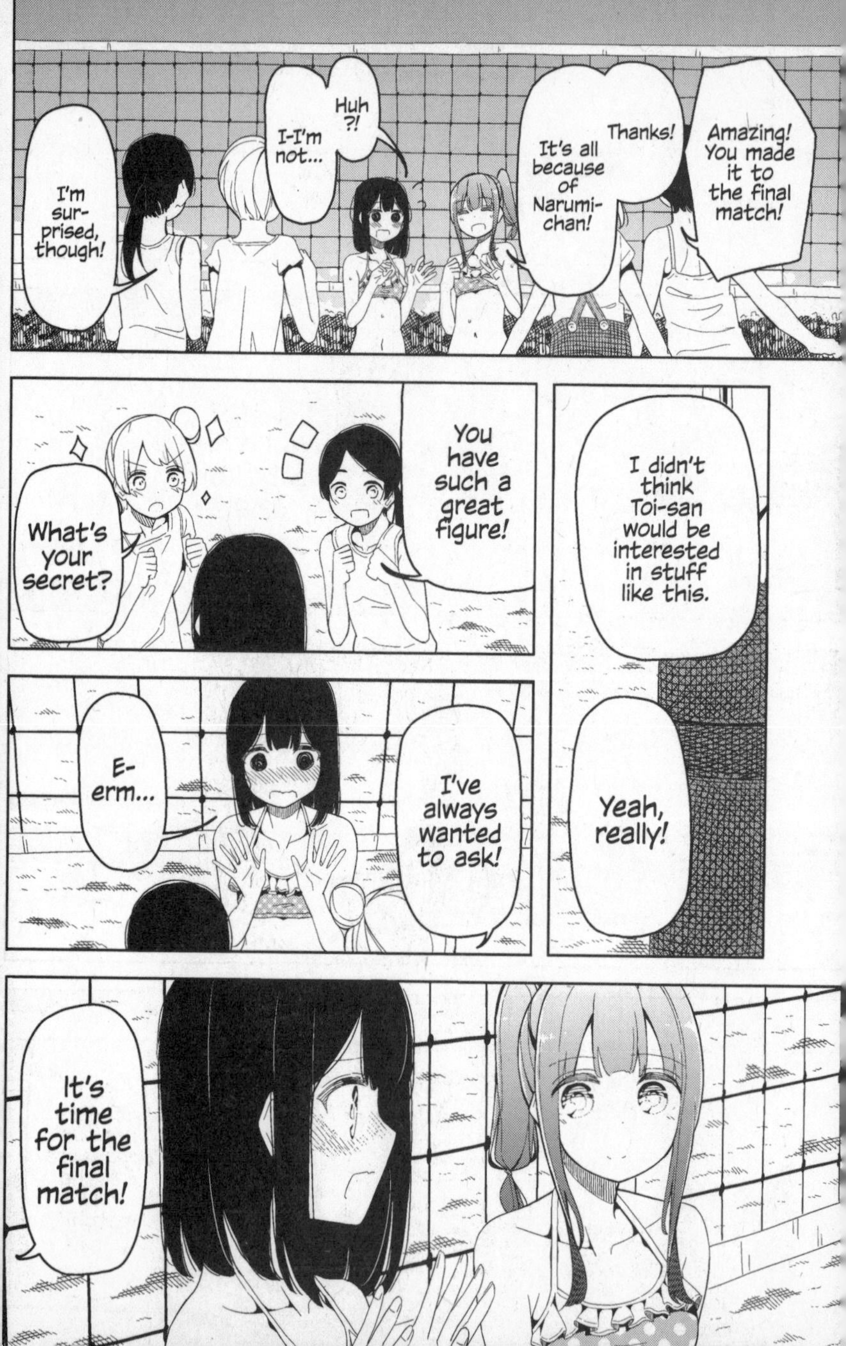
Amazing! You made it to the final match!
Thanks! It's all because of Narumi-chan!
Huh?!
I-I'm not...
I'm surprised, though!
I didn't think Toi-san would be interested in stuff like this.
Yeah, really!
You have such a great figure!
What's your secret?
I've always wanted to ask!
E-erm...
It's time for the final match!

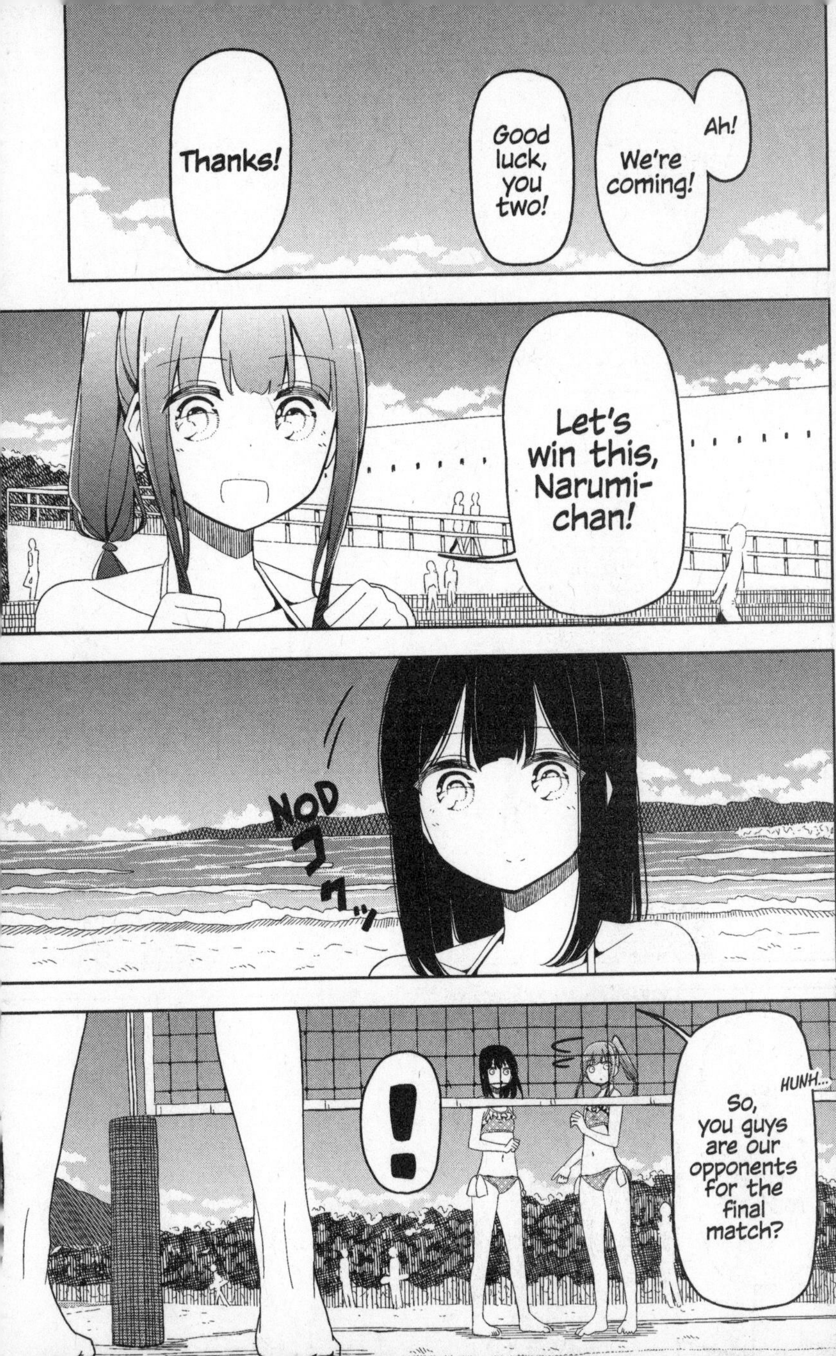
Ah! We're coming!
Good luck, you two!
Thanks!
Let's win this, Narumi-chan!
NOD
HUNH...
So, you guys are our opponents for the final match?
!

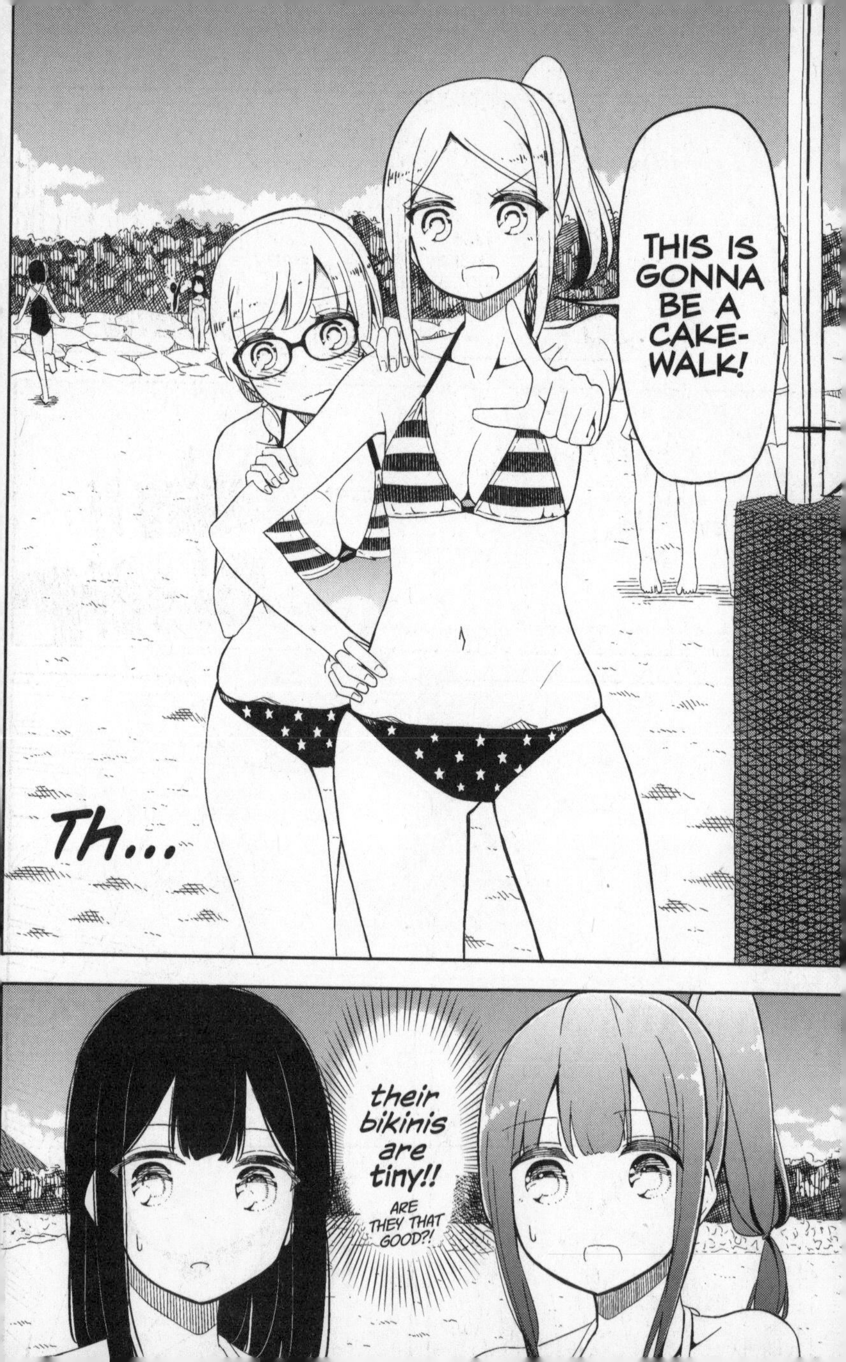
THIS IS GONNA BE A CAKE-WALK!
Th...
their bikinis are tiny!!
ARE THEY THAT GOOD?!

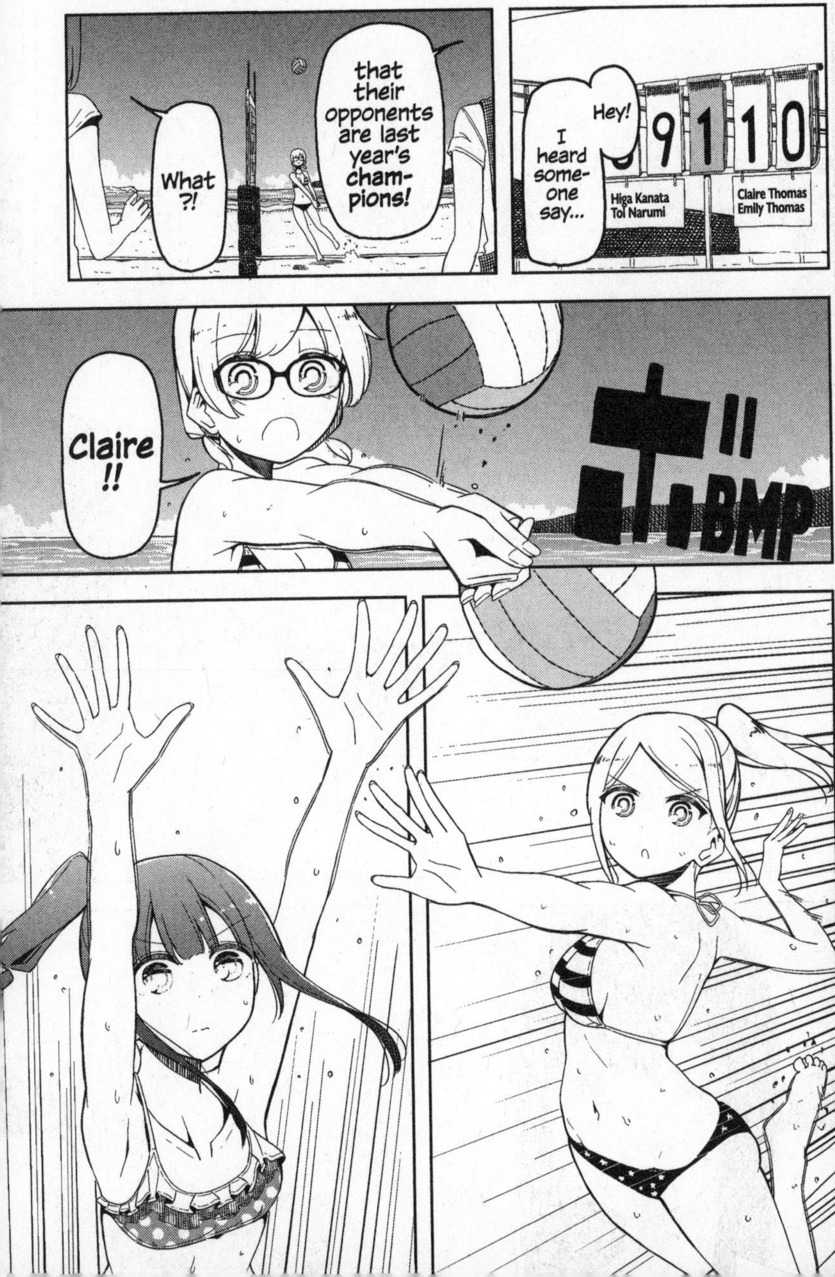
Hey!
I heard someone say...
9 1 1 0
Higa Kanata
Toi Narumi
Claire Thomas
Emily Thomas
that their opponents are last year's champions!
What?!
BMP
Claire!!

Chapter 18: We Only Have One Shot

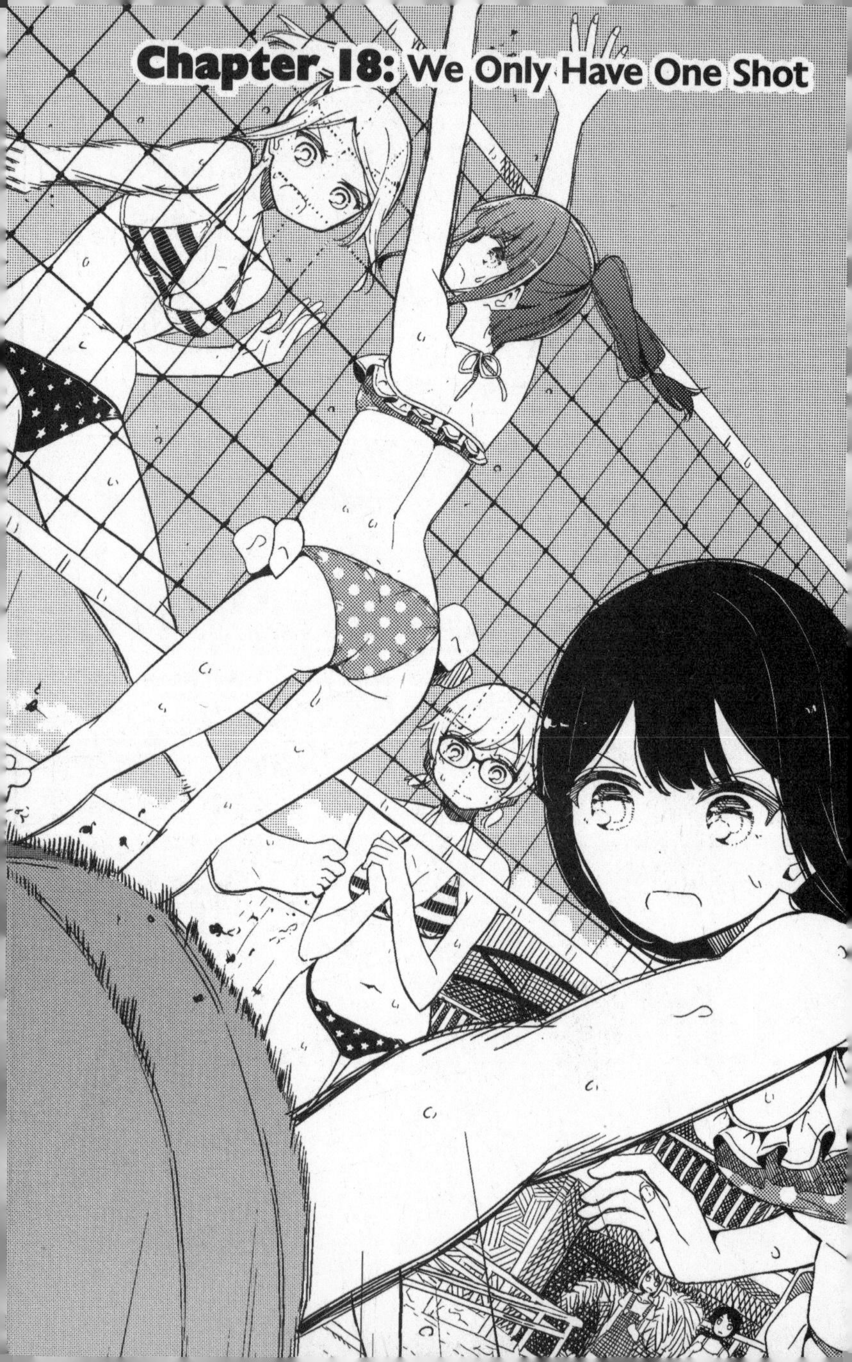

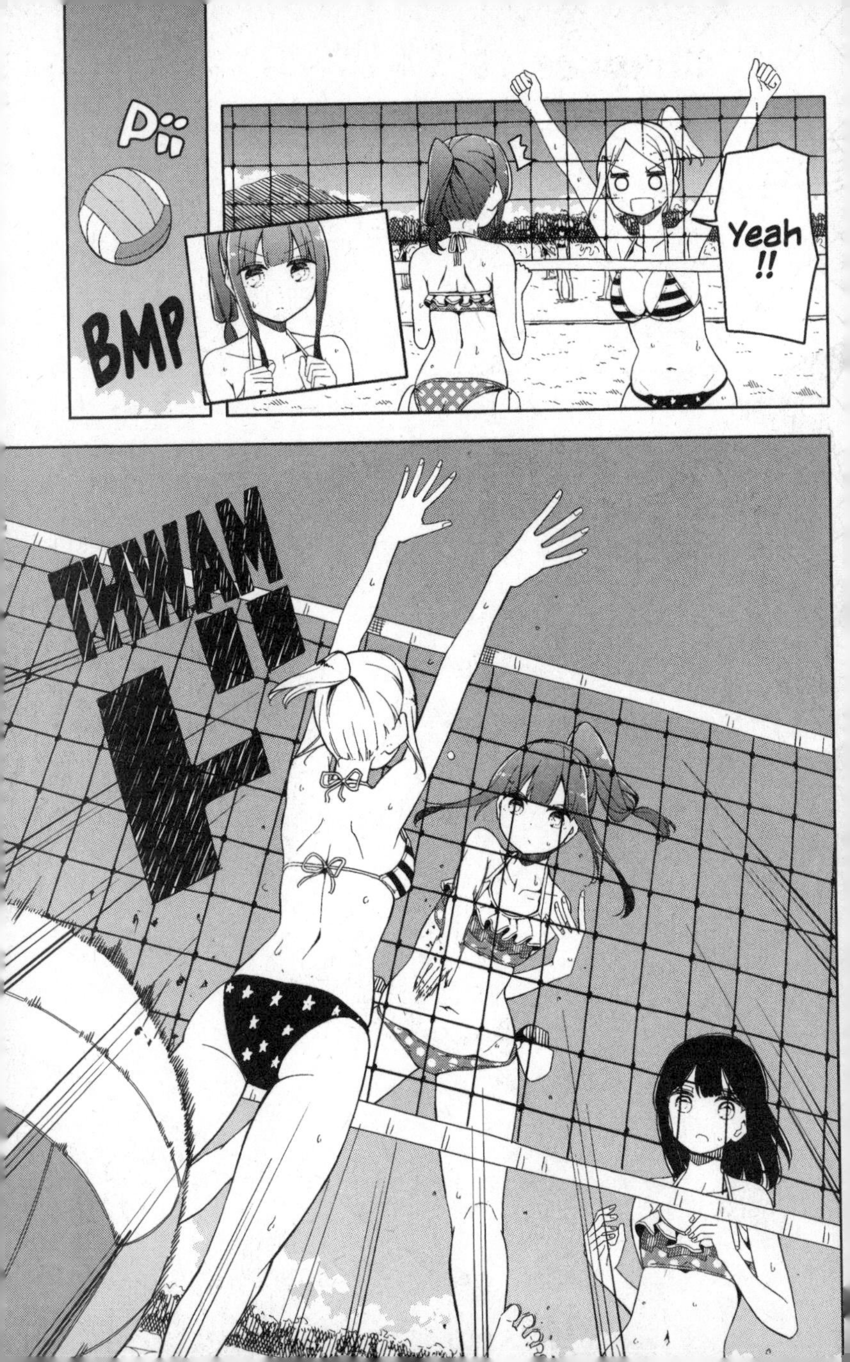
Yeah !!
Pii
BMP
THWAM

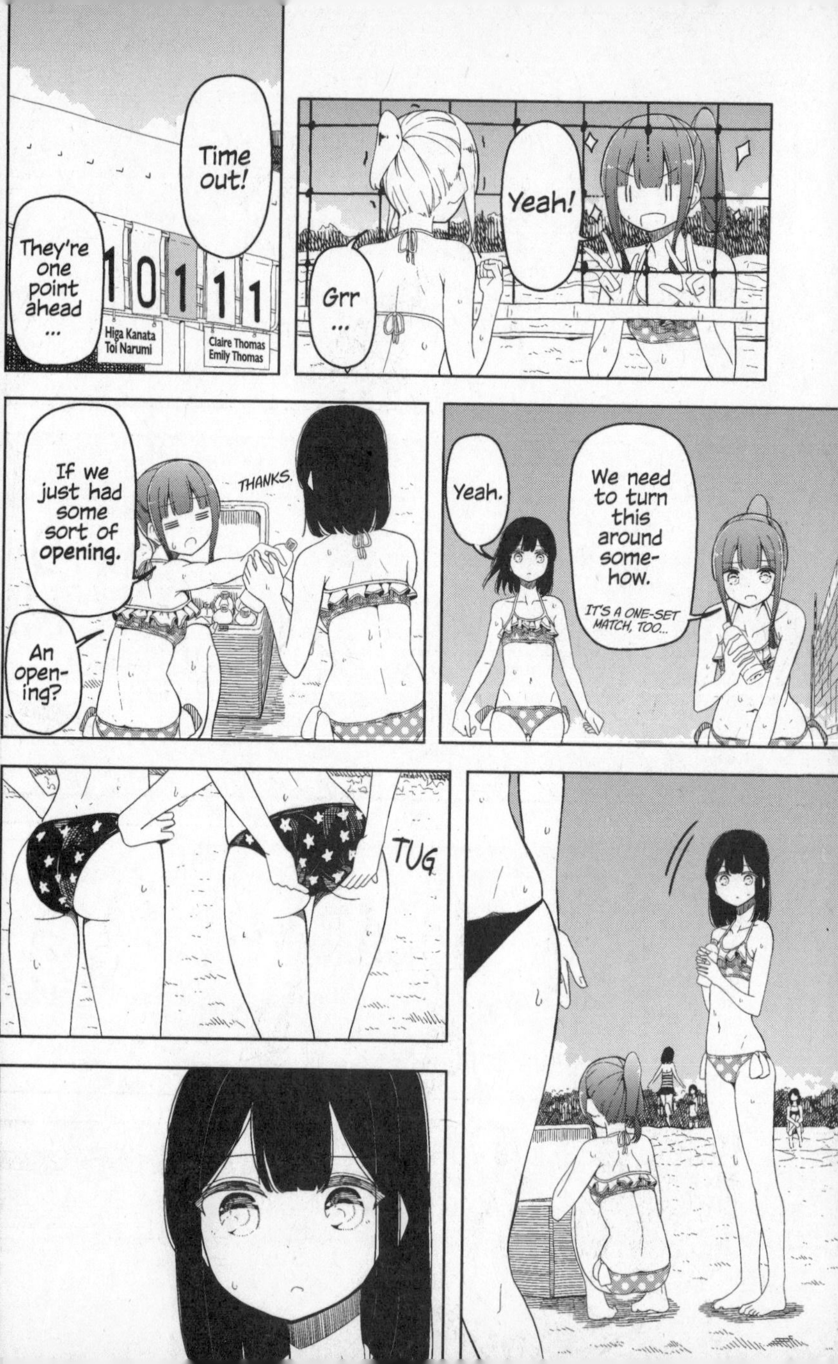

Yeah!
Grr ...
Time out!
Claire Thomas
Emily Thomas
11
10
Higa Kanata
Toi Narumi
They're one point ahead ...
We need to turn this around some-how.
IT'S A ONE-SET MATCH, TOO...
Yeah.
THANKS.
If we just had some sort of opening.
An open-ing?
TUG

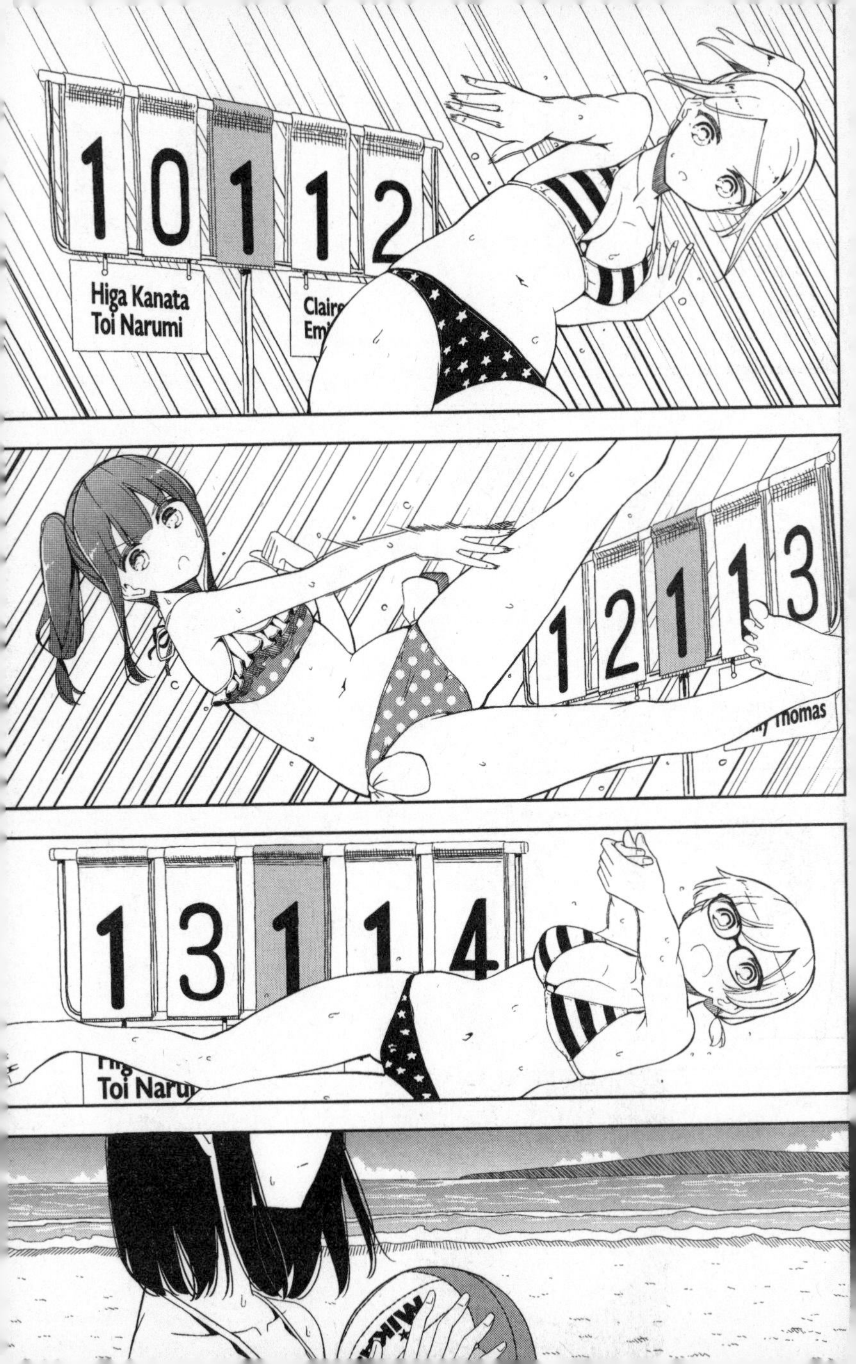
10 1 12
Higa Kanata
Toi Narumi
12 1 13
Thomas
13 1 14

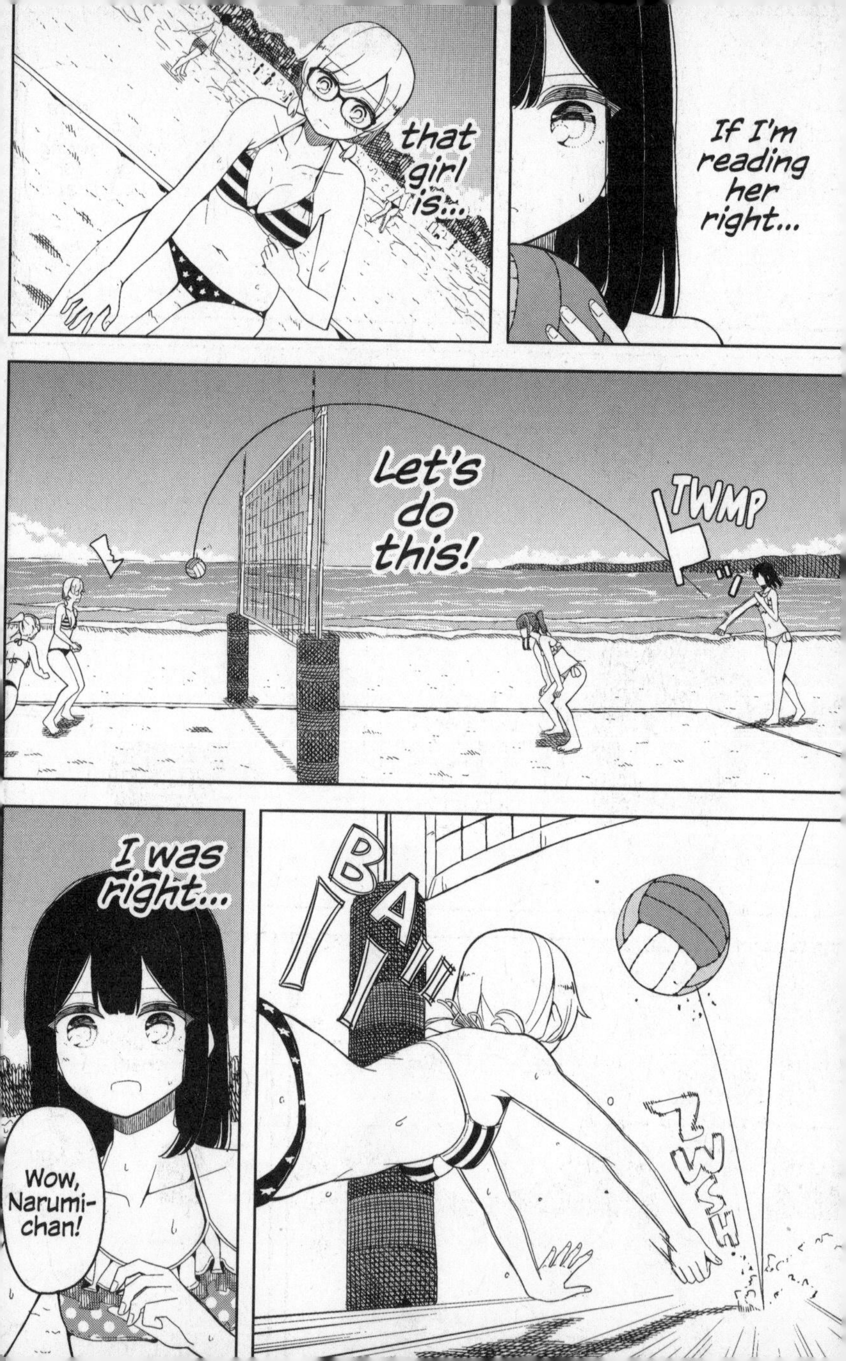
If I'm reading her right...
that girl is...
Let's do this!
TWMP
BA
ZWSH
I was right...
Wow, Narumi-chan!

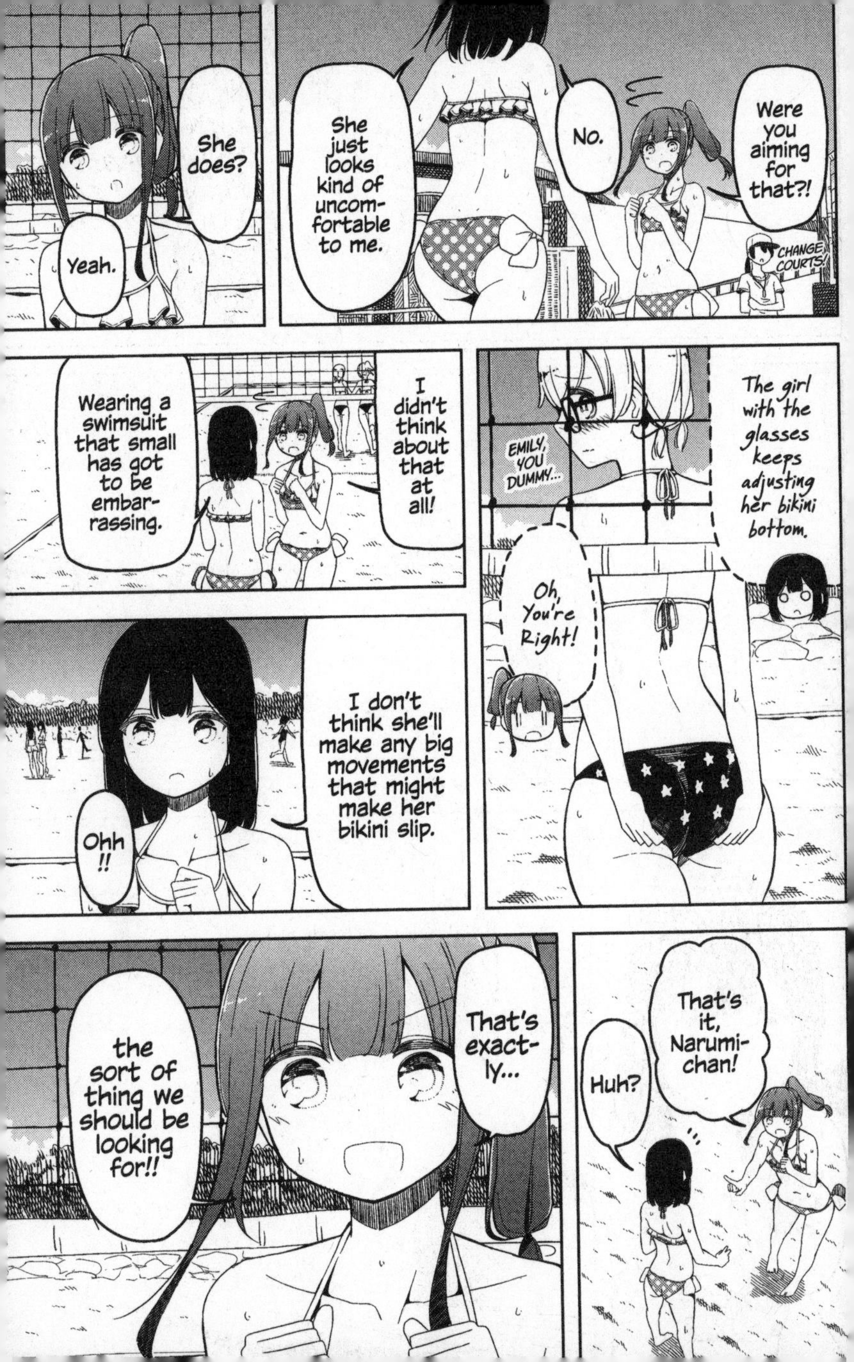
Were you aiming for that?!
No.
CHANGE COURTS!
She just looks kind of uncomfortable to me.
She does?
Yeah.
The girl with the glasses keeps adjusting her bikini bottom.
EMILY, YOU DUMMY...
Oh, You're Right!
I didn't think about that at all!
Wearing a swimsuit that small has got to be embarrassing.
I don't think she'll make any big movements that might make her bikini slip.
Ohh!!
That's it, Narumi-chan!
Huh?
That's exactly...
the sort of thing we should be looking for!!

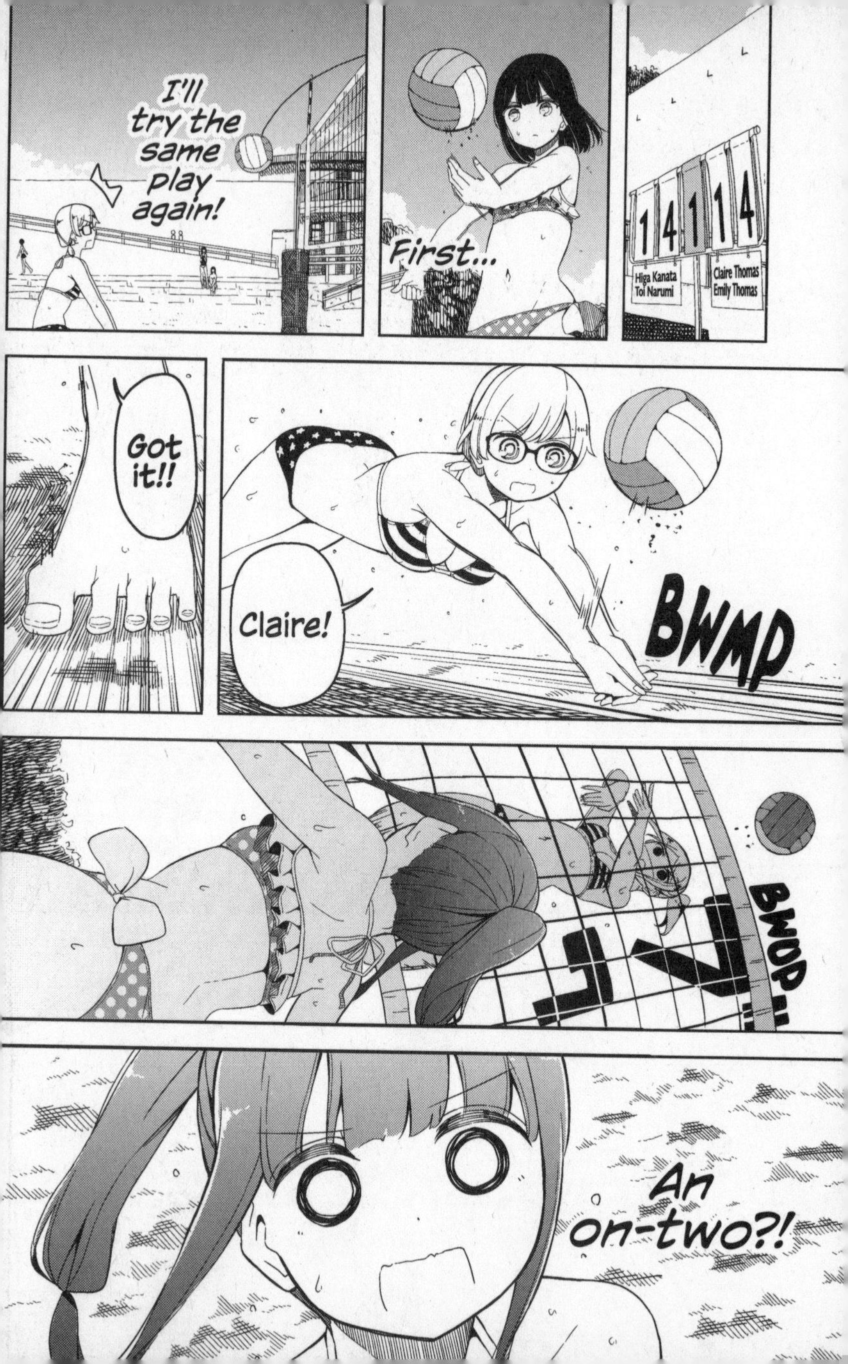
14 1 14
Higa Kanata
Toi Narumi
Claire Thomas
Emily Thomas
First...
I'll try the same play again!
Claire!
BWMP
Got it!!
BWOP!!
An on-two?!

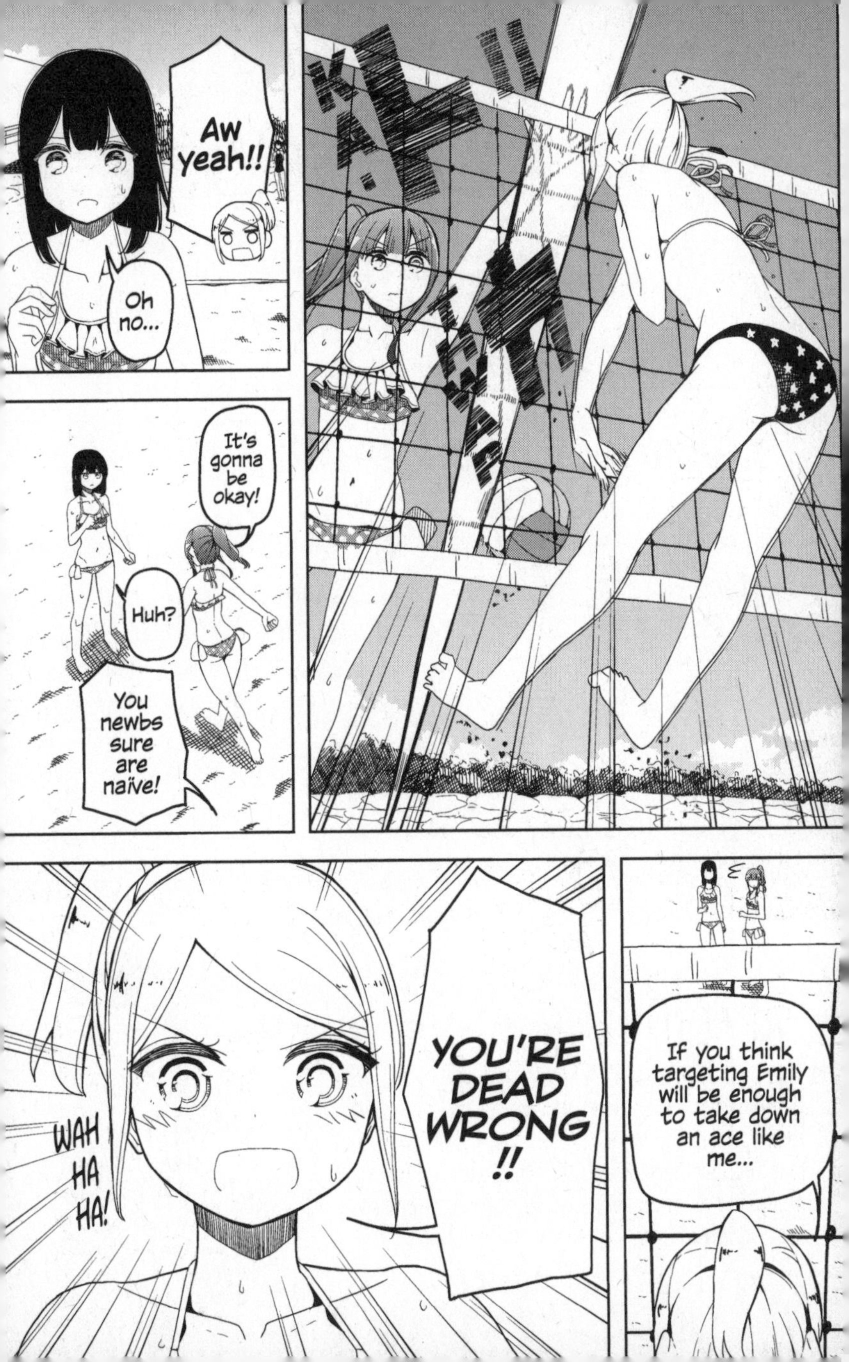
Aw yeah!!
Oh no...
It's gonna be okay!
Huh?
You newbs sure are naïve!
If you think targeting Emily will be enough to take down an ace like me...
YOU'RE DEAD WRONG!!
WAH HA HA!

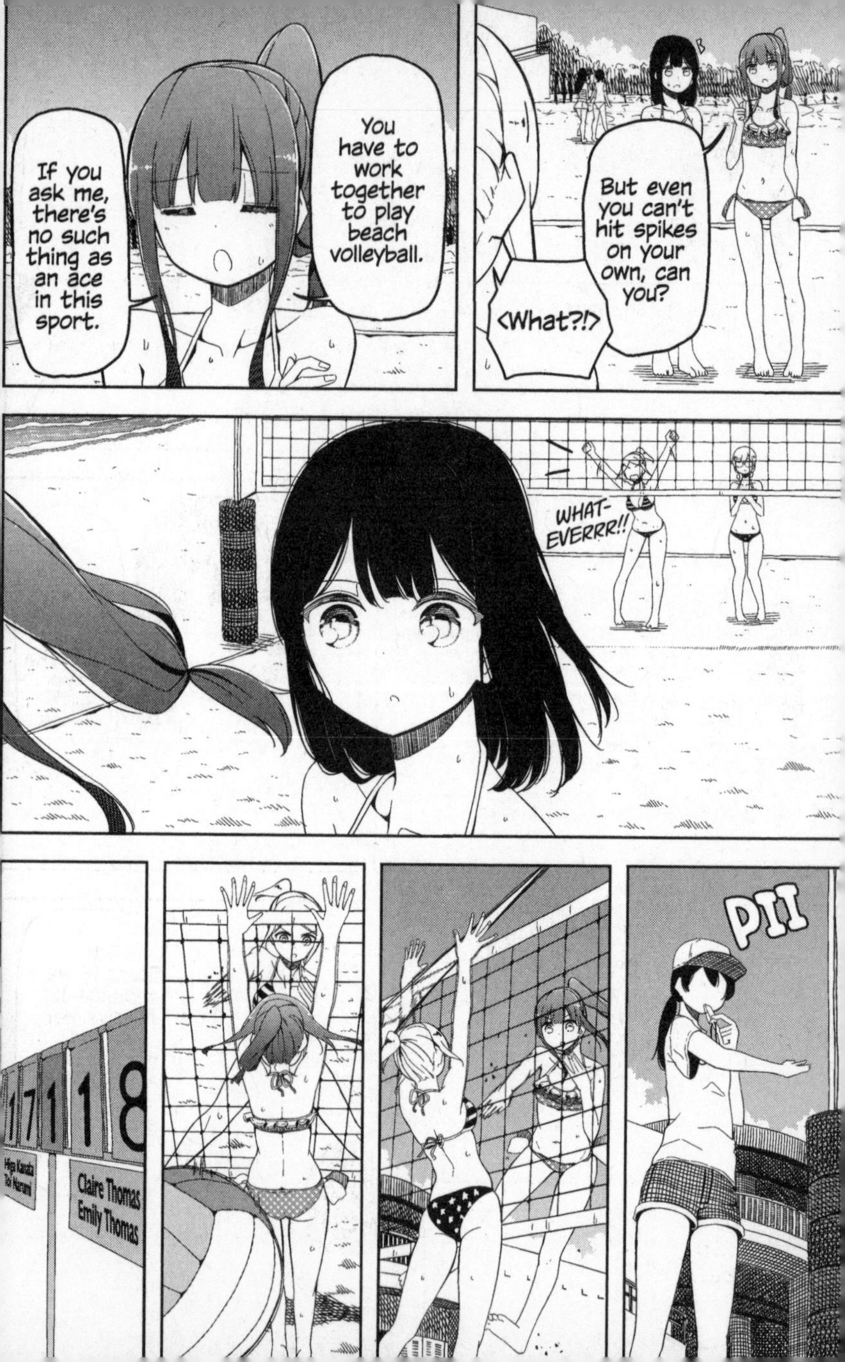
But even you can't hit spikes on your own, can you?
<What?!>
You have to work together to play beach volleyball.
If you ask me, there's no such thing as an ace in this sport.
WHAT-EVERRR!!
PII
Claire Thomas
Emily Thomas

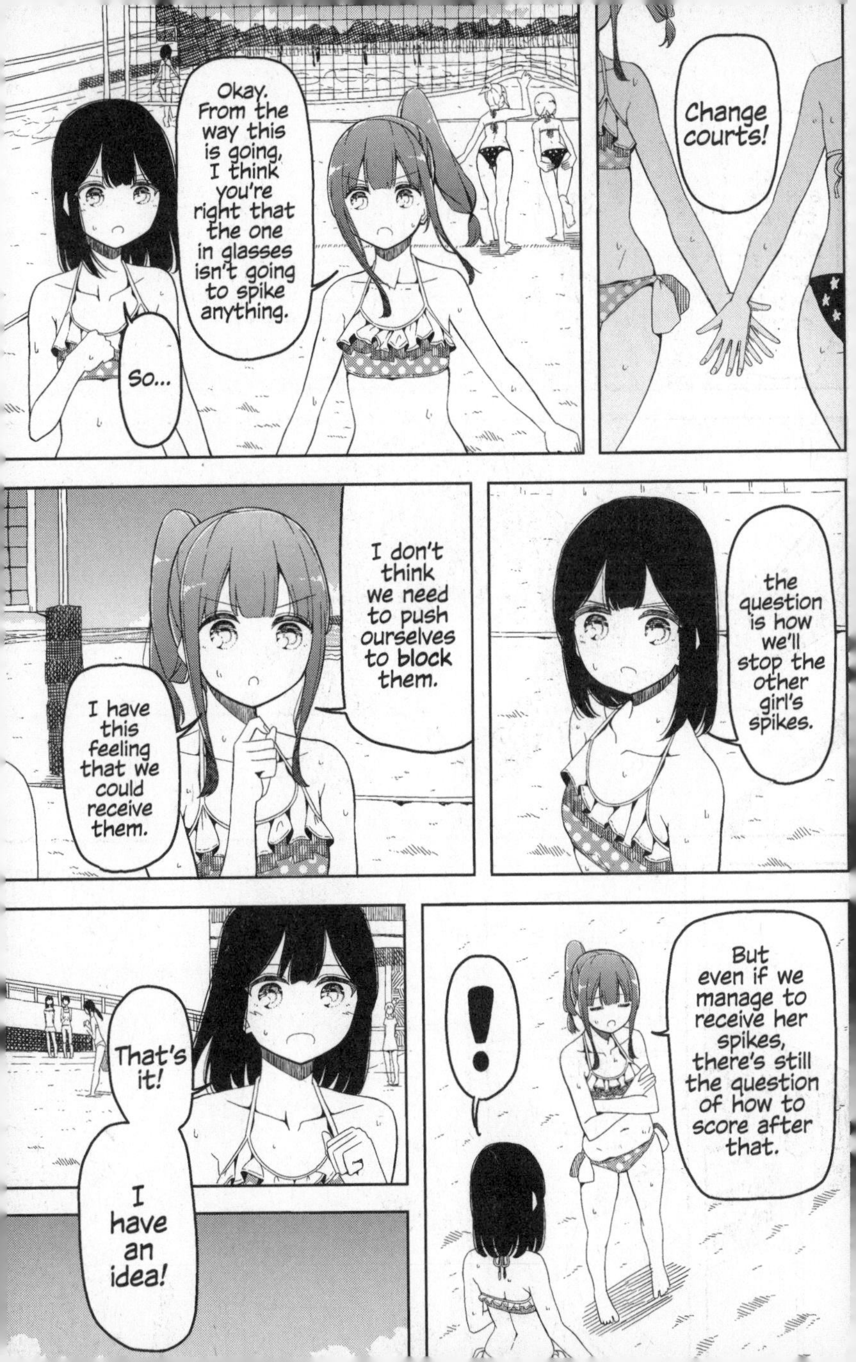
Change courts!
Okay. From the way this is going, I think you're right that the one in glasses isn't going to spike anything.
So...
the question is how we'll stop the other girl's spikes.
I don't think we need to push ourselves to block them.
I have this feeling that we could receive them.
But even if we manage to receive her spikes, there's still the question of how to score after that.
!
That's it!
I have an idea!

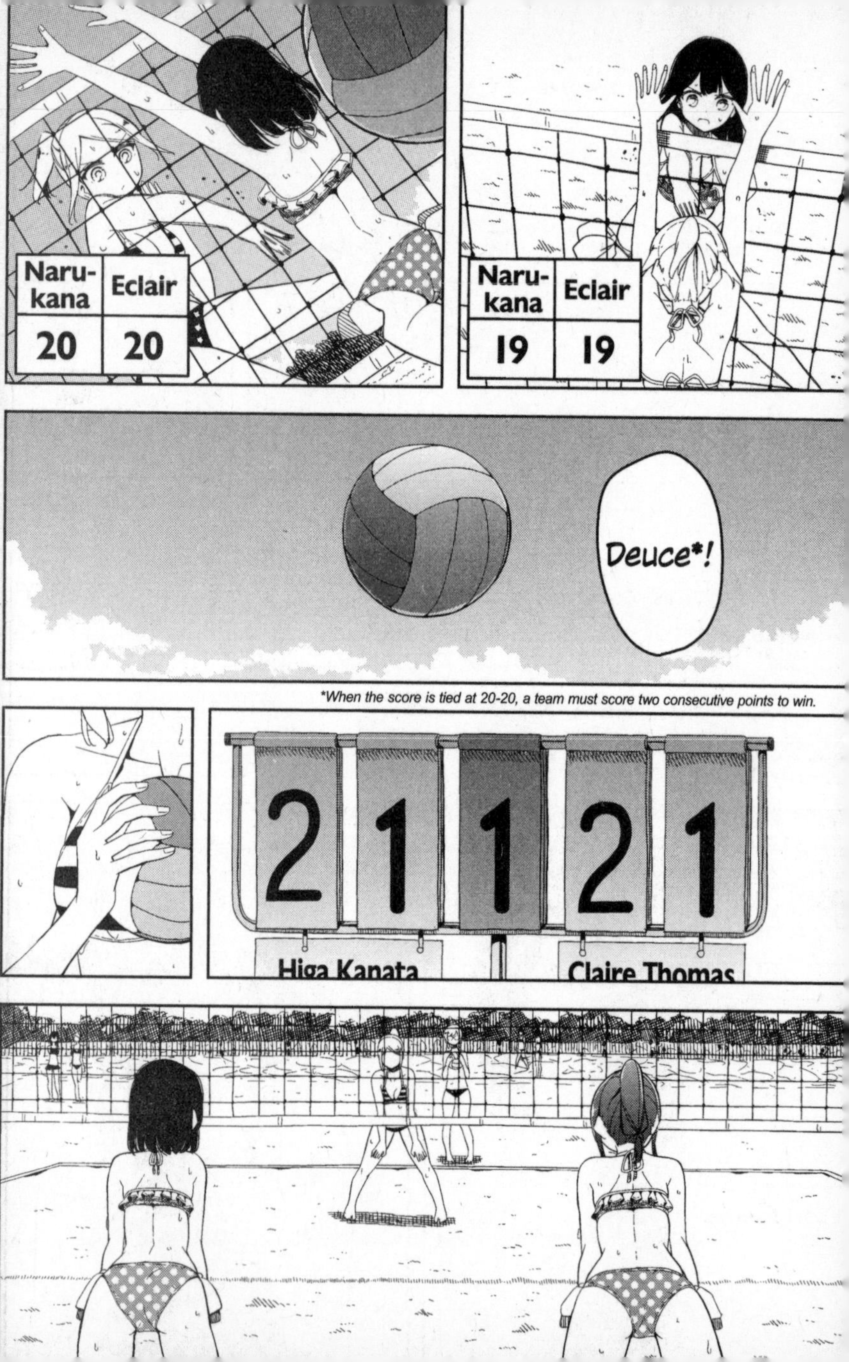
Naru-kana
Eclair
19
19
Naru-kana
Eclair
20
20
Deuce*!
*When the score is tied at 20-20, a team must score two consecutive points to win.
21 1 21
Higa Kanata
Claire Thomas

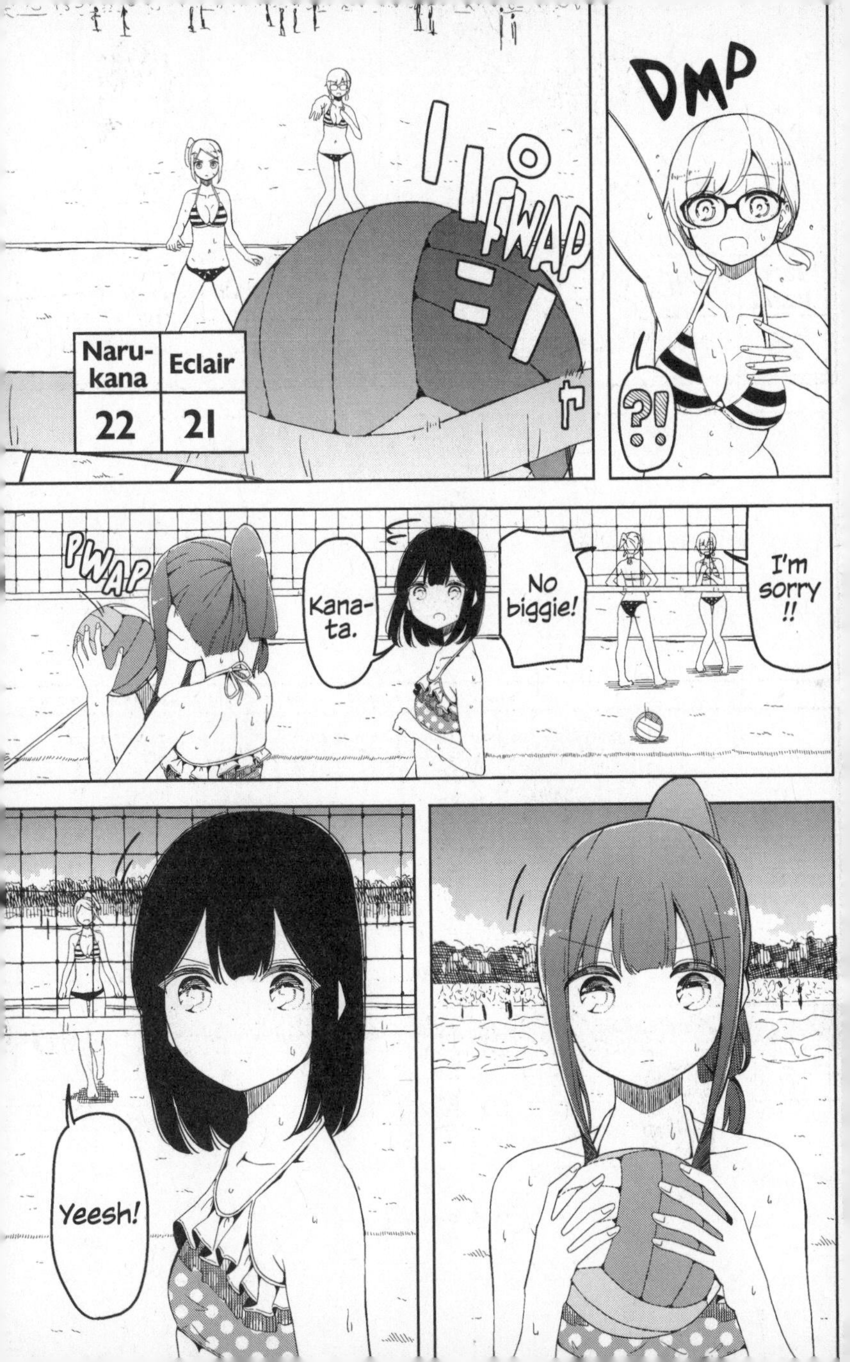
DMP
?!
FWAP
Naru-kana Eclair
22 21
I'm sorry !!
No biggie!
Kana-ta.
PWAP
Yeesh!

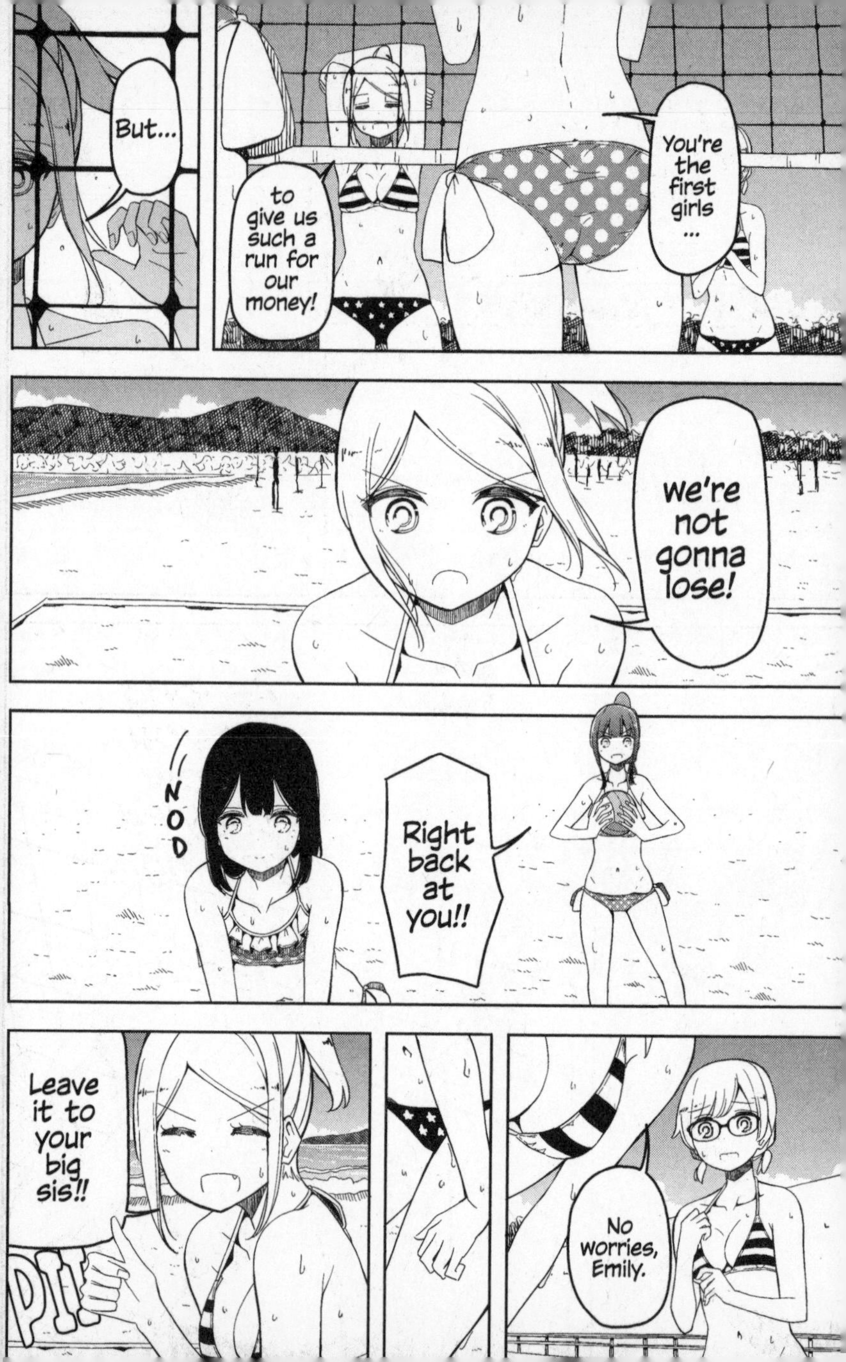
You're the first girls ...
to give us such a run for our money!
But...
We're not gonna lose!
Right back at you!!
NOD
No worries, Emily.
Leave it to your big sis!!
PI

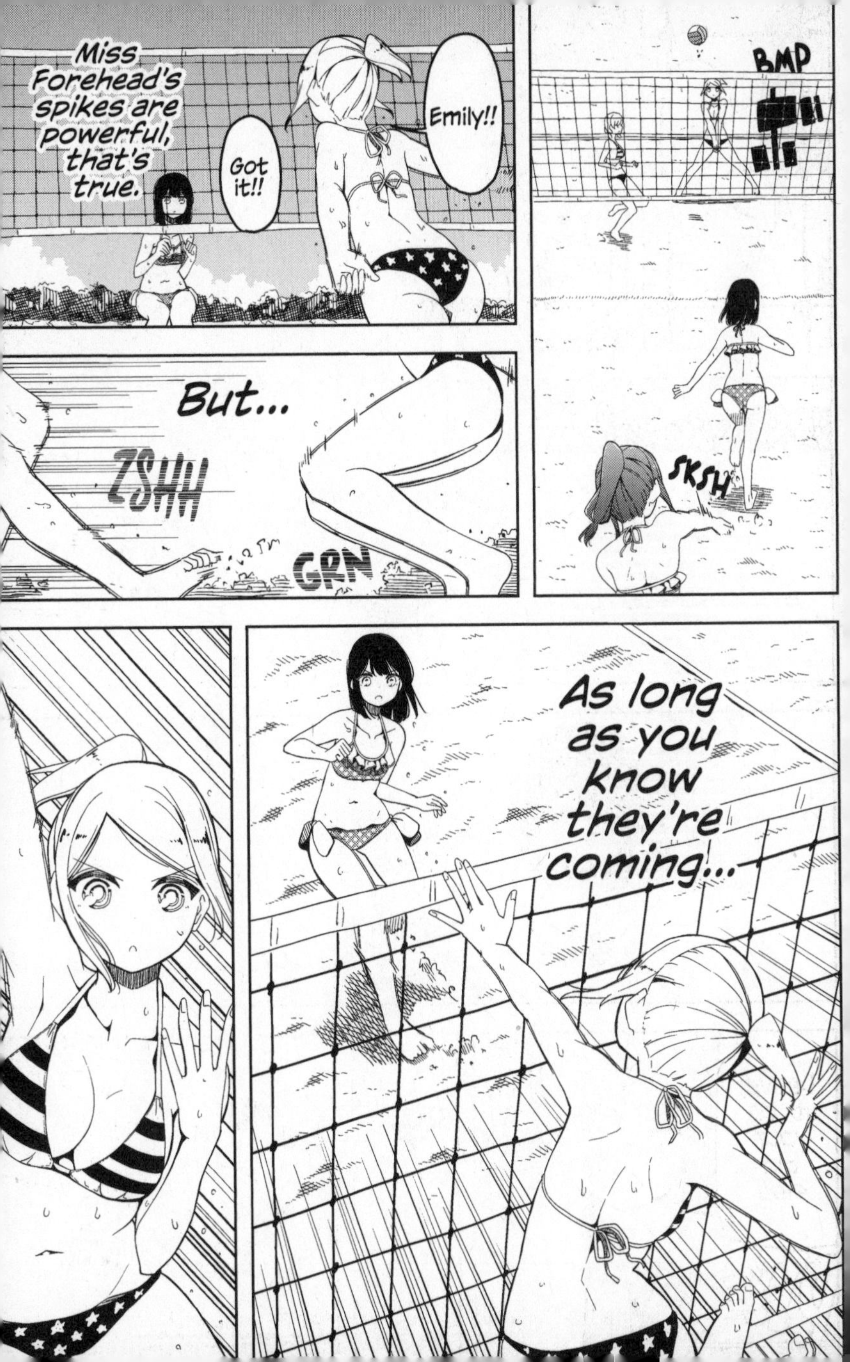
BMP
SKSH
Emily!!
Got it!!
Miss Forehead's spikes are powerful, that's true.
But...
ZSHH
GRN
As long as you know they're coming...

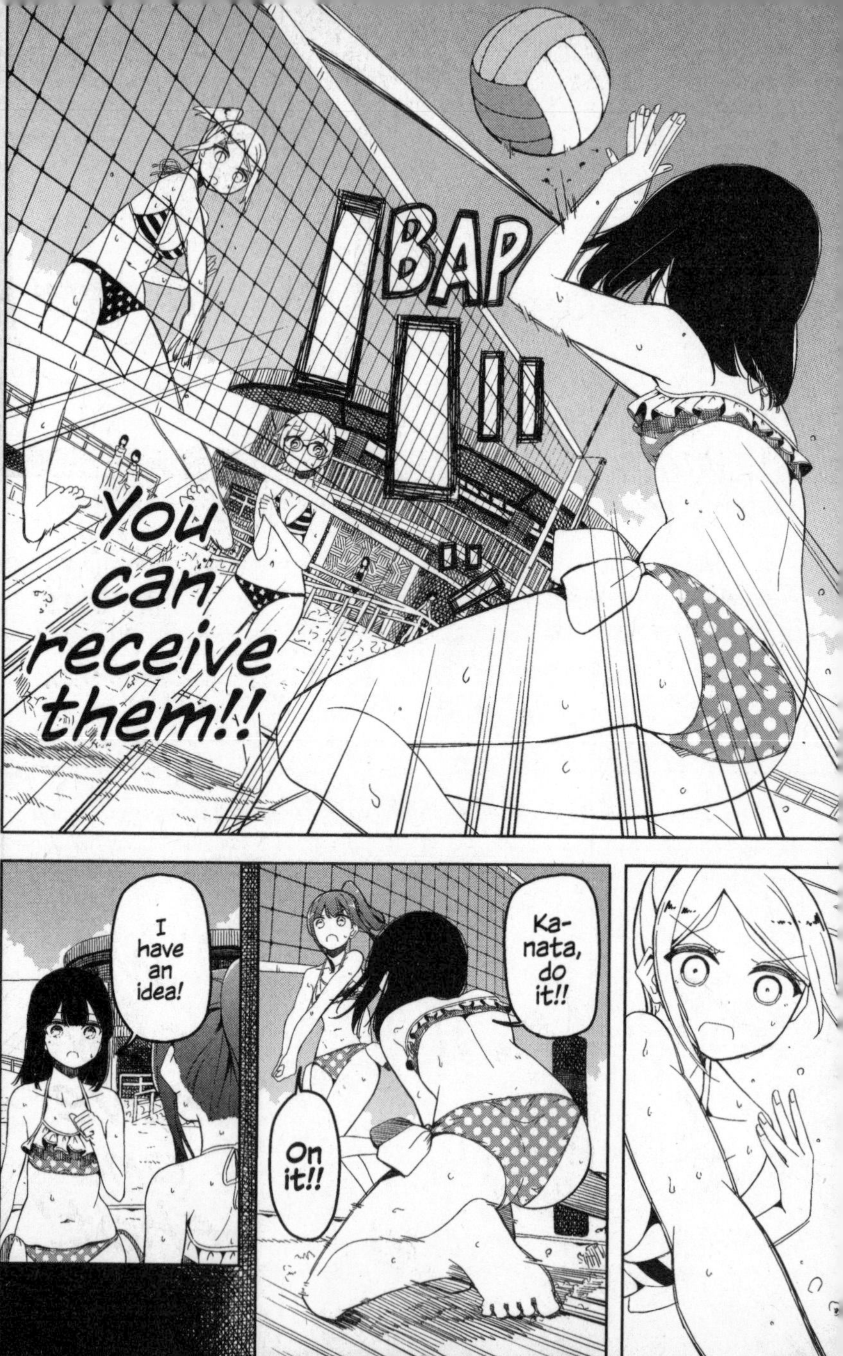
BAP!!
..
You can receive them!!
Ka-nata, do it!!
On it!!
I have an idea!

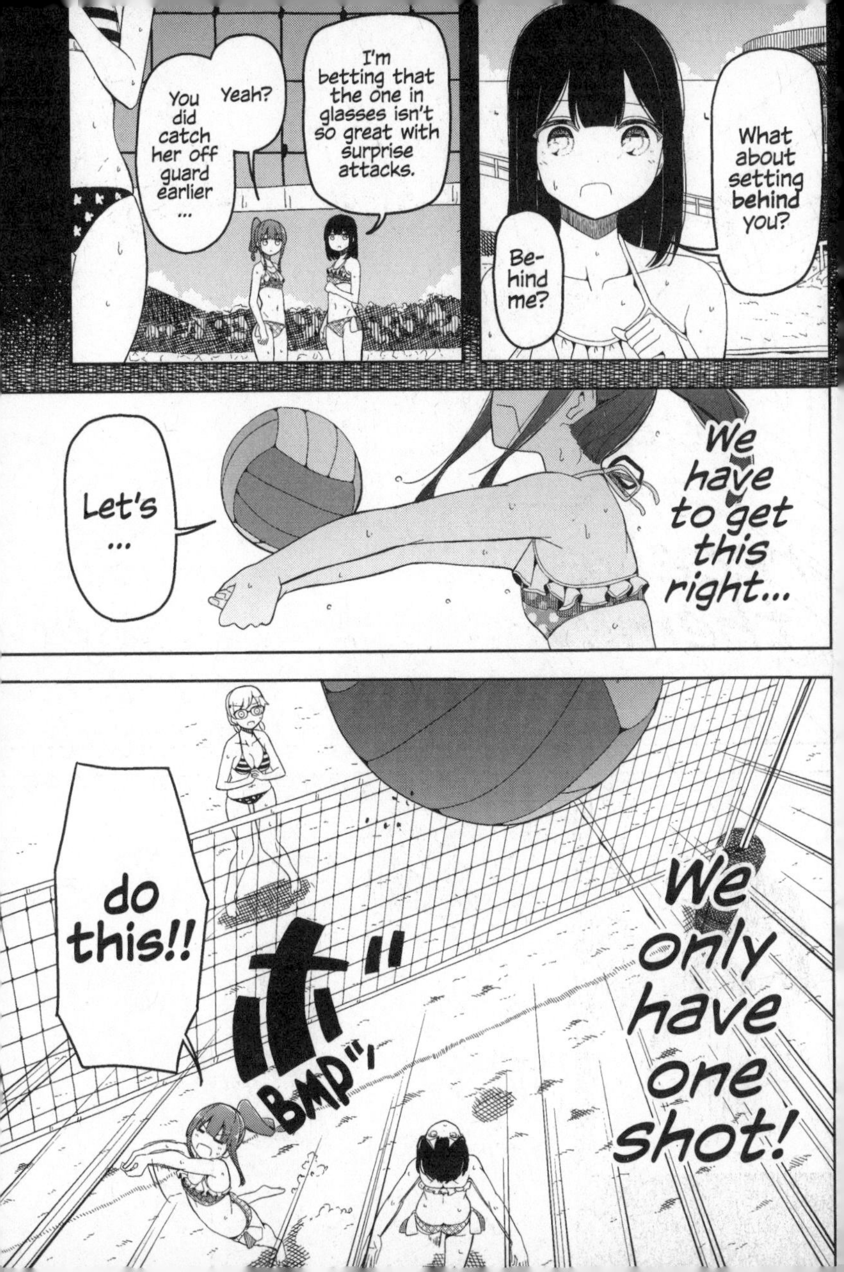
What about setting behind you?
Be-hind me?
I'm betting that the one in glasses isn't so great with surprise attacks.
Yeah?
You did catch her off guard earlier ...
We have to get this right...
Let's ...
We only have one shot!
do this!!
BMP

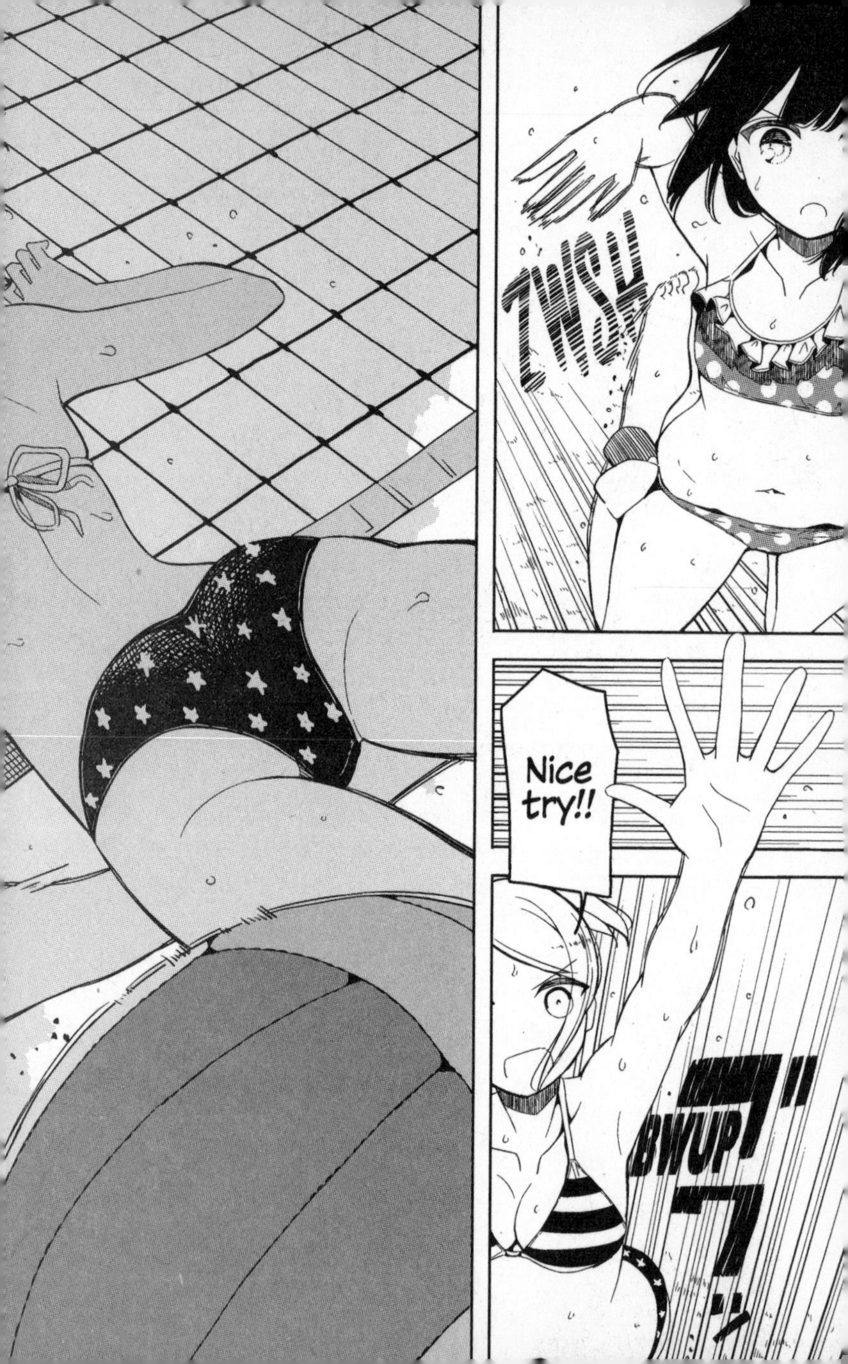
ZWSH
Nice try!!
BWUP

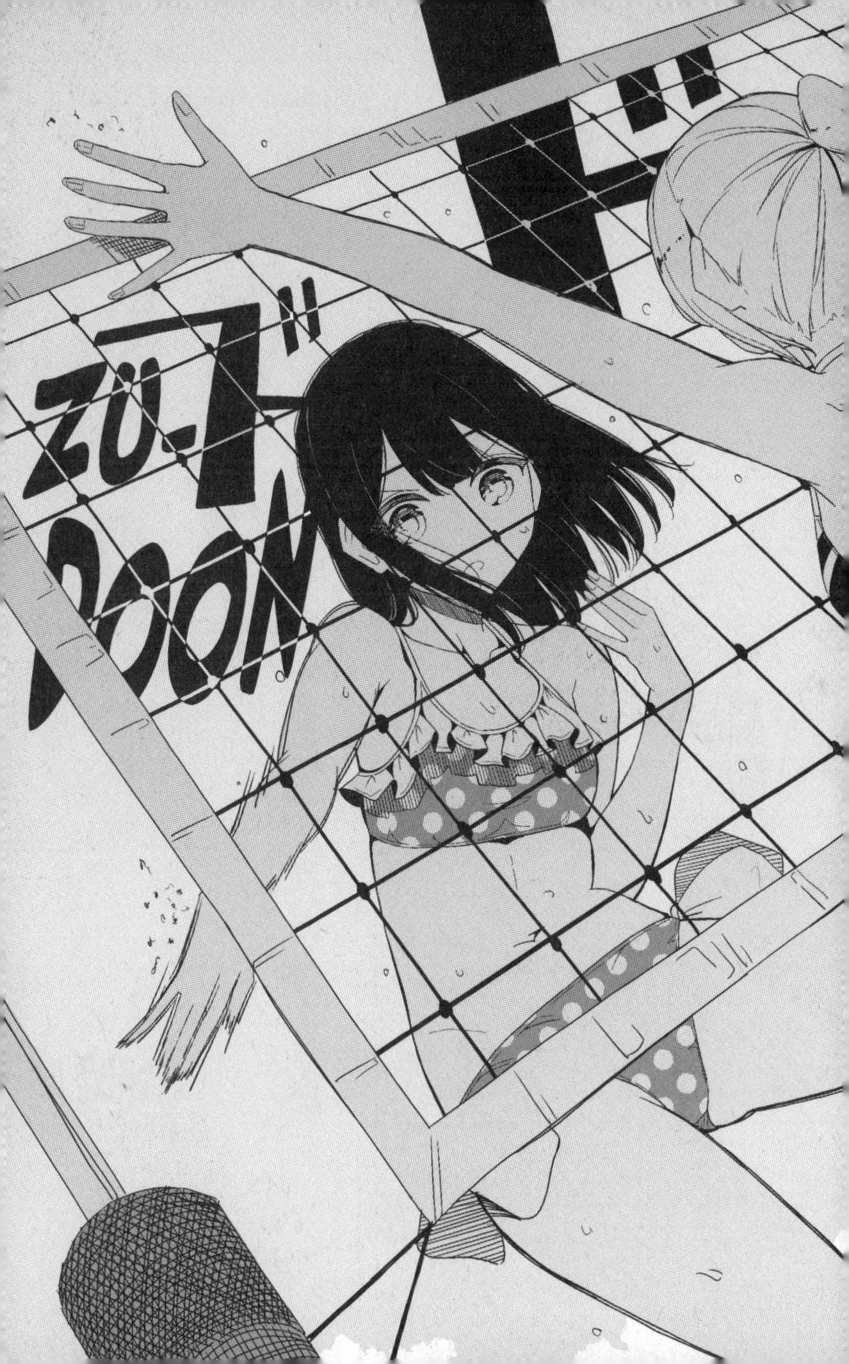

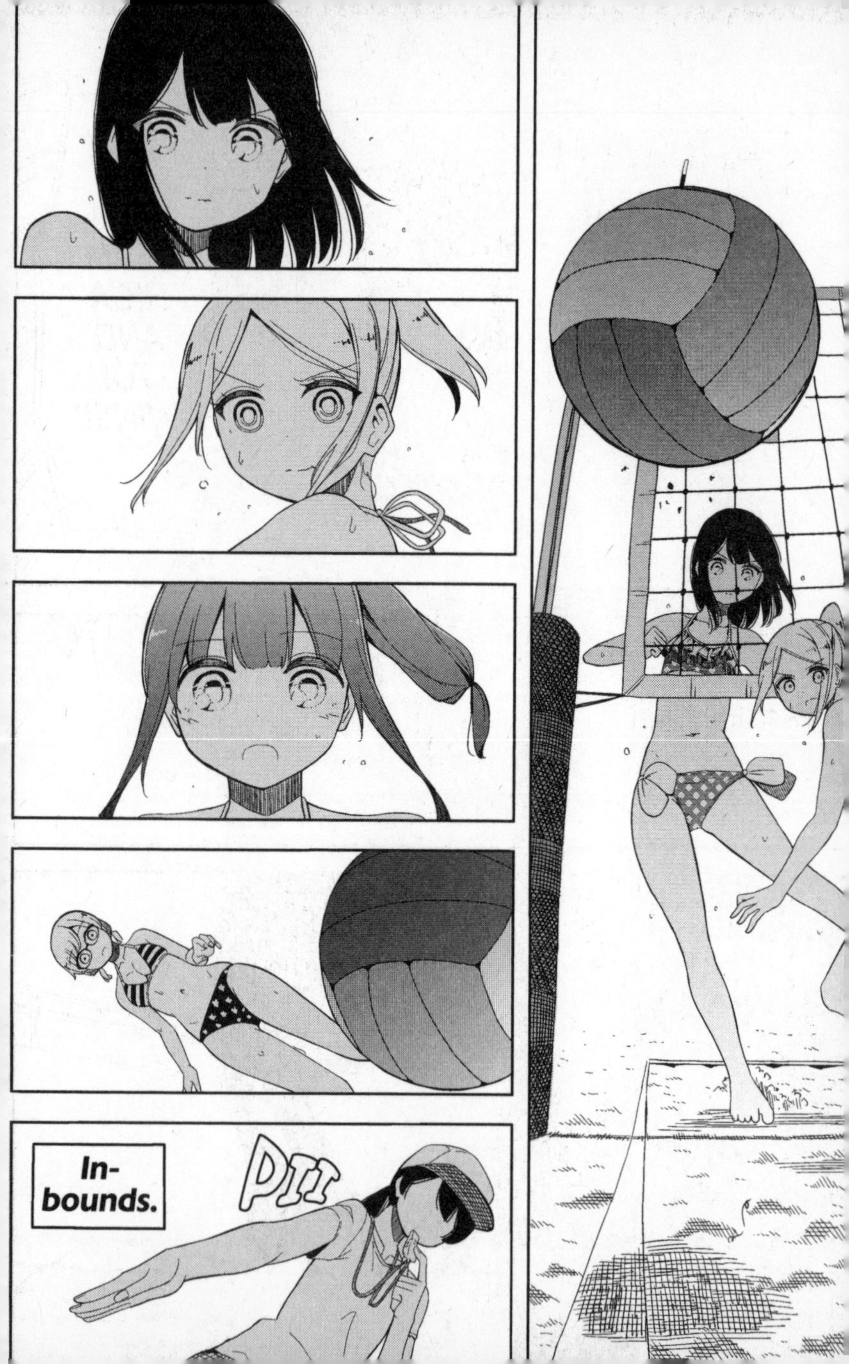
PII
In-bounds.

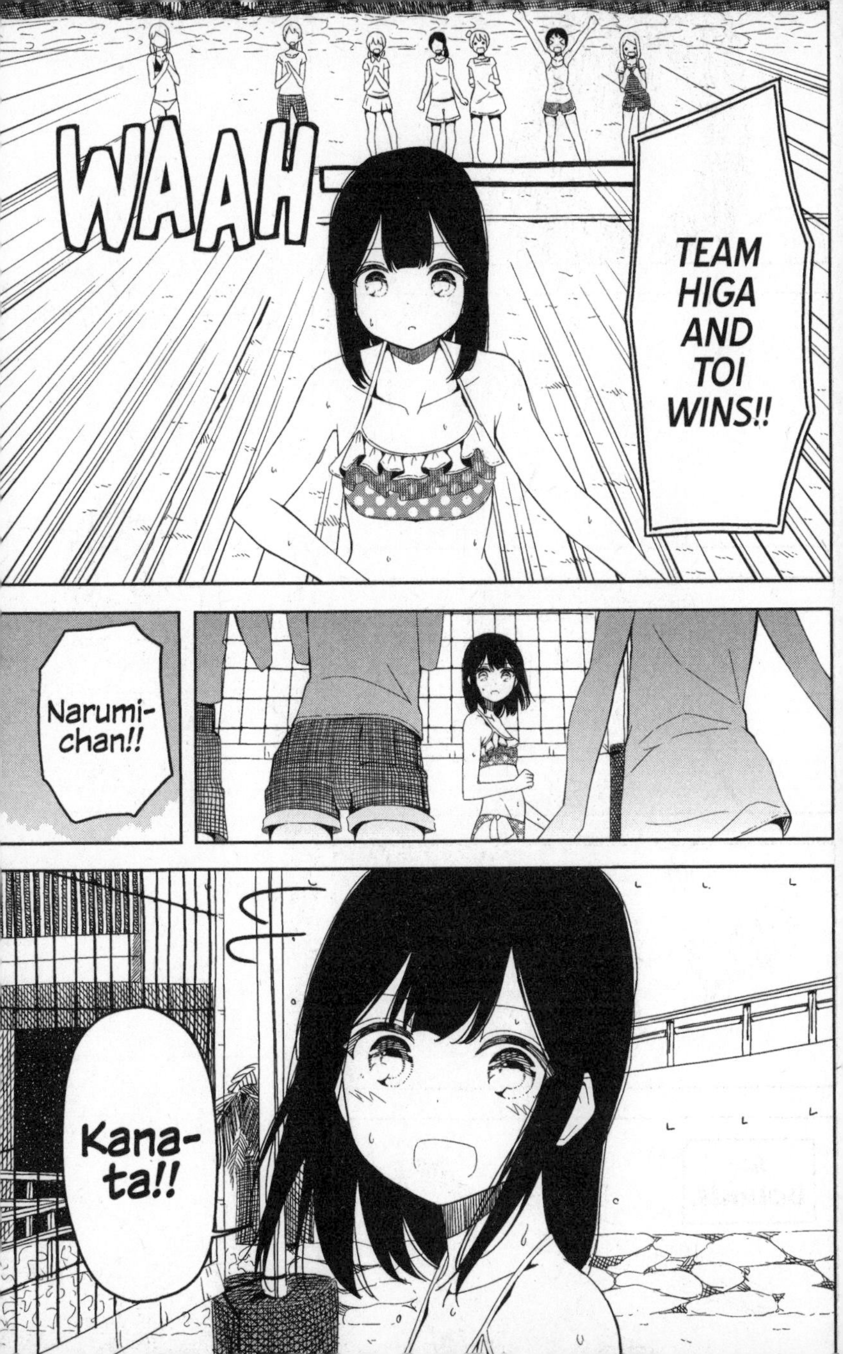
TEAM HIGA AND TOI WINS!!
WAAH-
Narumi-chan!!
Kana-ta!!

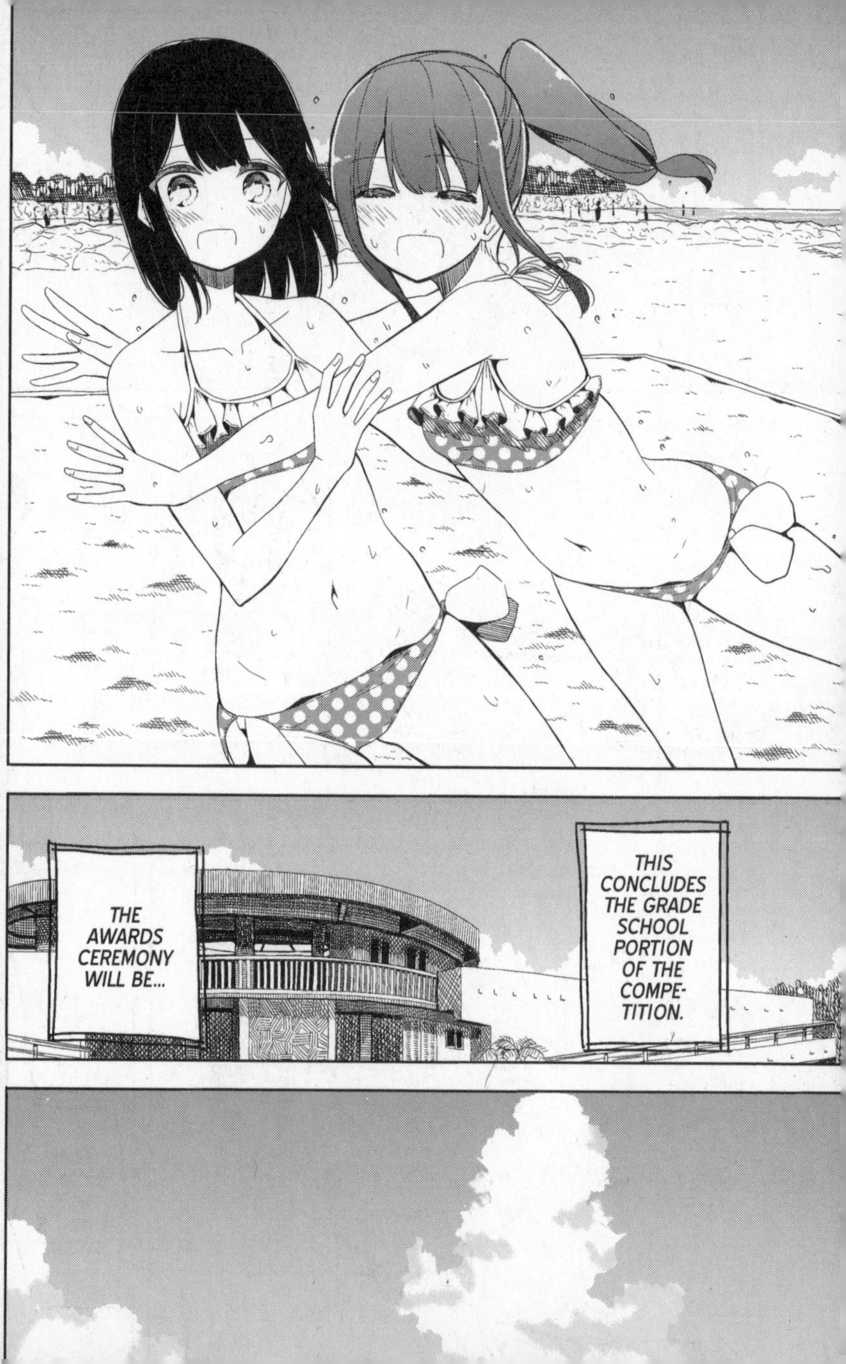
THIS CONCLUDES THE GRADE SCHOOL PORTION OF THE COMPE- TITION.
THE AWARDS CEREMONY WILL BE...

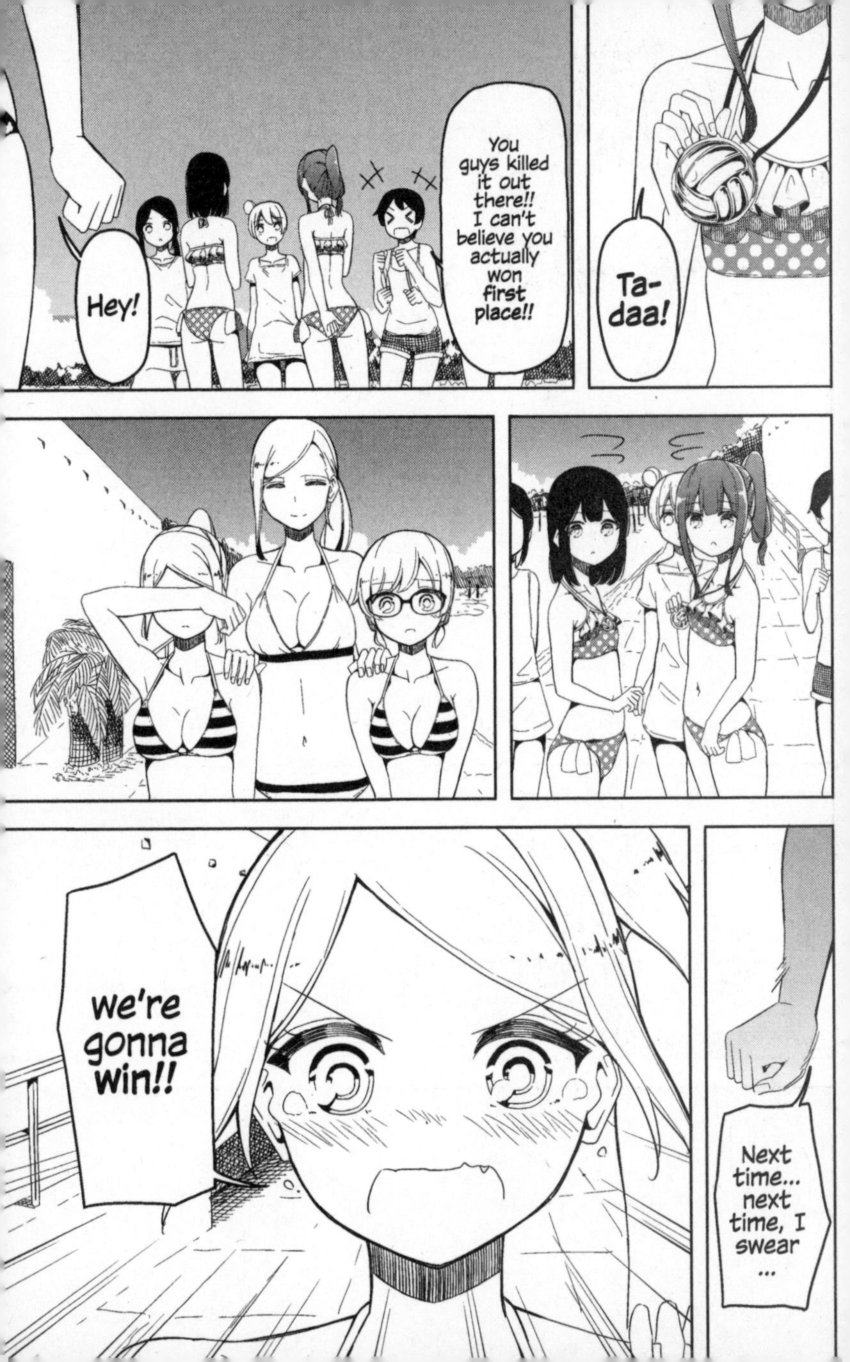
Ta-daa!
You guys killed it out there!! I can't believe you actually won first place!!
Hey!
Next time... next time, I swear ...
we're gonna win!!

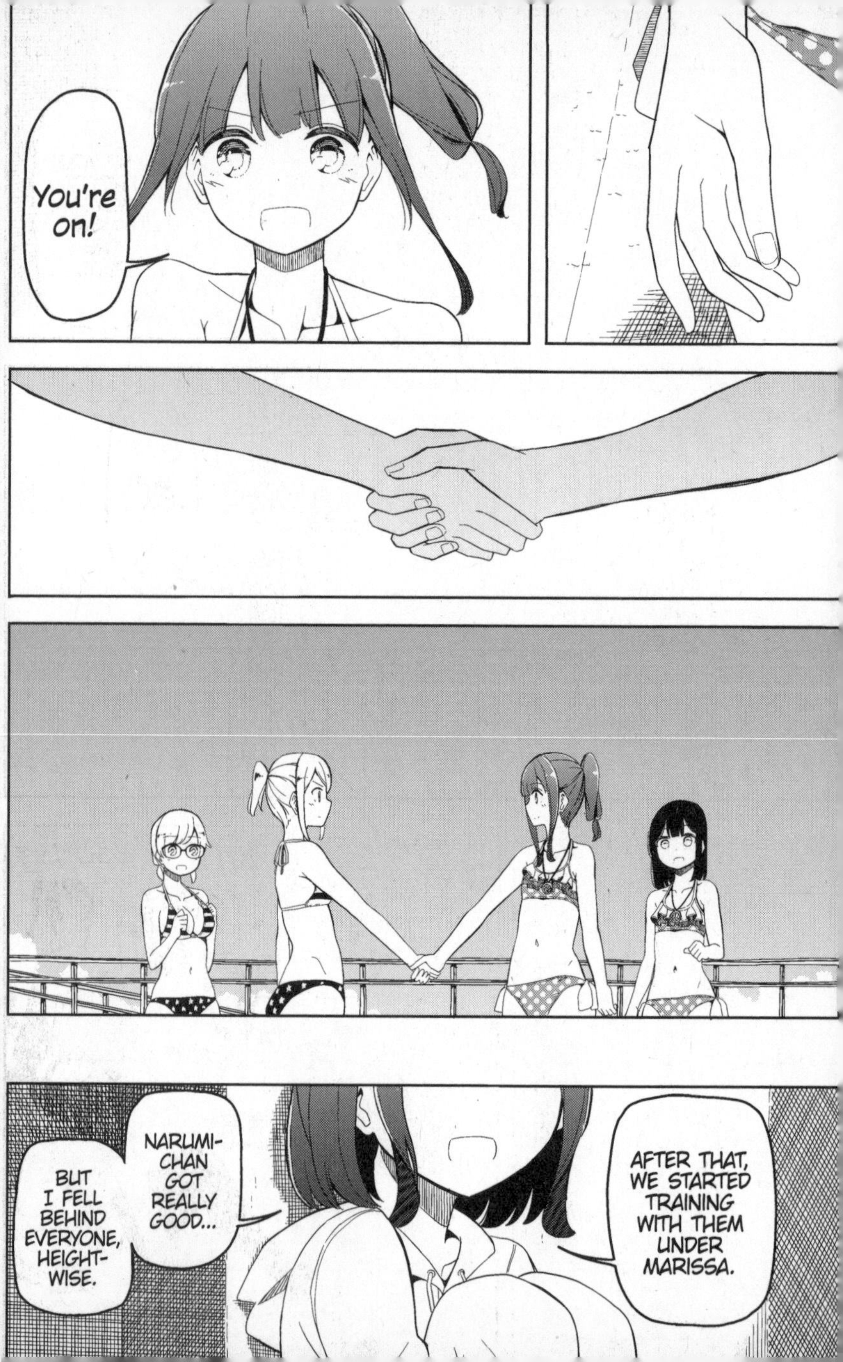
You're on!
AFTER THAT, WE STARTED TRAINING WITH THEM UNDER MARISSA.
NARUMI-CHAN GOT REALLY GOOD...
BUT I FELL BEHIND EVERYONE, HEIGHT-WISE.

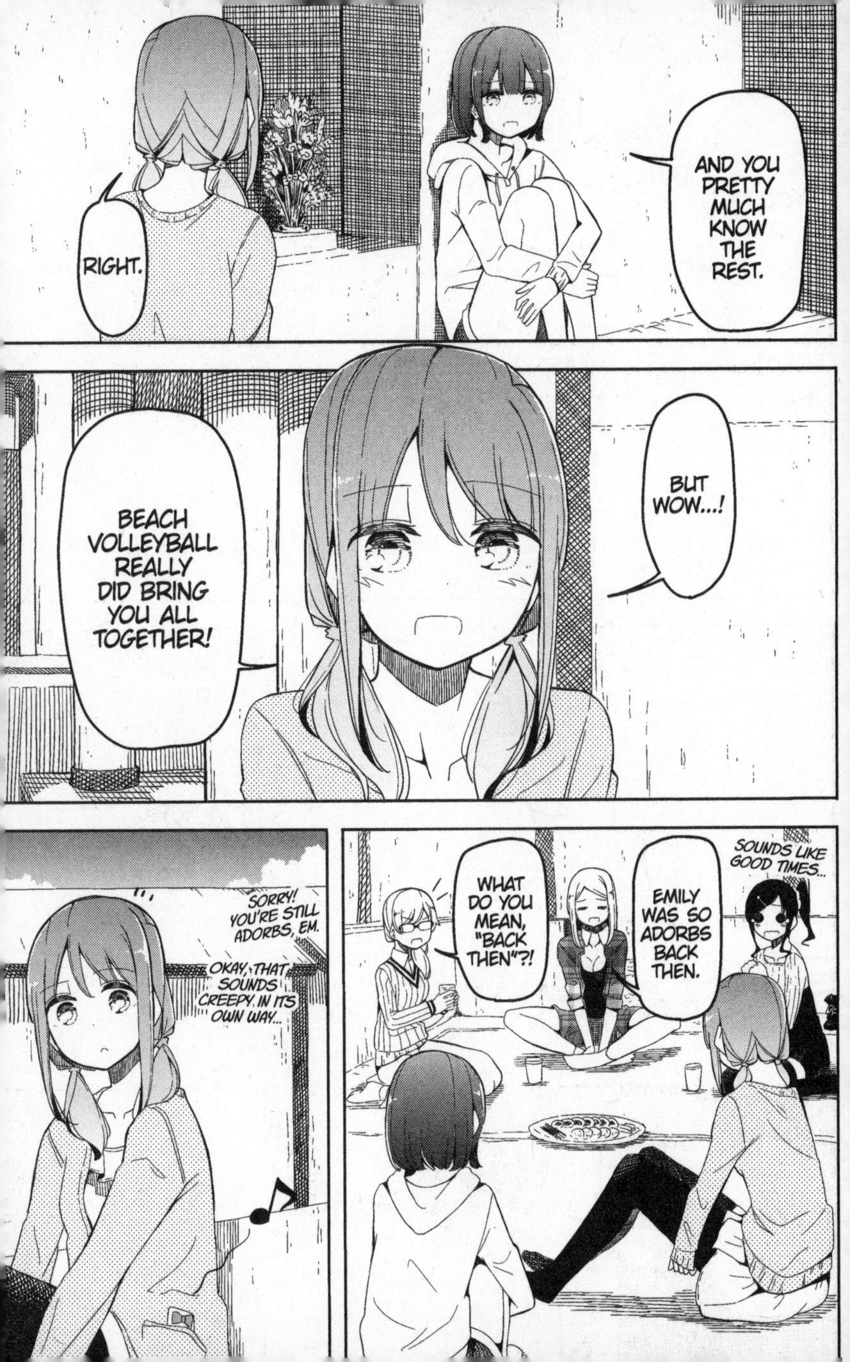
AND YOU PRETTY MUCH KNOW THE REST.
RIGHT.
BUT WOW...!
BEACH VOLLEYBALL REALLY DID BRING YOU ALL TOGETHER!
SOUNDS LIKE GOOD TIMES...
EMILY WAS SO ADORBS BACK THEN.
WHAT DO YOU MEAN, "BACK THEN"?!
SORRY! YOU'RE STILL ADORBS, EM.
OKAY, THAT SOUNDS CREEPY IN ITS OWN WAY...

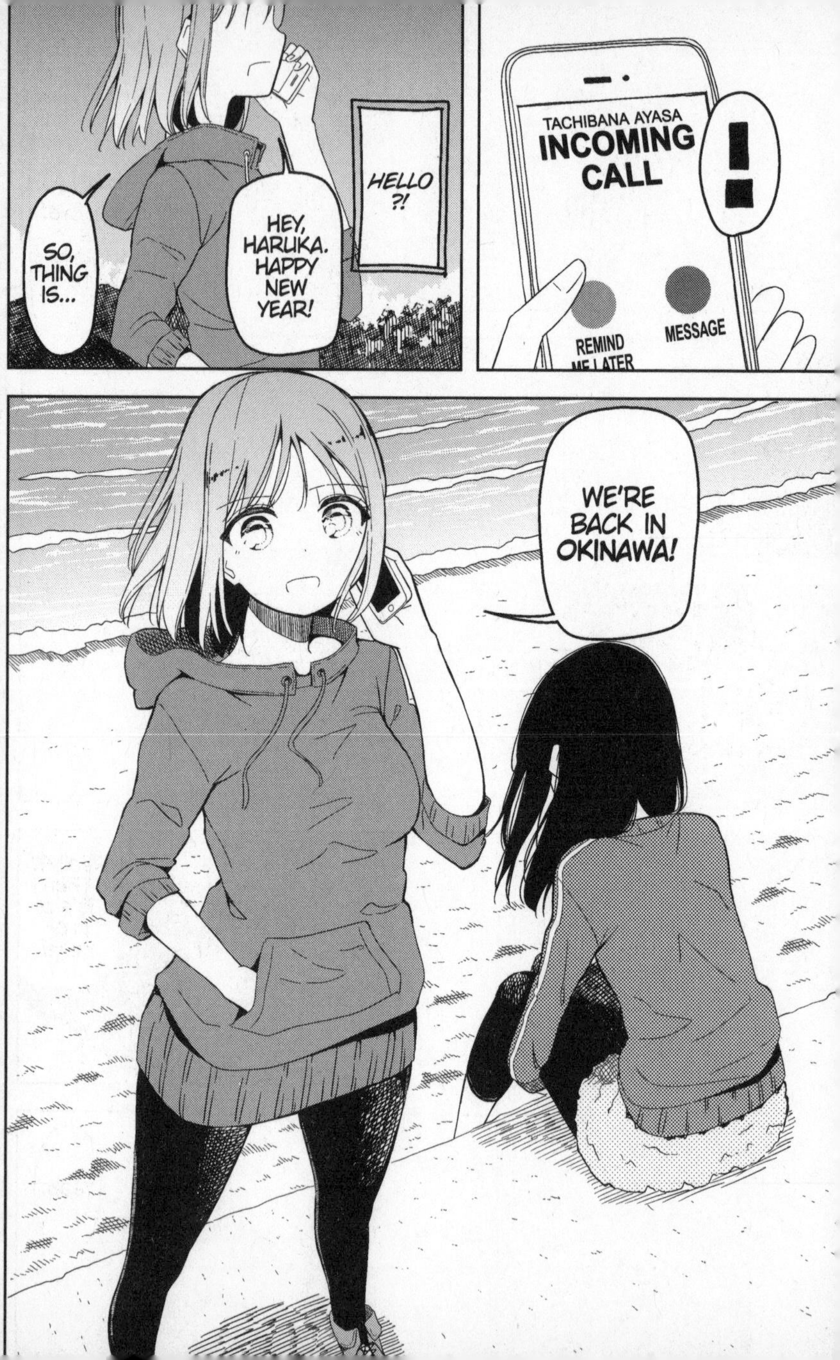
TACHIBANA AYASA
INCOMING CALL
!
MESSAGE
REMIND ME LATER
HELLO ?!
HEY, HARUKA. HAPPY NEW YEAR!
SO, THING IS...
WE'RE BACK IN OKINAWA!

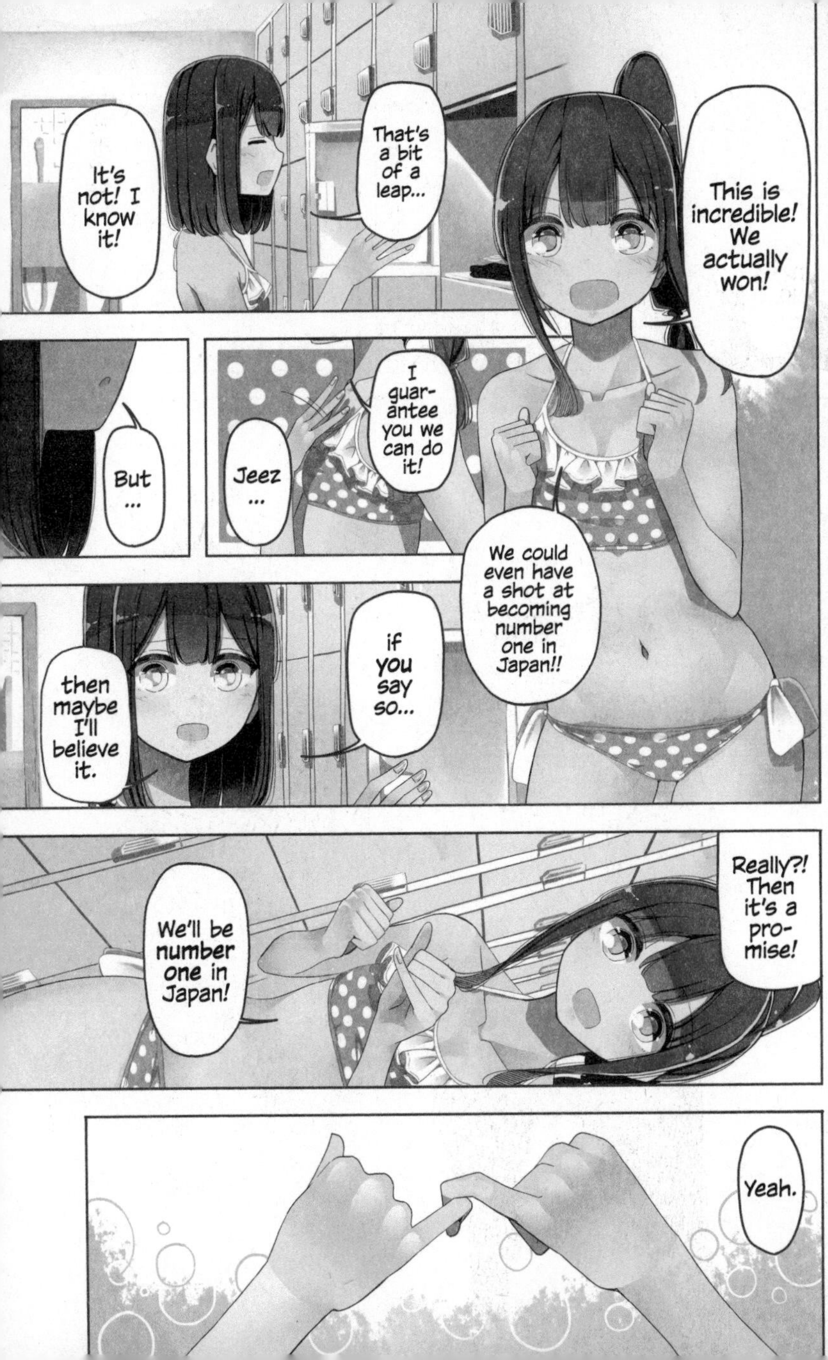
This is incredible! We actually won!
We could even have a shot at becoming number one in Japan!!
That's a bit of a leap...
It's not! I know it!
I guarantee you we can do it!
Jeez...
But...
if you say so...
then maybe I'll believe it.
Really?! Then it's a promise!
We'll be number one in Japan!
Yeah.

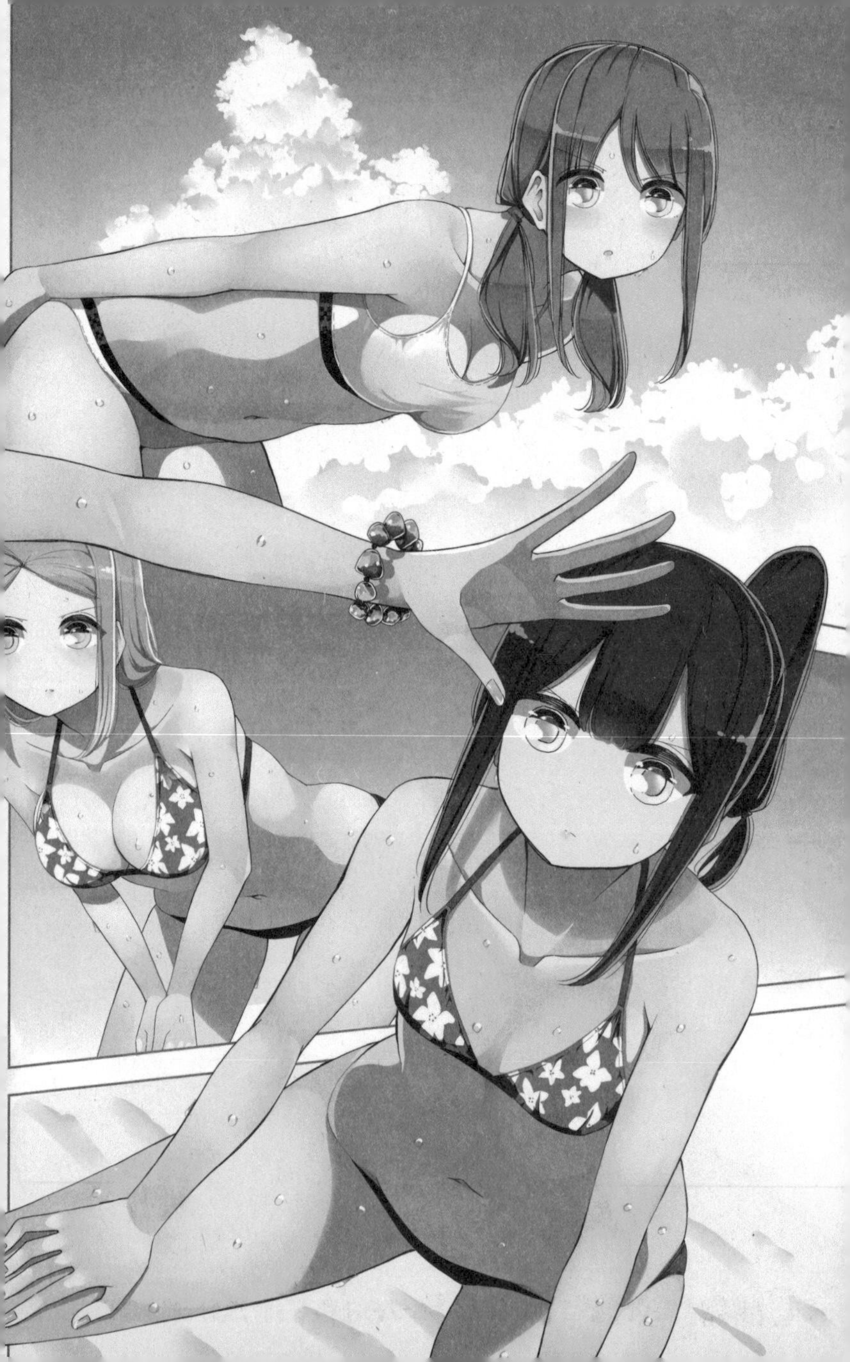

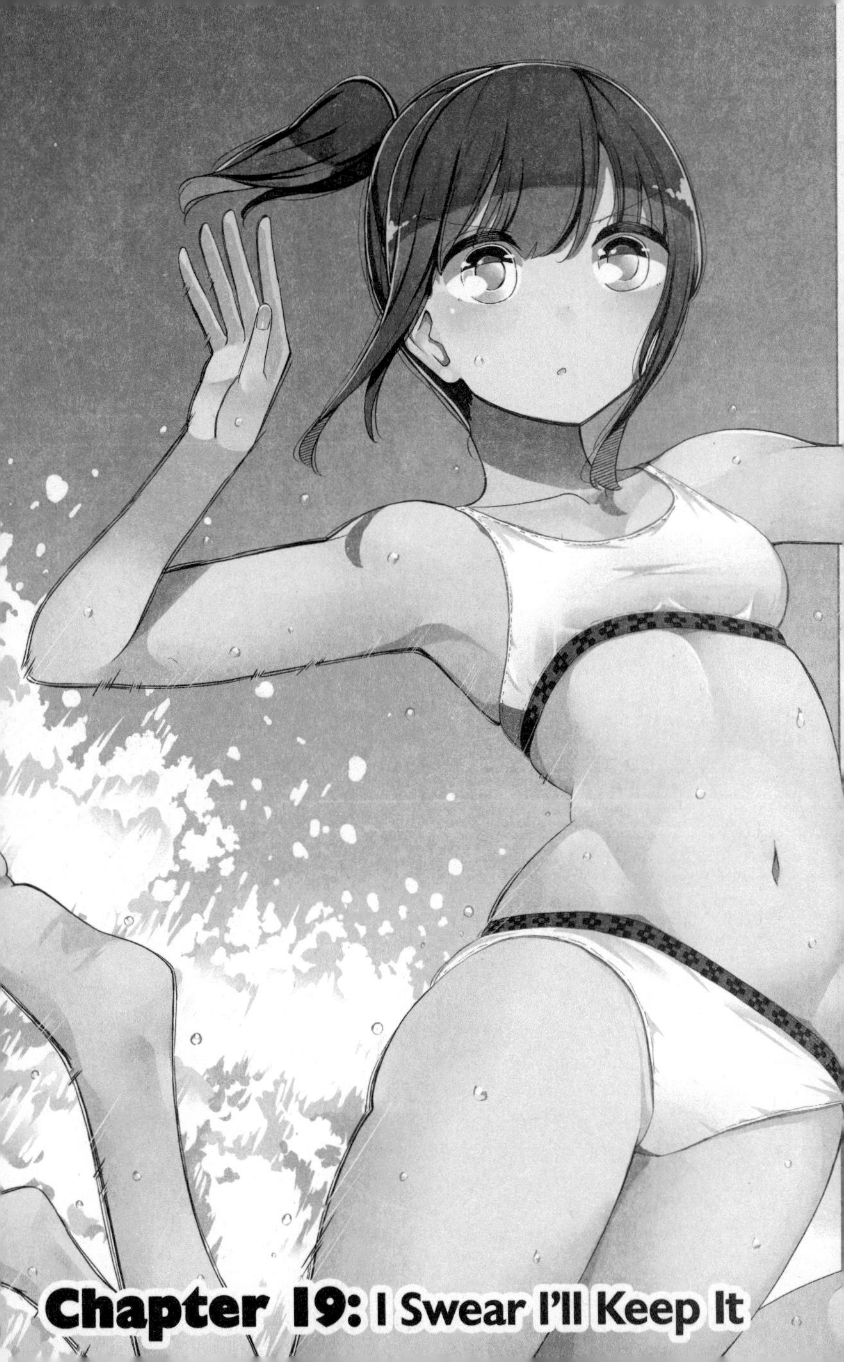

Chapter 19: I Swear I'll Keep It

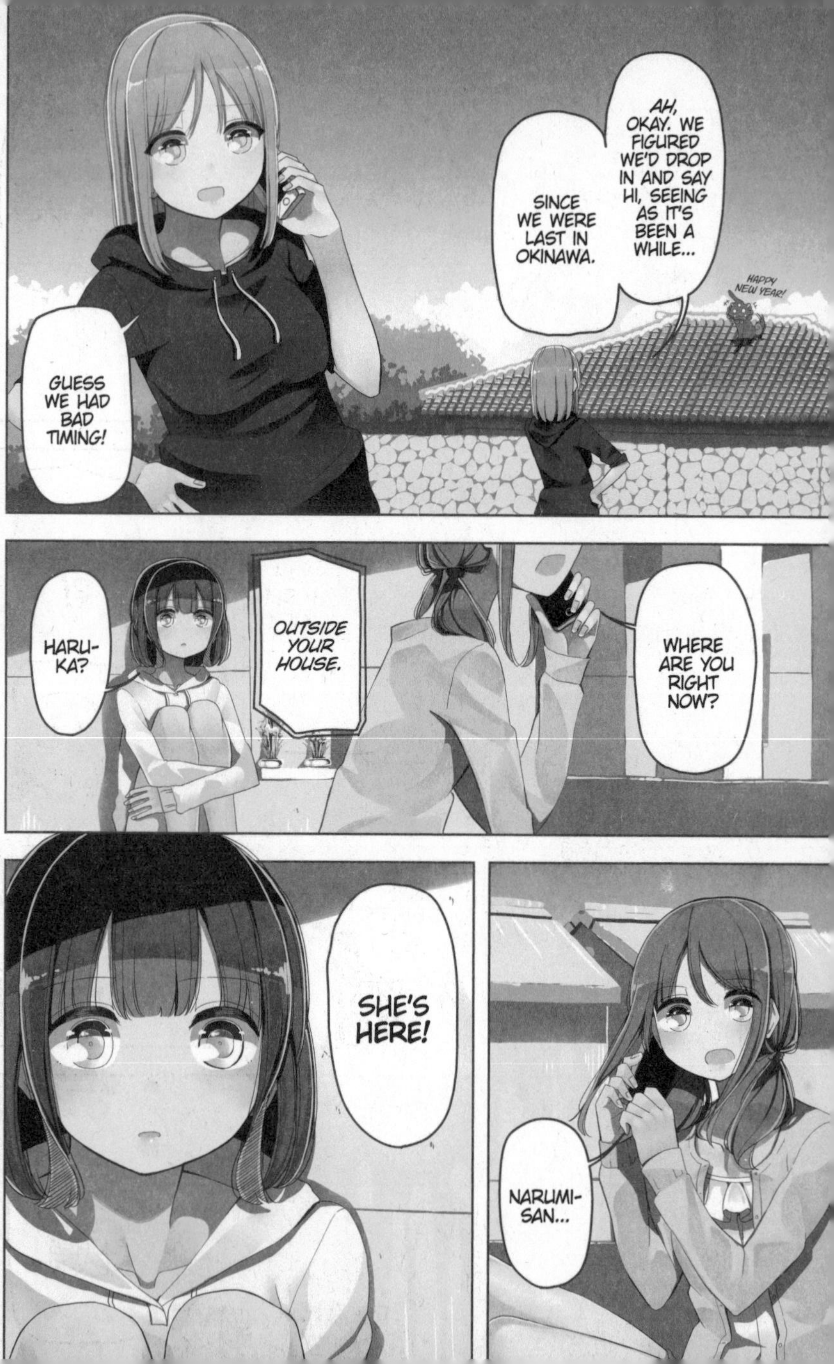
AH, OKAY. WE FIGURED WE'D DROP IN AND SAY HI, SEEING AS IT'S BEEN A WHILE...
SINCE WE WERE LAST IN OKINAWA.
HAPPY NEW YEAR!
GUESS WE HAD BAD TIMING!
WHERE ARE YOU RIGHT NOW?
OUTSIDE YOUR HOUSE.
HARU-KA?
NARUMI-SAN...
SHE'S HERE!

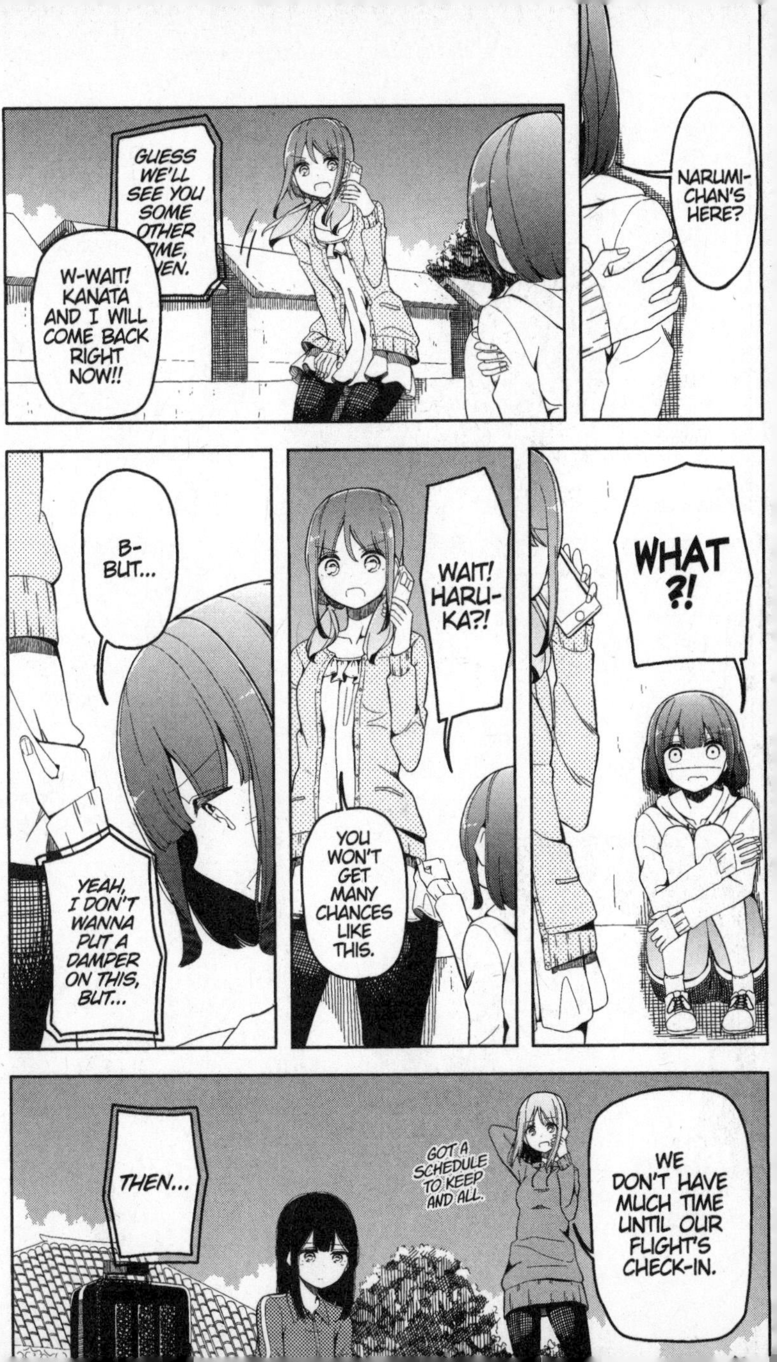
NARUMI-CHAN'S HERE?
GUESS WE'LL SEE YOU SOME OTHER
W-WAIT! KANATA AND I WILL COME BACK RIGHT NOW!!
WHAT?!
WAIT! HARU-KA?!
YOU WON'T GET MANY CHANCES LIKE THIS.
B-BUT...
YEAH, I DON'T WANNA PUT A DAMPER ON THIS, BUT...
WE DON'T HAVE MUCH TIME UNTIL OUR FLIGHT'S CHECK-IN.
GOT A SCHEDULE TO KEEP AND ALL.
THEN...

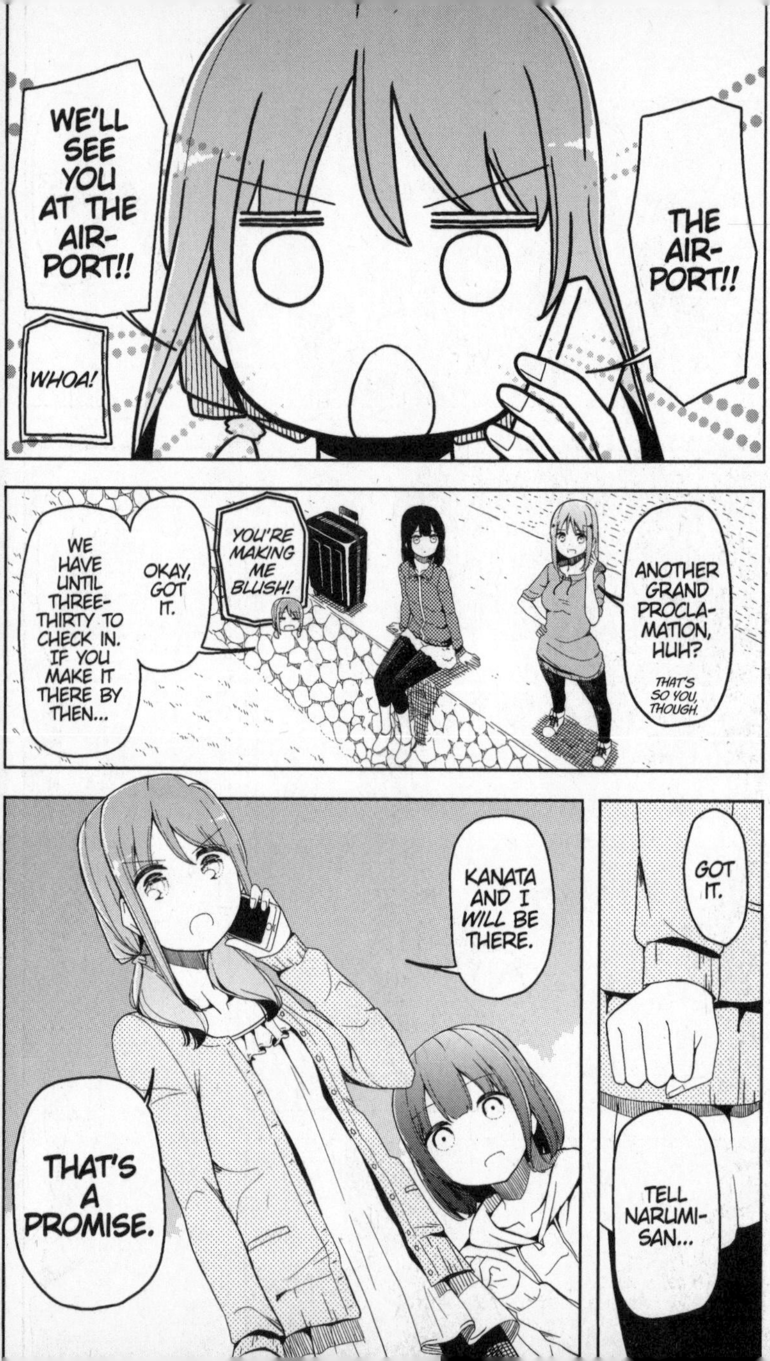
THE AIRPORT!!
WE'LL SEE YOU AT THE AIRPORT!!
WHOA!
ANOTHER GRAND PROCLAMATION, HUH?
THAT'S SO YOU, THOUGH.
YOU'RE MAKING ME BLUSH!
OKAY, GOT IT.
WE HAVE UNTIL THREE-THIRTY TO CHECK IN. IF YOU MAKE IT THERE BY THEN...
GOT IT.
TELL NARUMI-SAN...
KANATA AND I *WILL* BE THERE.
THAT'S A PROMISE.

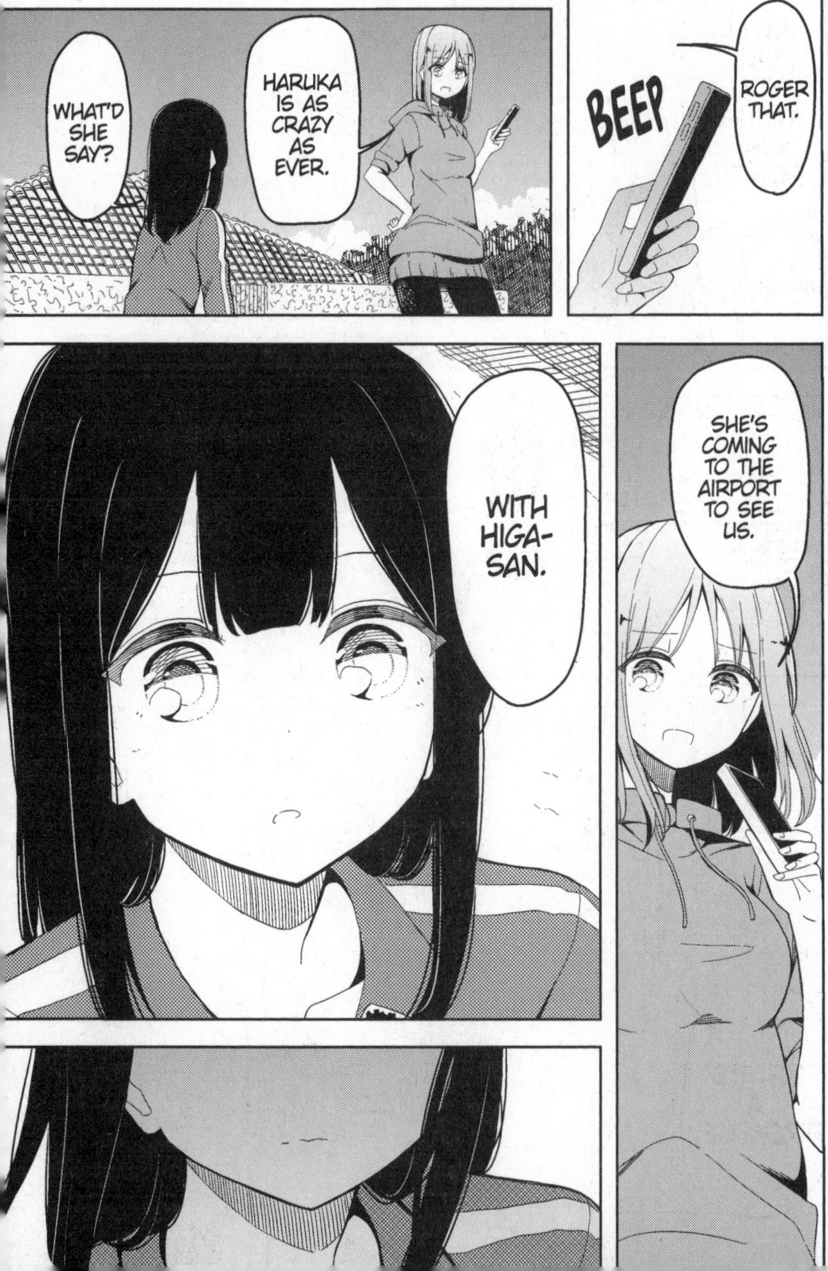
ROGER THAT.
BEEP
HARUKA IS AS CRAZY AS EVER.
WHAT'D SHE SAY?
SHE'S COMING TO THE AIRPORT TO SEE US.
WITH HIGA-SAN.

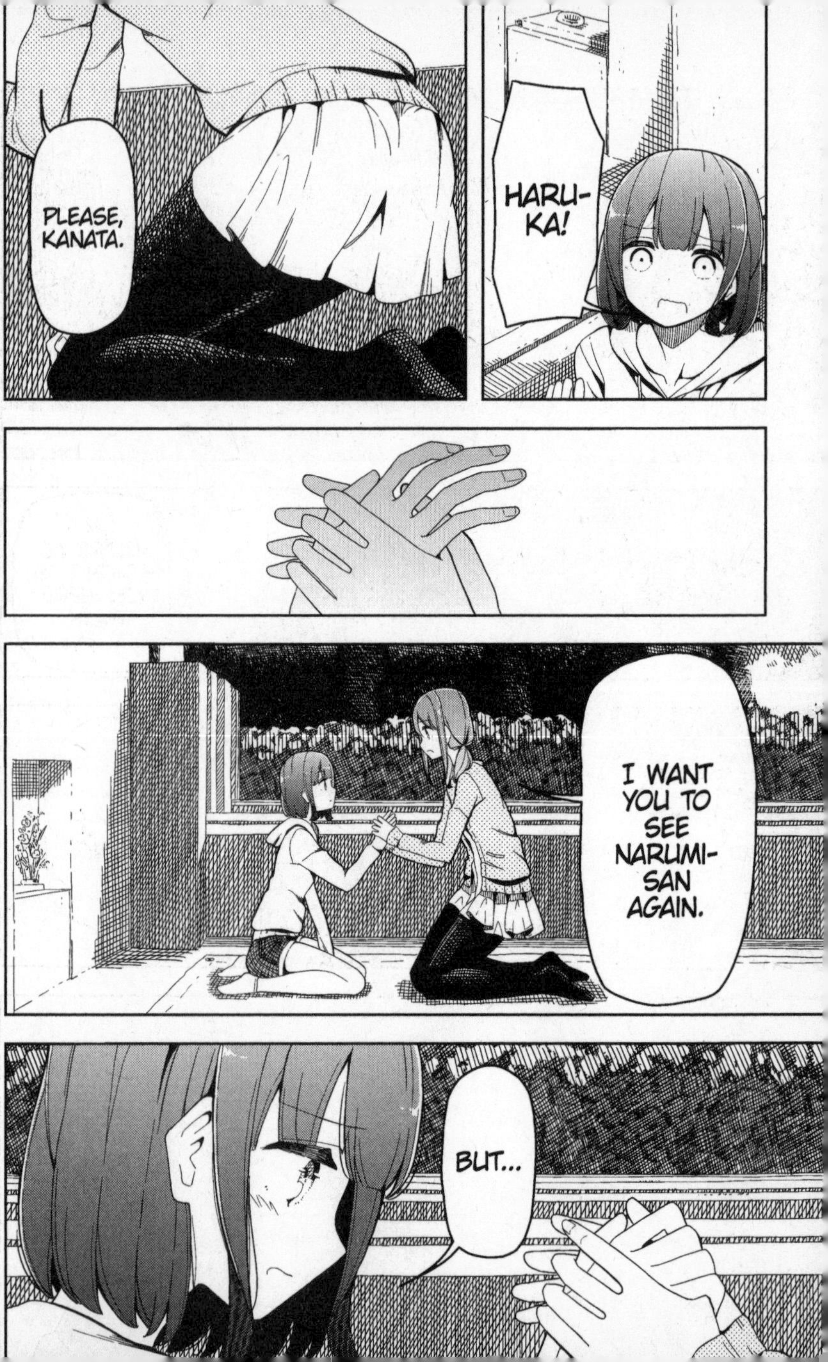
HARU-KA!
PLEASE, KANATA.
I WANT YOU TO SEE NARUMI-SAN AGAIN.
BUT...

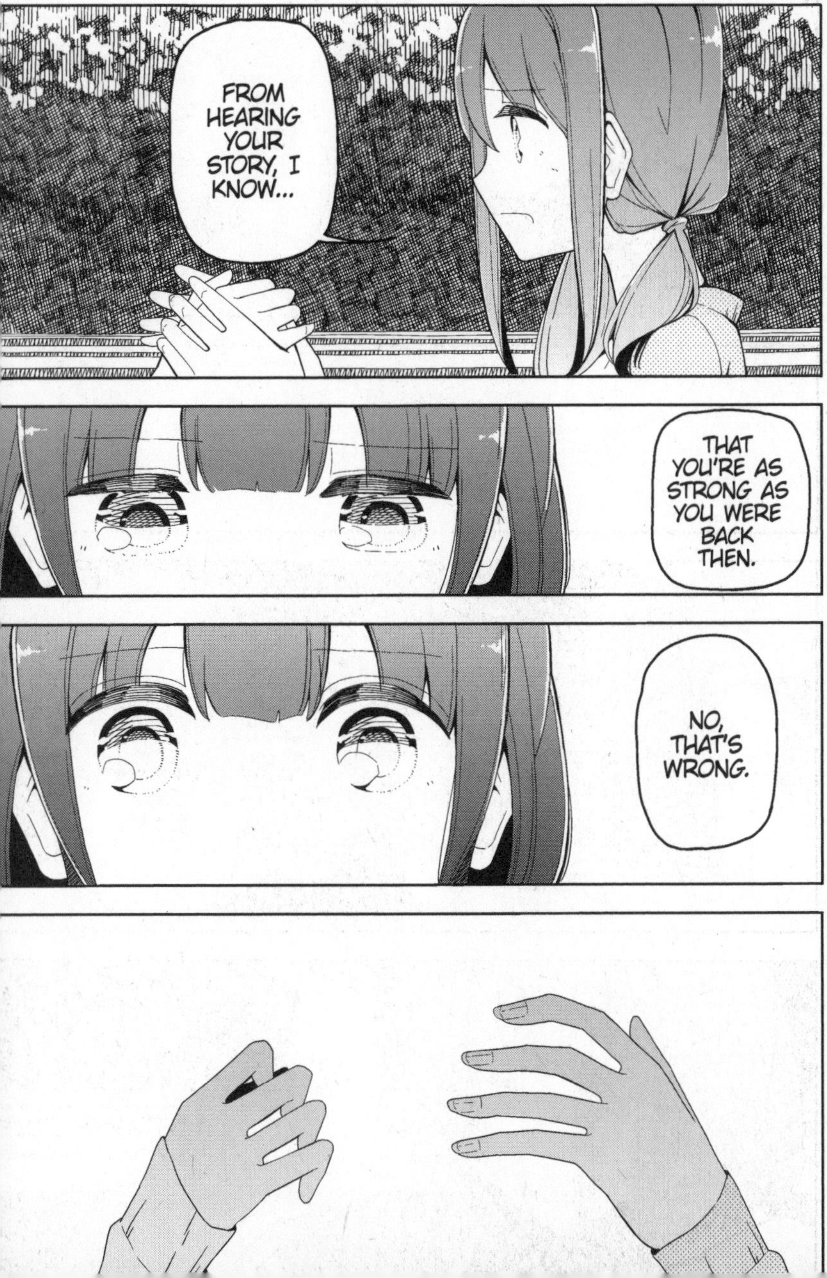
FROM HEARING YOUR STORY, I KNOW...
THAT YOU'RE AS STRONG AS YOU WERE BACK THEN.
NO, THAT'S WRONG.

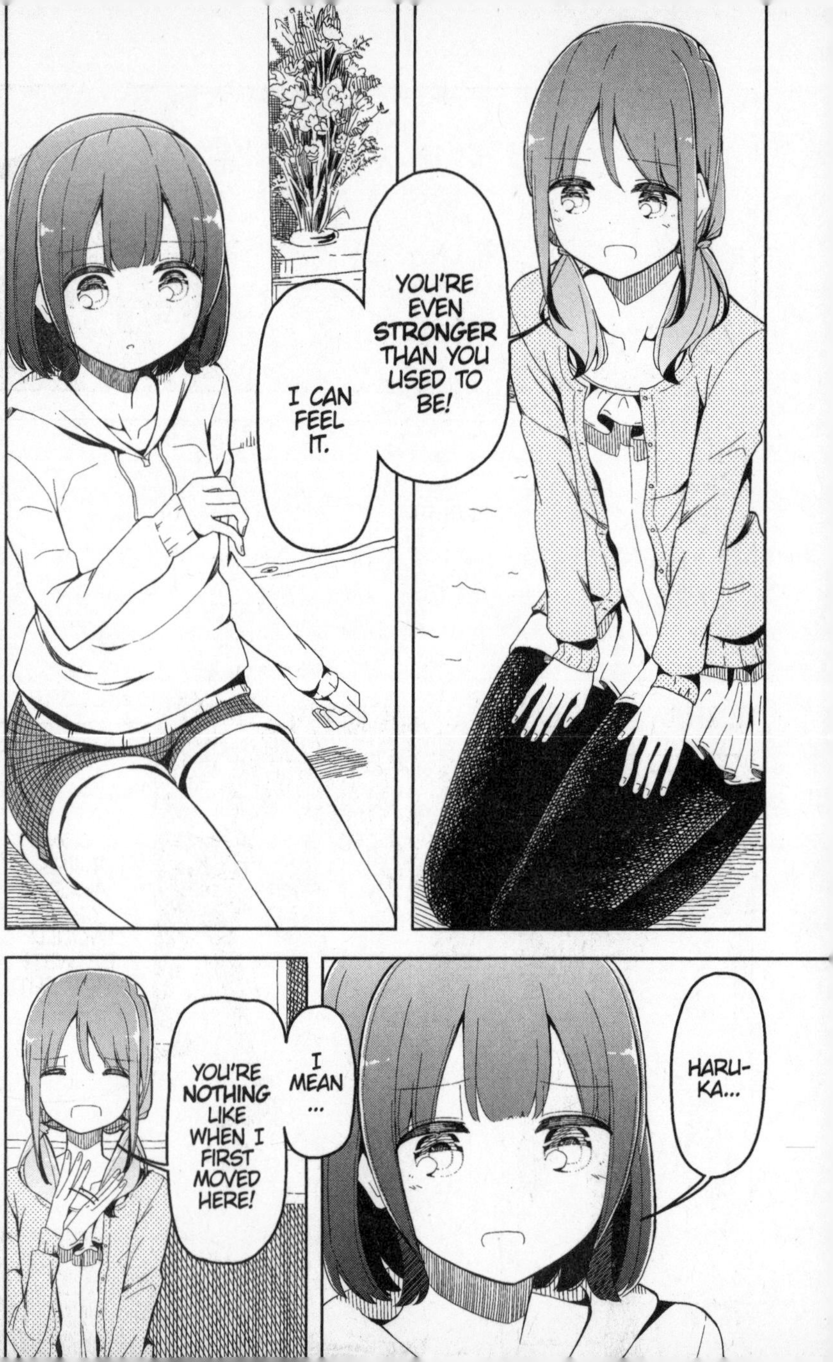
YOU'RE EVEN STRONGER THAN YOU USED TO BE!
I CAN FEEL IT.
HARU-KA...
I MEAN...
YOU'RE NOTHING LIKE WHEN I FIRST MOVED HERE!

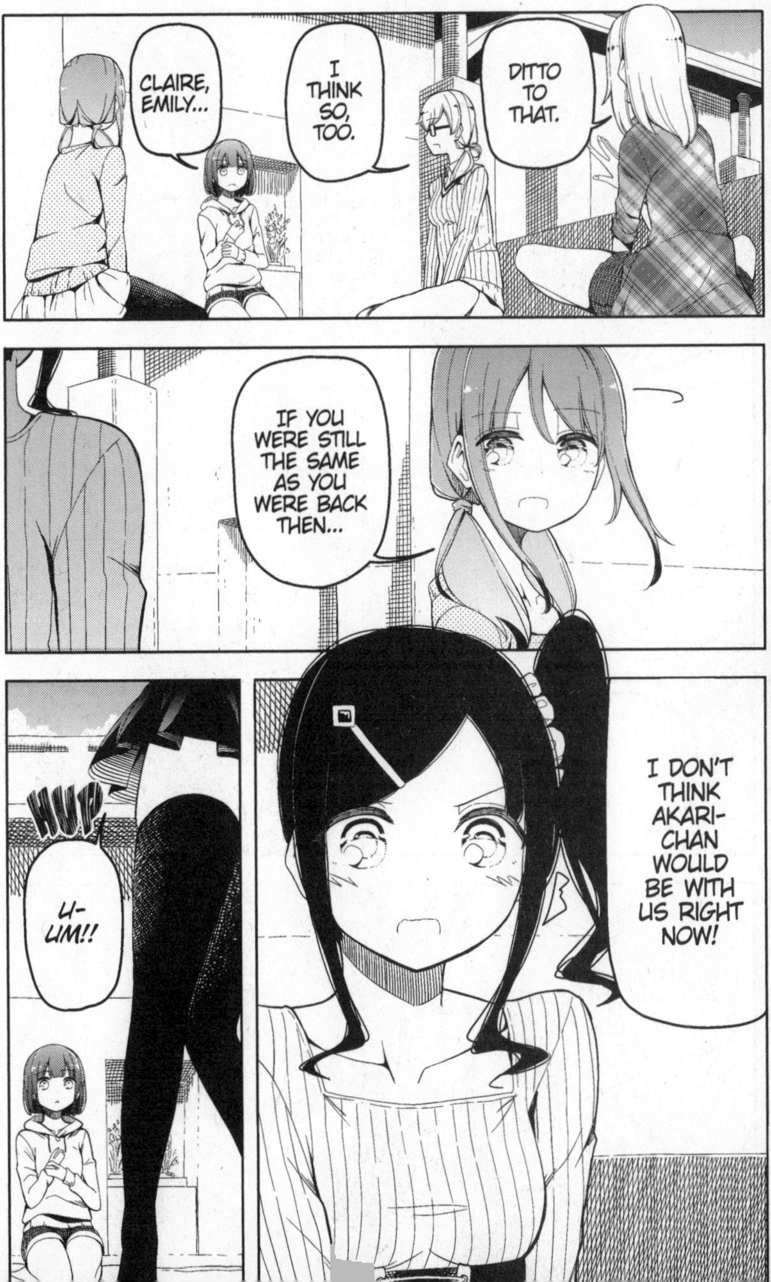
DITTO TO THAT.
I THINK SO, TOO.
CLAIRE, EMILY...
IF YOU WERE STILL THE SAME AS YOU WERE BACK THEN...
I DON'T THINK AKARI-CHAN WOULD BE WITH US RIGHT NOW!
HUP
U-UM!!

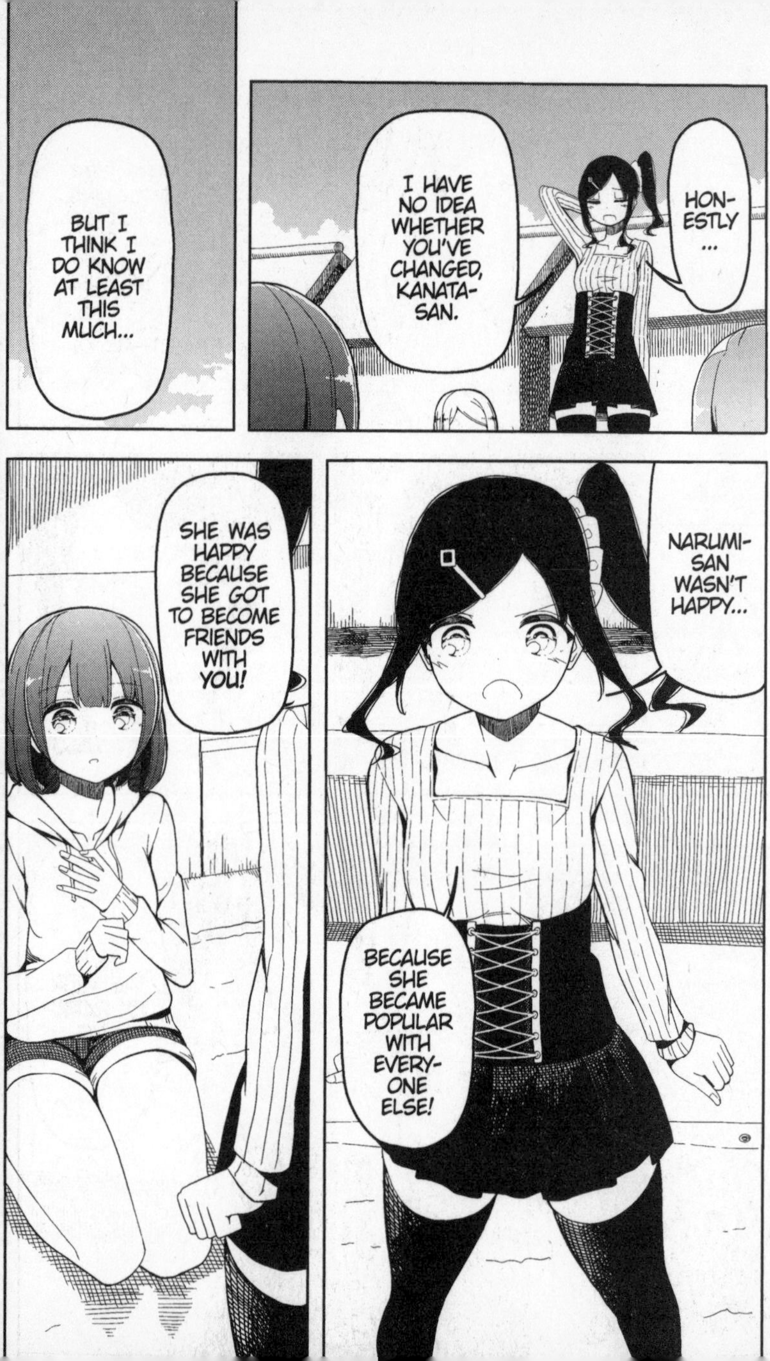
HON-ESTLY...
I HAVE NO IDEA WHETHER YOU'VE CHANGED, KANATA-SAN.
BUT I THINK I DO KNOW AT LEAST THIS MUCH...
NARUMI-SAN WASN'T HAPPY...
BECAUSE SHE BECAME POPULAR WITH EVERY-ONE ELSE!
SHE WAS HAPPY BECAUSE SHE GOT TO BECOME FRIENDS WITH YOU!

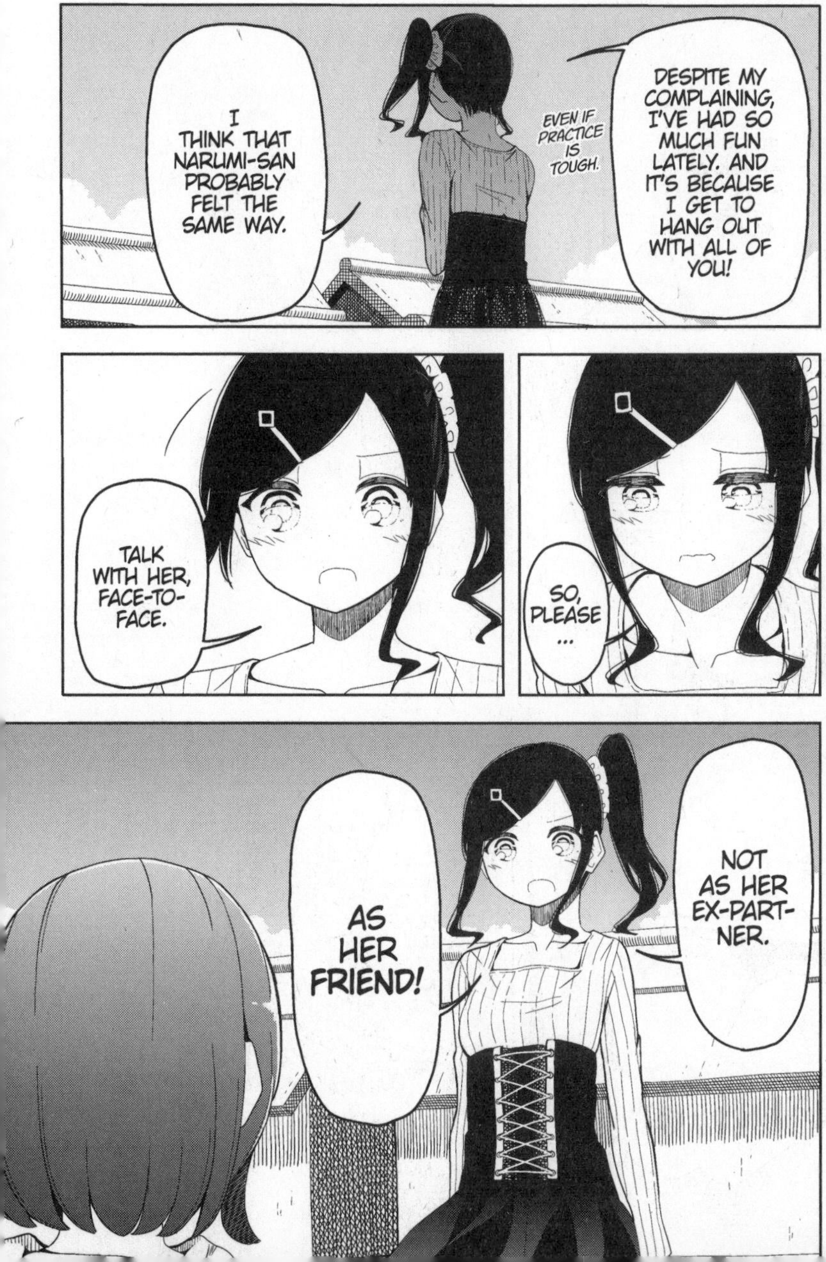
DESPITE MY COMPLAINING, I'VE HAD SO MUCH FUN LATELY. AND IT'S BECAUSE I GET TO HANG OUT WITH ALL OF YOU!
EVEN IF PRACTICE IS TOUGH.
I THINK THAT NARUMI-SAN PROBABLY FELT THE SAME WAY.
SO, PLEASE ...
TALK WITH HER, FACE-TO-FACE.
NOT AS HER EX-PARTNER.
AS HER FRIEND!

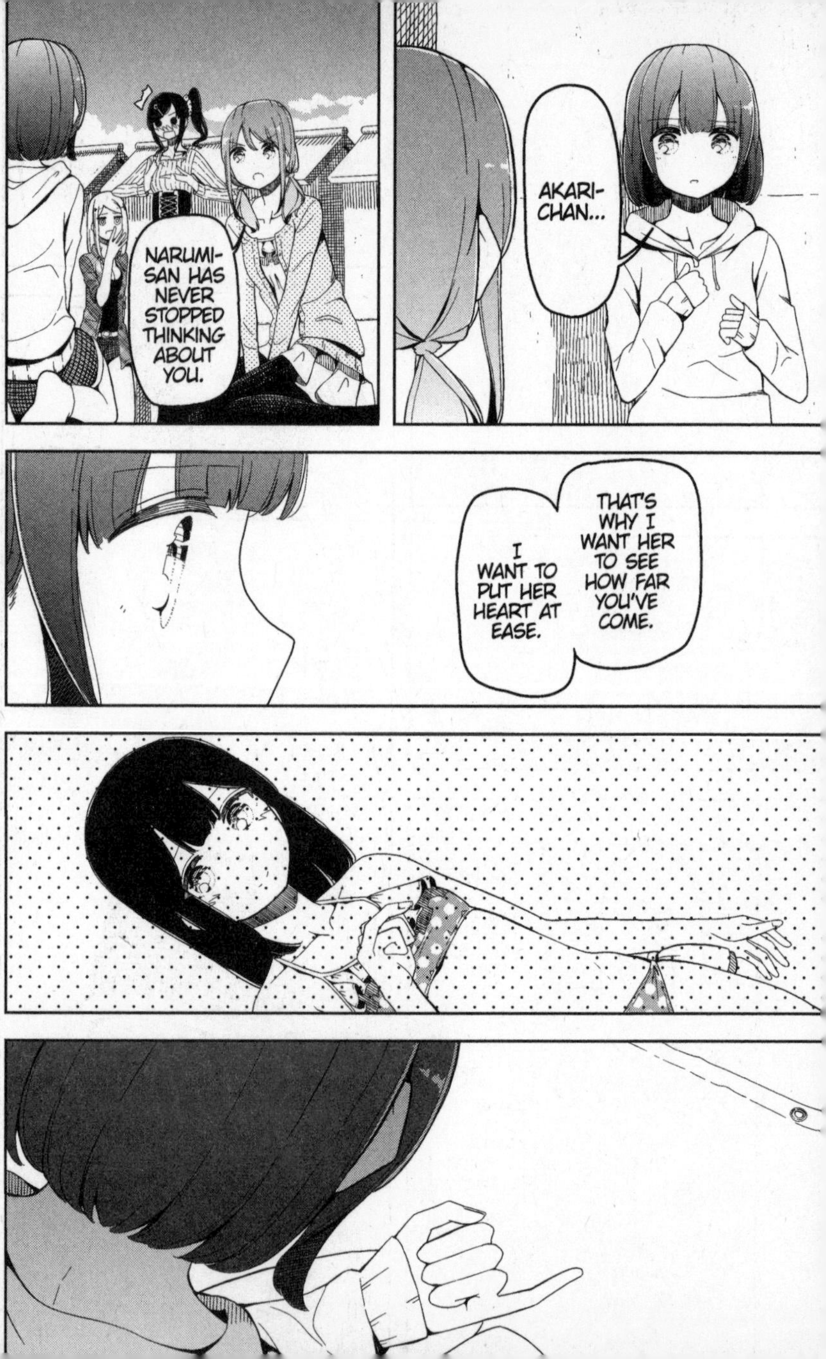
AKARI-CHAN...
NARUMI-SAN HAS NEVER STOPPED THINKING ABOUT YOU.
THAT'S WHY I WANT HER TO SEE HOW FAR YOU'VE COME.
I WANT TO PUT HER HEART AT EASE.

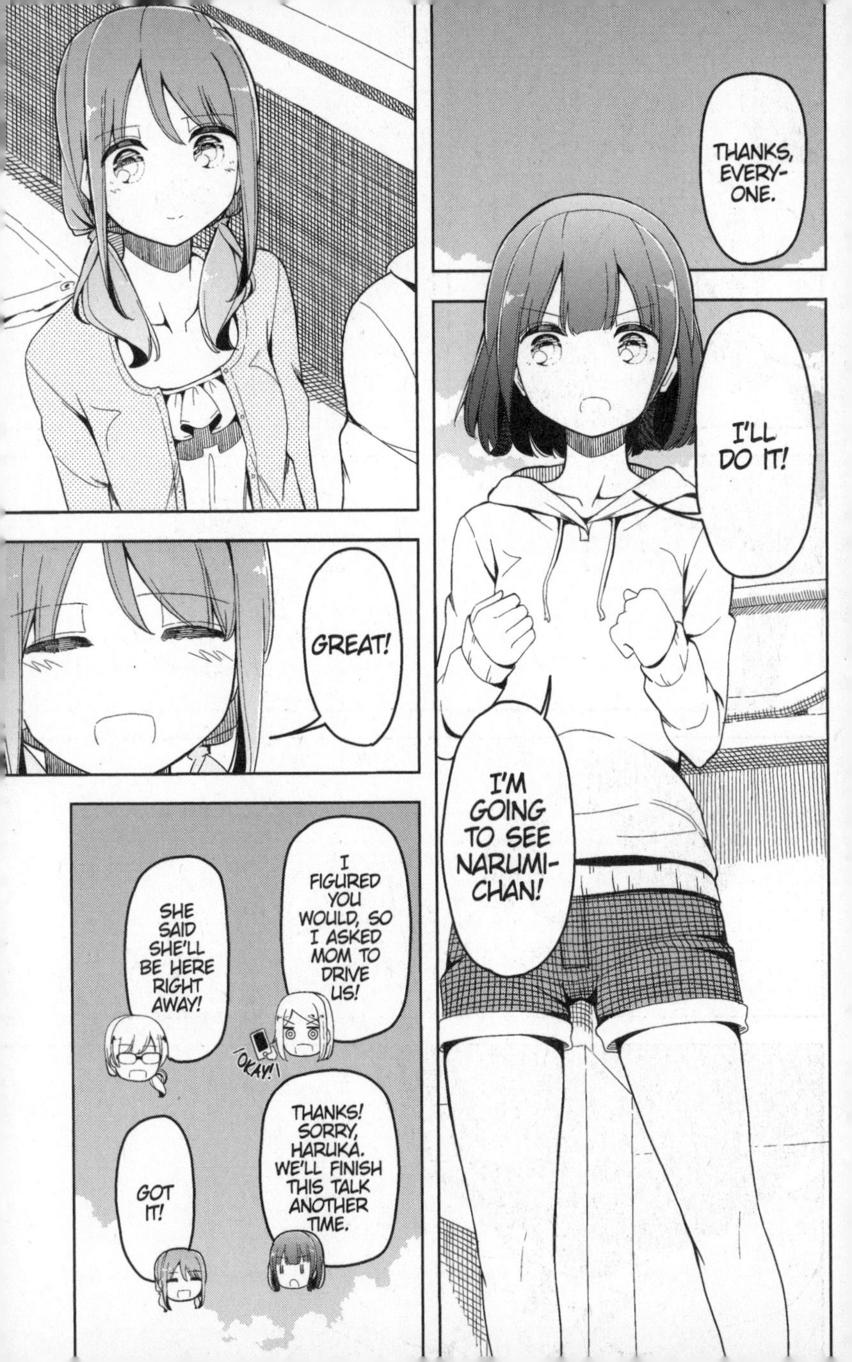
THANKS, EVERY-ONE.
I'LL DO IT!
I'M GOING TO SEE NARUMI-CHAN!
GREAT!
I FIGURED YOU WOULD, SO I ASKED MOM TO DRIVE US!
SHE SAID SHE'LL BE HERE RIGHT AWAY!
OKAY!
THANKS! SORRY, HARUKA. WE'LL FINISH THIS TALK ANOTHER TIME.
GOT IT!

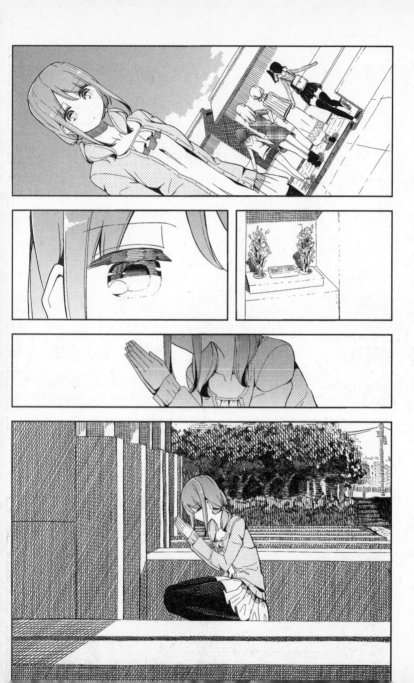

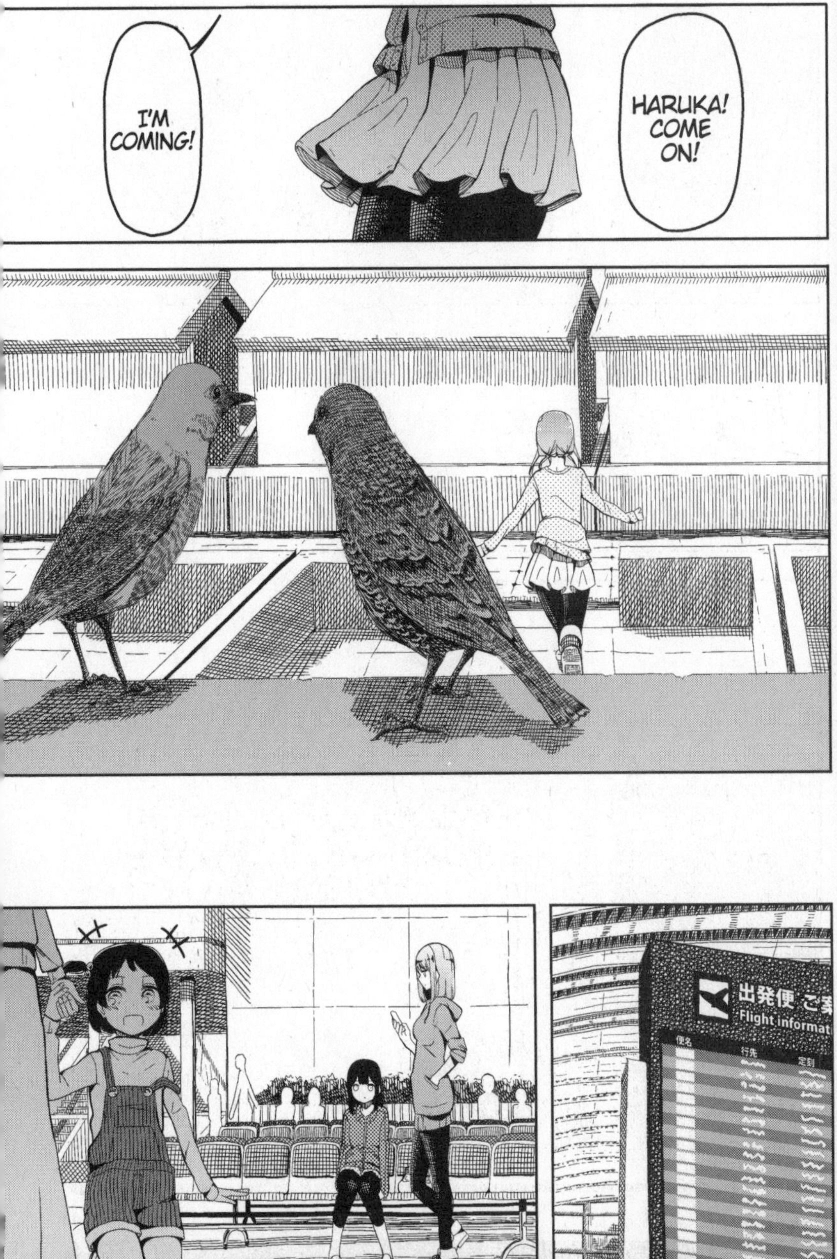
HARUKA! COME ON!
I'M COMING!
出発便

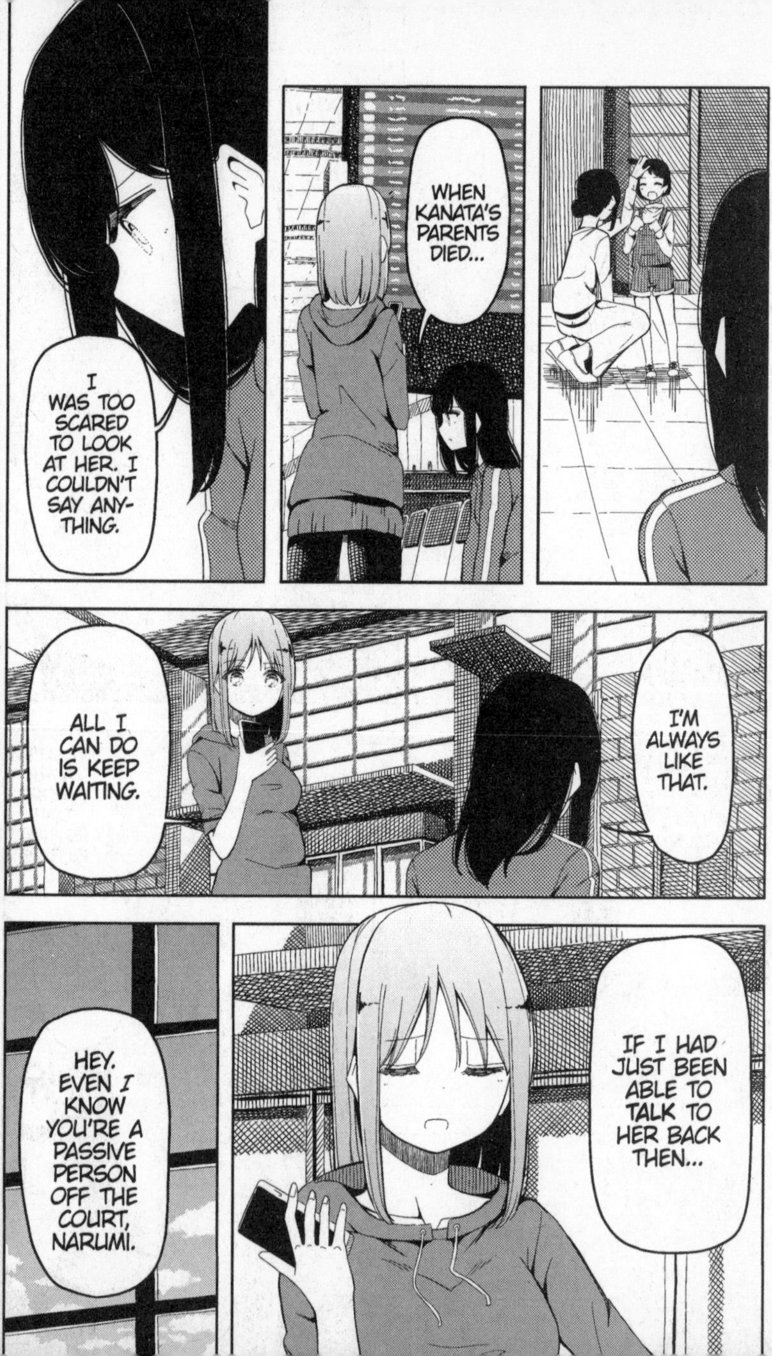
WHEN KANATA'S PARENTS DIED...
I WAS TOO SCARED TO LOOK AT HER. I COULDN'T SAY ANYTHING.
I'M ALWAYS LIKE THAT.
ALL I CAN DO IS KEEP WAITING.
IF I HAD JUST BEEN ABLE TO TALK TO HER BACK THEN...
HEY. EVEN I KNOW YOU'RE A PASSIVE PERSON OFF THE COURT, NARUMI.

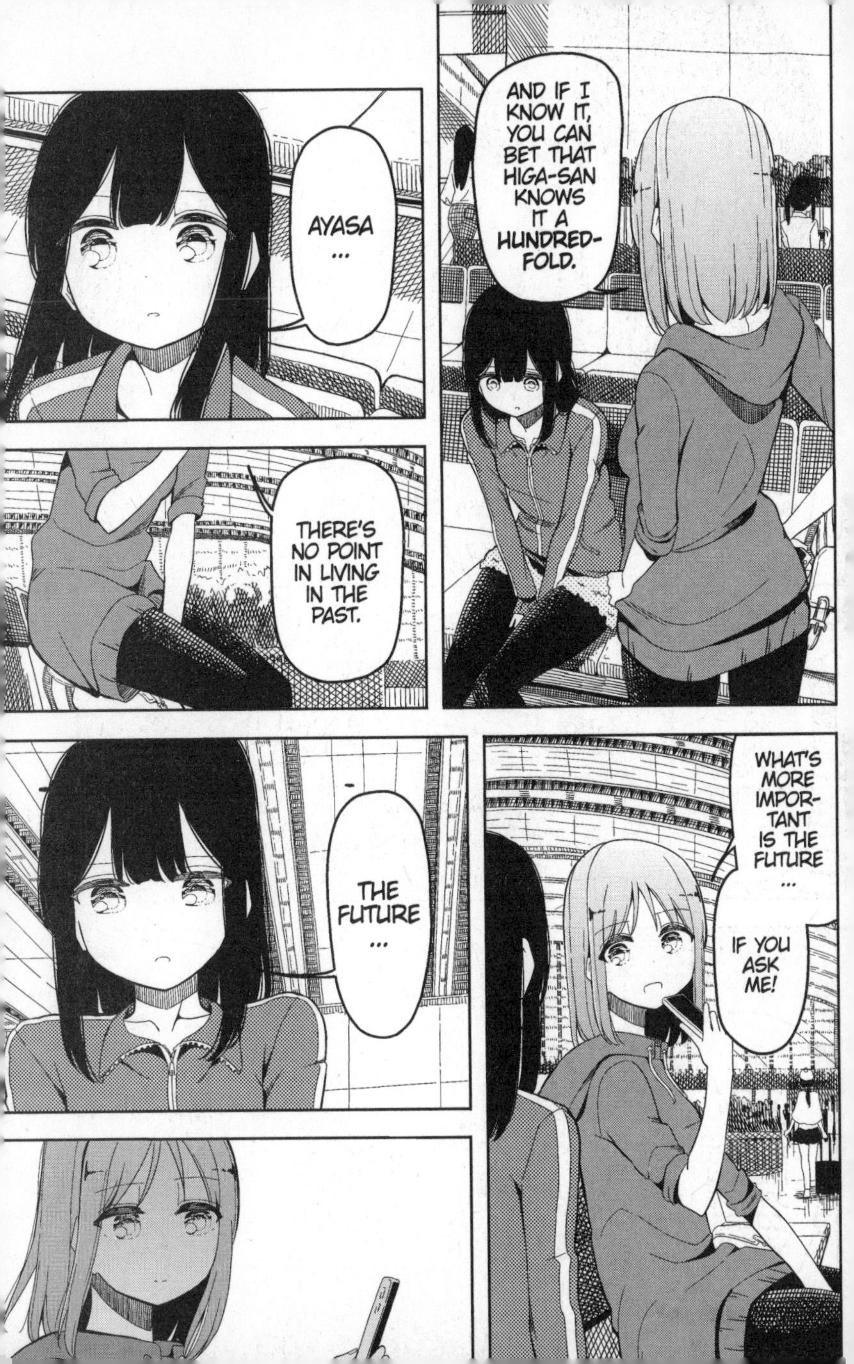
AND IF I KNOW IT, YOU CAN BET THAT HIGA-SAN KNOWS IT A HUNDRED-FOLD.
AYASA ...
THERE'S NO POINT IN LIVING IN THE PAST.
WHAT'S MORE IMPOR-TANT IS THE FUTURE ...
IF YOU ASK ME!
THE FUTURE ...

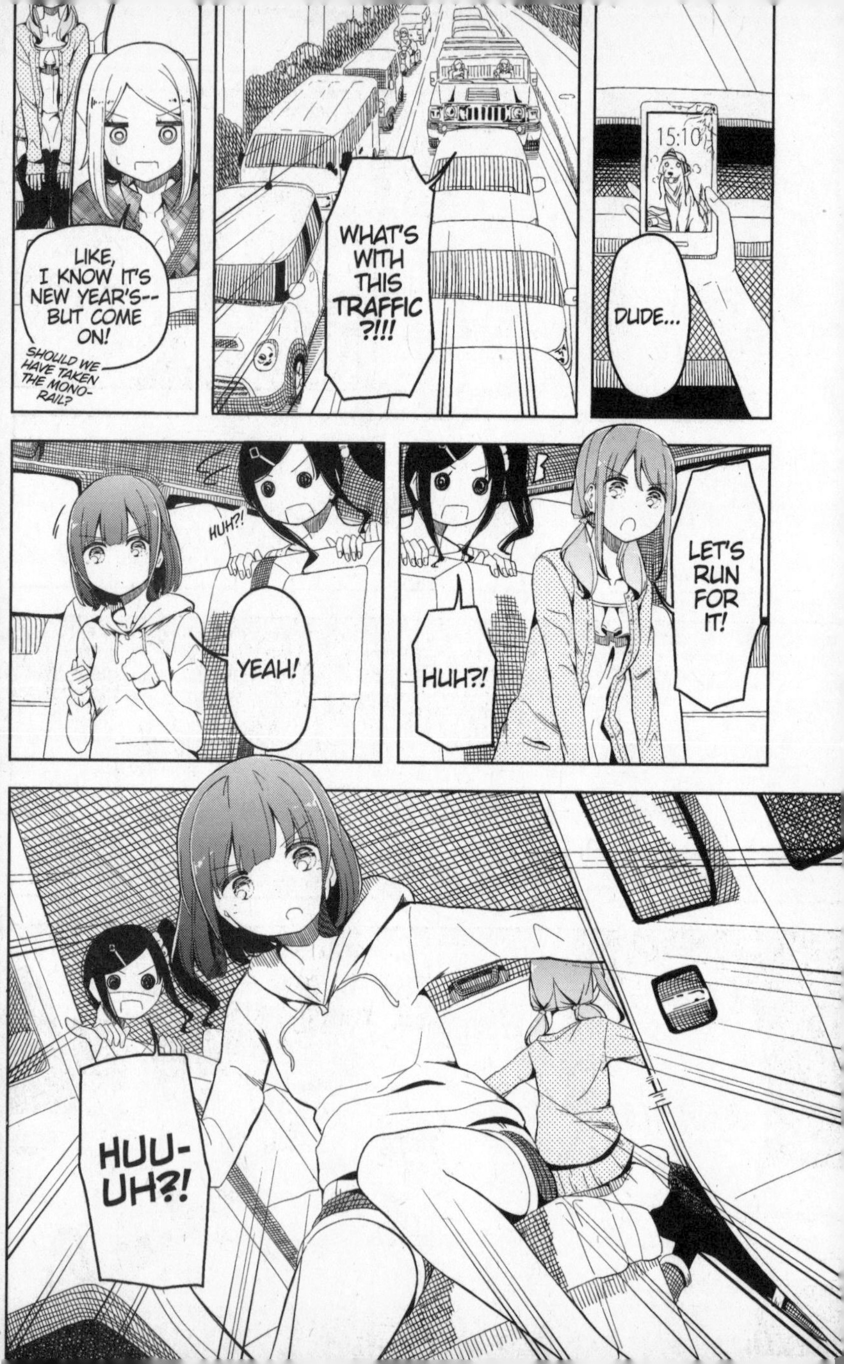
DUDE...
WHAT'S WITH THIS TRAFFIC?!!!
LIKE, I KNOW IT'S NEW YEAR'S-- BUT COME ON!
SHOULD WE HAVE TAKEN THE MONO-RAIL?
LET'S RUN FOR IT!
HUH?!
HUH?!
YEAH!
HUU-UH?!

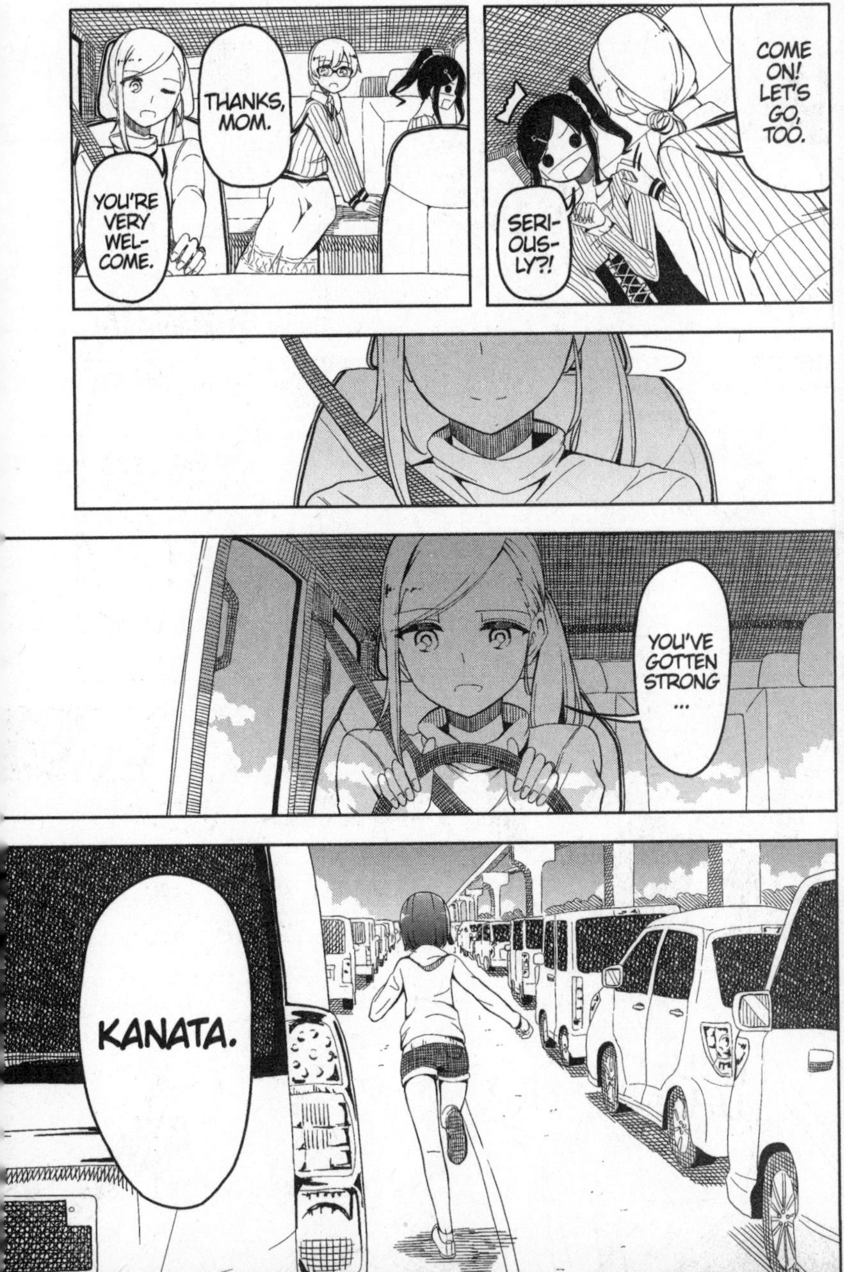
COME ON! LET'S GO, TOO.
SERI-OUS-LY?!
THANKS, MOM.
YOU'RE VERY WEL-COME.
YOU'VE GOTTEN STRONG ...
KANATA.

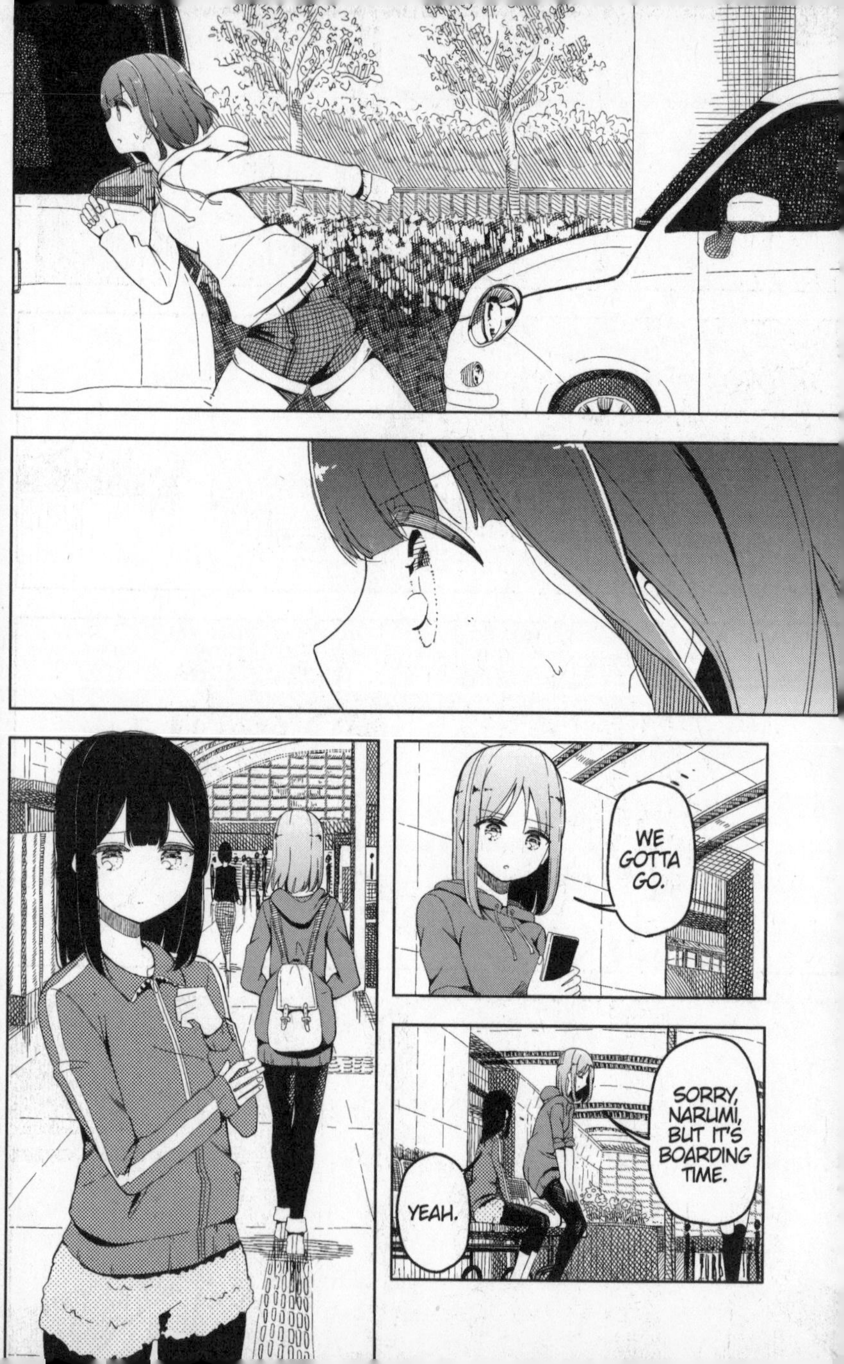
WE GOTTA GO.
SORRY, NARUMI, BUT IT'S BOARDING TIME.
YEAH.

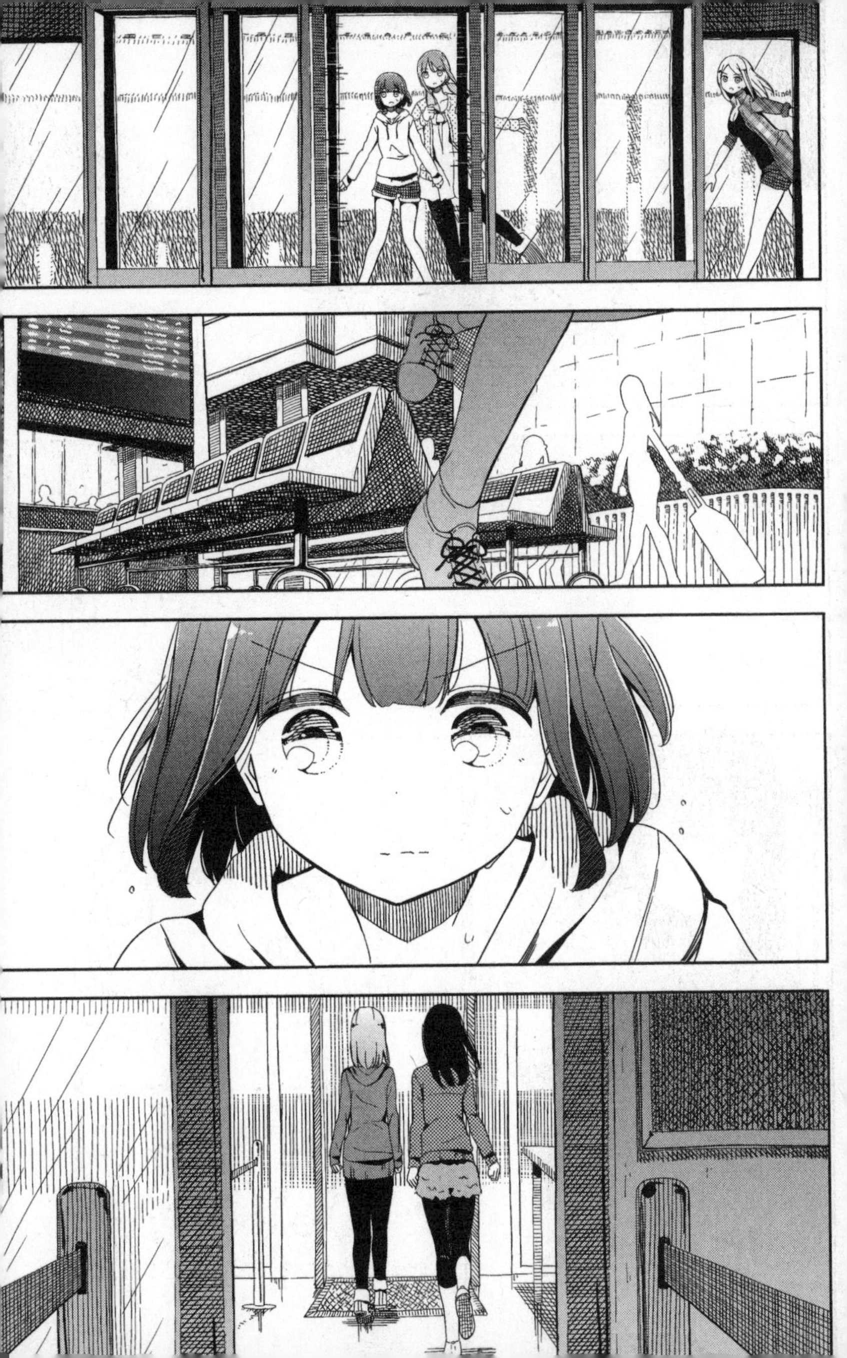

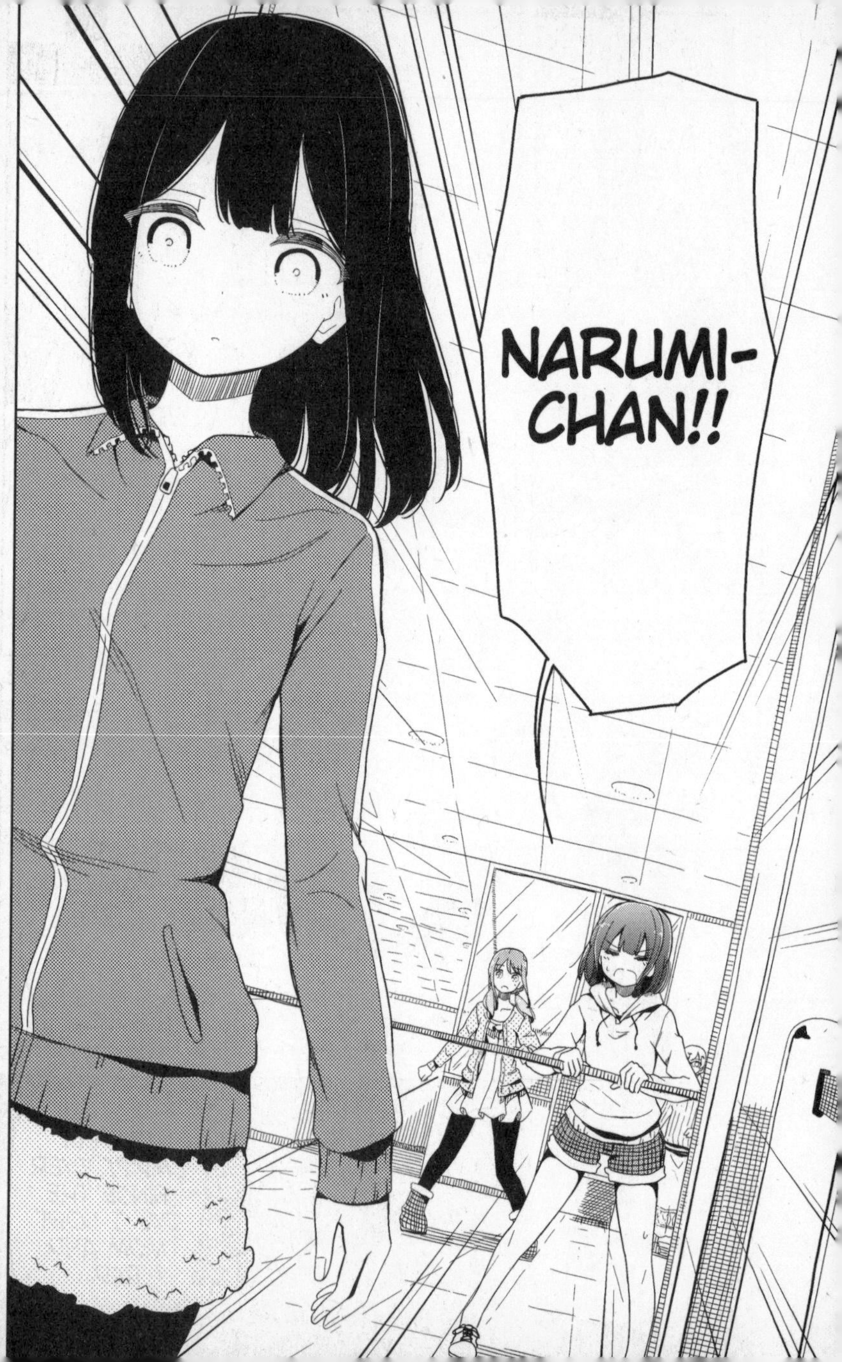
NARUMI-CHAN!!

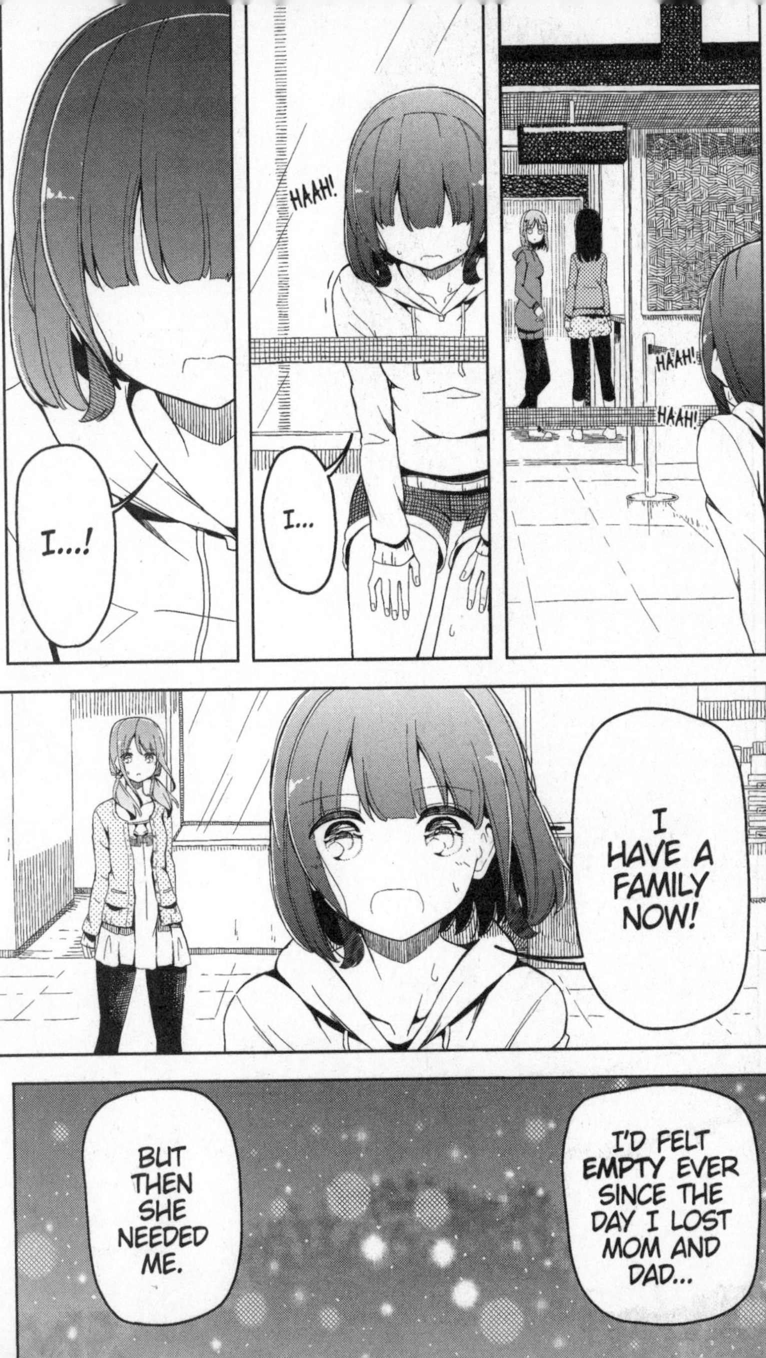
HAAH!
HAAH!
HAAH!
I...
I...!
I HAVE A FAMILY NOW!
I'D FELT EMPTY EVER SINCE THE DAY I LOST MOM AND DAD...
BUT THEN SHE NEEDED ME.

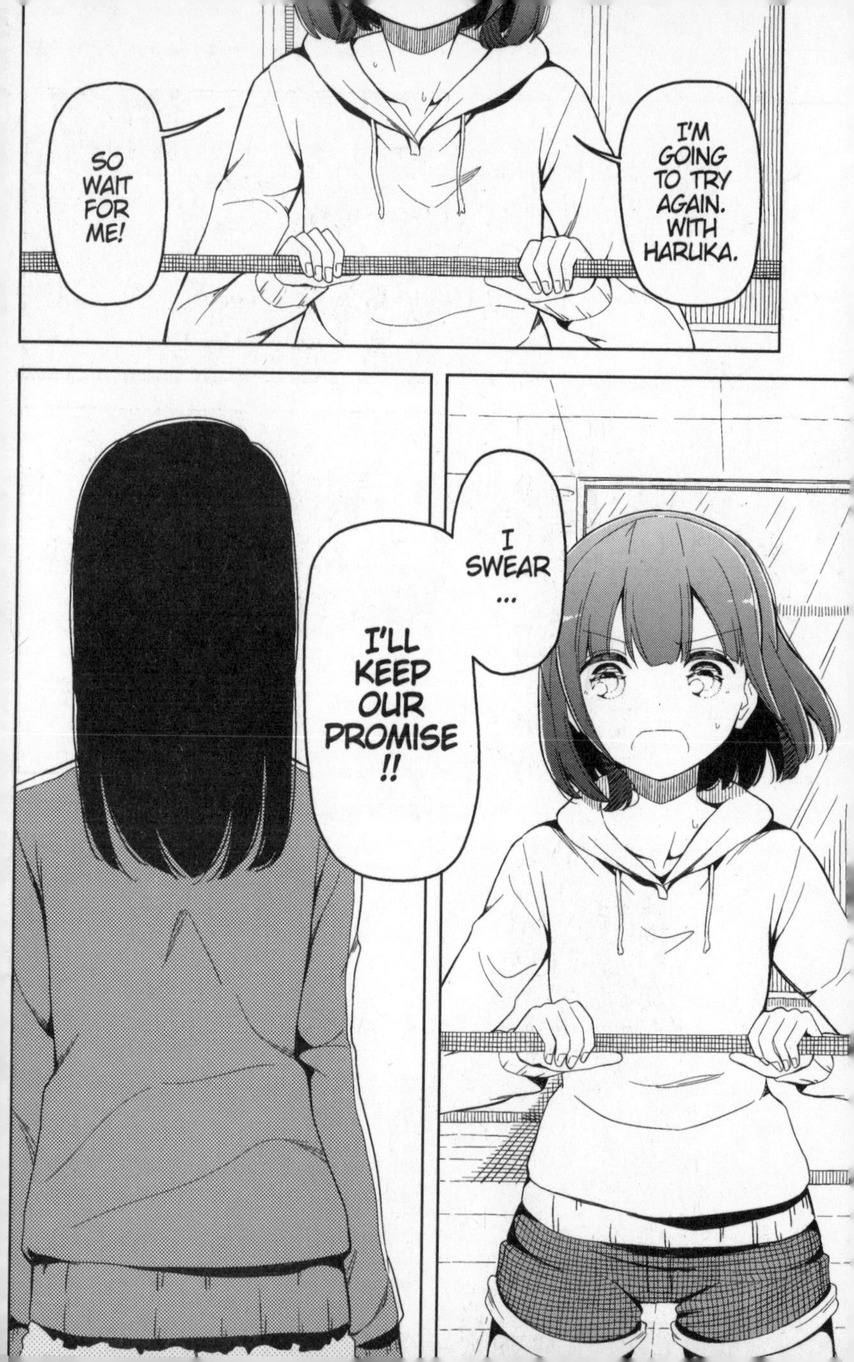
I'M GOING TO TRY AGAIN. WITH HARUKA.
SO WAIT FOR ME!
I SWEAR ...
I'LL KEEP OUR PROMISE !!

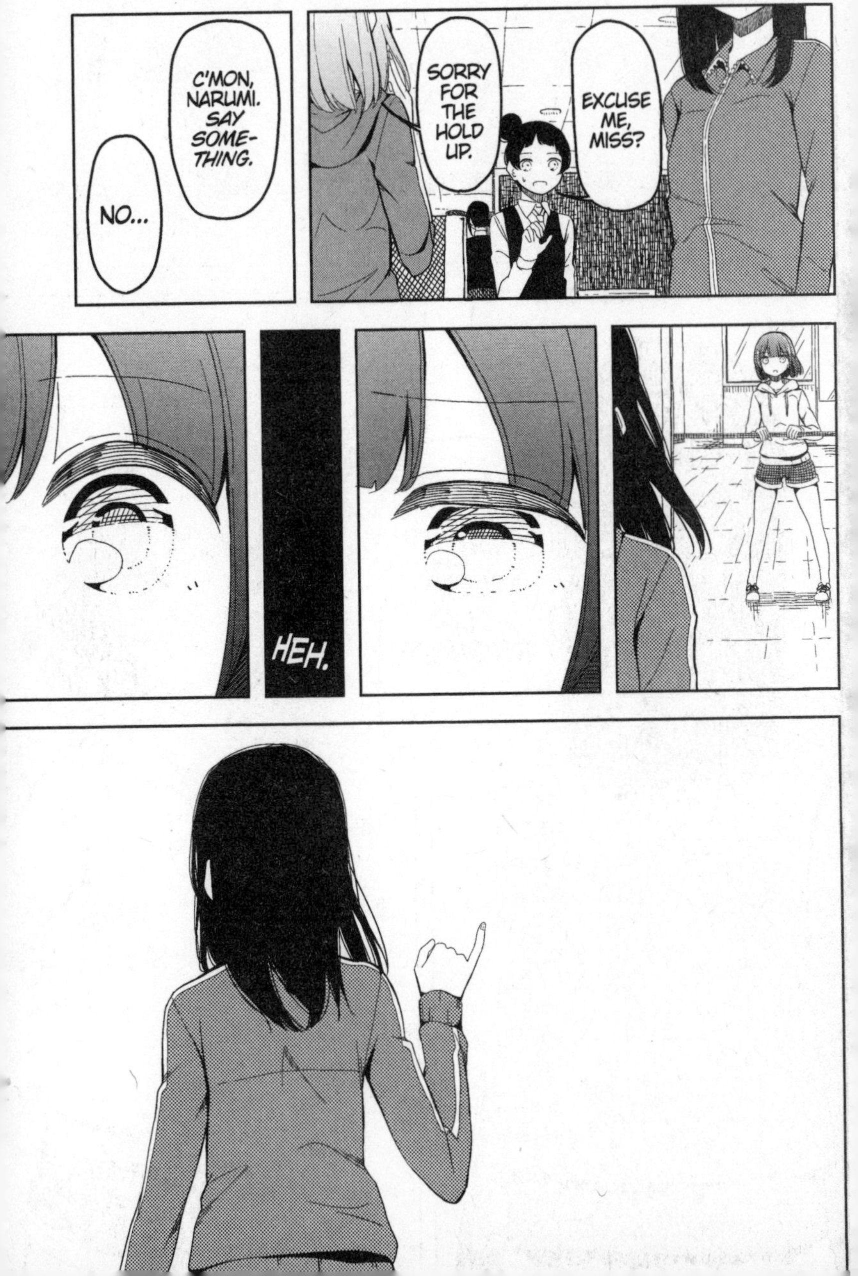
EXCUSE ME, MISS?
SORRY FOR THE HOLD UP.
C'MON, NARUMI. SAY SOME-THING.
NO...
HEH.

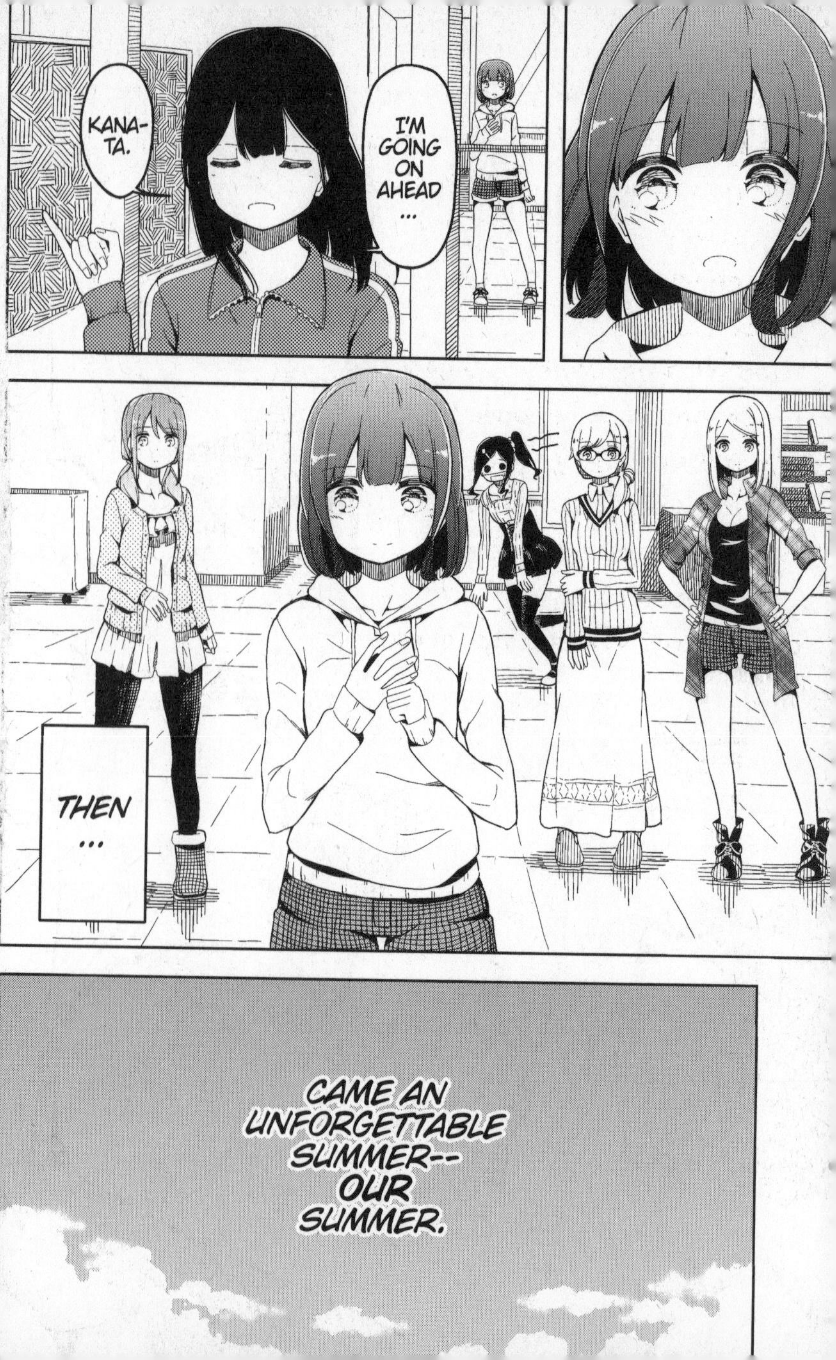
I'M GOING ON AHEAD...
KANA-TA.
THEN...
CAME AN UNFORGETTABLE SUMMER-- OUR SUMMER.

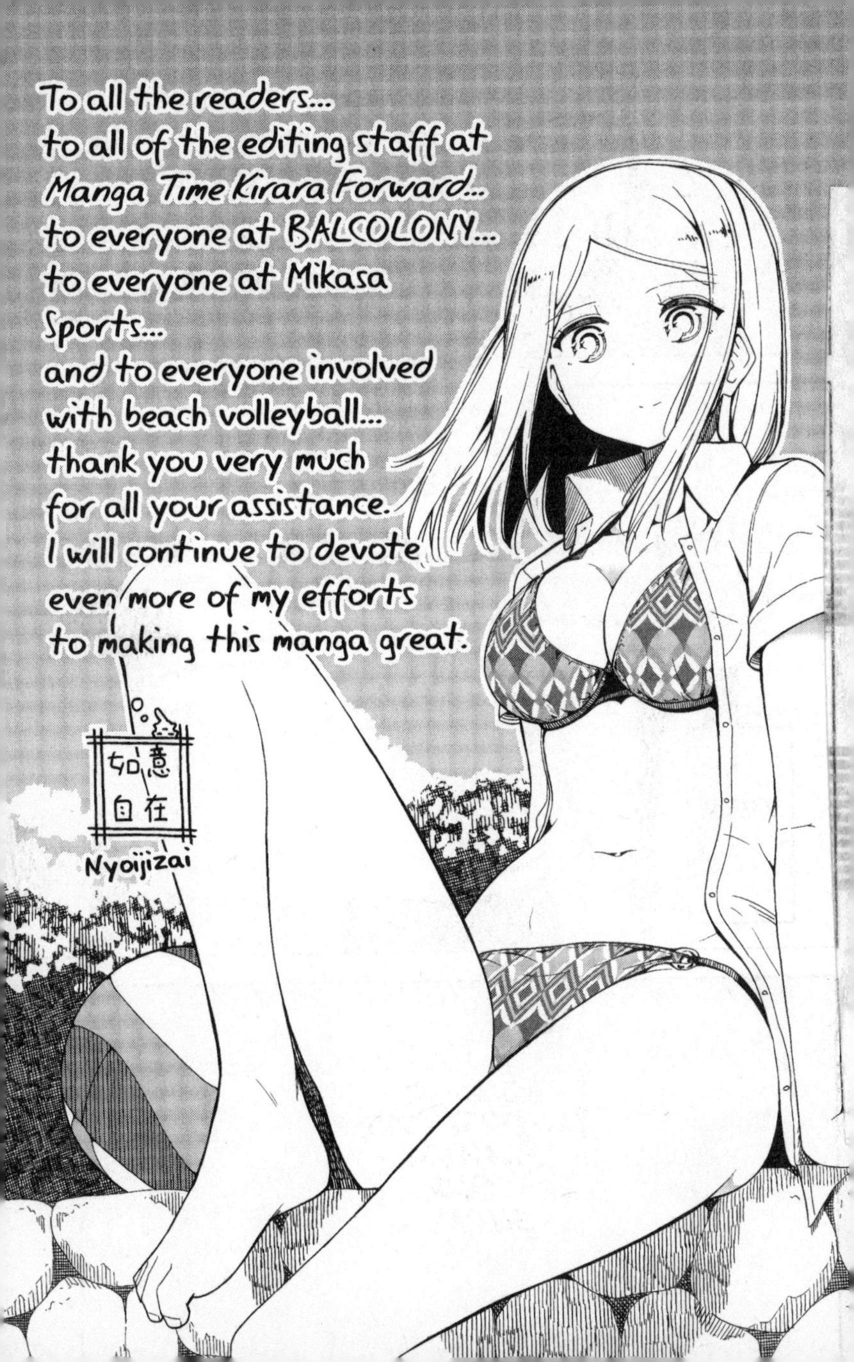
To all the readers...
to all of the editing staff at
Manga Time Kirara Forward...
to everyone at BALCOLONY...
to everyone at Mikasa
Sports...
and to everyone involved
with beach volleyball...
thank you very much
for all your assistance.
I will continue to devote
even more of my efforts
to making this manga great.
如意
自在
Nyoijizai

SEVEN SEAS ENTERTAINMENT PRESENTS

Harukana★ Receive

VOLUME 3 story and art by **NYOIJIZAI**

TRANSLATION
Amanda Haley

ADAPTATION
Claudie Summers

LETTERING AND RETOUCH
Ray Steeves

COVER DESIGN
KC Fabellon

PROOFREADER
Shanti Whitesides
Stephanie Cohen

EDITOR
Shannon Fay

PRODUCTION ASSISTANT
CK Russell

PRODUCTION MANAGER
Lissa Pattillo

EDITOR-IN-CHIEF
Adam Arnold

PUBLISHER
Jason DeAngelis

HARUKANA RECEIVE VOL. 3
© Nyoiiizai 2017

F_____ _____bunsha Co., LTD. Tokyo, Japan.
E_____

_____rm without
_____ion. Names,
_____imagination
_____, or persons,

_____ducational, or
_____illan Corporate
_____5442, or by

ISBN: _____

Printed in Canada

First Printing: March 2019

10 9 8 7 6 5 4 3 2 1

FOLLOW US ONLINE: *www.sevenseasentertainment.com*

READING DIRECTIONS

This book reads from *right to left*, Japanese style. If this is your first time reading manga, you start reading from the top right panel on each page and take it from there. If you get lost, just follow the numbered diagram here. It may seem backwards at first, but you'll get the hang of it! Have fun!!

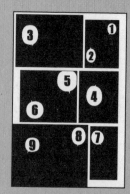